THEOLOGICAL
SCIENCE

THOMAS F. TORRANCE
Professor of Christian Dogmatics
in the University of Edinburgh

Based on the Hewett Lectures for 1959

OXFORD UNIVERSITY PRESS
OXFORD   LONDON   NEW YORK

OXFORD UNIVERSITY PRESS

Oxford   London   Glasgow
New York   Toronto   Melbourne   Wellington
Ibadan   Nairobi   Dar es Salaam   Cape Town
Kuala Lumpur   Singapore   Jakarta   Hong Kong   Tokyo
Delhi   Bombay   Calcutta   Madras   Karachi

To

Sir Bernard Lovell

in

Friendship and Admiration

The Library of Congress cataloged the first printing of this title as follows:

Torrance, Thomas Forsyth, 1913—
    Theological science by Thomas F. Torrance. London, New York, etc., Oxford
    U.P., 1969.

    xx,   368 p.   23cm   84/-
    "Based on the Hewett lectures for 1959."
    Bibliographical footnotes.
1. Philosophical theology   I.   Title
ISBN   0-19-520083-7   76-413012
BT40.T65   1969   230'.01

Printed in the United States of America

Preface

This volume represents in a considerably expanded form the Hewett Lectures on 'The Nature of Theology and Scientific Method', delivered in 1959 at Union Theological Seminary, New York, at Andover Newton Theological School, Newton Center, and at the Episcopal Theological School, Cambridge, Massachusetts. I should like to express my deep gratitude to the Trustees of the Hewett Lectureship for inviting me to lecture at such lively centres of theological learning, and to the Presidents and Deans for making possible discussion with many alert minds on the themes of the lectures, and not least for their wonderful hospitality to my wife and family as well as myself. We shall never forget the kindness and friendship showed to us all by teachers and students alike, nor the way in which we were allowed to share their daily worship of God.

The substance of these lectures was also presented in a different form to graduate students at Princeton Theological Seminary, New Jersey, in the same year. When I returned from the United States I had many questions to answer and these gathered even more as I offered the lectures on several occasions to postgraduate students in Edinburgh University. Thus, as I prepared the book for the Press, I found that the material had greatly expanded, but at one point I was held up. In a rash moment in New York in discussion with Professor Robert McAfee Brown I offered to include in the published form of the lectures a chapter on hermeneutics, but when I came to write it a book, instead of a chapter, appeared. I tried once again, and another book emerged. The matter bristled with so many epistemological problems and concealed assumptions that I determined to write an independent work on the subject, and then to offer a digest of that in a single chapter to go with the Hewett Lectures. This has proved a big undertaking, and the result will appear either in one very large volume or three smaller books. Meantime the publishers, who have been most patient with me, pressed for the original lectures, and so I set out to give them that material in a publishable form. But once again I could not shake myself free of many problems and questions and produced a much larger book than I had hoped. That is now presented in these pages, at the third time of writing, but without the chapter on hermeneutics. With this explanation I would like to offer to the Hewett Trustees and my many friends at the three Colleges my sincere regrets for the protracted delay in publication.

In discussing the meaning and place of authority in his second series of Gifford lectures delivered in St. Andrews, during the session of 1927–8, my revered teacher, A. E. Taylor, called for the locating of authority, neither in individualism nor in some institutional seat, but in a reality that is wholly given and trans-subjective, and simply and absolutely authoritative through its givenness. If knowledge is to be more than personal opinion, he argued, there must be control of our personal intellectual constructions by something which is not constructed but *received*. In our human knowledge of God this is humbly to acknowledge that what is genuinely given has unquestionable right to control our thinking and acting, just because it is so utterly given to us and not made by us. With that notion of authority clarified, Professor Taylor held that we might entertain hope for the future of theology as 'a genuine, assured, and yet progressive science of God'. (*The Faith of a Moralist*, vol. 2, p. 241.)

That is what I believe theological science to be and how I try to engage in it, but we are not concerned with that here in its positive and material content. This is a book about the philosophy of the science of God, a discipline which the theologian must undertake if he is really to do his job. What is required of us here is not a Philosophy of Religion in which religion is substituted in the place of God, but a Philosophy of Theology in which we are directly engaged with knowledge of the Reality of God and not just with religious phenomenality. Whenever religion is substituted in the place of God, the fact that in religion we are concerned with the behaviour of *religious people*, sooner or later means the substitution of humanity in the place of religion—the point at which our 'secularizing' philosophers of religion appear to have arrived. There is undoubtedly a place for the scientific study of religious people, of religious phenomena, and of religious language, but none of these can be a substitute for the Philosophy of Theology in which we are concerned with the meta-science of our direct cognitive relation with God. Science and meta-science are required not because God is a problem but because *we* are. As Austin Farrer has said, 'the existence of perfection requires no explanation, the existence of limited being requires explanation' (*Finite and Infinite*, p. 15). It is because *our* relations with God have become problematic that we must have a scientific theology.

If I may be allowed to speak personally for a moment, I find the presence and being of God bearing upon my experience and thought so powerfully that I cannot but be convinced of His overwhelming reality and rationality. To doubt the existence of God would be an act of sheer irrationality, for it would mean that my reason had become unhinged from its bond with real being. Yet in knowing God I am deeply aware that my relation to Him has been damaged, that disorder has resulted in my mind, and that it is I who obstruct knowledge of God by getting in between Him and myself, as it were. But I am also aware that His presence presses unrelentingly upon me through the disorder of my mind, for He will not let Himself be thwarted by it, challenging and repairing it, and requiring of me on my part to yield my thoughts to His healing and controlling revelation.

Scientific theology is active engagement in that cognitive relation to God in obedience to the demands of His reality and self-giving. In it we probe into the problematic condition of the human mind before God and seek to bring knowledge of Him into clear focus, so that the truth of God may shine through to it unhindered by its opacity and the human mind may acquire clear and orderly forms through which to apprehend and conceive His reality. That is to say, we seek to allow God's own eloquent self-evidence to sound through to us in His Logos so that we may know and understand Him out of His own rationality and under the determination of His divine being. In the course of this activity we begin to understand something of how the cognitive relation of men to God can be so sharply refracted that double vision results, in which human knowers are unable to trace the thought of God back to its proper ground in His reality. Although God does not cease to disclose His power and deity to them the truth becomes stifled, for at the very roots of their knowledge, as St. Paul said, they twist it into untruth. All a man may be able to do then in his sense of the presence of God is to give it oblique, or symbolic, meaning only to discover that he has thrust himself into its content, or he may try to straighten out the connections of his thought and make them point beyond him, only to find that they break off and point into emptiness and nothing, even though he remains haunted, as it were, by the ultimate rationality of God all round him.

This is where theological science must step in to help men refer their thoughts properly beyond themselves to God. We cannot communicate God to men directly, but we can engage in normal acts of communication in which we use language with a semantic intention, not so much to express our minds as to refer other minds to something beyond ourselves. While our linguistic and conceptual forms may be communicated directly to other minds, intuitable realities are not directly communicable: we may point them out, or refer to them through accepted signs or acquired designations, in the hope that others will perceive or apprehend them also, but unless that takes place communication has not achieved its end. Communication takes place between minds that are directed to the same or similar objects and so is necessarily indirect through a triadic relationship in which one mind directs another to an object by referring to it, and in which the other mind by following through the reference to the object understands the intention of the first mind.

This presupposes the rationality of the medium and the context in which communication takes place, that is, not only an intelligible language but an intelligible subject-matter. The things about which we speak to one another must be capable of rational apprehension and of semantic designation. This is something that we assume and operate with continually in ordinary experience and in science, without attempting to explain it. If the nature of things were not somehow inherently rational they would remain inapprehensible and opaque and indeed we ourselves would not be able to emerge into the light of rationality. It is because things are amenable to rational treatment that we can apprehend them at all; we understand them, or get light upon them, in so far as we can penetrate into their rationality and develop our grasp of it. Scientific knowledge is that in which we bring the inherent rationality of things to light and expression, as we let the realities we investigate disclose themselves to us under our questioning and we on our part submit our minds to their intrinsic connections and order. Scientific activity certainly involves a give and take between subject and object, while all knowledge is by way of being a compromise between thought and being; nevertheless it remains an awesome fact that if the nature of things were not intelligible and apprehensible, knowledge could not arise at all, far less communication. We communicate with others only when we get them to submit their thoughts to the same rationality in things that we experience. Thus communication from the very start involves an element of persuasion. So far as theological knowledge is concerned this is what we call, perhaps mistakenly, 'apologetics', but, whatever we call it, it is a necessary part of scientific activity in theological communication.

This basic persuasiveness is not one-directional, however, especially when we are engaged in a conjoint apprehension of things with other minds that communicate back to us, for in the fuller apprehension that we can have together of the same things there usually takes place a modification in our apprehension of them and of their rationality. If something is inherently rational, and not merely accidental or surd-like, then it is our fault and not that of the thing itself if we fail to understand it: we have probably overlaid it with some form of unreality by bringing to its apprehension preconceived ideas that are not appropriate or are wrongly extrapolated from another field of experience. This means that as we seek to penetrate into the rationality of something, our inquiry must also cut back into ourselves and into our presuppositions, for they must be brought into question if we are really to understand the thing concerned out of itself and in accordance with its own nature. In these circumstances persuasion or apologetics must argue for a reconstruction in our interpretative frame of thought, in order that the alien elements may be eliminated from it and new elements assimilated more appropriate to the nature of the things we are speaking about. It is always the nature of things that must prescribe for us the specific mode of rationality that we must adopt toward them, and prescribe also the form of verification apposite to them, and therefore it is a major part of all scientific activity to reach clear convictions as to the distinctive nature of what we are seeking to know in order that we may develop and operate with the distinctive categories demanded of us.

In this involvement with epistemological and methodological questions theological science is inevitably committed to dialogue with the other sciences and with philosophy, as well as with ordinary experience, for they too are engaged in disciplined activity to clarify the referential relations of human thought and speech and are continually at work refining and enlarging their range to take in hitherto unknown realities. They are all engaged in an unrelenting struggle to separate out from their entanglement in our experience and knowledge the elements that are ultimately and irreducibly given from the elements that are elaborated and constructed in our acts of consciousness, although without the latter we can never reach apprehension of the former, for we never apprehend anything without engaging at once in forming judgements and developing interpretations about it. But this is an unceasing task, for we can never reach completely clear and unambiguous apprehension of the real, both because it always outruns our experience of it and because we can never finally overcome our own artificiality—the least we can do is to devote all our powers to the refining and elaborating of methods that will take us as far as possible in this direction, methods that will carry in themselves self-correcting devices so that we may always be directed away from ourselves to the compulsive force of objective connections in the real world. In this theological science and the other sciences make use of the same basic tool, the human reason operating with the given, so that the theologian and the scientist are at work not only in the same room, so to speak, but often at the same bench, yet in such a way that each acknowledges the distinctive nature of the other's subject-matter and resists any *Gleichschaltung* of their categories and methods. Yet because each uses the same gift of reason and each seeks to establish the same kind of relation with the real in his own field, they cannot but interact with one another and learn from one another, if only in learning how to be religiously faithful to the nature of the reality into which they inquire and so to be real in their thinking.

As I see it, this is the great story of modern thought, whether it be in theology, science, or philosophy: the struggle for fidelity, for appropriate methods and apposite modes of speech, and therefore for the proper adaptation of the human subject to the object of his knowledge, whether it be God or the world of nature or man; but it is also the story of the struggles of man with himself, for somehow the more he comes to know, the more masterful he tries to be and the more he imposes himself upon reality, the more he gets in the way of his own progress. It is here that positive theology should have so much to offer, for it is concerned with right relations between man and God, with the healing and repairing of the human subject through humility before God, with the control of his convictions by what is ultimately given and real, with emancipation from arbitrary individualism, and thus with genuine objectivity in which man learns to love God and his neighbour, not for his own sake, but for their sakes.

In order to set the stage for the succeeding discussion, let me characterize briefly the basic and common problems of modern theology and science, as I see them. Modern theology in its distinctive form began with John Calvin's *Institute of the Christian Religion*, for in it there emerged three primary features of modern scientific thinking. (i) Calvin reversed the medieval order of scientific questions, *quid sit*, *an sit*, and *quale sit*, making the question *Qualis est?* primary in theological activity. But in making this question the first one, he altered its nature for it became a genuine interrogation without being governed by preceding abstractions and so the new kind of question that we have had to learn in the advance to new knowledge. Thus instead of starting with abstract questions as to essence and possibility, he started with the question as to actuality, 'What is the nature of this thing that we have here?' which in theological knowledge becomes the question as to who God is and as to what He reveals of Himself. It is only on that ground that we may go on to ask the other questions, which also become changed when put in this order, for then they are questions probing into the reality of our knowledge and testing its foundation. (ii) Calvin insisted that theology starts with the situation in which knowledge of God and knowledge of ourselves are already found together in a profound mutuality. We are unable to speak of knowledge of God cut off from the fact that He has addressed us and we have come to know Him, so that our knowledge of God must include the proper place given by God to the human subject. This means that scientific theology beginning with actuality cannot abstract itself from the subject-object relation, for it is there that it is locked in profound relations between the human subject and the divine Subject as its proper Object. Hence the immense stress that has been given in modern theology to personal relation with God. (iii) Within these actual relations our knowledge of God must be put to the test if we are to distinguish knowledge of God from knowledge of ourselves, especially in view of the fact that differences arise among us that are not overcome merely by appeal to the Holy Scriptures. The principle that Calvin brought into play here was what he called the *analogia fidei*, that is a movement of thought in which we test the fidelity of our knowledge by tracing our thought back to its ground in the reality known, in which we refer everything to God and not to ourselves. In this way we let the Truth of God retain its own authority and majesty, and allow ourselves to be questioned before it so that we may be delivered from distorting the truth through our untested preconceptions, for that is the root cause of error and division. In other words, this is the principle of objectivity and unification with which we operate in the scientific mode of inquiry.

The problem of modern theology, however, is that the second feature has got out of hand, for when the element of personal relation to God is not controlled by critical testing on the analogy of faith it degenerates into a gross personalism in which we obtrude ourselves into the place of God, making our relations with God the sole content of theological knowledge. That is the problem that faces us everywhere today in the so-called 'new theology' in which statements about God are reducted to anthropological statements. Whenever we try to transcend a subject-object relation or replace it by a 'pure' subject-subject relation, we are unable to distinguish God from ourselves, and lapse into irrationality, and then into the bitter futility of God-is-dead-ness.

The problem of modern science is not unlike that of theology. Modern science began with the emergence of the empirical approach in which we start with interrogation of actuality and operate through observation and experiment. That is to say, Calvin's first and third principles were brought into play, with appropriate change and modification in view of the determinate nature of the subject-matter, and in this movement modern science developed immense stress upon objectivity in every field of investigation, with the most startling results. But since the rise of quantum theory and the deepening exploration of nuclear activity, that is in the whole realm of microphysics, natural science has been forced to take the human subject into theoretical account in the development of its explanations. Since the interaction between the scientific observer and his object plays a necessary part in his knowledge, can we ever get beyond the observer to know things as they really are in themselves, independently of our observation? Is there not an impassable barrier between the subject and the object because the human subject keeps on getting in his own way, thus eclipsing the object from his proper view, as it were? Hence it is argued that we must leave the old conception of objectivity behind in the realm of classical physics, for objectivity of that kind is not attainable. Yet this itself seems to involve strangely the extrapolation from classical physics into modern physics of a feature that ought not to be there, namely, that scientific theories have a one-to-one correspondence with the realities they describe and are models in the sense of being theoretical transcripts of reality. This is certainly not the case, for they are actually models of a different kind through which we allow the realities to disclose themselves to us from beyond our theoretic constructions and through which we apprehend those realities in their distinction from and indeed in their critique of our models. That is to say, instead of re-garding the interaction between subject and object as positing a barrier to knowledge it ought to be regarded as the active means of communication between subject and object in which the subject directs his questions as a cognitive instrument to the object in order to reach deeper knowledge of it and in which the demand for the reforming of his question or re-moulding of his instrument means that he is thrust deeper and deeper into objectivity.

This is the struggle that is now going on in the epistemology of modern science, and it is strangely parallel to the struggle going on in theological science. Thus within physics, at the very moment, in the attempts to deal with the logical structure of quantum theory, hidden idealist (Cartesian and Kantian) presuppositions are being forced out into the open, and it is becoming increasingly apparent that these untested elements in our thought are seriously obstructing the advance and unification of scientific theory. On the other hand logical and mathematical forms of thought are now being developed in various countries to enable us to penetrate behind the subjective variables introduced by the observer. The measuring operations that gave rise to so much difficulty in the so-called Copenhagen Theory are now being treated as active links in the continuing relation between subject and object, so that in this way a critical and a realist epistemology becomes possible in which 'physical statements' are not ousted at decisive points for 'ideal statements'. It is one thing to say that since the act of observing interferes with a situation in nature that it is a necessary condition and element in our knowledge of it, but another thing to say that it is only a necessary step on our way toward knowledge of it, for then the constructions or theories we elaborate are employed as operational questions in a mode of inquiry that is progressively more profoundly objective.

But here also in modern science undue emphasis upon the place of the human subject leads quickly into an irrational situation, in which it is claimed that man himself imposes patterns of his own upon nature through his inventions. Not only is man unable to distinguish a given reality from his own constructions, but even to think of trying to do so, it is argued, is to fall from the pure ideal of science as complete technological control of nature. But all this can mean in the end of the day is that in his scientific activity man is only meeting himself, fulfilling himself, and that there is no meaning in anything except that which he puts into it out of himself. And so the real outcome of this line of thought is meaninglessness and futility, everywhere apparent in the social life of our 'scientific' civilization.

Thus it is apparent that theological and natural science share the same basic problem: how to refer our thoughts and statements genuinely beyond ourselves, how to reach knowledge of reality in which we do not intrude ourselves distortingly into the picture, and yet how to retain the full and integral place of the human subject in it all. When this is discerned the dialogue between theology and science takes a different turn, for then they are seen to be allies in a common front where each faces the same insidious enemy, namely, man himself assuming the role of the Creator, acknowledging nothing except what he has made and declining to allow any of his constructions to be controlled by unconstructed reality beyond. Man and nature are here organically related and 'God' is swallowed up between them. As Georgio de Santillana has said, 'The real conflict over these recent years of ours is not between "science and religion"; it is between romantic naturalism and a philosophy of order and design.' (*The Origins of Scientific Thought*, p. 301.) Yet romantic naturalism arises just as easily in 'religion' as in natural science. Hence I would add, that as long as we think of the dialogue as between *science* and *religion* we shall not escape from romantic naturalism—in any case that seems to me to be implied in just this contraposition. Rather must we be concerned with the dialogue between *science* and *theology*, and between the philosophy of natural science and the philosophy of theological science in the common struggle for scientific method on their proper ground and their own distinctive fields.

It is not the intention of this book to engage in that dialogue, although it is naturally unavoidable, any more than it is the intention of the discussion to engage in apologetics, although that too cannot but arise. Rather it is my intention to clarify the processes of scientific activity in theology, to throw human thinking of God back upon Him as its direct and proper Object, and thus to serve the self-scrutiny of theology as a pure science. At the same time it is the aim of the argument to draw out the implications for the human subject of the fact that he is addressed by God and summoned to faithful and disciplined exercise of his reason in response to God's Word, and therefore to call a halt to the romantic irrationality and bloated subjectivity with which so much present-day theology is saturated. This is then an essay in philosophical theology calling for objectivity and rationality within the positive and constructive task of theological science.

This volume is dedicated to Bernard Lovell, as he was then, who put to me the initial questions as to scientific method in theology which led me to examine more carefully the nature of theology as a science, and to select this theme for the Hewett Lectures.

I am most grateful to the Rev. Dr. Cameron Dinwoodie, of Langholm, for his careful revision of the proofs and preparation of the index. Mr. Andrew Louth and Mr. Iain R. Torrance, my son, both of Edinburgh University, have also read the proofs and helped to purge them of not a few errors. I am much indebted to all three of them.

It remains for me to express my cordial gratitude to the Oxford University Press, especially to Mr. Geoffrey N. S. Hunt and his colleagues, for much kindness and consideration, and to thank those who have helped me so nobly and ably with the typing, Miss E. R. Leslie and Miss Joan Morris of New College.

The University of Edinburgh   T. F. T.
The Feast of St. Athanasius, 1967

Contents

I

The Knowledge of God

(1) SOME INTRODUCTORY QUESTIONS

'It is part of our situation that we are inevitably and inseparably *inside* the knowledge relation, from the start to the end, and so cannot step outside of ourselves to an indifferent standpoint from which to view and adjust the relations of thought and being. Thought and being are together from the beginning. All discrimination of the contribution of the one side of the relation to the other is an analysis of a concrete togetherness of thought and being in a particular department of existence. Since, moreover, all possible Objects of thought come before the mind in a relation of Subject and Object—the wildest chimeras, the grossest illusions, as well as the soberest "matters of fact"—any discussion of the contribution of Subject to Object, of Object to Subject, of the proportions of subjectivity to objectivity in a particular topic, must have in view some particular sphere of actual concrete existence in which the Subject is more than the logical presupposition of knowledge in general, and the Object is viewed in relation to some actual concrete interest or pre-occupation on the part of the Subject.'

These sentences are taken from James Brown's fine study of the place of the Subject-Object relation in theological thinking of the last hundred years.[1] They are set down here not only because of their healthy rejection of dualism coupled with a refusal to admit that there is anything inherently wrong with the form of knowledge in the Subject-Object relation, but because in them Dr. Brown is concerned to maintain a principle that is still only imperfectly realized in many branches of knowledge, namely, that genuine critical questions as to the *possibility* of knowledge cannot be raised *in abstracto* but only *in concreto*, not *a priori* but only *a posteriori*.

[1] *Subject and Object in Modern Theology* (Croall Lectures for 1953), p. 170 f.

So far as modern theology is concerned this question has been posed by Søren Kierkegaard in two works of far-reaching importance, *Philosophical Fragments*, and *Concluding Unscientific Postscript to the Philosophical Fragments*. In them we have an attack upon a type of abstract thought which ignores the concrete and the temporal and abrogates the actual and the real. It is false, Kierkegaard argued, to answer a question in a medium in which the question cannot arise, and therefore it is wrong to pose the question as to possibility in abstraction from the reality which alone can give rise to it. That is why it is a contradiction to infer existence from thought, for 'thought takes existence away from the real and thinks it by abrogating its actuality, by translating it into the sphere of the impossible'.[1] This means that in any branch of knowledge we begin within the knowledge relation where we actually are, and seek to move forward by clarifying and testing what we already know and by seeking to deepen and enlarge its content. To do this we are forced at some time to raise questions as to the ground and reality of this knowledge, and only then can the question as to its possibility be meaningful or helpful.

In order to see something of the importance and scope of this principle we may glance at the different ways in which three very different philosophers speak of it, without necessarily committing ourselves to support their particular views.

Our first philosopher is Edmund Husserl.[2] Although he himself was concerned with philosophy as a rigorous science of essential being, dealing not with the real, but with transcendentally reduced phenomena, or, as he called it, an 'eidetic' science of pure possibility, he admitted that the natural sciences had grown to greatness precisely by fencing off their fields of research from all critical forms of inquiry into the possibility of knowledge, and so refusing to allow epistemological questions to obstruct the course of their inquiries. This is what Husserl called 'the dogmatic standpoint' of the positive sciences which insist in acknowledging the original right of all data and so take their start from the primordial givenness of the facts they deal with. '*The right attitude* to take in the *pre-philosophical*

---

[1] *Concluding Unscientific Postscript*, pp. 287, 281. See the whole of Part Two, ch. III; and also *Philosophical Fragments*, 'Interlude', pp. 59 ff.

[2] *Ideas: General Introduction to Pure Phenomenology* (1913, E.T. 1931), p. 95 f.

and, in a good sense, *dogmatic* sphere of inquiry, to which all the empirical sciences (but not these alone) belong, is in full consciousness *to discard all scepticism together with all "natural philosophy" and "theory of knowledge"*, and find the data of knowledge where they actually face you, whatever difficulties epistemological reflexion may *subsequently* raise concerning the possibility of such data being there.'[1]

In simpler language, this means that each special science, starting within the field of pre-scientific knowledge, presupposes the reality and accessibility of its own proper object and the possibility of knowing it further, and refuses to justify itself as a science by stepping outside of its own actuality, but leaves the question of its justification to be answered by its own positive content and inner rationality.

Our second philosopher is Eberhard Grisebach[2] who is concerned, unlike Husserl, to insist that even in the field of philosophy or metaphysics itself, epistemology has its proper place not at the beginning but at the end, for the logical questions it raises have normative rather than constitutive significance for knowledge. That is why, if we look at the history of philosophy, we find that authentic logic reaches its precise and developed forms at the end of great philosophical epochs, as with an Aristotle, a Leibniz, or a Hegel, while in all unfruitful times logic presses to the front and tends to displace philosophy, so that instead of being the self-critical discipline of creative thought it is too frequently *nur Technik*. It is not difficult to see that according to Grisebach our pre-occupation with logical analysis in much contemporary philosophy could only be regarded as obstructionist and ultimately sterile.

A similar line is taken by our third philosopher, John Macmurray.[3] 'If we limit the term knowledge as some philosophers would do, to that "logical certainty" which is the result of theoretical demonstration, we should have to confess that there is not and cannot be knowledge, and so relapse into complete scepticism.'[4] It is Professor Macmurray's contention

[1] Ibid. The italics are Husserl's.

[2] *Wahrheit und Wirklichkeiten, Entwurf zu einem metaphysischen System* (1919), pp. 333 ff., 362 ff. See also *Gegenwart, eine kritische Ethik* (1928).

[3] See especially *The Self as Agent*, chs. III, IV, and VIII.

[4] Op. cit., p. 168.

that knowledge in action is our primary knowledge, for the knowing Self is an agent having his existence in time where he is active both in pre-scientific and in scientific knowledge. Certainly there is a place even in the natural sciences for abstract critical thought; indeed the sciences could make no progress without it, but such critical thinking presupposes and depends upon the primary knowledge we gain in action. If, however, we start off with pure thought, we at once abstract from action, and so isolate our knowledge from that which sustains it, isolating the Self from existence as a purely logical subject concerned only with *idea*, that is, with the non-existent. It is precisely this radical dualism falsely posited between thinking and existence, knowledge and action, that lies behind so many of our modern problems, and therefore it must be rejected in order that 'a new logical form of personal activity' may be developed in which the theory of knowledge occupies a subordinate place within actual knowledge, and in which verification involves commitment in action.

In order to see how this fundamental question has affected modern theology we return again to the contention of Kierkegaard that although abstract thought considers both possibility and reality, it is unable to sustain the relation of possibility to reality, for it has falsified its concept of reality by trying to think it within the medium of possibility. To overcome this Kierkegaard called for a modification in traditional logical procedure in order to make room for thinking actual existence, without converting it into necessity—that is, he called for a mode of rational thought within the subject-object relationship which would be genuinely in accordance with and adequate to the nature of the object. Kierkegaard tackled this from both sides of the subject-object relationship. The object of the theological knowledge is Truth in the form of personal Being, that is Truth as active Subject, but this Truth must be known, must be an object of knowledge, in a way appropriate to its nature as Subjectivity, for only then will the knowing subject be in the truth in relation to it. Thus the very mode of apprehending the Truth belongs to the truth. This whole line of argument was expounded under the caption 'Truth is Subjectivity'.[1]

[1] *Concluding Unscientific Postscript*, pp. 169 ff.

It is at this very point that Kierkegaard has so often been severely misunderstood[1]—perhaps not altogether without reason because of his love for ironical and often exaggerated expression. Kierkegaard was certainly the avowed enemy of all objectivism, whether that was found in the rationalization of truth into a system of ideas or in ecclesiastical institutionalism, but his emphasis upon subjectivity was never intended to mean the abrogation of objectivity.[2] On the contrary, authentic subjectivity on the part of man, he held, is only possible when he collides with the objectivity of the divine Subject. This is the experience of faith, 'the highest passion of subjectivity', in which he so encounters the Truth that his own existence is involved and transformed in conformity to it. Apart from this the Truth is not known, but within the relation of knowledge truth is found not only on the side of the object known but on the side of the knower who must be in a relation of truth to the object in order to know it. Hence it can be said: 'The mode of apprehension of the truth is precisely the truth.'[3]

Through ignoring the fact that this subjectivity reposes upon and takes its rise from an objective ground in the divine reality, a whole host of 'existentialist' thinkers arose to interpret in their own way that 'truth is subjectivity', i.e. in a sense the opposite to that which Kierkegaard intended. He pointed out that when the question of truth is raised in an objective manner, the knower is directed objectively to the truth as an object to which he is related, but attention is not focussed upon that relationship. When the question of the truth is raised subjectively the knower is directed subjectively to the truth, and then the attention is focussed upon the nature of his relationship to the truth; but in this case it can be said, 'if only the mode of this relationship is in the truth, the individual is in the truth even if he should happen to be related to what is not true'.[4]

<hr />

[1] For discerning interpretations of Kierkegaard see H. Diem, *Die Existenzdialektik von Søren Kierkegaard*; J. Brown, *Subject and Object in Modern Theology*, chs. I, II, and VII; J. Heywood Thomas, *Subjectivity and Paradox*.

[2] This holds good for Martin Buber; see especially *The Eclipse of God*, in which he argues powerfully for a genuine objectivity against subjectivist tendencies in modern religion, philosophy, theology and psychology.

[3] *Concluding Unscientific Postscript*, p. 287.

[4] Op. cit., p. 178.

It is theoretically possible therefore to have a right 'existential' relation to X, that is to be 'subjectively' related to it, and yet to miss the mark entirely because X is not the Truth, but what is of ultimate importance is that he should be in a right relation to the truth. That 'truth is subjectivity' does not mean that the object of faith is to be confounded with faith, nor does it mean that the knowing subject constructs the object out of, or discovers the truth in, his own subjectivity.[1] On the contrary the very passion of faith is the opening up of the knowing subject to the most objective of all realities, God Himself as He actively communicates Himself to us in Jesus Christ. To know the Truth is to be in a right relation to Him, to be in the truth with the Truth. To know this Truth in a medium and in a mode appropriate to Him is to do the truth and to live the truth, to be true.

When in this tradition we turn to the theology of Karl Barth we find these basic issues in modern theology thrown into very sharp relief. In 1927 Barth published the first volume of *Die Christliche Dogmatik*, a volume of prolegomena, in which he sought to lay the foundations of a theology of the Word within the medium of the objective reality of divine Revelation, and beginning from within the actual knowledge of God, Father, Son and Holy Spirit, in the Church. In the great debates that followed Barth found himself under heavy attack on two fronts, mainly from Lutherans and Romans. Before long it became apparent that he was being understood within the existentialist misinterpretation of Kierkegaard, from which he himself was not altogether free, and was being misunderstood in his relation to the Romanist metaphysical presuppositions regarding subject and object. So far as Barth himself was concerned the debate called for a real *catharsis* in his theology in which he had to think out his relation to existential decision on the one hand and to the analogy of being on the other hand. It was during this period also that he engaged in his epoch-making studies of Anselm in which, as he says, he learned the fundamental attitude to the problem of the

---

[1] Cf. again Martin Buber, op. cit., p. 82: 'The soul can never legitimately make an assertion, even a metaphysical one, out of its own creative power. It can make an assertion only out of a binding real relationship to a truth which it articulates.'

knowledge and existence of God.[1] The upshot was his abandon-
ment of his project for a *Christian Dogmatics*, and the rewriting
of its first volume for the beginning of his massive *Church
Dogmatics* in 1932. In this he carefully expunged anything
that might lend itself to an existentialist interpretation, developed fully his doctrine of Grace over against every aprioristic
analogy of being, and elaborated a theological method in which
he learned from Anselm (*fides quaerens intellectum*), Calvin (*omnis
recta cognitio Dei ab obedientia nascitur*) and Kierkegaard (the
relation of *possibility* to the *reality* of the Incarnation)—although
the name of Kierkegaard is rarely mentioned in the subsequent
volumes. In other words, Barth found his theology thrust back
more and more upon its proper object, and so he set himself
to think through the whole of theological knowledge in such a
way that it might be consistently faithful to the concrete act
of God in Jesus Christ from which it actually takes its rise in
the Church, and, further, in the course of that inquiry to ask
about the presuppositions and conditions on the basis of which
it comes about that God is known, in order to develop from
within the actual content of theology its own interior logic
and its own inner criticism which will help to set theology free
from every form of ideological corruption.[2]

Barth's return to Anselm meant going behind the scientific
methods developed in scholastic theology (whether in its
Roman or in its Protestant form), which derived from the
sic et non procedure of Abelard and through the use of traditional
logic and dialectic operated with great antinomies in its doctrines of God and man, such as, mind and will, being and act,
election and freedom, justice and mercy, etc. Barth's way has
been to thrust behind and beyond these antinomies and dialec-
tics and under the influence of Biblical theology and the new
mode of questioning that arose in the sixteenth century to
build up a positive theology with 'new' logical forms derived

[1] *Church Dogmatics* 2, 1, p. 4. See also *Church Dogmatics* 1; 1 especially pp. 17
ff.,; 2, 1, p. 8 f.; and *Fides Quaerens Intellectum* (1931). Barth's peculiar interest in
Anselm is already evident in *Die Christl. Dogmatik* 1, pp. 97 ff., 226 ff., etc. See
my own study of Barth, *Karl Barth: An Introduction to His Early Theology*, pp. 180 ff.
[2] For illuminating accounts of Barth's theological method see especially F. W.
Camfield, *Reformation Old and New* (1947), Part I; and C. West, *Communism and
the Theologians* (1958), Ch. 5. Barth discloses his own method most clearly in
Church Dogmatics, 2, 1, Ch. V.

from the Word of God. The scientific theology that followed the Reformation (in great dogmaticians like Gerhard, Quenstedt, Polanus, Heidegger, etc.) was unable to achieve this in a way really appropriate to its nature for it lacked the necessary philosophical tools. Hence when it found itself under attack from the side of the Counter-Reformation with its revived Thomism, it also fell back upon the *philosophia perennis* to supply it with the instruments it needed to establish and defend itself.[1] In the course of this new scholasticism Protestant theology lapsed into the old antinomies once more and sometimes made them sharper than ever.[2]

The theology of Karl Barth is to be understood as a rethinking and restating of Reformed theology after the immense philosophical and scientific developments of modern times which have supplied us with new conceptual and scientific tools. While seeking to articulate Christian theology within this world of new thought-forms Barth has had to wage a fiercer war with modern philosophy than ever the medieval and Protestant schoolmen had to with ancient philosophy, but he has been no less appreciative of the contributions of scientific and philosophical thinking to the task of theology, which, just because it operates within the same world of speech and thought as they, cannot and must not isolate itself from them.[3] One of the interesting results of this new positive and dynamic theology in the modern style is the parallel between its method and that which has emerged in quantum physics. This is particularly evident in the way in which both physics and theology have had to treat the old antinomies between object and subject, thing and motion, being and act, determinism and freedom, etc.[4] Since Barth began to work out his rational method and develop his Dogmatics in a sustained integration of content and method, modern science has made even greater strides toward the clarification of the deep objective rationality in

[1] The old difficulties were not avoided, as many claimed, by the study of Aristotle in Greek rather than Latin, as the new formalistic Aristotelianism of Peter Ramus made clear.

[2] Cf. a similar situation which arose in Roman theology in the debate between Molinism and Jansenism.

[3] See the Introduction to the Eng. edit. of Barth's *Theology and Church*, 1962, and also *Karl Barth: An Introduction to His Early Theology*, 1962, pp. 148 ff., 180 ff.

[4] Cf. G. Howe, *Kerygma und Dogma*, 4. 1, pp. 34 ff.

the nature of things, e.g. in the periodicity or mathematical structure of the elements,[1] and the effect of this upon theology is to challenge every attempt to transcend the subject-object relationship as an irrational flight from objectivity and rigorous, exact thinking.[2]

Whatever be our views of the detailed teaching of any of the theologians mentioned, it is in the light of this development, and without forgetting for a moment the other giants in the field of theology, notably Thomas Aquinas and Friedrich Schleiermacher, that we will seek to answer the questions as to the nature of theology and its scientific method, questions that still press hard upon us in a day of unparalleled scientific rigour and methodological development.

In scientific theology we begin with the actual knowledge of God, and seek to test and clarify this knowledge by inquiring carefully into the relation between our knowing of God and God Himself in His being and nature. Then in the light of this clarification we seek to be more and more open and ready for God, so that we may respond faithfully and truly to all that He declares and discloses to us of Himself. It is through this disciplined obedience of our mind to God as He gives Himself to be known by us that we advance in knowledge of Him. It is in the course of this inquiry that we raise the question of the possibility of the knowledge of God—that is to say, in inquiring how God is actually known, we inquire also how far He may or can be known. In this procedure we have to reject as unscientific any attempt that begins with the question, *How can God be known?* and then advances to the question, *How far is this actual?* We cannot begin by forming independently a theory of how God is knowable and then seek to test it out or indeed to actualize it and fill it with material content. How God can be known must be determined from first to last by the way in which He actually is known.

[1] See S. Dockx, *Théorie Fondamentale du Système Periodique des Elements*, 1959.

[2] It is a pity that Barth's persistent attack upon rationalism, i.e. upon reason abstracted from its object and treated as *res cogitans*, operating solely out of itself without attention to the given, should be attacked, e.g. by H. J. Paton, so bitterly, as anti-rational, since it is Barth's aim to restore to the reason its true rationality through overcoming Cartesian dualism and romantic irrationality (e.g. in his criticism of Otto). What is really at stake here is Barth's *realism* as against the *idealism*, and often the subjectivism, of his critics.

It is because the nature of what is known, as well as the nature of the knower, determines how it can be known, that only when it actually is known are we in a position to inquire how it can be known.[1]

At this point we see right away a close resemblance between the road of theological inquiry and the road that modern science, e.g. quantum physics, is being forced to take in recognizing the impossibility of separating out the way in which knowledge arises from the actual knowledge that it attains. Thus in theology the canons of inquiry that are discerned in the process of knowing are not separable from the body of actual knowledge out of which they arise. In the nature of the case a true and adequate account of theological epistemology cannot be gained apart from substantial exposition of the content of the knowledge of God, and of the knowledge of man and the world as creatures of God. It is scientifically false to begin with epistemology. On the other hand it must be admitted that we operate with an inchoate epistemology as soon as we begin to engage in theological inquiry, that is with a tacit understanding of how we know God, although it can yield a proper epistemology only as we advance in the knowledge of God and submit our actual knowing to criticism and control in accordance with the nature of the object of our knowledge. This means that all the way through theological inquiry we must operate with an *open* epistemology in which we allow the way of our knowing to be clarified and modified *pari passu* with advance in deeper and fuller knowledge of the object, and that we will be unable to set forth an account of that way of knowing in advance but only by looking back from what has been established as knowledge.

It must be said right away, that what is offered in this discussion presupposes the full content of theological knowledge, and is an attempt to set forth the way of proper theological

---

[1] Cf. F. Heinemann: 'Erkenntnistheorie und die Sachwissenschaft stehen in einem Verhältnis wechselseitiger Abhängigkeit: Erkenntnistheorie ohne wissenschaftliche Kenntnisse bleibt leer, und wissenschaftliches Wissen ohne erkenntnistheoretische Besinnung bleibt blind.' *Die Philosophie in 20. Jahrhundert* (edited by F. Heinemann), p. 296. Likewise G. Ryle (*The Concept of Mind*, p. 30): 'Efficient practice precedes the theory of it, methodologies presuppose the application of the methods of the critical investigation of which they are the products.' And earlier A. E. Taylor, *The Elements of Metaphysics*, p. 38.

knowledge in accordance with that content—although, of course, little of that positive content can be expounded here. It is to be granted also that what is offered here is not fully meaningful if considered in abstraction from that material content. All we can attempt to do, therefore, is to examine what theological knowledge actually is in the light of its material content with a view to clarifying our understanding of its method and cleansing theological activity from impure mixture, i.e. from pseudo-theological thinking.

Before we go more deeply into the nature of our knowledge of God, we must pause to make several preliminary observations.

(a) Knowledge of God is essentially a *rational event*. It is not concerned at all with anything that is sub-rational or irrational. We are concerned in theology with a fully rational communication between God and man and a fully rational response between man and God.[1] Indeed we are concerned with the very essence of rationality before which all our other experiences appear inadequately rational. By rationality, of course, we do not mean something that lies in the reason itself, some sort of self-rationality—that is a very common error—but rather our ability to relate our thought and our action appropriately to objective intelligible realities. Reason is our ability to recognize and assent to what is beyond it.[2]

Here we may well take as our guide, if only by way of a preliminary definition, the account of 'rationality' given by Professor John Macmurray. 'The rationality of thought,' he says, 'does not lie in the thought itself, as a quality of it, but depends upon its reference to the external world as known in immediate experience.'[3] Or again, in a later work: 'Reason is the capacity to behave consciously in terms of what is not ourselves. We can express this briefly by saying that reason

[1] It does not seem to me helpful to speak of God as 'supra-rational', either, for how could we have rational knowledge of this? To know God is to know that He is more fully rational than we are. If He transcends our comprehension, it is because we are not able fully to apprehend Him, but to know this God is to partake of His rationality and to become more fully rational. Hence it is difficult not to think of 'atheism' as a form of irrationality. But cf. H. D. Lewis's way of speaking of God as 'supra-rational', which does not empty our thought of God of rational content: *Philosophy of Religion*, p. 154 f.

[2] Cf. 'Faith and Philosophy', *The Hibbert Journal*, April 1949, pp. 242 ff.

[3] *Interpreting the Universe*, p. 131.

is the capacity to behave in terms of the nature of the object, that is to say, to behave objectively. Reason is thus our capacity for objectivity.' [1] This is not to deny that the objective reality may have the nature of a subject, or to question the place of the subject in our human knowing.[2] After all, as Nels Ferré has reminded us recently, reason is a function of the self and must be thought of as the subject engaged in activity.[3] It should not surprise us therefore that it is another subject who confronts us with full objectivity, for it is when our own objectivity meets the objectivity of another subject that we have our fullest and most rational experience.[4] This is a question that we shall have to discuss later, but at this point all that we are concerned to claim is that our knowledge of God is in the fullest sense a rational experience, so that we cannot for a moment concede that religious knowledge begins where rational experience is limited or becomes marginal.

(b) Knowledge of God is *knowledge* in the proper sense of that word. Here we are using the term *knowledge* formally in the same way in which we use it in every branch of true knowledge or *scientia*. It is *formally* the same, but not, of course, *materially*, for the kind of knowledge in question depends upon

[1] *Reason and Emotion*, p. 19.

[2] The terms *subject, subjective*, and *object, objective* need not present great difficulty if we remember that not only are they correlative to one another, but that each has a proper ambivalence. Originally *subject, subjective* referred to that which is under our control or attention, so that *subject* might refer to the subject of a realm or to the object of thought or study. Originally *object, objective* referred to that which is placed before us, that which encounters us or opposes us, or that which is presented to and so relates to a subject. Today, when these terms are used *concretely*, they still tend to have their original meanings, especially in the verbal forms. Thus we speak about the subjects of a king, subjection, or subject in the sense of subject-matter, and we speak about an object in the sense of an obstacle, about objection, objectionable, or about the objective that lies ahead of us, etc. On the other hand, when we use them *epistemologically*, we reverse their meanings, so that subject refers to the self, the thinking or knowing agent, or it refers to the self over against us, who encounters us, whereas object refers to what is known or thought or is the subject of our attention, or it refers to a thing or object external to the mind, what is not ourselves but is in itself. In spite of this reversal the original meanings which are still powerfully evident in the verbal forms, to *subject* (subjection), and to *object* (objection), continue to influence the epistemological usage. See further James Brown, op. cit., p. 19 f.; R. Eucken, *Main Currents of Modern Thought* (E.T. 1912), Ch. 1; and E. Cassirer, *Substanzbegriff und Funktionsbegriff* (1910), Chs. 6 and 7.

[3] Nels Ferré, *Reason in Religion*, p. 3 ff.

[4] Cf. J. Macmurray (*Reason and Emotion*, p. 32): 'The capacity to love objectively is the capacity which makes us persons. It is the ultimate source of our capacity to behave in terms of the object. It is the core of rationality.'

its material content, that is, upon the nature of the objective reality known to us.[1]

By knowledge, then, we are concerned with a conscious relation to an object which we recognize to be distinct from ourselves but toward which we direct our thought as something intelligible and ascertainable. Actually to know we must be able to distinguish what we know from our knowing of it.[2] All true knowledge involves a two-fold operation, a positive relation of attachment in which we submit ourselves to an object, and a relation of detachment in which we discriminate between the object and our awareness of it. As Tillich has expressed it, 'cognitive distance is the presupposition of cognitive union.'[3] Wherever we fail to distinguish the object as a reality existing independently of our knowing it, or confound a subjective experience with what is actually objective, we do not have true knowledge; nor do we have true knowledge when we fail to conform our thought properly to the external world, or seek to manipulate the external world in order to make it conform to our own subjectivity. When we act in these ways we are falsifying our proper relation to objective reality and are behaving irrationally. In true knowledge we refer our thought appropriately to the nature of reality and at the same time distinguish it as objective to ourselves and independent of our apprehension of it, although, of course, we cannot know anything by leaving it alone to itself, that is, apart from our experiencing and apprehending it. This is the kind of knowledge that obtains in every science, and it is with this scientific knowledge that we have to do in theology. How far we have to adjust the relations of subject and object to one another in the act of knowledge depends upon the particular nature of the object which varies from field to field, but this is a question that will have to be discussed later.

(c) Knowledge of God is conceptual both in its acts of cognition and in its acts of expression. Right from the start it involves a structured understanding in formed acts of cognition, while the whole movement of theological thought consists in developing and clarifying the conceptual structure

---

[1] See *The School of Faith*, 1959, pp. XXI ff., and XLIII ff.

[2] Cf. A. E. Taylor, *The Elements of Metaphysics*, p. 410 f. and also *The Faith of a Moralist*, vol. 2, p. 212 ff. on the inexhaustible nature of the *given* in our knowledge.

[3] *Systematic Theology*, vol. 1, p. 105.

of this knowledge by constant reference to the object and by advancing in the cognitive modes of rationality set up between us and God as He communicates Himself to us.[1] This conceptual character of the knowledge of God arises out of His self-disclosure in His Word, in the Word which God is and which He reveals to us. We shall return to this again, but at this preliminary stage we are concerned to make it clear that theology is fully rational even in the sense of conceptual understanding and conceptual communication. Its conceptual character is not something that it has to acquire or which we have to give to it by borrowing from some other mode of rationality such as philosophy or natural science. It operates with a form of rational cognition which it claims to be valid in its own right, and which is basically conceptual in its own nature, and is therefore not to be distinguished as symbolic in contrast to what is conceptual.[2] We apprehend God without a discursive process, but not without an act of conceptual cognition. We must pause to ask what we mean by 'concept'. By derivation 'to conceive' means to lay hold of, to seize, to take in, to comprehend, but there are different ways of conception according to the nature of what is conceived. To conceive in the womb is different from conceiving in the mind, but even in the mind there are different modes of conception in accordance with differences in the nature of what is conceived. Thus the use of 'concept' is governed not only by the nature of the conceiver but by the nature of what is conceived, so that the kind of concept that arises in the cognition of what is entirely determinate, for example, will be different from the kind of concept that arises in the cognition of what is indeterminate or not determinate in the same way.[3]

[1] Cf. Martin Buber's attack upon 'the conceptual letting go of God' in which modern philosophy (of the existentialist type) 'cuts off its own hands, the hands with which it is able to hold and grasp God', *The Eclipse of God*, p. 125.

[2] This is the distinction that is basic to the whole of Tillich's theology, even though he admits that religious 'mythological symbols' have conceptual elements that can and must be developed—see especially *Dynamics of Faith*, 1957, pp. 89–95. Tillich's theology represents a conceptual rationalization, by the aid of the discursive reason, of the symbolic knowledge of faith. It is against the deeply-embedded element of romantic irrationalism here that classical theology protests in its claim that faith itself has a conceptual structure and cannot be contrasted with the conceptual in this way.

[3] This is of course one of the primary differences between the concepts of theological science and those of the natural sciences, although there is a necessary overlapping in their conceptual forms.

This calls for several remarks.

In the first place, we must make a distinction between *closed* and *open* concepts, even if we recognize, as we must, that this distinction can never be clean-cut. There are acts of conception in which, as it were, we can get our fingers round something and enclose it in our grasp, but there are other acts of conception in which what we are grasping at is too big to get our fingers round, for, as we grasp or conceive it, it transcends us, so that even in genuine apprehension there cannot be full comprehension. In other words, it belongs to our very understanding of it that it cannot be exhausted by our knowledge of it, and that by its very nature it reaches out so far beyond us that we are unable to delimit our concept of it or bring it within the four corners of a proposition. 'Closed concepts' are of the kind that we can reduce to clipped propositional ideas, whereas 'open concepts' are of the kind which by their very nature resist being put into a strait-jacket, for the reality conceived keeps on disclosing itself to us in such a way that it continually overflows all our statements about it. Closed concepts are rigid and easily manipulable but open concepts are elastic because they operate on the boundary between the already known and the new.[1]

We may illustrate this from two very different realms. Frequently in Byzantine art the figure of Christ is portrayed standing on a dais which is so depicted that its lines are not made slightly to converge as the laws of perspective demand, but are, on the contrary, made to diverge so that when produced even to infinity they could never meet. The background is filled in with gold, for it is only in this open perspective reaching out to a golden eternity that Christ may be truly conceived; He cannot be brought within a perspective in which the lines when produced meet at a point in finitude. Here the concept of Christ while definite at one end is infinitely open at the other, but it *is* a concept.

Our second illustration, which is very different, is drawn from modern physics which operates on the boundary between classical mechanics and quantum mechanics. The concepts of classical physics considered by themselves, are closed, for they are constructed by a science operating within a field

[1] Cf. Hans-Georg Gadamer on 'the logical structure of openness', *Wahrheit und Methode*, p. 344 f.

delimited by what is perceptible, so that even when it reaches out beyond what is actually perceived it cannot handle anything that is not describable in terms of perceptibility. Modern physics, however, has only been able to make its great advance by a break in the structure of classical science, through a dissolution of its rigid framework and an opening out of its concepts.[1] This means, as Heisenberg has shown so effectively, the acknowledgement that the concepts of classical science have only a limited range of applicability,[2] or as von Weizsäcker has put it, the renunciation of the final validity of the criterion of perceptibility.[3] Thus while the concepts of modern physics are more closed at one end through the limited validity of the classical framework,[4] they are widely open at the other end, for what is conceived beyond that in the nature of the case cannot be brought within the strait-jacket of the old closed concepts without radical falsification. As Heisenberg has said, 'the scientific concepts cover always only a very limited part of reality, and the other part that has not yet been understood is infinite. Whenever we proceed from the known into the unknown we may hope to understand, but we may have to learn at the same time a new meaning of the word "understanding".'[5]

Theological concepts are, naturally, different from those of physics or indeed of art, so that these illustrations are not altogether apt, but they may serve to show that closed concepts have a limited range, that not all concepts are closed, and that where we are concerned with the new or with what cannot be construed in terms of what we already know, we can only act rationally if we operate with open concepts. The way in which concepts are open is determined by what they are open toward, so that theological concepts are open in a different way from the concepts of quantum physics; they are *open toward God*.

[1] W. Heisenberg, *Physics and Philosophy* (Gifford Lectures at St. Andrews for 1955–56), pp. 29, 198.

[2] Op. cit., pp. 44, 56, 90, 125, 179, 201.

[3] *The World View of Physics*, pp. 29 f., 54 f., 93 f., etc.

[4] We shall see later that they must be open at both ends, in the sense that they must be open to critical reconstruction as well as open to the assimilation of new knowledge.

[5] Op. cit., p. 201.

In the second place, we require to clarify the relation between concept and image. So long as thought and being are held together, concept and image modify each other, but when a radical cleavage is posited between them, concept and image are both embarked upon a process of increasing abstraction. In many respects this is the great problem that modern thought has inherited from Cartesian dualism, the disastrous cleavage between the mental and the material, between form and matter, which has resulted in a radical bifurcation of man's knowledge so evident in the development of great symbolic systems on the one hand, e.g. mathematical logic, and in the development of empirical sciences based on observation and experiment on the other hand.[1] One of the exciting trends in our own day is the attempt being made in various directions to think symbol and concrete reality together again, but this can be done only by getting behind the split between form and matter, or between mind and what we think.[2]

The sharp distinction between concept and image has affected theology rather differently, for it is concerned primarily with man's knowledge of God, rather than of the world, and yet because this has to be expressed in the language and thought-forms we inherit from previous generations, it has hardly been able to escape serious involvement in the Cartesian dualism. The problem first arose in a sharp way when Christian theology had to be expressed in the thought-forms inherited from Greece. Hellenistic thought operated with a radical dichotomy between a realm of ideas and a realm of events, and it took its stand within the realm of ideas as the realm of the ultimately real. From this perspective it could only regard the Christian doctrines of God at work in history, of the coming of the Son of God into human and creaturely existence, of the Eternal entering the world of space and time, as unreal, or at best as a 'mythological' way of expressing certain timeless truths. Various attempts were made to solve this question, by the Gnostics who sought to give a philosophical interpretation to Christian 'mythology' and so developed a highly intellectual system in which *gnosis* and ritual, the conceptual and the

---

[1] Cf. F. Heinemann, *Neue Wege der Philosophie*, p. 34 f.

[2] This is one of the enduring merits of G. Ryle's *The Concept of Mind*, even though he often drives his cart and horse along tracks that will not take it.

symbolic, while sharply distinguished, were religiously correlated; and by some early apologists who sought to 'demythologize' the Christian Gospel by subjecting the crudities of faith (πίστις) to scientific treatment (ἐπιστήμη) and so producing a Christian understanding (γνῶσις) acceptable to the world of culture and science.[1] Both these attempts failed, although they have been revived from time to time, as in our own day, and of course with different thought-forms, by thinkers like Tillich and Bultmann.

However, there did develop out of the patristic theology a compromised answer to the problem which succeeded in holding concept and image together in a way that stood the test of a thousand years. This was the Augustinian doctrine of the sacramental universe, combining Plotinian and Ptolemaic notions in a 'Christian' cosmology, which was given its fullest and most powerful expression in the medieval synthesis of patristic theology and Greek philosophy, notably in the great work of Thomas Aquinas. This in turn came under attack, a double attack, from the Reformation which called in question its theological content from the side of biblical and patristic theology, and from critical philosophy and empirical science which called in question the presuppositions of its logic in Aristotelian physics and metaphysics. The great merit, particularly of Thomist theology, is the remarkable way in which it holds together concept and image through its doctrine of analogy, but one of its demerits is the extent to which it systematizes all knowledge of God in a rigid framework of concepts which inevitably become closed within that system even if they are not in themselves. Embedded in this lies a conception of perceptibility which is no longer tenable, while the insistence of St. Thomas that we have 'no direct knowledge of any existence save the world of nature as perceived by the five senses', and his reliance upon a discursive movement of thought for our basic knowledge of God,[2] lays him peculiarly open to attack from the side of critical philosophy and science. Some modern Thomists wisely seek to get past this difficulty by developing the notion of a direct apprehension of God

[1] Cf. here my contribution to the *Festschrift* for Oscar Cullmann, *Oikonomia. Heilsgeschichte als Thema der Theologie*, entitled 'The Implications of Oikonomia for Knowledge and Speech of God in Early Christian Theology', pp. 225 f, 232 f.

[2] See the excellent discussion by John Baillie, *Our Knowledge of God*, pp. 109 ff. and 167 ff.

through symbols that derive from sense-experience, and so seek to help out the inferential movement of the reason (*ratio*) by an immediate vision of the intellect (*intellectus*). In so far as this means that theological knowledge uses its symbols as transparent media for cognition, we cannot but agree, but this seems to require a better basis than either medieval or modern Thomism seems able to give it.[1]

But there is still a basic question here to be answered: What relation do images bear to God in theological knowledge? This is a question that arises in Austin Farrer's very attractive discussion, *The Glass of Vision*, in which he has a great deal to say that is of real importance. We must agree with him when he says: 'Faith discerns not the images, but what the images signify: and yet we cannot discern it except *through* the images.' But when he goes on to say, 'We cannot by-pass the images to seize an imageless truth',[2] we must ask, 'Do the images signify by *imaging* the reality, and does this mean that the reality is imageable in its nature?' If we can think of God only in images, and can operate only with image-truths, then is this not essentially a form of idolatry? The difficulty with Farrer is that he appears to 'think only with his eyes', like the Greeks who posited a 'mimetic' relation between the signs and the things signified. To use Wittgensteinian language, are these 'images' 'pictures' or 'tools'? Granted that images have and must have a place in our knowledge of God, are they not tools rather than pictures, pointing to a reality which they do not describe, and therefore making themselves in a real sense dispensable as they do their work and we apprehend the reality through them?[3] In other words, are the images

---

[1] When in this connection Thomists argue that knowledge of universals is prior to, and not subsequent to, knowledge of particulars, we must ask whether this is a historical priority or a logical priority that is envisaged. If the former, then must not analogy be reinterpreted in the historical context of the actual knowledge of God in Israel and in the Church, but if the latter, does this not mean that theological concepts come to us first *in vacuo*? Cf. E. L. Mascall, *Words and Images*, p. 124.

[2] A. M. Farrer, *The Glass of Vision*, p. 110, but see the whole of lectures IV and V.

[3] Cf. here Tillich's definition of a symbol, *Systematic Theology*, vol. 1, p. 265 f. 'A symbolic expression is one whose proper meaning is negated by that to which it points. And yet it is also affirmed by it, and this affirmation gives the symbolic expression an adequate basis for pointing beyond itself.' On Tillich's view this is possible because the symbol 'participates in that to which it points' (*Dynamics of Faith*, p. 42), but one must still ask for the mode of this participation, especially if the symbol is an 'image'

as images adapted to the human subject or the divine Subject?
When patristic theology struggled with the Greek concept of
eidetic image and of the mimetic or iconic relation between
words and the realities they signified, it insisted that images
have to be taken, not in a descriptive but in a *paradeigmatic*
sense, that is, as aids to our human weakness in apprehending
the indescribable God, to point Him out to us in such a way
that we may have some hold in our thought upon His objective
reality, but without actually imaging Him. As Hilary expressed it, the likeness or comparison the images entail is to
be regarded *as helpful to man rather than as fitted to God*, since they
suggest or indicate and do not exhaust Him.[1]

It must be admitted that the notion of images that do not
actually image while pointing to and signifying a reality is a
difficult one, yet surely this is the kind of image that is offered
to us in the biblical revelation, where images set the stage, as
it were, but where God is revealed through His Word in such
a way as to be entirely distinguished from the images employed.
In the biblical tradition image and word belong together, and
it is through *word* that the images are made to signify or indicate
that to which they point.[2] It is this powerful element of word
that makes us look through the images and hear past them to
what God has to say, and so to apprehend Him in such a way
that we do not have and are not allowed to have any imaginative or pictorial representation of Him in our thought. It is
through this word that we are able after all to point away
from the image to the reality it signifies, although that is what
Farrer denies can be done.[3] In this event we do not need to
bring in natural knowledge as 'a canon to interpret revelation',[4]
which has always proved to be damaging and distorting for
it gives our natural images an archetypal instead of an ectypal
relation to God's self-revelation. We do have to do here,
however, with a *natural* knowledge, but one *natural* to God and

[1] Hilary, *De Trinitate*, 1. 19; and cf. Athanasius, *Ad Serapionem*, 1. 20.

[2] Farrer himself seems to accept this, op. cit., p. 44.

[3] Op. cit., pp. 61, 94. Cf. here the 'signitive' art of the Catacombs in which, as
Vladimir Weidlé points out, the form and content are not fused, in which the form
does not embody thought, but signifies it within the sacramental context of the
Gospel, *The Baptism of Art*, pp. 7 ff. For a similar relation between word-language
and mathematical symbols, see below, pp. 257 ff.

[4] Op. cit., p. 110.

yet adapted, to cite Hilary again, to human understanding.[1] But since this is appropriate to the nature of God as Spirit, who cannot be known through eidetic images, our knowledge of Him cannot be construed in descriptive language.[2] How difficult it is to think and speak about God in this way should be evident from the Old Testament account of the ordeal through which Israel had to pass for many centuries until it got rid of thinking of God in εἴδη or εἴδωλα—we also require to be thoroughly schooled in Israel if we are to know and speak of God appropriately.

All this means that we must learn not to schematize our concepts to *percepts*. This is one of the points where Thomist theology needs to be questioned more profoundly, for the attempt to eke out the discursive process of knowing God by a direct cognitive act does not succeed in breaking free from the tyrannical assumption that all knowledge must ultimately rest upon a form of sense-perception—hence it can speak of this direct cognitive act of the intellect only in terms of *vision*. A similar problem is to be found in modern philosophy in its preoccupation with phenomenality, particularly in the continental traditions of phenomenology, but it is also evident in British empiricism with its obsession with questions of perception, and not least in the damaging notion of representative perception, or its earlier counterpart in the Middle Ages of 'images in the middle'. We also have the same problem in many contemporary thinkers who give to 'ostensive definition' a meaning tied to the model of perception.[3] In some ways an outstanding exception to this development of visual thinking is Kant's *Critique of the Practical Reason*,[4] in sharp contrast to his *Critique of Pure Reason* and *Critique of Judgment*, for the doctrine of the categorical imperative he develops in it appears to represent, if in a somewhat Stoic form, an attempt to give

[1] Hilary, op. cit., 1.4. Cf. also a powerful discussion of the same point in Novatian's *De Trinitate*.

[2] See *Theology in Reconstruction*, p. 19 f. 'Descriptive' is here being used in its normal sense, not as it is used in the expression 'descriptive metaphysics.'

[3] Cf. what A. D. Ritchie has to say about 'the visual epidemic', *Studies in the History and Method of the Sciences*, pp. 5 ff., 209 ff.

[4] I do not wish to suggest, in what follows, that Kant deliberately sought to interpret the activity of the Word of God in his notion of the categorical imperative, but that this notion is to be appreciated fully only against the background of his Lutheran inheritance. It could have arisen only out of the Reformation tradition.

philosophical expression to the Lutheran notion of the *Word* of God coming down directly from above—that is to say, here we have a serious attempt to deal with a concept not by interpreting it according to the pattern of optical experience but according to the pattern of auditory experience.

Christian theology has a peculiar interest in this question, for while it developed out of the Hebraic tradition with its own notion of *form* determined largely by its hearing of the Word of God,[1] it had to be expressed in the language and thought of the Hellenic tradition which operated with a different notion of *form* shaped by its perception of the true, the beautiful and the good, i.e. an essentially aesthetic form. It is to the Greeks that we owe what Professor Macmurray speaks of as 'the primacy of vision', and the tendency that has ever since dominated Western philosophy to take vision not only as the model of all sense-experience but of all knowledge.[2]

Looked at from this perspective, the Reformation must be interpreted as a great protest against the dominance of optical notions of form and thought, and as the insistence that these must be modified and corrected by notions of form and thought that are modelled upon *audition*. This is not to say that there is no place for knowledge construed on the pattern of visionary experience; on the contrary, it has an essential and unavoidable place, but it does mean that it would be false to construe all knowledge on the model of vision. It is in theological knowledge above all that we walk 'by faith and not by sight' (διὰ πίστεως, οὐ διὰ εἴδους) as St. Paul says,[3] but there are also other areas of knowledge where we can make genuine progress, as we have already seen, by the renunciation of the assumption that all knowledge must be describable in

---

[1] Of course the element of vision occupies a considerable role in the Hebraic tradition, but it is never primary. Typical of the combination of both audition and vision is the following: 'And the word of the Lord was precious in those days, for there was no open vision', I Sam. 3.1. On the other hand, the Hebrew O.T. is very much more alive with dramatic images than the Greek LXX.

[2] *The Self as Agent*, p. 105. 'From the time of the Greeks, and especially through the influence of Plato, "vision" has tended to be the model upon which all *knowledge* is construed. Thought is taken to be an inner vision.' This is what Martin Buber calls 'an opticizing of thought' or 'the hegemony of the sense of sight over the other senses', deriving from the Greeks, *The Eclipse of God*, p. 40 f. But cf. Aristotle's *De sensu et sensili*, 473 a3 and *Metaphysica* 980 b23–25 for the priority of hearing over seeing.

[3] 2 Cor. 5.7.

terms of perceptible experience. This is one of the reasons why genuine conversation is possible today between pure science and pure theology, if only on the ground that both have a similar battle to fight in order to made room for the knowledge of their proper objects, and room therefore for concepts appropriate to such knowledge. The outstanding characteristic of theology is that it operates with a direct act of cognition in *hearing* God and engages in the act of conception through *audition*. The concepts which derive from this hearing we may call, for lack of a better expression, 'audits'.[1] The nature of this hearing and therefore of theological statements appropriate to it, we shall have to discuss later, but at this stage, we are concerned mainly to insist that theological concepts have an aspect that cannot be appreciated so long as we insist on construing them only in modes of vision.[2]

A signal instance of the impasse we can reach when we neglect the auditory aspect of theological concepts is the attempt made by many people in modern times to interpret the life and person of Jesus only within the field of the observable and perceptible; that is the attempt to look at the life of Jesus 'in the flat', as it were, without attention to the dimension of depth behind it, in the Word of God become flesh, so that even the teachings of Jesus are ironed out flat into static ideas.[3] When this is done consistently the portrait of Christ breaks down again and again until the foolish cry is raised that it is impossible to give an account of the historical Jesus Christ at all. Jesus will always prove intractably enigmatic, indeed an impossible subject for plastic representation of any kind, precisely because He is a Subject who by His very nature resists being subjected to what we deem to be observable or being interpreted exclusively in terms of cosmic perceptibility.[4] The New

[1] See *Theology in Reconstruction*, pp. 21 f., 58 f., 87 f.

[2] It is unfortunate that both medieval and modern philosophy (since Kant) have tended to restrict *intuitive* knowledge to the model of vision, to the neglect of intuitive auditive, and intuitive evident knowledge. This has had the effect of narrowing unduly the discussion of 'natural theology' and has tended in Protestant thought, by limiting intuition to what is finite, to delimit objective knowledge within the same sphere, and relegate God beyond what is rationally knowable. For a line of thought in this direction see H. L. Mansel, *Metaphysics*, cf. pp. 275 ff.

[3] Cf. Barth, *Church Dogmatics*, IV, 2, p. 102 f.

[4] It was precisely the recognition of this that makes the Byzantine portrayal of Christ, we noted above, so profound.

Testament does indeed give us a portrait of Christ, although it is a portrait of a unique kind—never once, for example, does it drop even a hint of what He looked like—but considered from the perspective of vision it can only appear very fragmentary and elusive, for the aspects of the life of Christ that have to be interpreted in the language of vision, have their full meaning as predicates of the Word made flesh, the Son of God become incarnate. This is precisely the aspect of Christ that cannot be seen, but can only be heard. 'He that hath ears to hear, let him hear,' as Jesus said again and again. Because He has a visible aspect, the concept of Christ may be said to be relatively closed at one end, but it is open at the other because in Him we hear a Word from beyond, the eternal Word of God from beyond the observable, a Word which, while it is made flesh at this end, yet recedes into the eternity of God at the other end. Thus to consider only the aspect of Christ that can be construed in terms of vision, without the aspect of Christ that is to be construed in terms of audition, is to consider an abstraction without a Subject. The concept of Christ is as much an 'audit' as a 'percept'.

We may illustrate the nature of our problem here by referring to a famous doctrine of the earlier Wittgenstein to the effect that if sentences are 'pictures' of reality then in the nature of the case we cannot represent in sentences the way in which sentences are 'pictures' of reality, nevertheless this relation shows through.[1] In this doctrine Wittgenstein was attempting to speak about a relation that cannot be described in the language of vision, and yet found himself apparently forced to use the language of vision in order to say so—and was consequently much misunderstood. The point that Wittgenstein made is remarkably apt for our understanding of theological sentences and concepts, for theology is deeply concerned with the fact that we are unable to express in statements how these statements are related to that to which they are directed—hence the place of the sacramental relation in the very heart of Christian theology. But whereas the Western Roman tradition has insisted in construing this almost entirely in terms of vision, the Reformed tradition insists that this becomes nonsensical

---

[1] *Tractatus Logico-philosophicus*, 1922, 4.12 f. For a clear exposition see J. O. Urmson, *Philosophical Analysis*, pp. 87 ff., 126 ff., 141 ff.

unless it is also construed in terms of audition, for it is the relation created by the Word that is fundamental even to the sacramental relation.[1]

What has been said in this introductory section cannot stand alone apart from what follows, and must not be taken to provide the basis of a theological epistemology, as if all we now have to do is to apply this to the knowledge of God in particular. What we have been concerned to do, is to show that Christian theology has its place of inquiry within the field of rational knowledge, and to claim that in accordance with its attempt to behave in terms of the nature of its own proper object, it must be allowed to adapt and modify language, to shape and form its own concepts, and to delimit or expand its use of terms, like any other branch of knowledge or science. Because of the unique nature of its own proper Object—there is only one Lord God—its use of language and thought-forms will not unnaturally often be unique. Herein lies one of the great temptations of the theologian, to stretch ordinary language to the breaking-point. If he has a serious concern for communication, he will be constantly on his guard here, but if he is to be true and faithful to the nature of his own proper object, he will pass on the warning of Jesus that new wine will burst the old wine-skins.

(2) ITS ACTUALITY, OBJECTIVITY, AND POSSIBILITY

In this section we attempt to give an account of the nature of specifically theological knowledge, and then probe into the divine ground of that knowledge. Our primary task, epistemologically, is to focus our attention on the area where God is actually known, and seek to understand that knowledge in its concrete happening, out of its own proper ground, and in

---

[1] Cf. here my essay 'Abstractive and Intuitive Knowledge from Duns Scotus to John Calvin', published in the *Acta* of the Duns Scotus Congress, 1966, ed. by P. Balić, 1968, vol. iv, pp. 291 ff. Reformed theology must be equally critical of the kind of position taken up by Spinoza in which the proper rejection of imaginative, picturing and descriptive language of God leads only to abstract intellection and purely logical conceptions of God in which it is impossible to distinguish God from our idea of God. See the fine account of Spinoza's thought given by Stuart Hampshire, *Spinoza*, chs. 2 and 3.

its own proper reference to objective reality. Scientific procedure will not allow us to go beyond the boundary set by the object, for that would presume that by the inherent powers of our own 'autonomous reason' we can gain mastery over it.[1] We have to act within the limits imposed by the nature of the object, and avoid self-willed and undisciplined speculative thinking. It would be uncontrolled and unscientific procedure to run ahead of the object and prescribe just how it shall or can be known before we actually know it, or to withdraw ourselves from actual knowing and then in detachment from the object lay down the conditions upon which valid knowledge is possible. As against all loose arbitrary thinking, or rather romancing, of that sort, scientific theology is disciplined and positive. It keeps its feet on the ground of actuality.

It is with the knowledge of the living God that we are concerned here. We are engaged with the knowledge of a Reality which we cannot construe in terms of what we know already, and therefore we must be prepared to take heuristic steps if we are to go forward; or rather we must be prepared to be taken up by the Truth beyond the confines of ordinary natural knowledge as they are defined by the world of our familiar creaturely experiences. Our minds must be ready to behave in terms of what God reveals of Himself, and therefore be open to what is genuinely new.

1. *The Actuality of the Knowledge of God.*

Christian theology arises out of the actual knowledge of God given in and with concrete happening in space and time. It is knowledge of the God who actively meets us and gives Himself to be known in Jesus Christ—in Israel, in history, on earth. It is essentially positive knowledge, with articulated content, mediated in concrete experience. It is concerned with fact, the fact of God's self-revelation; it is concerned with God Himself who just because He really is God always comes first. We do not therefore begin with ourselves or our questions, nor indeed can we choose where to begin; we can only begin with the facts prescribed for us by the actuality of the object

---

[1] The 'autonomous reason' is, of course, a diseased form of rationality for it is the reason turned in upon itself, and claiming as inherent in itself the forms which it can derive only in relation to the objective world upon which it reasons.

positively known. Anything else would be unreal and un-scientific, as well as untheological.[1]

Here, then, our thinking is from inside the area delimited by actual knowledge of God, and does not operate at any time outside of it. It is from within this positive knowledge that theology puts its questions and seeks its answers and puts them to the test. It cannot, scientifically, put its questions from some point outside itself and then test them upon ground different from that on which actual knowledge of God arises—that would be quite artificial. Theology insists on being utterly genuine. An outstanding example of this theological pro-cedure is to be seen in MacLeod Campbell's famous work *The Nature of the Atonement*, in which, as he says, he sought 'to answer Anselm's question *Cur Deus homo* by the light of the divine fact itself as to which the question is put instead of seeking an answer in considerations exterior to that fact'.[2] That is to say, he attempted to understand the atonement 'in its own light', by keeping 'within the limits of its own self-evidence', so that he would not be misled by untested pre-conceptions—the wrong path to take, he held, was to ask for 'evidence not proper to the subject'.[3]

Two points must now be made clear.

(a) Theological knowledge pivots upon what is *given*, given from beyond it,[4] and which does not depend upon our dis-covering it. It is concerned with fact that has objective ontological reality. Not all facts are of the same kind, and not all are to be observed or cognized in precisely the same way. But here we have a fact beyond the ordinary range of facts—there is only one of its kind. There is only one true God, who is not known by reference to other facts beyond or behind Him. This fact is given to us within the range of our conscious-ness, and never apart from a complex of experiences, but it is a primordial reality given from beyond our consciousness, and it is important that we do not confound it with our subjective states or with the complex of what is *also given* in those states. Strictly speaking, however, we mean by *the given*, not this

[1] Cf. F. W. Camfield, *The Collapse of Doubt*, ch. 4, pp. 48 ff.

[2] Introduction, p. xvii, 6th edit., 1895.

[3] Op. cit., pp. xxxi f., 102, 275, 321 etc.

[4] For the ambiguity of the term 'given' see A. E. Taylor, *The Faith of a Moralist*, vol. 2, pp. 217–237, and H. J. Paton, *The Modern Predicament*, pp. 268 ff.

complex of experiences but that stubborn element in them which cannot be reduced to anything else and which we cannot reproduce at will, the ultimately hard objective reality without which we would have no such knowledge and which we must distinguish from our knowing of it.[1] Hence even though we know God in the givenne.s of faith, it is not faith that is the given subject-matter of theology but the God in whom we have faith.[2] We are not engaged in proper theological thinking if we do not refer our thoughts to what is beyond and try to distinguish what is primordially given to us from our manifold experience of it, or from the situations in which it is actually given to us. This is true of genuine knowledge in every field, and it is no less true of theology, but it is all the more important to recognize this distinction clearly in theology where we are given such a profound inner experience through the Spirit of the objective reality that it is a constant temptation to confound this objective reality with a subjective state, with feelings, or concepts, or even with words which are also given since without them we do not apprehend what is experienced. Genuine knowledge is of 'things' in their objective connections, not of shadowy states or habits of mind or formalities of thought and speech that come in between us and 'things'. While we do not have genuine knowledge anywhere apart from a complex situation, or apart from subjective experiences and intellectual or verbal articulation, nevertheless it is *through* these that we perceive the objective reality—logic and language should be used with scientific instrumentality and therefore used critically, but they ought to be transparent media through which we apprehend the objectively given reality beyond our subjective experience and its articulation in speech.

[1] See what Margenau has to say about the *irreducible* element in the object of natural scientific knowledge, F. Heinemann, *Die Philosophie im* 20. *Jahrhundert*, p. 387 f.

[2] To refer to MacLeod Campbell again, faith by its nature apprehends what is given to it as a gift, and the gift as given, so that it is not occupied with itself but with the gift which it apprehends, *The Nature of the Atonement*, p. 86. However, it has been the fault of some of the most distinguished thinkers of modern times, such as Schleiermacher and Troeltsch, that they were concerned with *Glaubenslehre*, that is with religious ideology rather than with theology, with reflection upon the phenomena of faith rather than with that in which we have faith. A similar mistake is made by those who appear to confuse theology with a species of phenomenology—cf. Gustaf Wingren, *Theology in Conflict*, pp. 159 ff.

Theological thinking is *theo*-logical, thinking not just from our own centres, but from a centre in God, from a divine ground. It is essentially *theo*-nomous thinking. It pivots upon the fact that God has made Himself known and continues to make Himself known, that He objectifies Himself for us, so that our knowledge is a fulfilled meeting with objective reality.[1] Apart from that, theological thinking is objectless, meaningless, and, as it were, 'in the air'. Theology does not have its meaning, therefore, in its self-articulation, in its symbolism, in its form or its beauty, that is to say, in aesthetic or poetic, in emotional or even ethical overtones to real knowledge. It is itself real knowledge working with a given factual reality, and it will not concede anything as genuine knowledge that does not arise out of the given or is not bound to what is given.

(b) The given fact is *not a mute fact*—that is the kind of fact we have in the natural world, a fact that is only made to 'talk' as it comes to cognition and expression in our rational experience. Here our fact is the living God, the active, willing and loving God, who communicates Himself to us, and it is through His self-communication and self-disclosure that He gives Himself to us. In other words, the given fact is the *Word of God*, God giving Himself to us as Word and in Word, God speaking to us in person (*Deus loquens in persona*), as Calvin used to say, and sounding His word through (*personare*) to us by chosen instruments.

It may be worth pausing here to note a parallel to this in exact science. We have said that the kind of fact we have in the natural world is mute and is only made to 'talk' as it comes to cognition and expression in our rational experience, but that is not to say that it only derives rationality from us. If that were so, there would be no science at all. Every science presumes that the object it investigates is accessible and

---

[1] Cf. Barth, *Church Dogmatics*, 3.1, pp. 344 ff., where he argues that this reality is not simply our self-consciousness and consciousness of the world raised into an objective reality, nor merely a reality of God for us, but *God's own inner and proper reality* in which He is independent of us and our knowing, the ground of His own Being, but who graciously gives us reality in the actualization of our relation to Him as creatures before the Creator. For a useful discussion of 'objective reality' as applied to God, see H. Gollwitzer, *The Existence of God as Confessed by Faith* (tr. by J. W. Leitch), p. 216 f.

amenable to rational interpretation, i.e. that rational patterns can be perceived in nature, and, as Professor Michael Polanyi has argued so clearly,[1] that this rationality of nature objectively transcends our experience of it and so commands our respect for it that we are ready to *let it speak for itself*, so to say, and to subject our formulations and apprehensions to its criticism and guidance. According to Polanyi it is in this vision of a reality beyond sense-experience, of a rationality with 'implications that extend indefinitely beyond the experience which they were originally known to control' that science has its deepest sense of objectivity.[2]

Now, formally, it is not otherwise in theology. In theology we have knowledge of an objective reality in which we hear a Word, encounter a *Logos*, from beyond our subjective experience, a Word which utters itself in our listening to it and speech of it, a Word which speaks for itself in guiding us to ever deepening understanding of the objective reality,[3] and to which we submit our subjective experience for constant criticism and control. But in theology this Logos is encountered as a Word to be heard, as Truth to be acknowledged, not just a rationality to be apprehended and interpreted, so that we have to learn how to distinguish the given *in its own self-interpretation* from the interpretative processes in which we engage in receiving and understanding it.[4] This means that theological thinking is more like a listening than any other knowledge, a listening for and to a rational Word from beyond anything that we can tell to ourselves and distinct from our rational elaborations of it. The words that we tell to ourselves are mere ideas, and we cannot do without them, but considered in themselves they are abstractions and are so far unreal because they are isolated from reality. As John Macmurray has said,

[1] *Personal Knowledge* (Gifford Lectures at Aberdeen for 1951–52), 1958, pp. 5 f., 15 f., 37, 63 f., 103 f., etc

[2] Professor Polanyi's words are: 'Man has the power to establish real patterns in nature, the reality of which is manifested by the fact that their future implications extend indefinitely beyond the experience which they were originally known to control', op. cit., p. 37.

[3] This form of words is adapted from Polanyi's statement, op. cit., p. 5.

[4] Hence I cannot agree with John Baillie's position that the 'propositional' element is derivative, and comes only in a second-order reflection upon faith (see *The Sense of the Presence of God*, pp. 88 ff.) for it arises out of the immediate conceptual content of our intuitive knowledge of God.

'to add idea to idea, to organise ideas and systems and to expand these systems without end, brings us no nearer to reality'.[1] To reach reality we have to refer our thought back to the external objective world, to *re-flect* it, listen to it and conform to it, and so overcome the abstractions of ideas and thinking in ideas only, and to reach and maintain knowledge of the divine reality we must distinguish what we hear from our hearing of it, and constantly allow our formulations of it to fall under the criticism of the divine reality itself. But all this involves an acknowledgement of the given as an objective self-revelation on the part of God Himself.

Unless we have a Word from God, some articulated communication from Himself to us, we are thrown back upon ourselves to authenticate His existence and to make Him talk by putting our own words into His mouth and by clothing Him with our own ideas.[2] That kind of God is only a dumb idol which we have fashioned in our own image and into whose mouth we have projected our own soliloquies, and which we are unable to distinguish from our own processed interpretation. In other words, we have no genuine knowledge of God at all, for we are left alone with our own thoughts and self-deceptions.

That was the problem of Schleiermacher. By his doctrine of the feeling of absolute dependence he sought to express the fact that God is ontologically and divinely independent of us, and that our knowledge of His presence is a pure finding and in no sense a fashioning on our part.[3] But because such a God was absolutely mute, Schleiermacher was thrown back upon his own subjective states, and could only claim that interpretation of these subjective states corresponded with what was beyond by a secret togetherness of the spirit of man with the Spirit of God,[4] and could only lend to this knowledge an air

---

[1] *Interpreting the Universe*, p. 34.

[2] Cf. F. W. Camfield, op. cit., pp. 48–53.

[3] *The Christian Faith* (E.T., 1928), pp. 12 ff.

[4] 'We have only to do with the God-consciousness given in our self-consciousness along with our consciousness of the world', op. cit., p. 748. 'To feel oneself absolutely dependent and to be conscious of being in relation with God are one and the same thing; and the reason is that absolute dependence is the fundamental relation which must include all others in itself. This last expression includes the God-consciousness in the self-consciousness in such a way that the two cannot be separated from each other'. p. 17.

of objectivity by laying the emphasis upon the historical consciousness of the community over against that of each believer. It was not difficult for Feuerbach to show that 'theology' of this kind is only a form of 'anthropology',[1] for its whole method rests upon a basic falsification, an ultimately irrational failure to distinguish the objective reality from the subjective states of our own consciousness, or to distinguish what is not ourselves from ourselves.

Apart from a real Word of God it is impossible, we do not say to be aware of, but to distinguish the objective reality of God from the subjective states of our own consciousness and therefore impossible to have genuine and rational knowledge of Him. In a true theology God's Word is the condition and source of real knowledge, for it is in and through His speaking that I am not cast back upon my own resources to establish His existence or to devise a symbolism in order to make it meaningful. It is in and through His Word that God distinguishes Himself from our self-consciousness, for He so addresses us that, as Camfield has expressed it, He is not left to the mercy of our questions and answers, but we ourselves are questioned by a Word from beyond which draws us out of ourselves and declares to us what we are utterly incapable of learning and declaring to ourselves.[2]

Thus, the given fact with which theology operates is God uttering His Word and uttering Himself in His Word, the speaking and acting and redeeming God, who approaches us and so communicates Himself to us that our knowing of Him is coordinated to His revealing of Himself, even though this does not happen to us except in a complex situation involving our cognition of the world around us and of ourselves along with it. It is within the area of this divine communication and revelation that theological thinking takes its rise and operates by referring itself to the given reality, that is, by the direction of

[1] *The Essence of Christianity* (E.T. 1893), p. 207: 'The secret of theology is nothing else than anthropology—the knowledge of God nothing else than a knowledge of man.' Cf. also pp. 12 ff., 89, 221, 231, 336.

[2] Op. cit., p. 48 f. This is rather different from Tillich's 'method of correlation', in which he seeks to relate the questions that arise out of man's self-interpretation to the answers implied in the Christian message. This Tillich calls 'answering theology', but is it not answer to man rather than answer to God? Cf. *Systematic Theology*, vol. I, pp. 8, 35, etc. The movement of Tillich's thought appears to suffer from the same kind of inversion in relation to God as that of Schleiermacher.

all its rational attention to the communicated Word. That is the meaning of faith. Faith is the orientation of the reason toward God's self-revelation, the rational response of man to the Word of God.[1] It is not only that, but more than that, as we shall see, but it is no less than that, i.e. than a fully rational acknowledgement of a real Word given to us by God from beyond us. In Alan Richardson's fine phrase, faith is a 'condition of rationality'.[2]

This is why a genuine theology is distrustful of all speculative thinking or of all *a priori* thought. Theological thinking is essentially positive, thinking that keeps its feet on the ground of actuality; *a posteriori*, thinking that follows and is obedient to the given and communicated Word and Act of God as the material for its reflection; and *empirical*, thinking out of real experience of God determined by God. It is because it is through this given fact that theological knowledge has reality, and on its basis alone that it can be established as knowledge, that it is incumbent upon us to put to the test all thinking that claims to be theological by referring it to the concrete reality of the object actually known. In this way we distinguish between what is genuine theology and mere paper-theology, that is, theology that is verifiable by reference to its divine ground in the actual region of experience in which knowledge of Him has arisen, and theology that is speculatively worked up

---

[1] It may be recalled that in Aristotelian and Stoic thought πίστις and συγκατάθεσις were equivalent ways of speaking of the mind's rational assent to the given. In Stoic thought there was also acknowledged an important moment of the will, προαίρεσις, involved in it, but this did not reduce the fact that the assent took place καταληπτικῶς or under the 'seizure' of the given reality. This was the language that early Christian theology, e.g. as found in the writings of Clement of Alexandria, used to speak of faith as 'conceptual assent' (ἐννοητικὴ συγκατάθεσις) to divine revelation. See 'The Implications of Oikonomia for Knowledge and Speech of God in Early Christian Theology', in *Oikonomia*, edit. by Felix Christ, pp. 223 ff.

[2] A. Richardson, *Christian Apologetics*, pp. 237 ff. This means that an antithesis between reason and faith must be ruled out, for faith is the behaviour of the reason in accordance with the nature of its divine Object. It is strange that Professor Macmurray should still operate with this false antithesis, although he defines reason as acting in this way—cf. *The Self as Agent*, p. 18. The term he evidently prefers, however, to describe the relating of reason toward its object, is '*love*', *Reason and Emotion*, p. 32. This is what St. Paul called *faith*, although he insisted that faith works through love. Cf. also the way in which Nels Ferré relates reason and faith as functions of the self or the rational subject, *Reason in Religion*, pp. 28 ff.

by a dialectical manipulation of ideas in answer to unreal questions (i.e. questions not controlled by empirical reference to reality).[1]

Unfortunately a good deal of modern theology, like much medieval theology, appears to be little more than paper-theology, for however true its argumentation may be within its chosen symbolism, it is often palpably unreal. Part, at least, of the reason for this lies in a common confusion between what is primordially given in the divine self-revelation, where we are thrown back ultimately upon the simple and absolute truth of the divine Being, and what is given by way of acknow-ledged premises or self-evident principles, where we are operating with the complex truth of statements. When this confusion is made there is a return to the theoretic questioning (*quaestio*) of the scholastic thought directed to the solution of mental problems, and a neglect of the active questioning (*interrogatio*) of scientific thought directed to the disclosure of realities in their profound and enlightening simplicities. This is not to say that the former can ever be neglected, but when it gets out of hand (this is the constant temptation of philosophical theology), the theologian tends to 'think statements' instead of 'thinking things' through statements.

2. *The Objectivity of Theological Knowledge*

As we have already stated, theological knowledge is know-ledge devoted to and bound up with its object—it will have nothing to do with objectless thinking. Therein lies its essential rationality.

Now, because theology is devoted to its own proper object, it loosens its hold upon all other presuppositions except its own proper object. We all have our presuppositions, our antecedent ideas and even theories, but when we engage in theological thinking we are summoned to renounce all other presuppositions in concentration upon the object. This is thinking that freely refuses to be fettered by *a priori* dogmatisms drawn from anywhere outside of what is given to it, whether

---

[1] By empirical reference to reality is meant one in the mode of the reality experienced. Theology protests against the arbitrary limitation of experience to sensory experience of the corporeal world—see the chapter 'The Range of Exper-ience' in John Baillie, *The Sense of the Presence of God*, pp. 41 ff. and also pp. 60 ff.

those presuppositions or dogmatisms come from some logical system, or metaphysics or natural science, from our own personal satisfactions and desires, or even the Church. True theology is free from all these and genuinely open to the self-disclosure of its object. Therein it is free to be unconditionally obedient to it, and ready for the realism demanded by it in the face of other objects.

It is important to distinguish this understanding of objectivity from a commonly held view that objectivity means detachment, impartiality, indifference toward the object—that is to say, the attitude in which we stand off from the object in order to contemplate it calmly and dispassionately, in which we suspend active relation to the object in order to prevent our commitment from warping our judgement or even to exclude the influence of our subjectivity upon the object. The principle that lies behind this is a sound one, namely, that we cannot pass a true judgement upon an object if our relation to it distorts our knowledge of it, or, in the case of exact science, that we cannot know a thing properly if we affect its nature by our methods of observation. To cite John Macmurray again, 'If we are to know the world we must see to it that it really is an external world. That means not merely that the world must remain external to us but that we must remain external to it.'[1]

This is a principle that must be acknowledged frankly. Admittedly it has a limited range of applicability, but far from implying that we must detach ourselves from the object and take up an attitude of indifference toward it, it implies that we must so submit ourselves to the dictates of the object that we think in terms of it, and not in terms of what we think we already know about it. We must certainly distinguish it as an object 'out there', or 'over against us', but it is our very engagement with it as such which disengages us from other attachment. We may put this briefly by saying that the detachment from all presuppositions, which scientific objectivity requires, is not the same as detachment from the object. On the contrary, it is attachment to the object which carries with it detachment from all *a priori* judgements. In other words, we are summoned not to be indifferent or impartial toward the object, but indifferent or impartial to anything and everything

[1] *The Boundaries of Science*, p. 85.

outside of or beyond the object which may influence our knowledge of it, in order that our knowing of it may be governed as far as possible by the nature of the object itself.[1] This involves us in a proper circularity. It is sheer attachment to the object that detaches us from our preconceptions, while we detach ourselves from our preconceptions in order to be free for the object, and therefore free for true knowledge of it.

We may now return to the point raised above that in objective knowledge of this kind the reason acts freely toward its object and yet is ready to submit to the demands of the object upon it. We are free and yet unconditionally bound—is that not rather paradoxical? When we enter into a room and look round, we are obliged to see what is there. We have no option to do otherwise, for our observation and cognition are unconditionally bound by what is external to us and not-ourselves. In spite of that, we know that we are free to reflect upon it, and free to use our knowledge and to direct our lives accordingly. Thus our obligation to the object is not inimical to freedom— what would limit our freedom would be a failure to realize that we are unconditionally bound to the object, for then we would be imprisoned in deception. No preconceptions are more enslaving than unconscious ones, but the same applies to the ignorance of which we are unaware. Only when we are ready for the realism demanded by the object can we be truly objective, and then objectivity and freedom belong together. To be actively attached to the object and therefore free from preconceptions, to be detached from the bondage of preconceptions and therefore free to submit to the object, is the aim of scientific objectivity. And that is also the concern of theology.

We cannot pretend for a moment that objectivity can be abstracted from the subject-object relationship all knowledge involves. Therefore it must be considered from the side of the subject in that relationship, that is, from the side of the knower who rationally directs his thought away from himself to the object, and from the side of the object in that relationship, which may, as is the case in theological knowledge, be a subject. We shall have occasion later to consider the problem that

[1] How far impartiality is actually possible is another matter—what we are concerned with here is impartiality as a methodological principle.

objectivity presents from the side of the knowing subject, but now we have to ask what we are to learn from the side of the object, and in this case from the side of God Himself, about the objectivity of theological knowledge.

Various factors have to be taken into account in considering this objectivity.

(a) The absolute *primacy* of the Object—the Lord God Himself. In our knowledge of Him, He remains the Lord, He comes first and remains first, and maintains His ascendency over all our knowing of Him. Here the Object takes us under its command and directs our very being and existence in relation to it, in a measure that obtains in no other field of knowledge. That is the primary element in the knowledge of the Lord God Almighty, the determination of our knowledge of Him from beyond ourselves by the very Godness and Lordship of God. Everything else depends upon this, just as all the Ten Commandments depend upon the primary Word, 'I am the Lord thy God . . . . Thou shalt have none other gods before me. Thou shalt not make unto thee any graven image or any likeness . . . .' Knowledge of this God cannot be moulded according to our plastic ideas or controlling archetypes; that would be idolatry. Rather must our knowing of God be brought into conformity with what He reveals of Himself, and under the control of what He gives us of Himself.

(b) The Object is given to us in a unique sense of *given*. It is given to us as all other objects are given to our knowledge in the whole field of science, within the subject-object relationship, but in accordance with the unique nature of this Object it is given in *Grace*. Natural objects, when we know them, *have to be* objects of our cognition—that is part of their determinate nature. This is not to deny that knowledge of them requires effort on our part, and indeed discovery. Even though we must engage in intuitive and discursive thought we do not discover God by our own efforts, and when we know Him He does not have to be an object of our cognition in the same way as in natural knowledge.[1] He gives Himself to our thinking; He objectifies Himself for us, in an act of pure freedom and

---

[1] By 'natural knowledge' is meant here knowledge of natural phenomena, but the point made ought to apply also to 'natural theology' properly understood, whether it claims to operate inductively or deductively.

Grace, and therefore in such a way that He does not resign that freedom and Grace, but remains free to give Himself to us as He pleases, or even to withdraw Himself.

As we shall see later, in natural science, that is in the science of natural objects which have to be objects of our cognition, when we know them, we can test our knowledge through experimental controls in which we force them to answer our questions. Moreover natural objects may be affected by our knowledge as they come under the coercive devices of our empirical methods of observation. But God is not subject to observation like that. He does not come under man's command, and therefore we cannot put Him to the test or bring Him under the power of our controlled scrutiny.[1] Nevertheless, here, as in all other genuine scientific knowledge, the method of knowledge must correspond to the nature of the object, so that where natural science has its controlled observation and experimental verification, we have to cast ourselves on the Grace of God and allow Him to determine the form our knowledge will take, and the kind of verification appropriate to Him. Thus, for example, the kind of inquiry we have to direct to God that is in accordance with His nature as Divine Subject is rather of the nature of prayer, and never the coercive questioning we have to devise for mute and natural objects.

(c) God is *Person*, and when He objectifies Himself for our knowledge He does not cease to be *Subject*, to be Himself. He does not give Himself to us as a mere object subjected to our knowing, but as Subject who maintains Himself in implacable objectivity over against us, objecting to any attempt on our part to subject Him to our own knowing. This is an objectivity that is the antithesis of all objectivism, for objectivism treats the object merely as an object and prescinds the relation of the knowing subject to the object in such a way that the relation of the subject to the object becomes purely theoretical

[1] This is the element of truth in the desire of a Schleiermacher or a Bultmann to transcend the subject-object relation, but behind their strange fear that we would damage God by having Him as the object of our knowledge lies the equally strange notion that an 'object' is limited by a subject's act of consciousness. Behind this lies the way in which Kant could sometimes speak of the 'object' as that which we 'make'. See the *Critique of Practical Reason*, II.7, Abbott's tr. pp. 231 ff. See also Kemp Smith, *A Commentary to Kant's Critique of Pure Reason*, p. 79 f. for a discussion of Kant's ambiguity of thought in this respect.

or logical, i.e. an abstraction. But God gives Himself to be known as personal Subject, as the one Lordly Subject who approaches us and assumes us into personal relation with Him as subjects over against His own divine majestic Subjectivity. Apart from being a primary element in the objectivity of theological knowledge, this means that our cognitive relation to the object is essentially and unceasingly dialogical. At no point can theological knowledge step outside this dialogical relation, without abstracting itself from the object, without falsifying itself, or without retreating into unreality. Thus theological knowledge is not reflection upon our rational experience or even upon faith; it is reflection upon the object of faith in direct dialogical relation with that object, and therefore in faith—i.e. in conversation and communion with the living God who communicates Himself to us in acts of revelation and reconciliation and who requires of us an answering relation in receiving, acknowledging, understanding, and in active personal participation in the relationship He establishes between us. It belongs to the essential objectivity of theological knowledge that it falls within this dialogical relation to the Lord as the Object-Subject or Subject-Object of our knowing.

(d) The Object of theological knowledge is *speaking* Subject, God addressing us personally—that is, *the Word of God*. We shall discuss later how this Word comes to us, namely, through creaturely objectivities and creaturely speech, through words which are the inescapable media of rational communication and personal relationship. In the language we used earlier, the object of theological knowledge is not mute; it is God uttering and declaring and communicating Himself rationally to the understanding of men whom He has made to know Him. The object of theological knowledge is articulating Word of God that requires on our part articulated thought and speech in answer to it if knowledge of Him is to be realized.

We must recognize, however, a distinction between the Word of God, and the words assumed in the media of its communication to us and among us. We may also draw a distinction between 'the inner word' as the Word of God to which we listen, including our listening of it, and 'the outer word' or the speech that is used in its articulation and communication. The distinction between the Word heard and the words used in its hearing and communicating, means that the concepts or audits we employ must always be open, and never closed. The Word of God as such can never be enclosed or boxed up in words even though there is no hearing or speaking of it apart from inner or outer word. On the other hand, it is just because the Word always transcends our speech that we must be critical and self-critical in all handling of theological speech. We are not given the Word in the form of delimited and tight propositional ideas but only in verbal forms that always point away from themselves to the Word itself, that is to God speaking in Person and communicating rationally with us. The words we have to use, therefore, and indeed the concepts and audits in which our hearing and understanding of the Word become articulated, are to be regarded as transparent media through which we submit to an objective articulation or pattern of truth in the Object, God uttering Himself in His Word. From the very start theological knowledge arises through the conformity of our rational cognition to that objective articulation of the Truth in the Word of God.

(e) The object of theological knowledge is the living, loving, acting God, God in His *action* toward us. God's objectifying of Himself does not cease to be His self-giving action, and therefore knowledge of God is correspondingly *in actu*, a knowledge that is spontaneous, free and active, analogous in nature to the freedom and motion in God's self-giving. It is not true knowledge if it steps outside of this movement, or seeks to abstract the content from it, and, so to speak, to freeze it, as something that we can return to at will, and handle and manipulate as we desire. Moreover the God who gives Himself as the object of our knowledge comes to us within the movement of time where we have our being and our knowing, so that we cannot know Him by seeking to step outside of this historical existence, or by seeking to abstract knowledge from that movement or relationship in time and turn it into timeless ideas or propositions that have their truth timelessly. This has very important implications for the verification of theological truth and for the relation of theological truth to logical necessity and to historical facticity to which we shall return. Our interest at the moment is to note that divine action, even action in time, is an essential element in the very nature of the truth we know and therefore in the objectivity of theological knowledge.

(f) The object of theological knowledge is engaged in *purposive* action—God fulfilling His creative and redeeming purposes. He is not known except within these purposes or in accordance with them. We cannot know God against His will, but only as He wills to reveal Himself; nor can we know Him apart from His purpose for us, apart from His claim upon the whole of our existence, or apart from His will to redeem and reconcile it to Himself. The truth with which we are concerned in theology is teleological truth, truth for us, truth laying hold upon us for a divine end, so that knowledge of it must be analogous to its teleological nature. Hence theological knowledge by its very nature is practical, directed to a supreme end prescribed for it by its object; it has an ordered objectivity all the more stubborn and irreducible because of the persistence of its undeviating purpose. Far from being able to bend the object to our will, or to fashion knowledge of it to our liking, we cannot know it without being drawn into its redeeming and reconciling activity, without being renewed and re-ordered in accordance with its saving will. In other words, we cannot truly know God without being reconciled and renewed in Jesus Christ. Thus the objectivity of our theological knowledge is immutably soteriological in nature.

Wherever we turn in our actual knowledge of God in Jesus Christ, in Israel, in history, on earth, we are confronted with its stubborn and insurmountable objectivity, but precisely because it is in and through that objectivity alone that knowledge of God has its reality, in the very act of confrontation, all our knowledge of God is called into question. Because the Word of God comes to us objectively from beyond, it requires us to be critical of all that claims to be knowledge of God. Genuine objectivity calls into question all unreality and therefore summons us to probe into the ground of our knowledge that we may distinguish true from all false objectivity. It is under the questioning directed to us by the Word of God that we discover how much false objectivity there is, how much there passes under the guise of objectivity which is but the objectification of inner subjective states of experience.

This is something we are consciously engaged in doing in various areas of our life, where our own inner desires, satisfactions or even dissatisfactions, the elemental motifs of the natural man, press upward for expression and recognition, and even create for themselves symbolic structures for that purpose. *Hominis ingenium perpetua idolorum fabrica.*[1] We can observe that taking place in our own dream-world, but it is also to be found in the background, and often even in the foreground, of our waking and reflective life, where our deepest and often inexpressible experiences assume the guise of objective forms in order to have a place among the realities to which we refer our rational thought.[2] Then they may even be rationalized and interpreted as arising from or reposing upon independent modes of being. It is in this way, for example, that the dogma of the physical assumption of the Virgin Mary seems to have arisen, as a projection out of the depths of popular piety into the sphere of the divine. But we must not allow ourselves to forget that this is precisely the way in which critics of Christianity attack the core and centre of the Christian faith, in the doctrine of Christ as very God and very Man, and it is lent not a little plausibility because as a matter of fact we are frequently engaged in mythological self-objectifications of this sort. It is incumbent upon us, therefore, to put all our doctrines to the severest test by probing into the ground of their objectivity and examining their truth or falsity, to distinguish divine objectivity from all idolatry.

There is another, if complementary, kind of false objectivity which we cannot afford to neglect, and this is also one in which we are constantly tempted to engage. This arises not so much through the objectification of our subjective desires, but from an objectification of divine things which abstracts them from dialogical objectivity and translates them into dialectical or institutional objectivity where they can be possessed and handled and manipulated without threat to our security or to our cherished desires and satisfactions.[3] An outstanding example of this is the objectification or the reification of grace and truth in the institutional and rational structures of the Church, whether in its Roman or in its Protestant forms.

---

[1] Calvin, *Inst.* I.XI. 8.

[2] See Hans Jonas, *Augustin und das paulinische Freiheitsproblem*, 1930, pp. 66 ff., and H. Diem, *Dogmatics*, E.T. 1959, pp. 25 ff.

[3] Cf. M. Buber, *I and Thou* (E.T., 1937, by R. G. Smith), p. 113 f. But if Buber is not to be misunderstood in the English translation of *Ich und Du* careful attention must be paid to what he says about *objectivity* in *The Eclipse of God*, especially the essay 'God and the Spirit of Man', pp. 123 ff.

Perhaps no one is more tempted to engage in this kind of false objectivity, or objectivism, than the systematic theologian, but like its twin (the self-objectification noted above) it is natural to the sinner who seeks by law or ethics, by religion or idealism, to interpose a barrier between himself and the living God in order to refract direct encounter with the Truth, and so to provide him with a measure of independence and security and what he imagines to be freedom over against it. Now it is just because we are all sinners and inevitably manifest the fruit of original sin in this way, by seeking to secure ourselves in a position of our own, that we have to subject all our theology to radical questioning by the Truth in order that alien and false objectivity may be pruned away.

This is not so easy to undertake because God objectifies Himself for us within the world of our natural objects, and so clothes His ultimate and divine objectivity with the kind of objectivity with which we are familiar in creation, in Israel, among men, in history, in our common human life—that is to say, within the space and time of this world. It is under this secondary form of objectivity, as Karl Barth has called it,[1] that all false objectivities take cover and gain their hold over us. In the terse language of St. Paul, 'the law is the strength of sin.'[2] On the other hand, it is because ultimate divine objectivity has assumed concrete, positive and particular form within our world that we are really able to put false objectivities to a decisive test—in Jesus Christ. It will be through ruthless and relentless Christological criticism of all our knowledge of God that we will be able to distinguish, as far as possible, between genuine and false objectivity.

3. *The Possibility of Theological Knowledge*

The question as to the possibility of the knowledge of God has to be asked if we are to gain a full understanding of the objectivity of theological knowledge, but we have kept this question back until now, because it is only meaningful when correlated with the actual knowledge of God.[3] Even so, the question has to be put in the right way in order to be real.

---

[1] *Church Dogmatics*, 2, 1, p. 16 etc.   [2] 1 Cor. 15.56.
[3] For what follows cf. again Barth, *Church Dogmatics*, 2, 1, pp. 64 ff.

When, for example, we examine the question 'how is it possible to know God', we find that it questions the very fact that the question implies in order to be a question at all.[1] It is not a scientific question, but a self-contradictory or empty movement of thought. Nevertheless its examination serves to show that we can begin meaningfully only with the fact of prior knowledge of God and then seek to test and clarify it. We cannot genuinely discuss the possibility of the knowledge of God outside of its own actual reality. Therefore to those who doubt the possibility of such knowledge we cannot scientifically seek a place outside the knowledge of God where its possibility can be judged before we acknowledge its reality, but we can only point to actual knowledge and seek to explicate and elucidate the possibility arising out of its actuality, and in that way bear witness to it.

But there is a genuine question here which we must seek to answer. It is the given Reality itself which poses it in its actual confrontation of us—the question as to its nature and ground. 'How do we actually know God? How is God known? How far is He knowable?' In the nature of the case this is not a question that can be put in general terms without making it unreal. Real questions must be asked in a real way, that is to say, without being removed from their proper setting and then considered in isolation in abstract or general terms. We shall return again to the place of scientific questions in theology, but here we are concerned with the inquiry into the ground, and therefore into the possibility, of our knowledge of God in order to test how far our knowledge of God really rests on God Himself, or how far it can stand up to the test of referring it to objective reality as its sole presupposition and the ultimate source of its necessity. This is particularly important because this is the kind of knowledge that has to be continually renewed and established on its proper object. It is then by raising the question as to the possibility of the knowledge of God, and by

[1] When this, or a similar question, e.g. 'How is it possible for man to think about God?' (cf. Basil Mitchell, *Faith and Logic*, 1959, p. 7) is posed in the abstract, it is meaningless, but then it would be just as meaningless to seek to answer it in its own mode and within its posited abstraction—hence the aridity of so much recent discussion of this question. But cf. the way D. M. MacKinnon treats the question 'Is the conception of a divine revelation philosophically tenable?' *God the Living and the True*, p. 32.

tracing its roots in the way in which God has actually objectified Himself for us and revealed Himself to us, that we can correct our thinking and make it genuinely theological. Thus whether to those outside who doubt the possibility of the knowledge of God or to those inside who seek its clarification, we have to point to the fact that God has given Himself to be known by us in Jesus Christ, and seek to elucidate the *mode* of that knowledge. As Karl Barth has argued so strongly throughout the volume we have had in mind in this chapter, God's decisive action in Jesus Christ invalidates all questions whether He might have acted otherwise.[1]

Our question is evidently two-fold. (a) How does God give Himself to be known? (b) How does man truly receive and know what is given? There is a two-fold movement, from the side of the object known and from the side of the knower, and both have to be fully considered—the way from God to man and the way from man to God. These are not two separate movements, each proceeding from its own independent ground to meet the other, but one two-fold movement, for even the movement from the side of man toward God, free and spontaneous as it is, is coordinated with the movement of God toward man, and is part of the divine movement of revelation and reconciliation. This fulfilling and actualizing of the knowledge of God in man can be elucidated only in a full exposition of the doctrine of Christ, for He is God as He has objectified Himself for us, He is the concrete embodiment of knowledge of God within our humanity, and so He is Himself not only the way of God toward man, but the way of man toward God. It is by positive and concrete reference of all our theological knowledge to Him, or rather by actual participation in the two-fold movement of knowledge in Him, that we have genuine knowledge of God.

In the light of the doctrine of Christ we may proceed to answer the question as to how we know God first *negatively*, and then positively.

Negatively, the way of true knowledge is indicated over against the two basic errors in Christology. In *Docetic* Christologies

---

[1] Fundamentally the same point is made by A. M. Farrer, *Faith and Logic* (ed. B. Mitchell), pp. 99 ff.

we see that we cannot take the way of deduction, beginning with a particular idea of God and then finding that fulfilled or confirmed in Jesus Christ, only then to relegate the actual humanity of Jesus to a place of ultimate unimportance compared to the idea of the Christ or of God as brought to light through Him. In *Ebionite* Christologies we see that we cannot take the way of induction (at least as 'induction' is usually understood), beginning with the manhood of Christ and seeking to rise toward God as the goal or end of man's thought, only then to end up in the idealizing of man himself.

As against both of these erroneous ways of procedure we begin positively with God Himself meeting us in Jesus Christ, giving Himself to us not simply in this Man but as Man, and yet without resolving Himself into the Man Jesus in such a way that He ceases to be the God who gives Himself even when He really gives Himself to us as Man in Jesus. It is as such that God objectifies Himself for us, gives Himself to be known, makes Himself accessible to us, and so makes possible knowledge of Him.

Now in probing into the ground of this possibility, in order to elucidate it and to allow it to become more fully evident to us, we may distinguish three 'moments' in the realization of our knowledge of God in Jesus Christ.

(i) In Jesus Christ God has condescended to reveal Himself to us within our creaturely existence and contingency, and has assumed our humanity to meet us as man to man and to make Himself known to us within the conditions and limitations of our earthly life, within our visible, tangible, temporal flesh. In so doing He has objectified Himself for us within our world and its natural objectivity, that is to say, within our world where we and natural objects are posited together and co-exist as creatures of God. Thus He reveals Himself to us within our subject-object relations and even within the structural relations of our minds to natural objectivity, whether it be in regard to objects or other subjects. But He does not thereby cease to be the Lord God, the Creator from whom we derive our being before ever we know Him, while He does thereby come to lay His total claim upon us and to redeem us.

Thus the possibility of our knowing God is grounded

ultimately in His divine freedom and grace to cross the boundary between Himself and us, and really to give Himself to be known by us in our condition as frail creatures of earth.[1] That is to say, in making Himself the object of our knowledge He confronts us as the one true God who is before all but who as the transcendent Saviour stoops down in boundless freedom and grace in order to lift us up to Himself in reconciliation and communion. While He is really the object of our knowing, He is object in an utterly unique way. It is in objectifying Himself for us that He takes control over us and is the sole Master of our knowing as well as the sole Author of our reconciliation. Thus while entering within our subject-object relationships and within the structural modes of our existence and knowledge He reverses or converts our whole relation of knowing, in directing it out beyond all possibility in ourselves to knowledge of God. It is a knowledge made possible under the commanding majesty of the Object which not only establishes itself in our knowledge but does not allow itself to be halted by our creaturely limitations and disabilities, for it creates, bestows, and controls a real knowledge on our part appropriate to it.

'Knowledge of God is thus not the relationship of an already existing subject to an object that enters into his sphere and is therefore obedient to the laws of this sphere. On the contrary, this knowledge first of all creates the subject of this knowledge by coming into the picture .... Only because God posits Himself as the Object is man posited as the knower of God. And so man can only have God as the self-posited object.'[2] In other words, it is not through setting aside our subjectivity, but on the contrary through positing it, and making it free and spontaneous, and fully responsible, that God establishes the possibility of man's knowledge of Him. In this approach to man God engages man in active responsibility toward Him,

---

[1] This is another way of saying that the possibility of knowledge rests upon divine *revelation*. Cf. H. R. Mackintosh, *The Christian Apprehension of God* (p. 70): 'All religious knowledge of God, wherever existing comes by revelation; otherwise we should be committed to the incredible position that man can know God without His willing to be known.'

[2] *Church Dogmatics*, 2, 1, p. 22 f.

and it is therein that man is established in his being a free and responsible person. That is the ground of his knowledge of God, of his being the human being called into fellowship with God, and therefore of his being man who spontaneously opens himself up to God and actively knows Him. Moreover, it is in this responsible act in which man steps out of his self-isolation and returns to God that he comes to find and know himself. It is then that knowledge of God really strikes home to him, and it is then that it is *his* knowledge, *his* action, *his* theology, that is, the knowledge of one who really knows himself in knowing God, who really becomes a self-possessed subject through the movement in which God stands him on his feet as a subject over against Him and in communion with Him.

(ii) In Jesus Christ God has come to reconcile man to Himself so that man may be delivered from his self-enclosure and be restored to true objectivity in God and true subjectivity in himself. The self-objectification of God for us takes place within the sphere of our alienation from Him, not only within a structured scheme of things in space and time where our modes of existence and knowing are already determined and predisposed toward natural objectivity, but where we are actively engaged in subjugating the external world to the processes of our thought in order to give us power and control over them so that we may use them to reassure and establish ourselves in the world, and also where in the midst of all that we have even sought to be independent of God, and so have estranged ourselves from Him by resisting His will and taking the way of self-will.

That is the situation revealed by the Incarnation, in which the majestic objectivity of God meets our objectivity both uncovering and arousing its hostility to the ways of God. Thus the very coming of God in Jesus Christ to give Himself as the object of our knowledge reveals that we need to be reconciled and adapted to that object if we are to have true knowledge of it. In other words, our possibility of knowing God is grounded not only in His adaptation of Himself to our humanity in the Incarnation, but in the corresponding adaptation of our estranged humanity to the Word and Truth of God in Jesus Christ. That is where the sharpest difficulty lies—in the overcoming of our estrangement and alienation. It is precisely because the majestic objectivity of God draws near and encounters us clothed with the objective forms of our very own world that the latent tension between us is revealed and brought out into the open where we actively resist and oppose Him, and indeed crucify Him. In so doing we finally reveal from our side a hostile disposition toward God and toward the Grace and Truth He manifests towards us in Jesus Christ. Nevertheless, out of His immeasureable love and infinite self-giving God suffers this contradiction of sinners against Him in order to enter into the very heart of our enmity and by revelation and atonement to overcome it and reconcile us to Himself.

In this whole movement of condescension and atoning reconciliation God reveals not only the depths of our God-lessness but the depth of our inadequacy for God, not only the fact that we are held fast in a form of existence that is severed from His Truth but that in ourselves we live in positive untruth, in contradiction and opposition to the Truth. It is not only that our ideas and conceptions and analogies and words are too limited and narrow and poor for knowledge of God, for it is within this poverty-stricken existence of ours that God has objectified Himself for us and He is more than able to overcome its limitations, but our ideas and conceptions and analogies and words are twisted in untruth and are resistent to the Truth, so that we are prevented by the whole cast of our natural mind from apprehending God without exchanging His glory for that of a creature or turning His truth into a lie.[1] Hence the demand of the Gospel for repentance (μετάνοια) on our part, for radical change even in the inner slant of our mind, and in the structural capacities of our reason. But how can we repent like that? How can we expel the untruth that distorts our reason and falsifies the habits of our knowing unless we receive the Truth into our minds, and yet how can we receive the Truth into our minds unless the whole shape of our mind has been altered so that it can recognize it, and unless we are made appropriate to receive it?

Here let us pause to see where our discussion of the first two 'moments' of knowledge of God has carried us. We have seen that the possibility of our knowing God is grounded in His

[1] Romans 1. 23, 25.

divine freedom to cross the boundary between Himself and us and to give Himself to be known by us within the conditions of our frailty on earth. We have seen that this possibility is grounded, in the second place, in an adaptation of humanity to God in which man is lifted up to know God above and beyond his natural powers, that is, in a way appropriate and adequate to the nature of the object of his knowledge. Thus the movement of knowledge, from the side of God who gives Himself to be known and from the side of man who knows, forms, as it were, a closed polarity. On the other hand, the Incarnation reveals that as a matter of fact man stands outside that relation with God in which true knowledge of Him is actualized, and cannot get inside it because in his very existence he is imprisoned in the closed circle of his own estrangement and self-will where he can only fulfil his own possibilities and indeed where he is shut up to believing only in his own possibilities. There is, therefore, no possibility for man really to know God unless he can be taken into the closed polarity where such knowledge is to be realized, that is, unless he enters into the required adaptation of humanity to God. That is the third 'moment' we have to consider in our knowledge of God.

(iii) In Jesus Christ God has condescended not only to objectify Himself for man and to bestow His truth upon him, but also to provide from the side of man, and from within man, full, adequate and perfect reception of that truth. Both of these have been fulfilled in Jesus Christ, for He is in Himself not only God objectifying Himself for man but man adapted and conformed to that objectification, not only the complete revelation of God to man but the appropriate correspondence on the part of man to that revelation, not only the Word of God to man but man obediently hearing and answering that Word. In short Jesus Christ is Himself both the Word of God as spoken by God to man and that same Word as heard and received by man, Himself both the Truth of God given to man and that very Truth understood and actualized in man. He is that divine and human Truth in His one Person.

Therefore, Jesus Christ comes to us as the one Being within our human existence in whom the Truth of God and human knowledge are fully and faithfully correlated, the one Being in our humanity in whose existence we have directly to do with the Being of God Himself, and the only One in whom God's revelation and reconciliation have taken place for all other men. In Him there has already been fulfilled what we are unable to achieve, the reconciliation and adaptation and union of man with God, without which there is no true knowledge of God, so that in Him, in His true and obedient humanity, the Truth of God has been given and received for all men, and as such is made openly accessible to us in the Gospel, not only as the objective Word of God to man but as the same Word subjectively realized and expressed within our human and historical existence.

It is thus in the historical actuality of Jesus Christ, very God and very Man, as the Creed speaks of Him, that the possibility of our knowledge of God is rooted. In Him and through Him God has actually become known by man. Now this means that in Jesus Christ God has broken into the closed circle of our inability and inadequacy, and estrangement and self-will, and within our alien condition has achieved and established real knowledge of Himself. It is in the freedom of God to do that, and in the fact that God actually has done that, that our knowledge of Him is grounded—that is, in His condescension to enter within our creaturely frailty and incompetence and so to realize knowledge of Himself from within our mode of existence, in the incarnate Son. We do not first have to achieve this knowledge, we do not even have to achieve the appropriation of it which first actualizes it within our creaturely existence, for that has already been achieved for us in Christ, and in Him we may now freely participate in the knowledge of God as an actuality already translated and made accessible for us by His grace. Thus our freedom in knowing and appropriating the truth is grounded in the objective freedom of God, and our decision for the truth is grounded in the objective and decisive act of God made on our behalf in the whole historical fact of Christ. We find and know God where He has sought us and condescended to communicate Himself, in His objectivity in Jesus Christ. We cannot seek to know Him by transcending His condescension or objectivity, or by going behind it, for that would be to go where God has not given Himself to be the object of our knowledge. We can only know God in His self-objectification for us, not by seeking non-objective knowledge of Him. This then is the given fact, the indispensable pre-supposition of theological knowledge, and with which Christian theology stands or falls, that God Himself, the only God, the living and true God, has condescended to enter within our creaturely and contingent existence, to objectify Himself for us there in Jesus Christ, so that Jesus Christ is the Way, the Truth, and the Life, in whom and through whom alone we go to the Father, and by reference to whom alone we have true knowledge of God.

We have set forth three 'moments' in our knowledge of God in which its possibility for us is grounded in the objective action of God in the Incarnation, but Christian theology is not satisfied to remain there; it goes on to speak of another 'moment' in which this objectively grounded possibility becomes a subjective reality in our actual knowledge, and in which, therefore, we can speak also of a subjective possibility on our part in our actual knowledge. But this 'moment' is not an additional 'moment', in the sense that anything has to be added to the objective reality and possibility of our knowledge of God in Jesus Christ, but a 'moment' in the sense in which the other 'moments' are subjectively realized within us. In other words, Christian theology goes on to speak of the Holy Spirit of God in His freedom not only to meet us and to reveal Himself over against us, but to come to us as Presence from within us and so to open us up subjectively toward Himself.[1] This is to say, it is through the gift of His Spirit to us and by the presence and power of the Spirit, that we are enabled to share in the knowledge of God grounded and established and once and for all made accessible to us in Jesus Christ. It is not our purpose here to expound the content of the doctrine of the Spirit, but merely to indicate the epistemological relevance of that doctrine for our present discussion.[2]

Our understanding of the possibility of the knowledge of

---

[1] It is difficult to understand why medieval theism neglected the doctrine of God as Spirit, but its failure to think of the Spirit as the presence to us of God in His *Being*, helps us to see why medieval thought rejected an intuitive *evident* knowledge of God *per modum entis*. This must be judged a serious defect even in its 'natural theology'.

[2] See further 'The Epistemological Relevance of the Holy Spirit', in *Ex Auditu Verbi, Theologische opstellen aangeboden aan Prof. Dr. G. C. Berkouwer*, 1965, pp. 272–296, and *Theology in Reconstruction*, 1965, pp. 194 ff., 213 ff., 235 ff.

God can only carry us up to a penultimate, never to an ultimate, point, for it belongs to the very nature of the object we
are concerned to know that we are unable to make our knowing
of it fully comprehensible as *our* action, or therefore as a possibility of *ours*.[1] In the nature of the case we are unable to think
out to the end just how we think this truth that transcends us.
If we could, it would not be the Truth of God. The demand that
we must be able to think it out to the end, if it is real, presupposes that we can gain ascendency over it and that we are
in fact transcendent over it. But that is to take the way of
mythology, in which we project ourselves into the place of
God and think out a god in man's image. Now it is this
mythologizing process that is sharply inhibited and set aside by
the doctrine of the Spirit in the concern to guard the transcendence and objectivity of the Truth of God, that is in
biblical language, His *holiness*. God is present to us, and gives
Himself to our knowing, only in such a way that He remains the
Lord who has ascendency over us, who distinguishes Himself
from us, and makes Himself known in His divine otherness
even when He draws us into communion with Himself. He is
present to us in such a way that He never resigns knowledge of
Himself to our mastery, but remains the One who is Master
over us, who resists, and objects to, every attempt on our part
to subdue or redact the possibility of knowledge grounded in
His divine freedom to an immanent and latent possibility
which we deem ourselves to possess apart from Him in virtue of
our own being. Hence we can never give an account of our
knowledge of God in such a way as to reduce His Holiness,
His Transcendence, His unapproachable Majesty, to a
vanishing point, but only in such a way that we are thrown
ultimately upon His mercy, upon His transcendent freedom to
lower Himself to us and to lift us up to Him beyond anything
that we can think or conceive out of ourselves. To know God
in His Holiness means that our human subjectivity is opened
out and up toward that which infinitely transcends it.

[1] This point is well made by John Baillie. 'The fact is that no true knowledge,
no valid act of perceiving or thinking, can be explained by beginning from the
human end—whether it be my perception of the number of peas in a particular
pod or my discovery of an argument for the existence of God. In either case my
cognition is valid only so far as it is determined by the reality with which I am
faced.' *The Idea of Revelation in Recent Thought*, p. 22.

On the other hand, to know God in this way, does not entail an abrogation of the subject-object relationship, nor does it mean that the knower in any sense loses possession of himself in some ecstatic experience. Knowledge of God does not entail any diminishing of our rational powers, but the very reverse, for in requiring of us sober and critical judgements of our own powers and possibilities, it does so through requiring us to be obedient to the rational Word of God and to acknowledge that we are face to face with a Reality which we cannot rationally reduce to our own creaturely dimensions. To know God does not mean, then, that we must leave our humanity, and its mode of knowing, behind, but it does mean that here on earth in the fullness of our humanity we are given to know that which really transcends us, and are therefore engaged in a knowledge that cannot ultimately be explained from the side of man. If God really is God then to approach Him or even to consider that we can know Him in any way except out of Himself and in a way appropriate to His transcendent nature would be a form of irrationality, but it would also violate an essential characteristic of the scientific mind that is emancipated from all external authorities, for it 'acknowledges no ultimate authority save the witness of reality to his own mind'.[1]

[1] John Oman, *The Natural and the Supernatural*, pp. 100, 102.

2

The Interaction of Theology
with Scientific Development[1]

In the previous chapter we discussed the objectivity of theological knowledge as the reality in its actuality and the ground of its possibility. We maintained that there is no factual knowledge of God except where He has condescended to reveal Himself in His objectivity. We cannot know Him by transcending or going behind His objectivity, for that would be to go where no God is to be found and where there is no divine object for our knowledge. We know God, in the proper rational sense of knowledge, only in His objectivity, not by seeking non-objective knowledge of Him.

It is this very devotion of theology to its proper object that is the scientific passion of theology, its rigorous and disciplined determination to be properly objective, that is, to be faithful toward, and truthful with, its object, and therefore to be concerned with penetrating through the subjectivities that inevitably arise in our knowledge to the ultimate ground of the given, and to distinguish it in its irreducible reality from the extraneous habits of thought and speech that we bring to it. Theology by its very nature is thus inherently interested in scientific activity and the development of adequate tools and methods in the service of knowledge.

Of course, if we are to be wholly faithful to the nature of the object, namely, to the living God and His purpose with us, then we must acknowledge that theology is only part of man's total response to God. It has its place within the whole complex of the Church's response in worship and obedience and mission. Therefore theology as a scientific activity cannot be regarded merely as a science in itself, independent and

[1] For the following see *Theology in Reconstruction*, ch. 4, pp. 62–75.

self-explanatory. No theology is justified by itself, but solely in response to the total claims of God upon us. Theology is therefore more than a science. It is not for that reason less than a science, but rather all the more rigorously scientific because of the total claims of its Object and its unconditional requirements for objectivity. Within that comprehensive understanding of our response to God, we must see that scientific theology has its own proper, if relative, place, and its own unrelenting conscience, in passionate and unreserved loyalty of the mind to the one Truth of God. Here the measure of its commitment to the object, and its refusal of detachment, is the measure of its dedication to objectivity. Our task will, therefore, involve an examination of the scientific activity which theology knows to be required of it. That we shall try to do in the following chapter, but before then, and by way of preparation for it and more that must follow later, there is something else that we must consider: the implication of the fact that theology takes place in a creaturely world.

Theological knowledge of God is not concerned with God in the abstract, with God as He is simply in Himself, as it were, as if our knowledge of God could be cut off from the fact that it is after all knowledge of God by man on earth and in time. Theology is concerned with God as the Creator of the world, and therefore with God in His relation to the world of creaturely realities. It is concerned with God as the heavenly Father who enters into communion with men as His children, and therefore with God in His relation to man and indeed with man in his relation to God. Moreover theology has to do with the God who placed man in this world which He made to reflect His own glory and which He gave to man for his inquiry and understanding, and so theology is the activity of man who in this world and as part of it seeks to know God in all the relations and connections which God has established between man and God within the world. In theology, then, we have to do with God only as He has established man in the world in a relation to Himself, only as He has revealed Himself to man as Creator and Redeemer within the creaturely objectivities of the world, but for that reason we are committed in all theological activity to maintain faithful and responsible relations toward worldly objectivities in accordance with their creaturely nature.

Thus arising out of the very heart of theology there is an unquenchable interest in the scientific understanding of creaturely being, and for the whole fabric of worldly existence as the medium within which God has placed man and constituted him what he is in relation to Himself, since all that is part of man's total response to God. This does not mean that theology will confound knowledge of God even in His relation to creatures with the knowledge of creatures in their contingent realities, but it does mean that theology cannot be true to itself unless it makes room for and indeed fosters knowledge of creaturely being in accordance with its creaturely and contingent nature. That is the reason for the peculiar interest of theology in the rise and progress of natural science, and for the fact that its own scientific pursuit cannot be separated from the scientific pursuits that are pursued in the same world about other aspects of creaturely being. This is indeed why, in spite of the unfortunate tension that has so often cropped up between the advance of scientific theories and traditional habits of thought in the Church, theology can still claim to have mothered throughout long centuries the basic beliefs and impulses which have given rise especially to modern empirical science, if only through its unflagging faith in the reliability of God the Creator and in the ultimate intelligibility of His creation.[1]

Science does owe its origin, certainly, to ancient Greece, and there can be little doubt that its development was often seriously hindered by the Christian Church, even when within it the beginnings of modern ideas were taking their rise. The reasons for this are deep and complicated. We must not forget that behind this lay the break-up of the Mediterranean civilization and its rescue, notably in the West, through the power and beauty of Augustinian theology, out of which flowed the magnificent contribution to the arts in the Middle Ages. But the dominance of Augustinianism over the religion and culture of Europe for a thousand years had other effects. Its eschatology which perpetuated the idea of the decay and collapse of the world, and of salvation as redemption out of it, directed attention away from the world to the superterrestrial, while its conception of the sacramental universe allowed only a symbolic

---

[1] Cf. here Whitehead's estimation of the part played by the Medieval Church in this respect, *Science and the Modern World*, pp. 14 ff.

understanding of nature and a religious, illustrative use of it. This led to the exalted harnessing of human activity to the glory of God that fostered the arts, but it also meant the absorption of all effort in the saving of the soul. It was this outlook that frequently obstructed the advance of science, for it took up and 'sanctified' a cosmological outlook that had to be replaced if scientific progress was to take place, but what discouraged the scientific mind, often rather seriously, was a hardened, and a somewhat misinterpreted, notion of authority, and its relation to the understanding, that went back to Augustine, an element from which the Roman Church is still struggling to free itself. It was this that first gave rise to the bitter complaints of science against the Church.

On the other hand, there were elements deriving from the ancient world, secular and Christian, nourished by the Church throughout the Dark Ages which, when quickened by contact with Arabian thought and built up through the rediscovery of Aristotle, produced the conditions required for the development of Western science. Our knowledge of these developments has been immensely enhanced by the recent works of A. C. Crombie who has shown how deeply embedded the origins of empirical science are in medieval thinkers, particularly in the development from Grosseteste to Ockham.[1] He claims, and, it would appear, with ample justification, 'that a systematic theory of experimental science was understood and practised by enough philosophers for their work to produce the methodological revolution to which modern science owes its origin. With this revolution appeared in the Latin West a clear understanding of the relation between theory and observation on which the modern conception and practice of scientific research and explanation are based, a clear set of procedures for dealing with physical problems.'[2] But why was it, then, that

[1] *Robert Grosseteste, and the Origins of Experimental Science, 1100–1700*, Oxford, 1953; id., *Mediaeval and Early Modern Science*, vol. i, *Science in the Middle Ages: V-XIII Centuries*, vol. ii, *Science in the Later Middle Ages and Early Modern Times, XIII-XVII Centuries*, New York, 1959.

[2] *Robert Grosseteste*, p. 9. Of Grosseteste himself Crombie says: 'Grosseteste appears to have been the first medieval writer to recognize and deal with the two fundamental methodological problems of induction and experimental verification and falsification which arose when the Greek conception of geometrical demonstration was applied to the world of experience. He seems to have been the first to set out a systematic and coherent theory of experimental investigation and rational explanation by which the Greek geometrical method was turned into modern experimental science.' (p. 10.)

modern science had to wait till the beginning of the seventeenth century for it to make its real advance, if the methodological framework it required had been created so early?

Before it could begin its actual work, modern empirical science had to be liberated from the domination of medieval scholastic theology. This it owed above all to the great movement of thought at the Reformation. Now this is of particular interest to us, for it is as we discern the close relation between the rise of modern scientific activity and modern theology that we can appreciate the claims of modern theology to engage in scientific activity, not, be it noted, because it wishes in any way to imitate empirical science, but because when it is true to itself it cannot but be scientific in the proper sense.

There are several main contributions to this development from the side of the Reformation that we have to consider.

(1) CHANGE IN THE DOCTRINE OF GOD

During the period of the Reformation there took place a significant change in the doctrine of God which had far-reaching effects, not only for theology, but, as M. B. Foster has shown so clearly, also for natural science.[1] It was the displacing of the Stoic-Latin view of God as *deus sive natura* by the essentially Biblical view of God, the Creator of all things, and the active Redeemer of His people. Medieval theology had fallen heir to the Patristic notion of the impassibility of God, and this notion had been considerably strengthened with the bringing together of Aristotle's doctrine of the Unmoved Mover and its traditional doctrine of God as Creator, with the result that there lay deeply entrenched in the high medieval theology the idea that God is impassible and changeless, and that all created things have existence only as the objects of the eternal knowing and willing of God, so that their creaturely existence is directly grounded in the eternity of God. Now medieval theology quite definitely rejected the conception of the world as an emanation of God and therefore the linking together of the necessity of the world with the necessity of the divine

[1] See his articles in *Mind*, xliii (1934), pp. 446 ff.; xliv (1935), pp. 439 ff.; xlv (1936), pp. 1 ff.; *The Christian News-Letter*, 299 (Nov. 1947); also M. B. Foster, *Mystery and Philosophy*, 1957, pp. 87 ff. Cf. John Baillie, *Natural Science and the Spiritual Life*, 1950, pp. 20 ff.; W. A. Whitehouse, *Christian Faith and the Scientific Attitude*, 1951, p. 60 f.

nature, but nevertheless it held on to a (modified) notion of a hierarchy of being, embracing both the lowest and the highest being, which seriously blurred the Biblical distinction between the Creator and the creature, and introduced into its doctrine of God an unfortunate ambiguity. What it implied was an eternal positing or even co-existence of creaturely being with God's eternal Being which made it difficult to deny the *aeternitas mundi*,[1] even if it could not be affirmed, or at least not to be convinced of the ultimate changelessness of nature, i.e. of all that is not God. No doubt it may be right to argue, as St. Thomas did, that from His eternity God sees all temporal things as present to Him, for His eternity is present to every moment of time and encloses it, but it is quite another thing to reverse that movement of thought, i.e. to argue that these things in their real physical being are eternally present to God and in some sense coexist with Him.[2] To have given up this view would have implied, within the framework of the medieval theology, at any rate, the ultimate irrationality of creation, and that in turn would have reflected on its doctrine of God, but so long as this view of the natural world and its changeless and timeless bond to the divine mind prevailed, the rise of empirical science was severely handicapped.

We may express this differently, by saying that for medieval theology nature was thought of as impregnated with ultimate causes, so that not only could an eternal pattern be read off the face of nature (thus in effect substituting nature for God and giving rise to natural theology), but apart from that understanding of the eternal pattern real knowledge of nature was ruled out. But to interpret nature in the light of final and primary causes left little room for the element of real contingency in nature, to the recognition of which modern experimental

---

[1] Cf. *De aeternitate mundi contra murmurantes* in which St. Thomas argues that there is no contradiction between affirming that something is created and that it never was non-existent. That God created everything out of nothing and that the world was not eternal but had a beginning, was defined by *Concil. Lat. IV*: Denzinger–Schönmetzer, *Enchiridion Symbolorum*, edit. xxxiii (1965), 800 (428) *et seq*.

[2] *Contra Gentiles* I, 66; and also *Summa Theologica* I q. 14, a. 13, q. 57, a. 3; *Scriptum super Libros Sent*. I d. 38, a. 5. For modern Roman discussion of this see F. Diekamp, *Katholische Dogmatik*, 11th edit. vol. i, pp. 163 f., 182 ff., 201 f.; M. Scheeben, *Handbuch der Katholischen Dogmatik*, 2nd edit., by M. Schmaus, vol. II, p. 102 f.

science owes its existence.[1] This had to wait until the period of the Reformation for its real beginning, when men learned to think differently of the nature of God and of His relation to creation as something utterly distinct from Him while yet dependent upon His will for its being and ultimate order, and therefore learned to think differently of the nature of nature, and of the creaturely nature of its order. Only when nature was liberated from medieval rationalism and disenchanted of its secret 'divinity', and only when it was realized that the order of nature, while intelligible to us theologically as a divine creation, precisely because it is a creaturely order, can only be known through observation and interpretation of the creaturely processes themselves, could the more or less static science of the ancient and medieval world give way to the great movement of modern science.

Now someone may very well agree that modern empirical science owes much in its great forward movement to the recognition of these two facts, an ultimate orderliness behind the flux of nature, and the element of contingency in creaturely existence, and behind that lies the Christian doctrine of God. Of course, the recognition of the orderliness of the universe is as old as astronomy, while the orderliness of what is contingent seems to have arisen out of Christian theology. But is not this, he may say, precisely what medieval theology taught, although it may well have been tempted to 'exaggerate the element of rationality in the universe in comparison with the element of contingency, and so to minimize the place of experiment in comparison with that of theory'?[2]

In reply to that we must say that quite a *new kind of question* had to be put to nature, expecting quite a different kind of answer, namely, one which would call for the revision of the premises that first lay behind the question, i.e. of the notion of nature with which it began. The questions which medieval thinkers asked were so philosophically controlled from behind that they were not properly free and open, nor were they put in the mode and idiom of a rationality that was congruent with real contingency. They were governed by a fixed notion of

---

[1] See John Baillie, *Natural Science and the Spiritual Life*, p. 22 ff.

[2] E. L. Mascall, *Christian Theology and Natural Science*, p. 98.

nature and were therefore of little use in opening up nature, for they excluded from consideration the kind of contingency and the kind of order upon which empirical science is based.[1] For really free questions to arise, there had to take place a radical loosening up and questioning of the whole medieval synthesis, and because that synthesis was knotted tight in and through its doctrine of God and nature, it was at that point that the real shift in outlook had to take place, before the great transition from a mainly static to a largely dynamic mode of thinking could begin either in theology or in natural science.

In this respect it is instructive to turn the spotlight as it were upon William of Ockham,[2] the great scion of the *via moderna* and the *logica nova*, for he appears to represent best the point where the medieval synthesis was breaking up from within into radical dichotomies, and yet where it was challenged to take a step forward which it was unable to do without allowing itself to be called radically into question. Thus Ockham called for a separation of the Church from the world, which pointed to a new freedom of life and action in the secular realms.[3] In advocating a clear distinction between the realm of faith and divine truth, and the realm of reason and argument, he loosened rational investigation from its subservience to the Church.[4] He did not oppose faith to philosophy, revealed knowledge to natural knowledge, as is often supposed,

[1] Medieval discussion of the problem of God's knowledge of future contingent events, shows that contingency could only be conceived in terms of potentiality or possibility; contingent events could only be known in so far as they contain elements of necessity—cf. Aquinas, *Summ. Theol.* I a, q. 86, a 3. Even Ockham held that God's knowledge of future contingent facts is determinate and immutable—*Tract. de praedestinatione et de praescientia Dei et de futuris contingentibus.* Medieval thinkers could not face up to the problem of contingency squarely, because it could not be given logical definition. Contrast the attention given to *randomness* by modern science in its refusal to agree that what is purely contingent or accidental is to be excluded from scientific knowledge, which was a universal assumption in medieval philosophy.

[2] See A. C. Crombie, *Mediaeval and Modern Science*, especially vol. ii, pp. 29 ff., 351 f.; H. M. Carré, *Realists and Nominalists*, Ch. IV.

[3] *Tractatus de imperatorum et pontificum potestate*, and *Dialogus de imp. et pont. potestate;* selections in S. C. Tornay, *Ockham, Studies and Selections*, pp. 196 ff.

[4] This is very apparent in *Quodlibeta Septem*, ii, q. 1–3; *Comm.in Sent.*, *prol. 1 QQ*, etc. and selections in Tornay, op. cit., pp. 182–195. (Cf. the spurious *Centiloquium theologicum*, e.g. 1, or 7 f.)

but he showed that they involved two very different approaches and therefore quite different notions of *scientia*. Again, Ockham's denial of 'reality' to universals, that is as an independent entity which can be present in many particulars and be in common to them,[1] was meant to question the validity of abstractions and the basic assumption that we can only conceive of the real in terms of changeless patterns and eternal ideas, opened up the way for freer investigation of individual existents and the development of an empirical habit of mind.[2] But behind all that, Ockham taught a doctrine of the ultimate inscrutability (not the arbitrariness) of God, that is, that His existence as One God cannot be demonstrated and His nature cannot be known through the discursive reason but only through divine revelation and 'infused faith', and he taught a doctrine of nature appropriate to a free creation contingent upon the pure will and wisdom of God rather than to one conceived as grounded upon the unchangeable essence of God.[3]

Some of Ockham's ideas had far-reaching implications for the development of modern science, several of which we may note.

(1) His doctrine of God called in question the applicability of final causes to the sequences between natural events, while his logic forced him to doubt whether we could establish direct causal connexions in nature. This involved him in a very

[1] In Ockham's terminology, universal concepts exist *objective*, not *subjective*, i.e. in modern terminology, subjectively, not objectively—*Comm. in Sent.* prol. q. 3 d; I d 2 q. 8 g; *Quodlibeta* iv q. 19. Although Ockham spoke of universals as existing in the mind, he held them to be *vere entia realia*, and as corresponding to existing realities (ibid.). What he denied is that there were such things as universals *in re*, in the world of concrete reality. It is not easy to grasp his views exactly, but what seems clear is that he wished to do away with unnecessary sensible and intelligible forms coming between the mind and its intuitive cognition of the object whether that was through or apart from sensory experience. He does seem to have succeeded in opening up a way through medieval rationalism for real knowledge in direct perception of contingent facts and particulars. Ockham denies that the images or representations, through which the intellect apprehends material things, for example, exist as substantive copies of the object, because it is only through them that we really apprehend the object, and it is the object that has substantive reality. See *Comm. in Sent.* ii q. 8, 13, 15 etc. Cf. also L. Baudry, *Lexique Philosophique de G. d'Ockham*, pp. 278 ff., and P. Boehner, Ockham, *Philosophical Writings*, pp. xxvii f., and 32 ff.

[2] See *Comm. in Sent.* prol. q. 1 QQ; ii q. 150; iii q. 8 d, where Ockham insists that knowledge of contingent things is only possible through experience of them as individual and singular existents. Cf. also *Quodlibeta* i, xiii–xv.

[3] Cf. R. Seeberg, *Lehrbuch der Dogmengeschichte*, 3rd edit., vol. III, pp. 609 ff.

significant attack upon the physics and metaphysics that were embedded in the medieval synthesis. As A. C. Crombie has said, "the effect of Ockham's attack on contemporary physics and metaphysics was to destroy belief in most of the principles on which the 13th century system of physics was based. In particular he attacked the Aristotelian categories of 'relation' and 'substance' and the notion of causation."[1]

(2) Another significant contribution of Ockham was his attention to and his theory of *motion* which was carried on and developed by his follower Buridan.[2] Our concern is not with the contents of that theory but with the fact that in it we see distinct signs of a mutation in the thought-forms of the medieval world in a modern direction.

(3) With Ockham there began to emerge the recognition of a different kind of order in nature, a sequence and regularity of events that could only be discerned properly if it were freed from logical construction and reversibility; it was not something that could be explained by tracing a line of logico-causal connexion backward (eventually to a final cause), but only through examination of it as an irreversible succession, for that is how we know it in sensory experience.[3] In other words, Ockham seems to have been one of the first to realize that we cannot understand the sequence or succession of events in nature by converting the movement they involve into a logical relation—but is this not what the medieval way of applying geometry and logic to nature almost inevitably involved?

Ockham's views have their relevance only within the framework of medieval scholasticism, and it is there that our interest in him lies. When he sought *within* that framework to develop a new mode of rationality and explanation appropriate to contingent nature, he could only do that by advocating views, the primacy of the will, nominalism, the divorce of faith and

[1] Op. cit., p. 32.

[2] Op. cit., pp. 32 f., 62 ff. See *Comm. in Sent* II q. 26, M; and *Tract. de Motu* in *Tractatus de Successivis*, edit. by P. Boehner, 1944, which is apparently a compilation out of Ockham's writings.

[3] See Crombie, op. cit., pp. 29 ff., 62 ff. When Crombie says of Ockham's view, 'The observed regularities of the world became mere regularities of fact, and the laws expressing them became at their strongest mere possibilities, at their weakest simply conventional devices for correlation and calculation,' is he not interpreting Ockham in a too Humean and modern light? Op. cit., p. 315.

reason, etc. which could only be regarded as the rejection of rationality and the advocacy of scepticism. If we hold that *within* this framework we must acknowledge the right of the realists against the Ockhamists and nominalists, we can also realize how extremely difficult it was for empirical science to achieve any real break-through in the medieval world. The whole medieval synthesis had to be questioned down to rock bottom, and only a new theology could do that, reaching behind the medieval development to its Biblical and patristic source.

That is what happened at the Reformation. The very foundations of medieval Roman theology were subjected to searching criticism in the effort to purge it of alien conceptions of deity and nature, and to restore in its fullness the biblical doctrine of the living, acting God as Creator and Father. The result was an immense upheaval which substituted a more dynamic and active way of thinking for that of the medieval schoolmen, and it was that foundation that made possible the equally great mutation in scientific thinking from static to dynamic and kinetic questions, resulting in a corresponding change in terminology. Thus as Professor E. A. Burt has written: 'It is obvious, from a casual observation of the medieval and modern methods of attacking the difficulties of metaphysics, that a radical shift has been made in the terminology used. Instead of treating things in terms of substance, accident, causality, essence and idea, matter and form, potentiality and actuality, we now treat them in terms of forces, motions and laws, changes of mass in space and time, and the like.'[1] These changes derived from the new science, and it is significant that the men chiefly responsible at first for initiating these changes were men like Bacon and Newton whose scientific work was so closely tied up with their faith, and their explicit rejection of Aristotelian notions of deity and nature.[2]

(2) THE DISTINCTION BETWEEN GRACE AND NATURE

Parallel to the distinction between the Creator and the creature in Reformed theology, there arose a corresponding

---

[1] *The Metaphysical Foundations of Modern Science*, 1932, p. 26.

[2] Cf. John Baillie, op. cit., pp. 15 ff. Descartes also falls within this description, for, as Prof. Baillie points out (p. 18), the reason why he broke with the authority of Aristotle was 'a reason of faith rather than a reason of science'.

distinction between Grace and nature. This was a distinction that guarded the Godness of God on the one hand, and the naturalness of nature on the other hand, by calling in question any blurring of the distinction between God and creation. Thus it attacked the fundamental basis of the medieval synthesis in the following way. It challenged the notion of reversibility in the relations between God and man, which allowed an argument from the coexistence of God with the creature to the coexistence of the creature with God. God made man in His own image, but we cannot reverse that, and beginning with an examination of the image in man go on to speak of God on the ground of what we have learned in man— that is the way of mythology. Therefore it challenged the assumption that there is an inherent relation between the form-structure of the reason and the form-structure of being. The structure of true knowledge does conform to the structure of being, but that does not allow us to posit such a relation between the logical forms of the reason and the nature of the truth that we can necessarily argue from conformity to our reason to the truth of being, or so manipulate the immanent forms of the reason that we can coerce knowledge of the truth.

On the other hand, the distinction between Grace and nature must not be interpreted as a dichotomy, as if there were only a deistic relation between the creature and the Creator. There is a relation of being between the creature and the Creator immediately maintained by the Creator, but it is the irreversible relation of Grace which He freely posits and preserves in His love. It is a Creator–creature relation which God establishes freely out of pure Grace; as such it is neither explainable from the side of the creature nor logically definable, and therefore is not reversible.

We may consider the relation between Grace and nature in another way, more in connexion with the change in the doctrine of God already discussed. In the Augustinian tradition, with its powerful ingredient of Neoplatonism, which dominated the Middle Ages, the universe was regarded as a sacramental macrocosm in which the physical and visible creation was held to be the counterpart in time to eternal and heavenly patterns. Thus the world of nature was looked at only sacramentally, i.e. looked *through* toward God and the eternal realities. As such the world had no significance in itself, or only significance in so far as it participated in divine and eternal patterns. It was the longing of the world for the ultimate realities that moved it and directed it and so gave it meaning.

With the Reformation, however, there emerged a new outlook involving the primacy of Grace and the rethinking of its meaning as the turning of God toward the world. This gave new significance to the world as the object of divine attention, and therefore as the object of human attention in obedience to the divine. If in the former outlook the world was interpreted in its attraction toward God, in the latter it was interpreted in God's action upon the world. In the former the danger lay in a world-denying movement (particularly apparent in monasticism and its sharp contrast between the religious and the secular), but in the latter the danger lay in a tendency to allow attention to the world to induce forgetfulness of God (as in modern secularism). God the Creator turns in Grace to create and preserve a world utterly distinct from Himself, but because it is utterly distinct, although entirely dependent upon His free will and wisdom, it is to be interpreted aright in its utter distinctness, that is, in its natural or material processes without direct reference to God. Hence the way was opened up for the development of empirical science which is inhibited so long as man looks only away from the world to God to find its meaning in its participation in divine patterns. But once this outlook is established and the primacy of Grace is undermined, there arise tendencies toward Deism, which has room for God only in the ultimate beginning of creation, or toward agnosticism, which takes seriously the purely contingent nature of all that is not God but is tempted to convert this contingency into a new necessity. Both these tendencies are fostered by what we may call 'the religious materialism' of Protestantism, but they can arise only when the all-important doctrine of Grace is forgotten or perverted, for while Grace asserts that the relation between God and the creation is irreversible, it does nevertheless insist that the relation between God and the creature is a two-way relation.[1]

---

[1] Thus the *risk* of Deism or agnosticism is the price that Protestantism pays for the liberation of nature.

This understanding of the relation between God and the creature through Grace Reformed theology expounds by using the biblical conception of the *Covenant*.[1] The Covenant of Grace, as it has been called, embraces not only man but the whole of creation, involving a covenanted correspondence between the creation and the Creator—that is, not one reposing upon some inherent relation of likeness between the essence of God as such and the essence of man as such, but solely upon the gracious decision of God to create a world utterly distinct from Him and yet to assume it beyond anything it possesses in itself into such close relation with Him that it may reflect His Glory and be the appointed theatre of His revelation. Thus Reformed theology sought to assert the relation between Creator and creature, Grace and nature, in such a way as to repudiate any confusion or reversibility on the one hand and any separation or dichotomy on the other, for it took as its guide in understanding that relation the fulfilment of God's Covenant of Grace in Jesus Christ. In His incarnation and redemption the Covenant is seen, as Barth has expounded it in our day, as the inner ground and form of creation, and creation is seen as the outer ground or form of the Covenant.[2]

This distinction between the realm of Grace as the ways of God and the realm of nature as the course of creation in its creaturely distinctness from God bore immense fruit, for it at once disenchanted the world of its alleged divinity and yet claimed the world for God as His creation, thus denying that it was the product of capricious forces.[3] In the realm of Grace, Grace has dominion, primacy and precedence in everything, for man's salvation is due to God alone and even his knowledge of God derives its possibility solely from God's Grace and condescension; but in the realm of nature, man is by Grace given dominion, primacy and precedence, for all things are given under his command. Both in the realm of Grace and in the realm of nature man is created and called to be a partner

---

[1] In contrast to this the doctrine of Leibniz of a 'harmony' between the kingdom of grace and the kingdom of nature was formed under the influence of Scholastic logic and the reintroduction of final causes. His conception of the relation of nature and grace corresponding to the relation between efficient and final cause is much closer the medieval view.

[2] This is the theme of *Church Dogmatics*, 3, 1 on 'The Work of Creation', especially § 41.

[3] Cf. W. A. Whitehouse, op. cit., pp. 27 and 60 f.

in covenant with God, to be a subject in communion with God, to live in dependence upon Him and in obedience and love toward Him, while the dominion he is given over the realm of nature he is to exercise as God's creature and as the recipient of His Grace. In theological studies this had the effect of giving man full place as knowing subject over against the object, and rehabilitating theology as a dialogical activity with its positive content in the Word of God; while in other pursuits it tended to enhance man's sense of his dignity and autonomy by acknowledging that God has subjected the whole of nature to him.

The effect of this teaching is nowhere better seen than in the thought of Francis Bacon, who quickly realized the opportunities as well as the duties it opened up for man, not only in his service of God in the Kingdom of God (*regnum Dei*) but in the building up of his own life on earth through inductive science in the kingdom of man (*regnum hominis*). Far from leading to a neglect of nature, the distinction between Grace and nature directed Bacon to the pursuit of natural science as a religious duty,[1] for he understood it to mean that God has kept the Godward side of nature hidden, that is, He has kept final causes or the ultimate law of nature 'within His own curtain', but whatever is not-God is laid open by God for man's investigation and comprehension.[2] It is therefore by keeping within the limits and ends of knowledge which God Himself has set in the creation of man, and which faith makes clear to him, that man can fulfil his function as an interpreter of nature and build up his kingdom on *scientia*.[3] This is man's right by creation, and by the Grace of God it remains his right even if he has fallen from God, although the fall means that that kingdom can be acquired only by the sweat of his brow and laborious discovery in the actual investigation of nature itself.[4]

Bacon claimed that the reason why natural philosophers up to his time had really failed to deal with nature was to be traced to the influence of Plato and Aristotle, notably the latter who so impregnated nature with final causes that he substituted

---

[1] *Instauratio magna, prooem. Distributio operis; Novum organum* I. lii; *Valerius Terminus* I; *Filum Labyrinthi* 1. 7, cf. Burt, op. cit., p. 194.

[2] *Val. Term.* I.

[3] *Ibid.; Nov. Org.* I.x, xxiv, cxxix; *Parasceve* x.

[4] *Val. Term.* I; *Nov. org.* II. lvii; *Cogitata et visa* (Works, ed. by Spedding, Ellis, and Heath, vol. iii, p. 611); *Advancement of Learning* I (Works, iii, pp. 265 f.; 296 f.); *De augmentis scientiarum* iv. 2.

nature for God and thus made the conception of nature useless.[1] 'For the handling of final causes in physics has thrown down and driven out inquiry into physical causes, and made men satisfied with those specious and shadowy causes so that they did not press their inquiry into the causes that are real and truly physical, to the great detriment of the sciences.'[2] Moreover, it was this pernicious attempt to find ultimate truths in nature that led to divorce of theoretic understanding from experimental contact with nature, and so allowed nature itself to slip through men's hands.

It seemed unreasonable to Bacon to hold that what had never been discovered could still be discovered by the old methods. New facts required new methods of inquiry and facts about nature required methods appropriate to nature.[3] Accordingly, he turned away from the rational deductions and abstractions of the past in order to concentrate upon nature in its concrete manifestations or 'instances', and to devise a new method (*novum organum*) for this purpose, in which the theoretical and experimental would be wedded together in a 'true and lawful marriage'.[4] That is to say, he sought to develop a new inductive procedure, or a mode of rational investigation of nature in which active inquiry (*activa inquisitio*) and real discovery (*inventio*) would proceed together,[5] in order to let nature declare itself, rather than to superimpose upon it patterns which we have already reached by logic. Logic can tell us nothing new;[6] all it can do is to order what we already know, and

[1] *De aug. scient.* iii. Cf. iv; *Nov. org.* i. liv.

[2] *De aug. scient.* iii. In the following chapter Bacon adds: 'Inquiry into final causes is barren, and like a virgin consecrated to God produces nothing.' See also *Delineatio et argumentum partis instaurationis secundae*, and *Redargutio Philosophiarum*. Thus Bacon held that the very possibility of natural science depends upon our sense of the limitation of nature and of our knowledge of it—cf. *Nov. org.* i. xlviii.

[3] *Nov. org.* i. vi.

[4] *Mag. inst. prooem.*; *Nov. org.* i. xcv.

[5] The language used by Bacon, *activa inquisitio, inventio*, has been taken from the works of Rodolph Agricola, *De inventione dialectica* (1515 and 1538) and Laurentius Valla, *Dialecticae disputationes contra Aristotelicos* (1499 and 1509) who applied the kind of interrogation employed in courts of law to historical investigation and rational induction. They were widely followed in this by the Renaissance lawyers, e.g. John Calvin, who studied the sources of Valla's and Agricola's new method in the writings of Cicero, *Topica, De inventione, De partitione oratoria*, etc.

[6] Cf. Karl Popper: 'There is no such thing as a logical method of having new ideas.' (*The Logic of Scientific Discovery*, p. 32.) This is precisely the point which Popper has failed to appreciate in Bacon.

therefore tends toward the rationalization of erroneous pre-conceptions.[1] Man's place is to be the servant and interpreter of nature which he can understand only in proportion as he observes 'the order of nature' and submits himself to 'nature in action'.[2] Mere contemplation of nature never gets us very far, nor will the haphazard ways of discovery employed in the past. The science of the future must rather be one in which inquiry is planned and actively controlled throughout by the use of experimental methods.[3] 'Our steps must be guided by a clue, and the whole way from the very first perception of the senses must be laid out upon a sure plan.'[4]

The first task of this science was to be undertaken by what Bacon called 'a natural and experimental history', i.e. the task of gathering information as 'the first food' of natural philosophy upon which inductive reasoning can then set to work by observation and experiment to classify all known instances agreeing in the same nature.[5] This involves a process of interrogation in which we progressively narrow down the limits of investigation in order to delimit and determine the nature of the given subject-matter. Because nature does not reveal itself easily and it is hard for us to become familiar with it, especially at first, and because we inevitably mix up in our own notions the nature of things with our own nature so that nature is obscured by our anticipations and abstractions, interrogation has to take the form of controlled practical experiment in order that we may rid ourselves of preconceptions and constrain nature to come to view.[6] That is not to change or alter nature—for nature can never be thwarted by our operations—but to recognize that 'the nature of things betrays itself more readily under the vexations of art than in its natural freedom.'[7] 'Prudent interrogation', Bacon asserts, 'is as it were the half of science.'[8] This means that we have to engage in a progressive inquiry, for true questions provoke and solicit further

[1] *Nov. org.* I. xi, xii, xx.

[2] *Mag. inst., prooem. Distributio operis;   Delineatio secundae partis, Nov. org.* I.1 f.; *De interpretatione naturae sententiae,* xii, 1 f.

[3] *Nov. org.* I. lxxxii, cxxvi, etc. This is the method Bacon called *experientia literata, De augm.* v. 2; *Nov. org.* I. ciii.

[4] *Magn. inst., prooem.*   [5] *Nov. org.* II. i–xi.

[6] *Dist. op.; Valerius Terminus,* 17.

[7] *Dist. op.; Parasceve ad historiam,* v   [8] *De augm. scient.* v 3.

questioning, so that progress in actual discovery involves the reformulation of our questions and the devising of new experiments.[1]

Bacon laid great stress upon the fact that this inductive inquiry proceeds at first by way of exclusion or rejection, both because sense experience needs constant correction, and because our minds are full of 'idols' (false notions or erroneous modes of thinking), so that the isolation and determination of the nature of the given subject-matter requires of us to divest ourselves of all our 'anticipations' however we may reach them.[2] Then we have to face the difficulty of grafting new knowledge, revealed in the active inquiry, on to our old knowledge, for the old will so easily assimilate the new that we will be no better off than before.[3] Hence we have to exercise 'suspension of judgement' (*acatalepsia*) and realize that access to new truth inevitably entails revision of our premises.[4] 'No man rightly and successfully investigates the nature of a thing in the thing itself, but after many laborious experiments, instead of coming to a halt, still finds something beyond to seek.'[5]

Bacon is not very clear about the more positive side of his inductive inquiry. He has been accused of repudiating altogether the deductive element in scientific inquiry, but while he insisted in rejecting the deductive procedure that operated with necessary or ultimate 'truths' this charge cannot really be substantiated.[6] He insisted that the whole inquiry must be 'guided by a clue', as we have seen, and that it must acquire 'direction', but this direction only becomes progressively clear as the method of exclusion directs our minds to 'the discovery of forms'.[7] The 'form' is the essential, active nature of a thing, its ordered action. From one point of view Bacon

---

[1] *Nov. org.* I. cxxx; *De augm. scient.* v. 3; *Parasceve,* ix, x. This means that Bacon recognized that his own new method was only a beginning, and would be superseded. All he claimed to do was to give natural science a new direction.

[2] *Nov. org.* I. xxiii *et seq.*, xxxix *et seq.*; II. xv *et seq.* *De aug. scient.* v. iv; *Val. Term.* 15 f. Bacon rejected the medieval notion of *phantasm, Del. op.*; *Adv. of Learn.* I (*Works*, iii, p. 287).

[3] *Nov. org.* I. xxxi–xxxiv.

[4] *Dist. op.*; *Interp. nat. sent. xii*, viii.

[5] *Mag. inst. prooem.*

[6] See *Nov. org.* I. cli; II. viii; *Parasceve,* vii. Bacon denied, however, that deductive thinking could lead to *new particulars.* Karl Popper's criticism of Bacon at this point does not do justice to this, *The Logic of Scientific Discovery,* p. 278 f.

[7] *Nov. org.* I. li, lxxv; II. ii, iv, xvii etc.

looks upon the form as the fruit of the inquiry, the *affirmative form* or *law*, as he calls it. From another point of view, he looks upon it as the *forma rei*, as *ipsissima res*.[1] This is not a contradiction, for since motion, order in action, belongs to the very nature of a thing, true knowledge congruent with it must be a dynamic construct of it, and itself a form of operation (*operari*). That is why Bacon speaks of knowledge as power.[2] Here we see how his active questioning of nature guided him into a more dynamic conception of it, and that the kind of questions he asked (search into 'motions' rather than 'dead beginnings or principles of things'[3]) affected the whole form of science and gave it a new direction.[4] It was essentially instrumental science.[5]

Bacon was not himself a great scientist by any means (perhaps due to his lack of mathematics), but there can be little doubt that his attempt to give science a new direction by the method of putting the question to nature, played a very important role. Our interest in him lies in the fact that this attitude to nature on his part was not only allied to a deep Christian faith, but was a product of his understanding of the relation between God and creation. The distinction between Grace and nature did not mean for Bacon a dichotomy between faith and reason, but rather that in the realm of Grace as in the realm of nature man is summoned to exercise his reason in a way congruent with the given reality and in obedience to it.[6] As in the realm of Grace, so in the realm of nature man is summoned to activity, but in the realm of nature his task is to regain and exercise the dominion over the world he lost at the Fall, and which belongs to him by the bounty of his Maker.[7] It is at God's command that he must occupy the earth, and it is in obedience to that command that he must engage in natural science, the aim of which is to extend the empire of man and enhance his power over

---

[1] See especially *Nov. org.* II. i, ff., xi f., xvi f., xx f.; *De aug. scient.* IV. iv. By 'form,' Crombie points out, Bacon meant 'geometrical structure and motion', *Med. and Mod. Science*, ii, p. 289. Cf. *Parasceve*, vii. In one passage Bacon speaks of *form* as *natura naturans*, *Nov. org.* II. i.

[2] *Nov. org.* I. ii, iii; II. iii, iv; *Dist. op.*

[3] *Val. Term.* 14; cf. *Historia soni et auditus* (*Works*, iii, p. 679).

[4] That is, to use the language of Ockham, a move away from *scientia rationalis*, to *scientia realis*, *Summ. totius logicae*, III. 2. 10; *Comm. in sent.* II. d 2, q. 4. c. n., etc.

[5] *Nov. org.* I. aph. ii f.

[6] *De aug. scient.* III. i; IX. i; *Val. Term.* I: *Mag. inst. prooem.*; *Dist. op.*

[7] *Nov. org.* I. cxxxix; II. lii.

nature.[1] The whole fortune of the human race is at issue in it.

For as the servant and interpreter of nature man only does and understands as much as he has observed, in action or in thought, of nature's order. Beyond that he knows nothing and can do nothing. For there are no forces which can loose or break the chain of causes, nor can nature be conquered except by submitting to it. And so these twin objectives, human knowledge and human power, really amount to the same thing, and it is from ignorance of causes above all that our work is frustrated. And all depends on never letting the eyes of our mind stray from the things themselves, so that it may receive its images plainly. But God forbid that we should give out a dream of our own imagination for a pattern of the world, but rather may He graciously grant to write an apocalypse or a vision of the foot-steps and imprints of the Creator on His creatures.[2]

By this Bacon did not mean that through 'natural theology' we may know God, for it was 'natural theology', in which final and physical causes had been improperly mixed together, that had been the source of so much false theology and false science.[3] Therefore Bacon replaces 'natural theology' with natural science, to the benefit both of sacred theology and of natural science, for it throws theology back upon its own proper subject-matter, 'giving to faith what is of faith',[4] and it frees natural science for the interpretation of nature and the building up of the empire of man through obedience to nature.[5]

[1] *Nov. org.* i. cxvi, clxxxi; ii. xlviii; *Fil. lab.* v; *Val. Term.* i.; *New Atlantis* (*Works*, iii, p. 156).

[2] *Dist. op.; Cog. et visa* (*Works*, iii, 611).

[3] 'The prejudice hath been infinite that both divine and human knowledge hath received by the intermingling and tempering of the one with the other, as that which hath filled the one full of heresies, and the other full of speculative fancies and vanities.' *Val. Term.* i; cf. also 25; *Adv. of Learn.* I (*Works*, iii, p. 287).

[4] *Mag. instaur. prooemium; Cogitationes de scientia* 3; *Val. Term.* I. Bacon does allow natural theology a negative function in demolishing atheism. Bacon's difficulty with natural theology can be stated in the following way: If it operates with final causes embedded in nature, it must proceed deductively, but then its conclusion must already have been latent in its premisses; but if it does not operate with final causes and seeks to proceed inductively it cannot rise to God, for it cannot rise above the limitations of its chosen approach. This reminds us very much of the later position taken up by David Hume in his *Dialogues on Natural Religion.* I am inclined to think that Bacon and probably Hume would have agreed with the point made by H. D. Lewis that 'where the arguments fail is in trying to break into a series of steps what is in fact one insight, and also in seeking to start from purely finite factors and reason to conclusions about the infinite.'—*Our Experience of God*, p. 41.

[5] *Nov. org.* i. cxxix.

It was thus that there arose, as F. Heinemann has pointed out, the concept of modern man as *homo faber*.[1]

This had its danger as well as its advantage. In theology, for example, precisely because man is given his full place as the human partner in God's Covenant of Grace, he is constantly tempted to usurp the major role in the realm of Grace and to exercise there the dominion he is given by Grace only in the realm of nature. Indeed, modern man has carried this inordinate sense of his own creativeness into the whole realm of knowledge until it has become almost axiomatic for him that he only understands what he fashions and shapes and controls with the powers of his active reason. That has proved a serious hindrance for natural science as well as for scientific theology, for it has tended to superimpose upon them both the very artefacts of the reason which Bacon saw were the greatest impediments to interpretation in 'the books of God' as in 'the books of nature'. These are the artefacts which have once more become the object of attack in our day from the empiricists in their demand for real objectivity, and under this attack as under that of Bacon's they stand revealed as 'idols of the mind'— but it is just here that theology has made another significant contribution to the rise of modern science.

3 SCIENTIFIC OBJECTIVITY

It is once again to the Reformation that we must turn for the modern emphasis upon unbiased and disinterested truth, which arose particularly in the conflict between Reformed theology and Roman tradition. Concentration upon the Word of God, upon the self-utterance of the Truth, and the acknowledgement of its absolute primacy, cut the strings of prejudice and prejudgement and determined theological procedure. This was a passion for the truth from the side of the object which inculcated a repentant readiness to rethink all preconceptions and presuppositions, to put all traditional ideas to the test face to face with the object, and therefore a readiness to submit to radical testing and clarification. It is this masterful objectivity that is one of the great contributions of the Reformation to the modern world. It is going too far to say with

[1] *Neue Wege der Philosophie*, p. 272; cf. also p. xiii.

Professor Macmurray that 'the one creative achievement of the Reformation was science and the scientific spirit',[1] but we can surely agree with him when he says, in another work: 'It was Christianity that gave us science by its insistence on the spirit of truth. . . . Science is sustained by the love of the truth. Apart from a passionate belief in the supreme value of truth, and from the willingness to sacrifice pleasant illusions to that faith in the truth, the whole truth and nothing but the truth, science could neither begin nor continue.'[2]

Once again, it is Francis Bacon who provides us with an outstanding example of this scientific spirit, particularly in his attack upon the fallacious notions or idols of the mind which we bring with us to the interpretation of nature and with which we distort understanding of it. How modern he sounds when he complains that among these impediments are to be found none more harmful than metaphysical abstractions and the enslaving power of words.[3] Access to the truth requires of our minds submission to cleansing from all kinds of idols, 'all of which must be renounced and put away with a fixed and solemn determination, and the understanding thoroughly freed and cleansed, the entrance into the kingdom of man, founded on the sciences, being not much other than entrance into the Kingdom of Heaven, into which none may enter except as a little child (nisi sub persona infantis).'[4]

However, this masterful objectivity, as we have called it, did not have its way very easily within Protestant theology, as it has not had its way very easily in Roman theology, for in both, although in different ways, there developed the conception of the active reason as fashioning what it apprehends and as exercising determining control over the object. Applied to the realm of Grace, this is to exchange the glory of the Creator for the image of a corruptible creature, and to turn the truth into a lie, as St. Paul expressed it. This is to humanize theology by making man himself the measure or the central point of

---

[1] Reason and Emotion, p. 172.

[2] Freedom in the Modern World, p. 33 f.

[3] Nov. org. I. xxxviii et seq., lxviii et seq.; Mag. instaur. dist. op.; Val. Term., 17; De aug. scient. v. iv.

[4] Nov. org. I. lxvii. Cf. also Val. Term., 1: 'It is no less true in this kingdom of knowledge than in God's Kingdom of Heaven, that no man shall enter into it, except he become first as a little child.' And Cogitata et visa (Works, vol. iii, p. 617).

reference, and anthropology or ecclesiology the ultimate concern.

Medieval Roman theology operated with a conception of the active intellect (*intellectus agens*) along with the passive, or, as they preferred to call it, the possible intellect (*intellectus possibilis*). Its task is to make intelligible as its object what the possible intellect receives from the senses. Thus out of the *species*, or the image through which the mind is engaged with the object, the active intellect forms its intelligible impression or *phantasm*. This active intellect, then, is the power of the mind to frame and shape what it knows, and so to form concepts, but this is carefully balanced by the possible intellect which operates passively. This is a complicated way of stating that while our knowledge is an intellectual effort on our part, it is the activity in which we conform ourselves obediently to the object.[1]

In that respect we have no quarrel with it, but a difficulty does arise from the notion, implied in it, that the intellect is unable to apprehend particular or concrete existence directly but only in the medium of an intelligible phantasm in which it disengages the form from its material expression in order to allow it to apprehend the nature of the object or the concrete existent. The phantasms of the mind thus come in between the intellect and the external object, for only in them is thought provided with its proper object. It is this fact that gives the active intellect a much more masterful position than it would appear to have, particularly when it operates along with the discursive power of *ratio* (in abstraction, comparison, inference etc.), for while the mind cannot exercise control over the external objects it can exercise some real control over the phantasms in its intelligible act. In this highly intellectual notion of knowledge the passage from the conformity of thought to reality to the conformity of reality to thought becomes deceptively easy.

This difficulty becomes more acute when this intellectual activity takes place within the Church regarded as a sacramental

<hr/>

[1] See especially Aquinas, *Summ. Theol.* 1a. q. 5, a. 2 ad 2; q. 79, a. 3–5; q. 84, a. 1–6; q. 85, a. 1 ad 4; *Contra Gentiles*, 1, 56; ii, 77. Cf. H. Meyer, *The Philosophy of St. Thomas Aquinas*, E. T. 1946, pp. 326 ff.; and V. Remer, *Summa Philosophiae Scholasticae*, vol. v., *Psychologia*, Rome, 1935, pp. 1, 2 ff.

institution of Grace rooted in and extending the Incarnation into history. Medieval theology held that there was an intrinsic relation of Grace between the being and existence of the Church and the nature of the truth of revelation once and for all deposited in the apostolic foundation of the Church.[1] Because the Church is full of Grace it is held to represent in its forms and dogmas the objectification of the truth in its institutional and rational structure, that is, in the ordinances, decrees, and dogmatic definitions promulgated in the Church. Thus the expression of the mind of the Church in its dogmatic definitions is held to be the expression of the nature of the truth. That is the material upon which theology works with its passive and active intellect and all the power of its reason. Now theology is the work of the whole Church, so that we are concerned here with an intellectual activity at work in a corporate way, through which the mind of the Church is actively expressed from generation to generation.

The significance of this becomes apparent when we recall the Roman distinction between the passive and the active tradition, the former being the deposit of faith handed down through the ages from the Apostolic Church, and the latter the same deposit as interpreted and unfolded and worked up in the consciousness of the Church and from time to time defined in unalterable dogmas.[2] That which is transmitted and the transmitting of it are identified in a dynamic self-evolution, for the tradition is a living reality developing in ever richer forms under the continued inspiration and guidance of the Holy Spirit dwelling in the Church. This growing tradition comes to manifestation through the *communes sententiae*, and the *communes doctrinae*, in the thinking of the Church from age to age, and finally in the definitions given from time to time by the teaching office of the Church.

In this development the active intellect operates upon whatever it receives from previous generations and frames it

[1] Cf. E. Przywara, *Religionsphilosophie Katholischer Theologie*, E. T. *Polarity*, 1935, p. 61, who speaks of 'the free operation of the decisive metaphysico-religious relationship between the Creator and the creature, the self-operation of the *analogia entis*, which as "the" Catholic description *par excellence* of the relation between God and man is alive in the whole structure of the Church as it freely develops.'

[2] See K. E. Skydsgaard, *One in Christ*, 1957, pp. 62 ff., and G. Hök, 'Holy Spirit and Tradition,' in *Scot. Journ. of Theol.* vol. 10, 1957, pp. 389 ff.

as phantasms, as it were, of the mind of the Church. This operation always involves a further elaboration of its content in the living and creative consciousness of the Church and in the discursive reasoning of its representative theologians. Thus the active tradition may be described as a corporate form of the active reason that frames and interprets whatever it finds in the living soul of the Church, provides it with the rational form required by Catholic 'instinct' which then becomes the passive or possible reason of later generations, and so exercises a controlling and directing influence upon the process of development. In other words, from the original treasury of the faith the Roman Church progressively abstracts and elaborates universal forms which are acknowledged to be the unalterable patterns of the truth, so that all future knowing of the truth is governed by these final forms, and all determination of the nature of the faith is controlled by them.

In this way the Roman Church appears to have evolved a new notion of truth! The only reality it acknowledges is that which it finds in the developing forms of its tradition and continuously makes real for itself through doctrinal formulation, so that the tradition of a thing is its reality, and truth is that which conforms to this tradition as it is formed and shaped in the consciousness of the Roman Church. Thus the truth of a doctrine is what has become of it in the development of the active tradition, so that in this way the element of objectivity in the tradition is subordinated to a massive subjectivity in the mind of the Church. Hence it can be argued that for the Roman Church 'objectivity' actually and practically denotes conformity to its own mind. The ultimate criterion of truth with which it operates is appeal to its own self-consciousness which it assumes uncritically to be identical with the Mind of Christ. Truth is subjectivity, corporate subjectivity—that is what we may call the notion of the active reason in its corporate form, the *intellectus agens* combined with the dynamic creative subjectivity of the Church. According to Roger Bacon God is the active intellect of all mankind, but according to this line of thought it would appear that the Roman Church is the active intellect of all theological truth! There can be no doubt about the fact that when the Roman Church in the Middle Ages made use of thought-forms inherited from the Platonic and Aristotelian philosophies it made a massive attempt to bend all its thought into conformity to the nature of the objective reality revealed in Jesus Christ, and in so doing stamped the whole medieval world with the Christian imprint, but there can also be no doubt about the fact that far more than it ever realized the content of its thought was bent into conformity to the forms of thinking it took over from ancient Greece and Rome, and that through canonizing these forms it has made it almost impossible for it to break through them into radical and critical testing of its mind in accordance with the apostolic source and foundation of the faith. Yet this is precisely what is now taking place in the Roman Church.

It is in Protestantism, however, that the active reason has been given an unparalleled development in its individualist form, in the notion of the autonomous, self-legislating reason. In the Reformation itself, as we have seen, the stress was quite different, upon the concrete objectivity of the Word and Truth of God, given unalterable form in Jesus Christ, that ever remains identical with itself and will not be confounded with our traditions and formulations of it. Its objectivity is that of the object, God Himself who gives Himself to us in His Word in the midst of the Church and requires of us obedient and repentant conformity to Him in Jesus Christ. To this corresponds a positive theology and a positive Church, and it is precisely because of its devotion to the positive objective nature of the Truth and Word of God, and to the Church correlative to it, that the Reformers revolted from the false objectivities located in the dogmatic constructs out of the developing consciousness of the historical Church or in its rationalized institutions. Its very stress upon objectivity carried with it detachment and freedom from the shackles of external authority grounded in traditional institutions or in fixed frames of thinking, especially when derived from outside the Christian faith.

As such, however, the Reformation provided a medium, against its own trends, for the germination of another masterful idea that developed straight out of medieval pietism and spiritualistic individualism fostered by mystical and monastic spirits like Bernard of Clairvaux, but also out of what R. A. Knox has called 'the underworld of the Middle Ages',[1] namely the idea that faith has its centre and source in the religious

[1] *Enthusiasm*, 1950, pp. 71 ff.

subject, in the depths of the soul, in religious immediacy and illuminism. Behind the heretical exuberance and welter of medieval enthusiasm lay the ancient antithesis between spirit and matter which kept fermenting reaction against all institutionalization and rationalization of the Spirit, and presenting the appeal of religious excitement and abandon through internal intimacy with Deity. Hardly had the Reformation got under way when more extreme elements broke through the restraints of Roman authoritarianism and staged spontaneous outbursts in various parts of Europe, notably in the Anabaptist movements, but more sober elements of medieval spiritualism were carried right into the heart of the Reformation through its continuity with the Augustinian stress upon religious self-consciousness, inward conviction, and the passion of the soul. This subjective aspect, more evident in the Lutheran than in the Calvinist Reformation, was fostered everywhere by the spirit of the Renaissance in its humanism and individualism.

It was only when the classical forms of the Reformation began to harden and to provoke reaction, or when its classical expression began to be corroded, that it became apparent to what an extent this other idea had been gaining ground. Then, when it did emerge it was claimed over a wide area to be the real essence of the Reformation, namely, the religious inwardness and immediacy which allowed every one to form his own understanding of Christianity. That transformation may be illustrated in the change that came over the expression *for me*. That Christ loved me and gave Himself *for me*, meant, in the theology of the Reformation, decisive stress upon the objective reality of salvation in Christ. Thus justification by Christ alone, by Grace alone, meant that the attention of the Church in its proclamation and of the faithful in their response, was directed away from themselves to Christ, and His objective decision and acts on their behalf. But soon the emphasis in 'for me' came to be laid upon *me*, for the attention was then not directed upon Christ alone or to the glory of God, but toward the self, and its internal experience, or understanding, or appropriation of salvation. Thus justification by faith alone meant stress upon 'justifying *faith*' or 'acceptance' of Christ rather than upon Christ. Now certainly 'for me' involves a polar relation, but the stress came to be laid not so much upon the objective pole of that relationship as upon the subjective pole. That is the very essence of Neo-Protestantism which came to its great expression first in pietism and then in the movements of subjective idealism in the nineteenth century.

The story of that development need not detain us further, but we may glance at two significant stages in it. The first of these is the immense impact of Cartesian dualism upon Protestant Christianity—that was an influence from the side of Roman Catholic philosophy, but it had its strongest impact in Protestantism where there had been asserted such a clear distinction between Grace and nature, the Creator and the creature. Once that distinction became distorted into a dualism, it tended to breed Deism, and Deism provoked the old antithesis of spirit and matter, and rampant spiritualism broke loose only to find itself faced with the menace of a positivistic and mechanistic interpretation of nature.[1] It was in the midst of this that there took place the great 'Copernican revolution' initiated by Kant, which presents us with the other significant stage in the development of Protestantism which we must note. This is the stage in which the categorical imperative is identified with the self-legislating ego, the divine Spirit is identified with rational self-consciousness, or the inwardness of the human spirit, and the divine 'Word' which the Church proclaims and out of which it lives, is the 'Word' which it hears in the depths of its own subjectivity.[2]

The 'God' of this Neo-Protestantism is the God who is correlated with the religious subject and its spiritual potentialities, the God who meets and satisfies the needs and answers the questions of 'modern man' (that creature that takes himself so frightfully seriously and imposes himself upon everything).[3] Truth about Him is discerned within the religious subject himself, so that the business of theology is to examine the structure of the religious consciousness, particularly—so the stress developed as the nineteenth century wore on—in its historical

[1] Behind the rise of Deism also lies the idea of a perfect creation as one which can continue in operation on its own—Cf. Aquinas, *Summ. Theol.*, 1 q. 104, a. 1. 2.

[2] Cf. E. Troeltsch, *Der Historismus u. seine Probleme*, p. 109; F. Flückiger, *Philosophie u. Theologie bei Schleiermacher*, 1947, p. 128 f; and K. Barth, *Church Dogmatics*, 1.2, p. 606 ff.

[3] See K. Barth, *God, Grace and Gospel*, *S.J.T. Occasional Paper* no. 8, 1959, p. 62.

and universal manifestations. It was within this context that Christianity was subjected to such exhaustive historico-psychological examination in the late nineteenth and early twentieth centuries, which meant that Christianity was regarded essentially as a process, while the Reformation was regarded simply as a development in that process, when the essence of religion in the human spirit began to break free from its childhood bondage under external authority and the sovereignty of inward religious experience was asserted, and its right constantly to create for itself new forms through which to express itself in 'modern culture'.

In this light it was inevitable that Christianity even in its origins should have been interpreted as the product of the human spirit, and so from Strauss to Bultmann the thesis has been maintained that the Gospel does not go back so much to Jesus Himself as to the creative spirituality of the early Church, and therefore if we are to be true to Jesus who in His way provoked that creation we ought to create new forms of Christianity for our own day. This whole conception has been helped on immensely by the application of the concept of evolution to the development of the religious spirit and by the new 'modern' notion of history, stemming from Dilthey, as that which man himself creates and for which he is responsible.[1] Thus the historical truth of the Christian faith is only that which man can envisage for himself, what he can make real for himself, and for which he can make himself responsible through his own decisions. Christian truth is that which has become and continues to become true in and through the history which man himself creates by his existential decisions. That is the only reality which he can acknowledge—that is to say, whatever submits to the creativity of his active reason.

We commonly suppose that this active reason plays in Neo-Protestantism an individualist role in contrast to the corporate role it plays in the corporate decisions of the Roman Church, and that is certainly true, if we are to take modern existentialism as our guide to interpret Neo-Protestantism; but when we examine the history of the nineteenth century and of the first quarter of the twentieth century, it is really another picture that we get. For all the richness and variety of its

[1] For an exposition of this see F. Gogarten, *Demythologising and History*, 1955, pp. 21 ff, 25 ff.

manifestations, Neo-Protestantism actually presents itself as a developing process, unfolding its own inward spirituality, with its own continuous and dynamic forms of tradition, remarkably parallel to those of the Roman Church. Here too the Holy Spirit is conceived as the ultimate Author of this development, for it is He who operates in the depths of the historical self-consciousness of the religious community, and it is the task of theology to interpret and systematize the insights that emerge out of it. In the later Schleiermacher, for example, this corporate tradition of the Spirit is conceived in a way that brings him very close to the position of nineteenth century Romanism, as seen in J. H. Newman or J. A. Moehler or even in M. Scheeben.

It cannot be admitted that the line of development we have discussed presents a true picture of the whole of Protestantism; it gives us only one aspect of it, but one with which every branch of Protestantism has its affinity. On the other hand, it remains true that Protestantism has maintained within it throughout, as one of its chief elements, a factor deriving directly from the Reformation, its readiness to submit all its traditions to the criticism of the Word of God as heard in the Bible, and therefore to reform its own judgement and to think through its theology in obedience to the objective Revelation in Jesus Christ. This, and not the other, has been the main line of Protestant tradition, and it is this that is now thrusting itself forward so vigorously everywhere in the Evangelical Churches. Here once again the basic position of the Reformation has reasserted itself with greater force than ever in the recognition that the only real objectivity is that of the object, God Himself who gives Himself to us in His Word and summons us to submit all our traditions, and all our attempts to impose ourselves with our culture upon the Christian faith, to obedient conformity to His self-revelation in Jesus Christ. It is in Him that we are confronted with the transcendent objectivity of the Word and Truth of God that refuses to be domesticated to our subjectivity, or our active reason, whether in its individualist or in its corporate form.

Thus while the history of Protestant theology in the last three hundred years is the history of a great struggle between the objective Word of God and the masterful usurpation of the autonomous reason, it is also the story of how theology has been driven steadily back upon its proper object. Empirical science, to which the Reformation contributed through some of its basic doctrines, has in its turn helped theology to refer its thought away from itself to its proper object and to learn again the discipline of real objectivity. In this event a theology faithful to its object is in a position to show other sciences the real meaning of objectivity, precisely because in theological science above all we have to do with an object that encounters us as the Lord and Master, who will not be subdued to the forms of our subjectivity, but who will be known only in His Lordship over us. It is this humility and submission of theological knowledge to the sheer mastery and objectivity of the Truth that can help to shed light upon every struggle for objectivity, and every attempt at scientific knowledge. Utter respect for objectivity is the *sine qua non* of scientific activity.

4 THE PLACE OF THE HUMAN SUBJECT IN KNOWLEDGE

It is a truism that knowledge of an object is knowledge by a subject, for the subject has always had a logical place in knowledge. As we have seen, however, the great change that came over theology at the Reformation involved giving man in his life and knowledge full place as a human subject over against God who was thought of as addressing him personally through His Word and summoning him to active obedience. So long as we think of the human knower only as logical subject, we presuppose that the object of knowledge is entirely determinate and posit a timeless and necessary relation between the knower and the object, for the activity of the knower does not enter into the content of his knowledge at all. But when we think of the object as the living God who enters into living and personal communion with man through revelation and reconciliation then the place of the human subject in knowledge of God can no longer be excluded from the full content of that knowledge. Our knowing of Him is part of our knowledge of God—the inclusion of that fact in the Reformation doctrine of the Grace of God had immense repercussions.

We have already seen how modern man, particularly within Protestantism, has not been slow to seize upon the new status of the subject and with the help of the Renaissance idea of the autonomy of man to develop out of it the masterful conception of the active reason with dire consequences in philosophy and science as well as in theology. We have also seen how an inordinate subjectivity has come under heavy attack from empirical science and philosophy as well as from the Reformed theology, but now we must be careful to discern in these developments the rightful place of the subject as active knower, as in theology so also in empirical science.

We cannot talk about knowledge of God without taking account of the fact that it is we, human beings, who know Him. There is, therefore, an anthropomorphic element here to which we cannot shut our eyes, and which we cannot do without if we are to have knowledge at all, for this applies to all human knowledge. But our concern here is with a profounder fact which received considerable attention at the Reformation, especially under the influence of Calvin, who taught that God reveals Himself to man in such a way that he does not need to stretch himself beyond his humanity to know Him, and while there will always remain an element of impropriety in human statements about God, man's knowledge is not for that reason false.[1] Behind this lay two doctrines which have ever since been characteristic of Reformed theology. The first is the doctrine of *accommodation*, that God condescends to our ignorance, lets Himself down to us, adapts Himself to our knowing, and lifts us up to communion with Himself through reconciling and adapting us in conformity to Himself. The second is the doctrine of *election*, which rejects every projection of man and his creaturely forms into the eternal and divine, and teaches the incarnation of the divine purpose (πρόθεσις), the projection, as it were, of the divine into the human, in Jesus Christ, and the establishing in Him of true relations between God and man and man and God. These doctrines mean that Reformed theology operates with a Truth that upholds both sides of the knowledge relationship, the side of the object over against the human knower, but also the side of the human subject in the human form of his knowledge. It is because God has become man in Jesus Christ and our knowledge of God is rooted and grounded in Christ and shaped through

[1] This seems to echo the argument of Anselm in *Monologium*, 65.

conformity to Him that the very humanity embedded in our knowledge of God is an essential part of that knowledge, for it belongs to the essential nature of the Truth. Thus the active obedience and conformity of the human mind to the Word of God is part of the full content of our knowledge of God, and therefore, as Zwingli showed at the beginning of his Commentary *De vera et falsa religione*, and Calvin pointed out in the opening sentences of his *Institute*, the knowledge of God does not really strike home to us unless it issues in a deep knowledge of our own selves. That does not mean that self-understanding is our criterion for the knowledge of God, but that we are truly discovered to ourselves only when we are brought into conformity of heart and mind to Jesus Christ, for it is in Him that God has turned toward man and turned man toward Himself. To know the Truth is thus to be actively participant in it, so that our activity in knowing the Truth is part of its content. The conformity of the subject to the divine Object reposes upon the accommodation of the Object to the human subject.

So far we have been thinking of this mainly in terms of strictly Reformed theology but in some respects it had an even greater development in Lutheran theology particularly through its doctrine of *communicatio idiomatum* interpreted (beyond the patristic understanding of it) to mean a mutual interpenetration of the divine and human natures in Christ. On one side of it this meant that divine attributes are to be ascribed *realiter* to the human nature of Christ, which to the Reformed theologians appeared seriously to compromise the true and complete humanity of Christ. But when we remember that the humanity which the Son of God assumed is our humanity, in which we are given to share, then can we stop short at applying all the divine attributes to the humanity of Jesus, and not apply them to humanity in general? That is, in fact, what German idealistic theology and philosophy did do, so that it is very difficult to dissociate the deification of man which we find in nineteenth-century German philosophy from the Lutheran doctrine of the Incarnation. We shall return to that development later, but meantime it is the other side of the doctrine that we are interested in, the conformity of the divine to the human, which had its extreme form in nineteenth century kenotic Christologies. It was a form of this idea that came to be transferred from theology proper to general knowledge and especially to scientific knowledge.

Here it is most illuminating to turn the spotlight upon Immanuel Kant, who, as Eddington claimed, 'anticipated to a remarkable extent the ideas to which we are now being impelled by the developments of modern physics.'[1] We need not go further than the famous Preface to the second edition of the *Critique of Pure Reason*, where Kant set forth his revolutionary programme. 'Hitherto it has been assumed that all our knowledge must conform to objects. But all attempts to extend our knowledge of objects by establishing something in regard to them *a priori*, by means of concepts, have, on this assumption, ended in failure. We must therefore make trial whether we may not have more success in the tasks of metaphysics, if we suppose that objects must conform to our knowledge.' We cannot enter into the arguments he advanced for this 'Copernican revolution', but we may note his consideration of the way in which empirical science had developed in the century and a half since Bacon. Scientists, he pointed out, 'learned that reason has insight only into that which it produces after a plan of its own, and that it must not allow itself to be kept, as it were, in nature's leading-strings but must itself show the way with principles of judgement based upon fixed laws, constraining nature to give answer to questions of reason's own determining.' He went on to say that while we must approach nature in order to be taught by it, we 'must not do so in the character of a pupil who listens to everything that the teacher chooses to say, but of an appointed judge who compels the witnesses to answer questions which he himself has formulated.' We are at once reminded of Bacon's *activa inquisitio* and his stress upon the planned activity of the reason. But Kant held, as Bacon did not, that the resulting knowledge gained is determined by the coercive nature and purpose of the questioning, and drew the conclusion (which Bacon by rejecting all 'anticipations' could not draw) that in so far as the object is known it must conform to *a priori* elements which make possible its establishing as a knowable reality. We do not know the object, therefore, as a thing in itself, but only so far as it conforms to the power of the reason in knowing it.

[1] *The Philosophy of Physical Science*, p. 189. Cf. also the sustained thesis of v. Weizsäcker in *The World View of Physics*, espec. ch. 4.

All-important here is the famous notion of the *Ding an sich* upon which, as Kant saw it, the whole notion of science depends. Science cannot operate where nothing at all is given, for we cannot produce knowledge out of nothing, and cannot conduct any experiments apart from certain determinate conditions on the side of the object making it capable of being acted on. On the other hand science does not arise where the object is completely transparent and is directly and immediately knowable. It is precisely because it is opaque and hidden that we have to have recourse to coercive questioning and experimental inquisition in order to extract knowledge of it. Thus while Kant sought to give firm philosophical expression to the objectivity upon which the whole of science rests, he also sought to do justice to the spontaneity and productive activity of the reason in wresting objective knowledge from nature. At the same time the distinction he maintained between the object as the thing in itself and the object as real appearance, or the object so far as it is known to us, was a sharp reminder to science of the limitations of the human reason. In so far, then, as Kant claimed that scientific knowledge must be evaluated in accordance with the prior structure of our consciousness which makes rational experience possible at all, and in so far as he held that the results of scientific knowledge are relative to the coercive devices we employ in order to put nature to the question, we may not want to disagree with him.

Where we must disagree violently with Kant, however, is in his attempt to convert the fact that nature only yields her secrets to us when we constrain her to act within limits we impose, and according to specifications we bring to her in our coercive questioning, into a general principle, in which the conformity of the object to the mind of the knowing subject is attributed to our power of knowing or is predicated of our human nature.[1] It is precisely because Kant did do this that the temptation to discount the thing in itself as a mythological projection was so strong, that when it was discounted or denied the notion of 'the active reason' developed with a vengeance.

---

[1] Similarly a theological ethic is forced to disagree with Kant's identification of the categorical imperative with the will of the self-legislating ego, and its translation into a general statement through maximization, for this would be to identify the Will of God with man's alleged 'higher nature'.

At this point there is another element in the development of European thought that we must pick up for consideration. We may take as our starting point here the first two questions and answers in Calvin's *Geneva Catechism* of 1541. '*What is the chief end of human life?*—To know God.—*Why do you say that?*—Because He created us and placed us in this world to be glorified in us. And it is indeed right that our life, of which He Himself is the beginning, should be devoted to His glory.' The glorification of God expresses the supreme objectivity of Reformed theology and worship. But because God wills to be glorified *in us*, man is bracketed together with the glory of God, and therefore comes to share in that glory. Thus the turning of God to man means that God wills to be glorified in such a way that man as the recipient of His Grace may also become glorious in his way, in the fulfilment of his chief end to glorify God and enjoy Him forever.[1]

There is nothing there about the glorification of man by man, but the central place it gave to man's knowledge and life could easily be misinterpreted in that direction. Even Bacon came rather close to it when he could say that the function of human knowledge is 'to extend more widely the limits of and power and greatness of man'.[2] At any rate, if Bacon was right in holding that the pursuit of natural science was part of man's duty to God, then it was all the more necessary that a scientific study of man and his powers should be carried out. It was, however, through the humanism of the Renaissance that this became deflected until it could even be said that 'the proper study of mankind is man'.

That was the outlook that lay behind the Enlightenment, and behind the thought of Immanuel Kant. He combined, more than most, powerful emphases stemming from the Reformation, such as the littleness of man before the Majesty of God, the categorical imperative, the conception of law or order of nature, and the limits of the human reason, with the assertion of the rights and powers of man stemming from the Renaissance such as the notions of spontaneity, freedom, rational autonomy. That helped to give his thought a rigour

---

[1] Cf. Karl Barth, *The Faith of the Church*, a Commentary on the Apostles' Creed according to Calvin's Catechism, p. 25 f.; and *Church Dogmatics*, III. 2, pp. 41ff.
[2] *Nov. org.* I. cxvi

and critical depth denied to others, but once his conception of the conformity of the object to knowledge became detached from his own relentless self-criticism and grafted on to the glorification of man, the unique anthropocentric outlook, so typical of modernity, began its rapid advance. Perhaps one of the most unfortunate elements in the Kantian contribution was the rigid and unchanging character of the categories (substance, causality, etc.) that made up the structure of the understanding;[1]   Kant regarded them, not as determinations correlative to our experience, but as the conditions or pre-suppositions of experience, and independent of it, which were therefore beyond any possibility of criticism and modification by experience. In the realm of natural science this implied that the mode of knowledge correlative to this hard, fixed structure was the only possible mode, and therefore it postulated that what was as yet unknown could only be known according to a model in conformity with it. In other words, this laid the basis for the world view that was to dominate science until our own day, that every part of the universe must be observable or objectifiable in the same way and be amenable to the same kind of coercive experimentation as obtained in traditional physics and mechanics, and amenable to the logical forms that arise out of thinking of determinate objects. But by deter-mining in advance and by limiting like that the kind of results it would accept, this way of thinking made it extremely difficult for natural science to advance beyond certain limits, since advance could only be made beyond those limits through a radical change in the whole structure of scientific conscious-ness.[2] That is, of course, precisely what had eventually to take place through the work of Einstein and Bohr and others, for

[1] This element of rigidity corresponded well to Newtonian mechanics, and helps to explain why the epistemology of science remained stationary until the emergence of relativity and quantum theory. On the other hand we must not forget, as Einstein has reminded us (*Out of My Later Years*, p. 61) that it is the rigidity of the concepts, like rules in a game, which makes the acquisition of knowledge possible, even though we must agree that there are no final categories in the sense of Kant.

[2] If the structure of the understanding or the framework of our thought involved permanent forms, then we could gain our knowledge of nature through examina-tion of those forms without recourse to empirical observation and inquiry at all. Advance to new knowledge is only possible along with a change in the structure or framework of our thought.

the great advances in our own day (notably in physics) to take place.

In the realm of philosophy and theology, however, the Kantian way of thinking implied that the innermost structure of the human reason was fundamentally appropriate to and akin to the nature of ultimate reality, so that a massive idealism was built up on the basis of the subjective consciousness and under the guidance of the active reason. But, as we have already seen, that whole development eventually revealed itself as an exalted form of anthropology. That was the great dénouement of Neo-Protestantism, for the whole method of approach from its starting-point in man imported such a powerful ingredient of subjectivity into the nature of the object that it became impossible to distinguish between what was objectively real and the subjective states of experience.

What has been the upshot of this development in modern science and theology?

(a) There has taken place a critical reassessment of the place of subjectivity in knowledge. Of course throughout the whole history of modern science since the end of the sixteenth century there has been a steady critique of subjectivity, and an insistence, as we have seen, upon the primacy of objectivity. Scientific thinking involves a methodological abstraction from all subjective factors in its concern for strict impartiality and disinterestedness. However, when this rigorous scientific method came to be applied beyond the realms of mathematics and physics, e.g. to history by Dilthey, it soon became evident that there is no such thing as impartial science (*voraussetzungslose Wissenschaft*) although methodological impartiality retained its place. The really great change has come about in our own day through the theory of relativity and quantum mechanics, when it became evident that the development of classical science had reached the point when there had to take place a considerable change in the whole structure of scientific consciousness. Einstein had to wrestle for some twenty years with Newtonian and Kantian conceptions of space and time before the theory of relativity could be formulated,[1] whereas the advances in nuclear physics through the work of Maxwell and Rutherford

[1] See the illuminating discussions of this by M. Polanyi, *Personal Knowledge*, pp. 9 ff, 109, 144 f.

forced physicists like Bohr to carry through a change in the whole structure of knowledge as it lay embedded in classical physics and mechanics.[1] These changes revealed that modern science, far more than it ever realized, had been operating uncritically with a subjective structure of the understanding which had inevitably limited the range of its observation and discovery. All this meant that real advances in knowledge involve fundamental changes in the structure of the mind and profound changes in the meaning of basic concepts. These facts are still having seismic effects in various branches of knowledge.

One of the interesting things about this critical reorientation of modern thought is that it entails a double critique of subjectivity and objectivity. That knowledge proceeds by the conformity of the reason to the nature of the object has been re-established on a much wider, and in some respects, a deeper basis, for the fundamental modes of rationality, the basic states of consciousness, and even the primary concepts of science, are on the move and in need of constant modification and alteration. On the other hand, abstract objectivism comes under severe criticism, for it conceals a static subjectivity in the uncritical acceptance of fundamental categories of the understanding, which is all the more powerful in its influence upon the course of scientific development just because it is concealed. Thus, for example, A. Eddington,[2] M. Polanyi,[3] and von Weizsäcker[4] in their different ways, have successfully shown how the personal factor inevitably enters into scientific knowledge for the very fact of our knowing explicitly enters into what we know. It is therefore unscientific to pretend that the subjective element is eliminated when it cannot be. Scientific thinking must operate with a severely self-critical and controlled subjectivity, for we can only advance to new knowledge by rigorous re-interpretation, and sometimes only by renunciation of previous modes of knowing.

This has different applications in natural science and in theology. In neither does it mean that the subject can project

---

[1] See *Atomic Theory and the Description of Nature*, 1934.
[2] Sir Arthur Eddington, *The Philosophy of Physical Science*.
[3] Michael Polanyi, *Personal Knowledge*.
[4] C. F. von Weizsäcker, *The World View of Physics*.

himself into what he knows or allow his own nature to distort the nature of the object, nor does it mean in any way that we can only know something if we subdue it to the forms of our own subjectivity. In natural science, however, it does mean that the very nature of our inquiry, by which we create certain conditions within which we force nature to disclose itself to us according to our will, affects the content of our knowledge, and gives it an unavoidable ambiguity. It bears the impress of our questions and analysis. Therefore as von Weizsäcker has expressed it, 'two basic functions of consciousness enter into every proposition in the description of nature: knowledge and volition'.[1]

In other words, in so far as our scientific propositions are of stages in nature which we help to produce, they are statements about what we can do as well as statements about nature in itself.[2] Hence scientific laws are expressions of our modes of cognition as well as of realities in themselves. Thus the whole subject-object relation is such that we are unable to distinguish completely between things in themselves and our ways of knowing and speaking of them. Mathematical formulae really hold good for the inner order of nature. Number or at least something corresponding to it, is embedded, as it were, in nature,[3] and therefore not only is nature amenable to rational inquiry, but the mathematical formulations that arise out of it can only be in a form which expresses at once the nature of the object and the mode of its cognition. Because we can arrive at these formulations only by operating within the possibilities and necessities of our thought as well as within the framework of our experimental observation of nature we cannot project them as such into nature as if they are actual laws objectively inhering in nature. Rather are they to be understood as noetic constructions that reflect and point to ontic structures in nature,

---

[1] Op. cit., p. 102 f.

[2] The issue here is put very bluntly by Eddington (op. cit. p. 108 f): 'How much do we discover and how much do we manufacture by our experiments?'

[3] This is pushed to its extreme point in the view of Sir James Jeans that number is embedded in nature because it was created by a Pure Mathematician. At the opposite extreme is the view that it is we alone who inject number into nature. If the first extreme rests upon a univocal relation between mathematics in nature and mathematics in God the latter does not take seriously that some real co-ordination is involved between our scientific theories and the rational structures of nature.

and as such they are both like and unlike those structures. They cannot be confounded with them without directly projecting our subjective characteristics into nature itself, but because it is only through these noetic constructions that we can have knowledge of nature we must recognize that they cannot be eliminated from the content of that knowledge.

This applies above all, of course, to nuclear physics, where as von Weizsäcker has shown, the knowledge we have of nature enters explicitly into it.[1] In contrasting the outlook of modern physics with that of classical physics he declares that

what has been objectively determined here is no longer a being, but a give-and-take between acting and perceiving. We may speak of objects only in as much as they are possible objects of a subject. This sentence, too, is almost a truism since we define knowledge as the knowledge of an object by a subject. But we could not anticipate that the form of our statements would, in terms of pure logic, no longer permit us to pass over in silence the fact that, in each case, they are being pronounced by a subject.[2]

The reason why physicists sometimes go as far as this, in relating the objective to the subjective factors in scientific knowledge, is found in their recognition of the powerful element of the will that enters into modern science, that is, into its construction of the empirical world.[3] 'Every experiment is an act of violence which we impose upon nature. It must react to the violence, and the law of this reaction can be stated in formulae.'[4] Thus experimental science may be described as a planned and guided give-and-take between man and nature with a view to knowledge and power. It cannot be said to be concerned with purely objective states or merely with realities in themselves.[5] 'Natural science', to cite Heisenberg, 'does not simply describe and explain nature, it is part of the interplay between nature and ourselves, it describes nature as exposed to our method of questioning'.[6]

[1] Op. cit. p. 100 f. In the same passage he adds: 'It is the definitive difference of quantum mechanics from classical physics that it cannot even enunciate its propositions without at the same time expressing the way in which they are known.'

[2] Op. cit. p. 200.

[3] C. F. von Weizsäcker, op. cit. p. 123.   [4] Op. cit. p. 57. Cf. pp. 195 ff.

[5] Cf. E. Schrödinger, *Mind and Matter*, ch. 3 'On the Principle of Objectification', pp. 36 ff.

[6] W. Heisenberg, *Physics and Philosophy*, p. 80; cf. p. 58.

This must not be taken to mean, however, that in scientific knowledge we force subjective factors upon the world of nature or that we are unable to acquire any knowledge of the onto-logical structure of things. As Heisenberg himself insists in re-gard to the Copenhagen interpretation of quantum theory,

the introduction of the observer must not be misunderstood to imply that some kind of subjective features are to be brought into the description of nature. The observer has, rather, only the function of registering decisions, i.e. processes in space and time, and it does not matter whether the observer is an apparatus or a human being; but the registration, that is the transition from the "possible" to the "actual", is absolutely necessary here and cannot be omitted from the interpretation of quantum theory.[1]

As de Broglie has said,

scientists have come to feel more and more keenly that there exists in nature an order, a harmony, which is at least partially accessible to our intelligence, and that they have devoted all their efforts to discover each day more of the nature and the extent of the harmony. Thus was born what we often call "pure science", that is, that activity of our mind which has as its goal the knowledge of natural phenomena and of establishing among them rational relations, independently of all utilitarian preoccupation.[2]

Yet what we do in science is to penetrate into the ontological and objective order in things by reducing our relations with nature to careful formalization, for as this is done it results in a theoretic system coordinate to reality through which the systematic connection of things inherent in reality comes to view and is cognized.

What application, then, does this shift in our understanding of the subject-object relation have to theological knowledge? The Reformation taught us that we do not know God in His isolation from us but only in personal communion, that is, in a two-way relation between subject and object; nevertheless along with this the Reformation brought into great prominence the doctrine of *election* which asserts that we do not know God or worship Him through acting upon Him but through being acted upon by Him. Our knowledge of nature may be gained

---

[1] Op. cit. p. 137 f; see also E. Schrödinger, op. cit. p. 50.
[2] Louis de Broglie, *Physics and Microphysics*, p. 206.

through violence, through acting upon it in such a way as to force it to reveal itself by reaction to our stipulations and experiments, but that is precisely how we do not and cannot know God—we cannot coerce God; we do not experiment with Him or put Him to the test in accordance with our volitions. It is we who are questioned before Him, we who are acted upon by His Grace, and yet He acts upon us in such a way that He does not negate but rather posits and fulfils our subjectivity. We are never allowed to impose ourselves with our notions upon Him, but we are freed and lifted up as rational subjects in communion with God, and summoned to decisions and acts of volition in that communion, so that knowledge of Him arises and increases out of obedient conformity to Him and the way He takes with us in revealing Himself to us.[1]

Here it is indeed true that the fact of our knowing of God enters into the content of that knowledge, so that there is a real interplay between human subject and divine Object. Justification for that is found in the fact that God comes to us and acts upon us as the Word, but in such a way that the Word becomes incarnate, is accessible to us, and also upholds our side of the subject-object relation through revelation and reconciliation. Thus our theological formulations arise out of and can only take a form which expresses at once the nature of the object and the mode of our cognition of it. As the propositions of empirical science reflect not only the structure of the world as it discloses itself to us, but the ways in which we know it, so *mutatis mutandis* theological propositions reflect not only the nature of the Word of God as He reveals Himself to us, but also the way in which we know Him through incarnation

[1] Cf. P. Tillich, *Systematic Theology*, I. p. 105: 'Knowing is a form of union. In every act of knowledge the knower and what is known are united; the gap between subject and object is overcome. The subject "grasps" the object, adapts it to itself and at the same time adapts itself to the object, but the union of knowledge is a peculiar one, it is a union through separation. Detachment is the condition of cognitive union.' Excellent as this statement may be in some areas of knowledge it fails to leave room for the distinctive element in theological knowledge: the primacy of the fact that *the object acts upon us* while we *react* to it, but do not act upon it or adapt it to ourselves. On the other hand when Tillich wants to do justice to the 'unapproachableness' of God, he insists that ultimately 'God can never become an object for man's knowledge or action' (op. cit. pp. 191, 301, etc.). This, however, is at the expense of making faith non-conceptual, and is to pass by the fact that God has adapted Himself and objectified Himself for us in Jesus Christ.

and reconciliation. From beginning to end, however, we operate in theology through response to a Word addressed to us, in obedience to an act of Grace upon us, and in a life of decision that is correlative to divine election. Thus whereas in empirical science we are concerned with statements that are pronounced by human subjects in a forced interplay between a subject and a mute object, in theology we are concerned with statements that are pronounced primarily by God and only pronounced after Him by human subjects as hearers of His Word. Here, then, we are concerned with a subject-object relation in which the subject is given freedom and place before God and yet in which the subject is summoned into such communion with Him that he can only engage in it with self-criticism and repentance (μετάνοια) that is, through an alteration in the structure of his consciousness, in which he is brought into conformity with the Truth. Nowhere more that in Christian theology does knowledge involve such a profound change in the attitude of man, or such a radical break in the structure of his natural mind, or such a complete reorientation in his life. That is to say theological knowledge takes place only through a critical reconstruction of subjectivity in accordance with the nature of the object.

One of the chief difficulties we have to face in theology is the difficulty of relating the subject-object relation in the worship of God to our statements about it. In worship or meditation we have more freedom to distinguish between the object of our knowledge and ourselves as knowers and even in listening to a sermon we are freer to distinguish between the Word of God which we hear and the preaching or hearing of it, but when we come to formulate this in words and put it down on paper, we have great difficulty in putting into statements the relation between the Object and our statements about it. Nevertheless unless we are able to make this distinction in some way, real knowledge is not possible and certainly not capable of being communicated.[1] In other words the place of what Tillich has called 'cognitive distance' is all-important, as is also the place of repentant self-criticism, if we are not to abolish altogether the

---

[1] We are always in danger in communication of mistaking the formal structure of our knowledge, which is easily communicated, with the material content, which in its deepest elements cannot be communicated, except indirectly.

relation between subject and object which knowledge involves.[1] Thus the problem of the nature of our theological statements will have to be discussed in a later chapter.

It falls to us now to look at another important element that has emerged in the development of modern science and theology.

(b) There has been taking place a critical revision of our attitude to 'nature'. Earlier in this discussion we noted that in the beginnings of empirical science in the sixteenth century there was a strong protest against the substitution of nature for God through the habit of regarding nature as impregnated with final causes. That led to a humbler view of nature, but it helped to release nature from the strings of a rationalist theology. Once this took place, however, and nature began to be investigated in itself through a methodological exclusion of theological questions, then for a great many nature came to occupy the whole of their attention and so there was a lapse back into the very attitude that Francis Bacon protested against, the substitution of nature for God. This took place in more than one way. In the thought of Spinoza, there was a lapse back into the notion of *Deus sive natura*. The idea of infinity came back directly into nature with such theoretical notions as Newton's space and time, but on the whole the change took place indirectly. Theoretically the notion of the infinite or the absolute was held in suspense or in reserve, but practically scientific inquiry came to no resting place in reaching behind facts to other facts, and so it operated, ideally at any rate, with an infinite regress. This had its most powerful influence in the notion that the mode of knowledge developed in empirical science with such positive results could be extended without limit, that is, in the claim that the whole universe was accessible to the methods of natural science, and that apart from what could come under the experimental observation and detection of these methods there existed nothing at all. Thus nature, but now with scientific man lodged in its heart, took the place of God. Of course the positivist notion of nature met with

[1] Cf. The interesting remarks of von Weizsäcker, 'I believe that the distance which in the modern mind exists between the subject and the object is a direct legacy of the Christian distance from the World.' *The History of Nature*, E.T. 1951, p. 172.

sustained opposition in the rise of idealism, but as the nine-teenth century wore on it became apparent again and again that idealism was after all probably but the obverse of natural-ism, with the human reason as the common factor through which the one could, and in fact often did, pass over into the other.

In our day, however, the whole situation has substantially changed. There were clear adumbrations of this much earlier, for example, in Kant's criticism of the notion of infinity, and his reminder of the limits of the human reason, but it was with the formulation of the theory of relativity, which destroyed the notion of absolute space and time, and revealed the limited possibilities of observation, that the change is clearly marked. It is above all, perhaps, the results of nuclear physics and quantum theory that bring this home to us. If the knowledge of nature is inescapably bound up with the human subject, if it is *his* knowledge, then it is finite and limited, not only because practically he is limited and finite, but because knowl-edge is limited by the fact that his knowing is inescapably a part of it, limited therefore at its very root which it can never transcend without ceasing altogether. Experimental science can never transcend its starting point, or its own limited instruments and therefore attain to God's knowledge, i.e., from an absolute point where it transcends all anthropomor-phism. In other words, the whole notion of the infinite or absolute goes, for the profounder the knowledge of nature becomes the more it becomes evident that man is not and never will be in a position through empirical science to attain a knowledge that passes beyond the interplay between himself and nature.

There is a very moving passage in von Weizsäcker's book to which we have referred so frequently, when he comes to this point and then asks:

Must we rest content with this? Does the world mean nothing? Is only that man happy—if such a one there be— who can forever evade the question of the meaning and the right with which he uses his knowledge and his power? Does nothing remain for the others, who have run through the movement of modern times, but that in addition to the two ancient aspects of the world, suffering and guilt, meaninglessness has entered as a third?

And then he answers:

I do not believe it. I do believe, however, that we must first see the abyss, must bear the emptiness. But I believe that this emptiness means, not end, but the demand for a decision. Does God no longer speak to us? Our substitute symbolism has broken down, not because it was a symbolism, but because it was a substitute, but the silence which has taken its place is eloquent enough for it puts before us our real situation. We must in fact know only whether we want to hear God at all—not where we wish to hear Him, but where He really speaks to us.[1]

We may look at the same point through quite different eyes, those of Jean-Paul Sartre who appears to stand for the conviction that we must abandon all notion of infinity and choose the fact that the world really leads to nothing in itself, to emptiness. Only when we choose that are we deliberately being real—that at least is something, and that at least should be authentic.

What does theology have to say to this? The Reformation would remind us of the distinction between Grace and nature, of the fact that nature (both matter and form) is created out of nothing, and that it can be known as a contingent reality only through examining its contingency. But its sheer contingency, indeed its emptiness, is but the obverse of its utter dependence upon the Grace of God, of its creation out of nothing. Creation lives not by and out of itself, but solely by the Grace of God, so that apart from Grace the creation borders on nothingness or chaos. This does not mean that through examination of the nothing we can reach God; it means that through the examination of nature as nature (if we refuse to cheat by secretly importing 'divinity' into it) we can only find nature and the limits of nature, the emptiness or the silence. But, as von Weizsäcker says, that is where we are put into our real situation where we must know whether we want to hear God or not. We cannot coerce Him by our questions; rather does He coerce us by this silence or emptiness to listen to Him. As the Bible puts it, He shuts us up to vanity, that He may have mercy on us. In other words, the way of natural science in its relentless questioning, in which it calls in question all natural theology, in its determination to let nature speak for itself out of itself,

[1] Op. cit. p. 178.

is to be looked on as the partner of a pure theology. Both natural science and scientific theology operate through a methodological exclusion of one another, for by their very nature they move in opposite directions. Moreover one operates through a situation which we set up at will, in which we bracket off an aspect of natural reality and subject it to controlled experimentation of our own devising, whereas the other operates through a situation set up not according to our will but according to the divine will in which we are not left alone with nature or with ourselves, but are directed beyond to our Creator. Thus natural science and scientific theology depart from opposite starting points, and operate with very different premises. Here some words from Kant's preface to the *Critique of Pure Reason* to which we referred earlier are to the point. 'We do not enlarge but disfigure sciences, if we allow them to trespass on one another's territory.' But it is perhaps rather the modern notion of complementarity in quantum mechanics that one might invoke here (at least in an applied form), according to which two mutually exclusive ways of knowledge and description are held to be complementary to one another without any possibility of their combination, because in different approaches we have delimited and differentiated the concepts of objective nature at the very source of our knowledge. Therefore the more exactly natural science and scientific theology are pursued, the sharper the distinction but the greater the complementarity exists between them.[1]

In this light it becomes evident that natural theology may offer the greatest hindrance to natural science and to scientific theology alike. The purer theology is, the more strictly it behaves in terms of the nature of its Object, which is revealed as Grace—that is why justification by Grace alone not only sets aside natural goodness, but sets aside natural theology, for both belong to the life of the natural man. Just as justification by Grace is not a factual denial of natural goodness, so it is not a metaphysical denial of natural theology, for in neither case is it a denial of natural man in his actual existence, but

[1] Our urge to discern a logical relation (even indirectly) or some correspondence between them is due to the persistence of habits of thought formed through classical physics and mechanics. Complementarity involves relation which is not less actual but which cannot be conceived through the old logical forms.

in both cases it does mean that man is set upon a wholly new basis in Grace. Thus the questioning of natural theology is grounded upon the event of divine grace as relativizing it or excluding it, at least as far as positive approach to God or positive theological inquiry is concerned. We are reminded here of the conception of natural law that arises out of Fermat's principle in which the selection of one way invalidates all others and sets them aside as *a posteriori* unentertainable.

Thus the exclusion of 'natural theology' by scientific theology as a sort of 'foreign body' (however useful within its own limits, e.g. in helping to remove the grounds of rational doubt) results from its determination to act in strict conformity with the nature of its proper object, and to behave toward God as He has actually chosen to reveal Himself and to act upon us in human, historical existence. This is, however, a *methodological*, not a metaphysical, rejection of 'natural theology', just as theology by the nature of its subject-matter and corresponding method involves a methodological exclusion of natural science from the body of its knowledge. Natural science starts from premisses that do not include God, and moves in an opposite direction to theology in accordance with the nature of its subject-matter, but 'natural theology' starts from the same premisses and the same phenomena as natural science and seeks to move toward God, and in so doing brings itself into conflict with natural science and with pure theology, proving to be a source of confusion to both if not an actual obstacle in their progress.

This is not to deny that there is indeed a form of natural knowledge, for the reality of God presses upon us everywhere in nature, not only in the ultimate rationality which our scientific knowledge of nature must assume in order to be what it is, but in a 'sense of the presence of God'[1] which all men have unless they obstruct or suffocate it. It is to claim, however, that this natural knowledge cannot be worked up into a 'natural theology', for in it we operate with a refraction in our relation to God at the very source of our attempt to reach and articulate ordered knowledge of Him on our own. Even in our refracted relation to God there is truth, even in our disobedience to Him there is a form of knowledge, but we

[1] Cf. John Baillie's Gifford lectures for 1961–2, *The Sense of the Presence of God*.

are unable to bring it out in clear and convincing steps of thought. What we reach by our argumentation cannot be equated with the living God, and can only distort knowledge of God if it is. That is to say, what scientific theology rejects is the attempt to treat 'natural theology' as a foundation upon which positive theology can be made to rest, or to use it as a criterion by which to assess the content of what we apprehend through divine 'revelation'. This would seem to be a form of cheating, for it is to assume what it claims to establish. Even St. Thomas used to point out that it is only the baptized reason that can properly engage in 'natural theology', that is, the reason as endowed with supernatural grace, for it is only as the reason is given knowledge of God that it acquires that adaptation by and through which it may think of Him and reason toward Him.

This seems to be the significant point which the development of theology, science and critical thought has reached in our own day, where it is more and more recognized that 'natural theology' is a sort of mixture pursued by men of faith reasoning within the natural realm, *remoto Christo*, as it were. It is not something that can stand on its own feet, purely as *natural* theology erected on natural grounds, but is, taken at its best, a form of rational argumentation on natural grounds in which a believer attempts to elaborate chains of reasoning which will remove from sceptical minds that which obstructs direct intuitive apprehension of the living God.[1] But if so, it must be recognized to be just this, and no more, not only in the interests of clear and exact thinking but in the interests of an authentic dialogue between scientific theology and natural science in which each declines to mishandle the evidence of the other or to demand that the other must produce convincing arguments outside its own proper framework of knowledge. To echo the words of Francis Bacon, we must learn to give to faith what belongs to faith and to nature what belongs nature. In this way we must develop a scientific theology, operating on its

[1] 'It is being more and more widely admitted that a disposition towards theistic belief is a necessary antecedent to the presentation of a reasoned case for theism.' Geddes MacGregor, *Introduction to Religious Philosophy*. p. 173. Cf. also the point made by A. E. Taylor in *The Faith of a Moralist* that natural theology flourishes only in a soil and atmosphere of historical religion, apart from which it quickly degenerates into naturalism, vol. 2, pp. 7 ff.

own proper grounds and with its own distinctive categories determined by the nature of God as known, and developing its own proper philosophy of science, the philosophy of theology, and from this position engage in scientific dialogue with other science and philosophical dialogue with other philosophy.

3

The Nature of Scientific Activity

In the Introduction to his book *Studies in the History and Methods of the Sciences* A. D. Ritchie has rightly reminded us that there is no Science in the singular, for there are only sciences. 'Sciences have arisen out of certain special human relations and consist of special human practices and thought about the practice.'[1] The implications of this are considerable. It means that we cannot know what a science now is unless we understand how it has come to be what it is, and that we cannot advance in it without a careful review of what has already been done, and so without building securely upon the foundations laid in the past. This is why some of the most significant forward leaps in modern science have been taken by men with a profound historical grasp of the developments within their own field. But it also means that we cannot abstract 'science' from the actual processes of scientific inquiry and discovery and consider it as a method that works *by itself*. There is no one scientific method that is universally applicable; there are only the actual methods which each science has developed in relation to certain special things and in which it 'has solved its own inductive problem of how to arrive at a general conclusion from a limited set of particular observations'.[2] Hence to have engaged successfully in one special science does not give a man the right to pontificate beyond it for the methods developed in relation to certain special things cannot be made to apply to other special things, although in analogical ways they may provide valuable hints as to how appropriate methods should be developed in regard to those things.

All this is not to say, however, that there is not such a thing as a scientific way of acting and thinking which is to be pursued

[1] p. 1.
[2] p. 7. Cf. John Oman, *The Natural and the Supernatural*, p. 109: 'Each kind of reality has its own kind of witness, and this must determine its own kind of method. This cannot be laid down before-hand, and the chief requirement is an open mind to learn as we go on our way.'

in every field of learning and discovery. This is the way of acting and thinking that is no more and no less than the rigorous extension of our basic rationality, as we seek to act toward things in ways appropriate to their natures, to understand them through letting them shine in their own light, and to reduce our thinking of them into orderly forms on the presumption of their inherent intelligibility. Scientific activity of this kind is essentially open and flexible through fidelity to the manifold character of reality and is therefore universally applicable, but as such it is the antithesis of the paranoiac rigidity manifest in every form of 'scientism'. The latter is clearly what Professor Ritchie has in mind when he rejects 'the common error of supposing that physics is the one and only science and that all other studies just creep in as hangers-on or else are not scientific at all.'[1] Nevertheless, there is an important sense in which physics has played an exemplary role, and may still be allowed to stand out as a model of pure science, when its intrinsically developed methods are shown to be determined by the nature of its own special subject-matter, for then it may serve to show us how basic rationality when rigorously extended in *appropriate* ways to some particular field may yield quite startling results. *Appropriate*, however, is the operative term here, for pure science can yield results only when the method and the matter are purely matched.

When we look at scientific activity in this way it should not surprise us that the development of theological thought and the development of natural science have influenced each other especially in regard to questions of method, not only because theological and natural science are pursued side by side within our common existence on earth but because of the scientific attitude which respect for their proper subject-matter begets in both. All this makes it important for us to clarify our understanding of scientific activity and to distinguish clearly the special requirements of theology as a science in its own right from those of other sciences such as physics, biology, or history.

1. *General and Special Science*

In proceeding to examine more fully the nature of scientific knowledge we may recall the old distinction between *scientia*

[1] Op. cit. p. 5.

generalis and *scientia specialis*. That has certainly meant different things from time to time. In the teaching of Aristotle, which dominated the conceptions of science for nearly two millennia, science is characterized by both unity and plurality. There is one world of nature which lies behind and requires a corresponding unity in our knowledge of it, but within this world there are different classes of things with their peculiarities providing different subject-matter and therefore requiring different branches of science appropriate to them, each with its own scope and with its distinctive characteristics in method.

That is an obvious and fundamental distinction which we cannot but affirm and must never allow to be blurred. If there were no basic unity in natural science, then the more profound and specialized our knowledge in the particular fields became, the greater would be our bewilderment and confusion. But if there were no special sciences, we would have an extremely monotonous world with one uniform method, eliminating, or at least failing woefully to do justice to, the manifold riches of nature and experience. Appreciation of 'the one and the many' in the world of nature is thus a heritage we derive from Greek science. On the other hand, it is worth noting that although it was Aristotle who developed and built up a formal method of scientific thinking in the *Organon* and gave us formal logic, nevertheless he did not think of that as a special science but thought of it as describing the rules of correct thinking, of testing evidence and of demonstration, basic to all science. Thus while Aristotle held that there were special principles that operated in special realms of knowledge—his strong biological interest did not allow him to be mesmerized by the importance of number in geometry or astronomy or music—he recognized that common principles obtained in all realms of knowledge, and so related the unity of science to logic.

According to Collingwood the polymorphic nature of primitive science was not uninfluenced by polytheism, but polytheistic science developed into monotheistic science through the influence of Patristic theology by giving natural science a very different set of fundamental presuppositions through the doctrines of the oneness of God, and of creation. This established further the unity of knowledge and yet developed the notion that there are diverse realms in nature through the doctrine of the self-differentiating activity of God.[1] On the other hand, it must be added that it was largely through the Christian tradition that elements of the Aristotelian and Platonic traditions were blended with the result that in a mono-theistic science Aristotelian logic acquired a quasi-mathematical dominance throughout all science, natural and theological alike. Thus there developed the conception of a uniformity of logico-causal connections throughout the whole universe which constituted a serious obstacle to the development of empirical science.

As against that trend the radical distinction between God and nature asserted at the Reformation released nature for independent and experimental investigation. But the more attention was directed to nature itself in all its manifold characteristics and the more the investigator sought to be a servant of nature in order to interpret it, the more inevitable it was that distinct special sciences should arise, jealous of their particular realms of inquiry and of their own characteristic methods of investigation and modes of thinking. And yet it remains true that the notion that there is one God, and one world which He has created and ordered in His wisdom, made stronger than ever the concepts of the underlying unity of natural science upon which the whole of modern science depends.

Into this unity of science, however, there was injected another powerful ingredient, the notion of a uniform method. That was initiated by Descartes through his attempt to develop a *scientia universalis* by rigorous application of the method of analytical geometry to all the other *scientiae speciales*, from which he excluded theology—for he did not presume to subject revealed truths to the impotency of his reason, as he expressed it.[2] There are several elements in Descartes' programme that are worth noting. He saw very clearly that scientific thinking involves 'assigning in thought a certain order even to those objects which in their own nature do not stand in a relation of antecedence and sequence.'[3] He held that 'all things, to the knowledge of which man is competent, are mutually connected

---

[1] R. G. Collingwood, *Metaphysics*, 1940, pp. 201 ff., and 213 ff.

[2] *Discourse on Method*, Part II, Everyman edit. p. 7 f.

[3] Op. cit. 15 f. Descartes' temptation, however, was to assimilate this with order in a mathematical series.

in the same way', and therefore if we preserve in our thoughts
the order necessary for the deduction of one truth from another,
we shall be in a position to reach clear knowledge of them.[1]
This involved a conviction of the organic unity of all science.
The nature of the world of objects and their connection according
to Descartes was such that they were amenable to order and
measurement, and therefore were to be elucidated by mathematical methods which alone can give us certitude and
exactitude.[2]

Two elements in this programme had an unfortunate effect
on the history of science and philosophy. It involved from the
start a sharp distinction between observation and thought[3]
which really made Cartesian natural science of little use and
left a legacy of radical dualism that has been extremely difficult
to get rid of. The attempt to apply a strictly mathematical
method to all sciences led to a one-sided passion for methodological monism in some of the greatest thinkers, from Leibniz
and Kant to Husserl and Russell.[4] As against that, two elements
in Descartes' method have been inordinately fruitful, the insistence that our thoughts of objects must be arranged in orderly
sequences if we are to intuit them, and the application of
geometry to nature, which Descartes himself inhibited by his
radical dualism, but which, when married to the experimental
methods of empirical science, contributed to the production
of the hypothetical deductive method that has been the great
instrument of power in all modern science.[5]

The importance of methodological monism and pluralism
in natural science has become even more apparent since the
rise of the theory of relativity and of quantum mechanics.
According to Einstein 'science is the attempt to make the
chaotic diversity of our sense-experience correspond to a

---

[1] Ibid.

[2] Cf. the curious remark of Descartes about his own method in *The Principles
of Philosophy*, IV. XII: 'Though I have endeavoured to give an explanation of the
whole nature of material things, I have nevertheless made use of no principle
that was not received and approved by Aristotle, and by the other philosophers of
all ages.'

[3] *Discourse on Method*, IV, p. 26 f.

[4] Cf. F. Heinemann, *Neue Wege der Philosophie*, p. 37.

[5] Cf. H. Reichenbach, *The Rise of Scientific Philosophy*, p. 100. The combination
of experimental knowledge and mathematics derives from Galileo and Newton.

logically uniform system of thought'.[1] That was precisely what he carried out in his work on relativity for it achieved an enormous simplification of prevailing conceptions through a simple yet momentous generalization.[2] Quantum theory has contributed startlingly to the unity of science in a similar way, yet it has shown with greater force the limited range of our methods of inquiry and fundamental differences in scientific approach and explanation. That is of course particularly clear in the notion of complementarity which, as Oppenheimer has stated it, 'recognises that various ways of talking about physical experience may each have validity, and may be necessary for the adequate description of the physical world, and may yet stand in a relation of mutually exclusive relationship to each other, so that to a situation to which one applies, there may be no consistent possibility of applying the other.'[3] If that applies within the realm of physics alone, it is obvious that it applies, as Bohr himself has shown, to the relation between organic and inorganic sciences.[4] Thus, to cite Oppenheimer again,

Every science has its own language. . . . Everything the chemist observes and describes can be talked about in terms of atomic mechanics, and most of it at least can be understood. Yet no one suggests that, in dealing with the complex chemical forms which are of biological interest, the language of atomic physics would be helpful. Rather it would tend to obscure the great regularities of biochemistry, as the dynamic description of gas would obscure its thermodynamic behaviour.[5]

It is apparent, then, that there is little need in the modern world to apologize for a distinction between *scientia generalis* and *scientia specialis*. However, this distinction is not intended to mean, and could not mean, that in addition to the special sciences there is a distinct 'general science', or some sort of super-science, although claims have been put forward in that

[1] *Out of My Later Years*, p. 95.
[2] See the paper by L. de Broglie, 'A General Survey of the Scientific Work of Albert Einstein' in *Albert Einstein, Philosopher–Scientist*, p. 116; and Max Born, *Einstein's Theory of Relativity*, p. 289.
[3] *Great Essays in Science* (ed. by Martin Gardner, 1957), p. 189,
[4] *Atomic Theory and the Description of Nature*, p. 21 and 117.
[5] *Science and the Common Understanding*, Reith Lectures for 1953, p. 87.

direction.[1] There are only particular sciences, but these particular sciences all have certain fundamental principles in common, for all knowledge as knowledge has a certain structural form in order to be knowledge at all. Within the whole realm of knowledge it is obvious that natural science has its own and a profound unity in spite of its manifoldness or plurality, although the understanding of that unity has been greatly altered by the discovery of the limited range of physics built up on the mechanical model, for the profounder natural science becomes the more it must be prepared to be concerned with the non-observable or the non-objectifiable, at least in the sense in which those terms held in the Newtonian framework. This makes it all the more necessary to discern the principle of demarcation between the special sciences and to work with a clear and applicable distinction between *scientia generalis* and *scientia specialis*. But we shall be concerned with a principle of demarcation that is applicable not only to the world of natural science but to the whole universe of knowledge which must include the *Geisteswissenschaften* or the human sciences, and include theological science, not to speak of philosophy.

In all science the reason behaves in terms of the nature of the object. Therefore the formal procedure appropriate to that behaviour is universal in its range. There is thus a procedure common to every science, *formal* scientific procedure. But in each particular field science requires a modification of its formal procedure in a way appropriate to the distinctive nature of the object or the matter under investigation, so that there is a *material* scientific procedure appropriate to each particular field of scientific research. Hence there arise the procedures of the special sciences. Thus while theological science shares with other sciences a generally recognized scientific procedure based on the principle of objectivity, theology has its own particular scientific requirements determined by the unique nature of its own particular object, just as every other special

---

[1] Husserl's conception of pure logic as *mathesis universalis*, under the influence of Leibniz, and of philosophy as *strenge Wissenschaft* (*Logische Untersuchungen*, Bd. 1, and *Logos*, Bd. 1, 1911) come very near this. As the science of *pure possibility* he looked upon philosophy as providing the *form of possible method*, in contrast to the *determinate methods* that are dependent on the structural forms of the sciences of fact (the dogmatic sciences, see *Ideas*, p. 95 f.), but as preceding them and giving them the guidance of its logical analysis of pure consciousness. All special methods have to link themselves up to it. *Ideas*, pp. 13, 63 f. 73, 175 f., 21 f. See also Heinrich Scholz, *Mathesis Universalis, Abhandlungen zur Philosophie als strenge Wissenschaft*.

science has its own peculiarities owing to the special features of its object. There is thus a *scientia generalis* common to all sciences, but each special science has its own mode of rationality or objectivity, and its own aim and method as a *scientia specialis*.[1]

This distinction arises also in a somewhat different way. In all knowledge we are concerned with the nature of the knower and with the mode of knowing appropriate to human nature—that is, it takes place within the possibilities and necessities and limitations of human observation and thought. Therefore there are general principles of knowledge relevant to every field of knowledge where the human knower is involved. But because we have also to operate within the framework provided by what is known and are concerned with the nature of the object in each field of knowledge, we must have particular principles of knowledge relevant to each particular field or object. Thus in theology we are concerned with our human knowing of God, i.e. with a mode of knowing appropriate to human minds and subjects, wherever there is a subject-object relationship. That theology shares with every branch of knowledge—*quidquid cognoscitur, cognoscitur per modum cognoscentis*, as the Medievals used to say. But in theology we are concerned with God in Jesus Christ as the Truth, and therefore we are concerned with a mode of knowing appropriate to His unique nature. Hence theology must have its particular principles relevant to this unique object or field of knowledge where divine self-disclosure is involved.

It is important to discern the right relation between *scientia generalis* and *scientia specialis*, i.e. in our case, theological knowledge or science. We must beware of distinguishing these as if they were two disparate forms of scientific procedure, or of separating them as the general and the particular too sharply for they only operate together. They are not two independent procedures but rather two modes of one scientific procedure which inevitably involves some measure of adaptation to the particular field of knowledge in question. But *scientia generalis*

---

[1] This rules out the idea that there is some *basic scientific language* to which the language of any special science could ultimately be reduced, the so-called 'physical thing-language' advocated by Carnap (*International Encyclopedia of Unified Science*, Vol. I, 1, 1938). Apart from presupposing here the materialistic ideas of seventeenth-century physics, this does not succeed in separating uniformity in language from uniformity in explanations, for it implies that the basic logical structure of all sciences is identical.

does not have any place by itself, for it could not be what it is, or be at all, without the particular sciences. It is not an abstract generalization from the *scientiae speciales* but is common to them all. Nor, on the other hand, are we to think of a *scientia specialis* as simply a particularization of *scientia generalis*.[1] Its formative movement is rather in the opposite direction, for each special science must reach out to what is general or universal in order to be a science at all. Wherever there is scientific knowledge, both are found, for the *scientiae speciales* in their mutual independence suggest a *scientia generalis*, common to them all, with which they are in mutual dependence, and which therefore is not independent of them. It can hardly be emphasized enough that while the *scientia generalis* is a way of knowing with certain minimal structural forms and relations fundamental to all scientific knowledge, it cannot be abstracted from the concrete sciences and erected into an independent *scientia universalis* without becoming artificial and arbitrary, and indeed imperialistic.

Now the area where *scientia generalis* overlaps with the *scientiae speciales* is that which specially interests the philosopher, but it is important not to confuse philosophy with *scientia generalis*. Science is a way of discovery, a way of attaining new knowledge, but philosophy is a way of thinking without being a way of adding anything positive to our information.[2] The actual work of discovery is carried out by the *scientiae speciales* which all presuppose and overlap with one another in *scientia generalis*, but the *scientia generalis* is bound to what is known like the *scientiae speciales*. Philosophy, however, is not bound in that way for its activity is not limited by a particular object or a set of objects and therefore has a considerable range of freedom within the possibilities and necessities of thought. It is concerned with what Whitehead called 'complete generality' or 'necessity in universality'.[3] It is much more like abstract

---

[1] We must bear in mind here Husserl's contrast between formalization and generalization (*Ideas*, p. 72): 'A sharp distinction must be drawn between the relations of generalisation and specialisation on the one hand, and, on the other the *reduction of what has material content to a formal generality of a purely logical kind*, or conversely the *process of filling in with content* what is logically formal.'

[2] Thus A. E. Taylor, *The Elements of Metaphysics*, pp. 191 f., 414. However this is not meant to reject the view, so strongly held by Whitehead, that metaphysical thinking and the speculative reason play an essential part in scientific discovery and advance.

[3] A. N. Whitehead, *Process and Reality*, 3 f.

mathematics which is not bound by the limitations of the concrete or of space and time, but because it is like abstract mathematics and because it is concerned, like *scientia generalis*, with the overlap between the *scientiae speciales*, philosophy is constantly being tempted to identify itself with *scientia generalis*, and through schematization to abstract mathematics to conceive of itself as a *scientia universalis*.[1] In so doing, however, philosophy confounds itself as a way of thinking with a way of discovery, and so lays down principles for verification which do not coincide with the actual ways of discovery in the special sciences, and would, if taken seriously, cut away the ground from beneath the special sciences and make them meaningless. This is the force, for example, of Einstein's critique of Reichenbach,[2] or of M. Polanyi's criticism of Ayer.[3]

Another way of distinguishing philosophy from *scientia generalis* is to note that they handle the same terms and concepts in very different ways. The terms and concepts in science are handled not only within the framework of the possibilities and necessities of thought but within the framework of concrete experience and existence, and are never without factual and experimental reference, but it is that concrete particular experimental reference that vanishes in the philosophical handling of the same terms and concepts. As Collingwood has expressed it in a clear-sighted essay:

There are words which are used in two different ways, a philosophical and a scientific; but the words are not on that account equivocal; they undergo a regular and uniform change in meaning when they pass from one sphere to the other, and this change leaves something fundamental in their meaning unaltered, so that it is more appropriate to speak of two phases of a concept than two senses of a word.[4]

This is a point that does not appear to be recognized by some critical philosophers who presume that the logical structure with which they operate, even when it has been schematized

---

[1] This can be done in very different ways, for example, by Hegel or Russell. Hegel however had learned from Kant a proper distinction between philosophical and mathematical thinking. The notion or practice of *scientia universalis* can arise also from the side of positivist science, e.g. Haeckel.

[2] *Albert Einstein, Philosopher-Scientist* (edit. by P. A. Schilpp), p. 289 ff., and 676 ff.

[3] *Personal Knowledge*, p. 13 f. Ayer is not mentioned by Polanyi, but seems to be indicated.

[4] *Philosophical Method*, p. 33.

to mathematics, can and must apply to the logical structure in scientific statements, theories and laws.[1] This idea is precisely what modern nuclear physics has so successfully shattered, and thereby has contributed immensely to the understanding not only of scientific method but indirectly of philosophical method as well.[2]

2. *Theology and General Scientific Method*

We have already considered much that must come under this heading, and there is no need to go over that ground in detail. It will be sufficient at those points to indicate briefly what is involved.

(a) The primary element we have already noted about scientific theology is its devotion to its proper object, sheer respect for objectivity. It will not concede as genuine knowledge what does not correspond to the given reality.

(b) A scientific theology is what the Germans call *wissenschaftlich*, that is, a rigorous, disciplined, methodical and organized knowledge. It is knowledge that insists upon the truthfulness of its undertaking and is dedicated to the detection of error and the rejection of all that is unreal. It will have nothing to do with a method that is not governed by the material content of its knowledge, or with confused, disorderly or loose thinking, or with hypothetical objects. Everything has to be tested and undertaken in a reliable and trustworthy way, with strict attention to correctness. Therefore it must be controlled knowledge that operates with proper criteria and appropriate methods of verification, knowledge that is answerable to inexorable conscience. This is an aspect of scientific theology with which we shall be concerned especially in two later chapters, so that we leave detailed discussion of it until then.

(c) Scientific activity engages in a search for elemental form in which to reduce the multiplicity of its knowledge to the

---

[1] Thus when Ayer maintains that the function of the philosopher is 'to clarify the propositions of science by exhibiting their logical relationships, and by defining the symbols which occur in them' (preface to the 1935 edition of *Language, Truth and Logic*), he fails to appreciate the logical stratification of scientific structure and treats their logical terms as if they are all on the same level. Cf. Heisenberg, *Physics and Philosophy*, p. 181 f.; M. Polanyi, *Personal Knowledge*, pp. 343 ff.

[2] Cf. W. Heisenberg, *Physics and Philosophy*, pp. 167 ff.; and von Weizsäcker, *Komplementarität und Logik*, *Naturwissenschaften*, 1955.

basic order into which our thought is forced under the pressure of objective reality. It is the movement from the many to the one, from the complex to the simple. This methodological principle has long been known as 'Ockham's razor'—*pluralitas non est ponenda sine necessitate*, or *frustra fit per plura quod potest fieri per pauciora*.[1] Its significance in modern times is nowhere better seen than in the work of Einstein who has himself given many statements of this principle. In one of his later discussions of the method of science he stated it in the following way. 'The aim of science is, on the one hand, a comprehension, as *complete* as possible, of the connection between the sense experiences in their totality, and, on the other hand, the accomplishment of this aim *by the use of a minimum of primary concepts and relations*. (Seeking, as far as possible, logical unity in the world picture, i.e. paucity in logical elements.)'[2] He also speaks of this as 'logical simplicity' or 'logical economy'.[3] That does not mean that the formulation of scientific theory is not difficult. On the contrary it may take very intricate and complicated processes of thought to arrive at it, but the elemental forms reached will be minimal and basic and will have the effect of illuminating a great variety of otherwise incomprehensible facts, and will thus represent a vast simplification of our knowledge over a wide area.[4]

Apart from giving form and order to our knowledge an essential requirement of these primary concepts and relations is that they have to be 'natural', that is, closely co-ordinated with the concrete subject-matter we are investigating and compatible with our actual experience. The theories or laws formulated to bind together these elemental forms must not be identified with ontic structures for they are only theoretic constructs, yet as such they must be determined by and point

[1] According to P. Boehner, *Ockham, Philosophical Writings*, p. XX f., the form usually given (*entia non sunt multiplicanda sine necessitate*) does not seem to have been used by Ockham.

[2] *Out of My Later Years*, p. 62. Cf. also p. 95 f. The italics are Einstein's.

[3] *Albert Einstein, Philosopher-Scientist*, p. 23, from Einstein's autobiographical notes.

[4] An example Einstein gives of this is the de Broglie-Schrödinger theory of wave fields. Of his own work Einstein has said, 'The theory of relativity arose out of efforts to improve with reference to logical economy, the foundation of physics as it existed at the turn of the century.' *Out of My Later Years*, p. 101. Cf. *The World as I see It*, p. 138.

to ontic order inherent in the material of our inquiry. That relationship Einstein called 'naturalness' which is just another way of expressing logical simplicity or economy. This relationship provides a real problem, as Einstein has frankly recognized. 'Nothing can be said', he has declared, 'concerning the manner in which the concepts are to be made and connected, and how we are to co-ordinate them to the experiences.'[1] Or, as he had expressed it elsewhere, speaking of it the other way round: 'Nobody who has really gone deeply into the matter will deny that in practice the world of phenomena uniquely determines the theoretical system, in spite of the fact that there is no logical bridge between phenomena and their theoretical principles.'[2] In other words, this is the problem raised by David Hume when he showed that the notion of causality does not arise on logical grounds. Because there is no logical road to these laws the scientist, in formulating them, must rely upon his 'intuition',[3] that is upon the sheer weight or impress of external reality upon his apprehension, although once formulated he can test them indirectly through their success in bringing the widest range of experience under their illumination.

On the other hand, this a-logical relation or hiatus between the theoretic constructions and the order inherent in nature constitutes a temptation. Logical simplicity is more easily reached through making our concepts independent of nature and working them up into an abstract system. Then when we clamp this artificial unity down upon nature it becomes a constant source of error and a serious hindrance to further knowledge. Here Einstein[4] and Wittgenstein[5] were at one in pointing out how easily we are deceived by our own words and language. It is because there is no logical road to the formulation of the laws of nature that there is no road back through logical reduction of our language to the structure of reality.[6] Nevertheless it remains the *sine qua non* of scientific advance that we penetrate through the mass of our concepts

[1] Op. cit. p. 61.   [2] *The World as I see It*, p. 23.

[3] The element of 'intuition' is strongly stressed by Einstein, e.g. in passages cited above, *The World as I See It*, p. 23; and *Out of My Later Years*, p. 61.

[4] Op. cit. p. 107 f.

[5] See especially *The Blue and Brown Books*, p. 25 ff.

[6] So far as theology is concerned this was the point of Kierkegaard's dictum that 'there is no retreat backwards into the Kingdom of God'.

and correlations to primary and elemental forms that *through* them, constructions of ours though they are, we may attain a profounder and clearer knowledge of nature.[1] The principle of logical economy implies that the simpler and poorer the basic forms we employ, the wider and the richer will be our knowledge. It enlarges the interconnection and simplifies the vision.[2]

With Einstein's discussion and achievements in our eye we have naturally been thinking mostly of scientific procedure in physics, but it stands to reason that the principle of logical economy will operate differently in descriptive as opposed to the explanatory science, for one operates with given forms and the other has to 'construct' them.[3] Appropriate modification is required in the application of the principle to theological activity, but theological science no less than any other requires penetration down to the basic 'forms' if extensive illumination and profound understanding are to be reached, although it suffers more than any other from abstract and artificial systematization.[4] Here too, therefore, it is most important to use only those concepts which can be co-ordinated as fully as possible with the given reality. That is what we shall later discuss as 'the interior logic' and 'the material mode of speech' of theology deriving from Christology.[5]

(d) We must now proceed to discuss the nature of scientific *inquiry*. The importance of questioning as a method of knowledge goes back to Socrates, but the Socratic questioning implied a sharp distinction between philosophical thinking and natural science. Its aim was to clarify what we already know and to

[1] Cf. Eddington, *The Philosophy of Physical Science*, pp. 66, 117.

[2] This is what gives scientific theory its 'inner perfection', as Einstein calls it (*Albert Einstein, Philosopher-Scientist*, p. 23), or beauty.

[3] Cf. S. Toulmin, *The Philosophy of Science*, p. 53 f.

[4] Cf. what Wittgenstein has to say about 'the craving for generality' that may arise out of preoccupation with scientific method, op. cit. p. 18. He has philosophy in mind, but it is relevant also to theology.

[5] Cf. the remarks of Professor D. M. MacKinnon about Karl Barth with reference to the suggestion of Bertrand Russell, 'Whenever possible let us substitute logical constructions out of the observable for inferred, unobserved entities'. 'There is in Barth something analogous to this recommended logical economy. We must, he insists, substitute for abstract, general statements concerning the being and purposes of God, and of men, statements that show them in terms of, or set them in relation to, Jesus Christ.' *Essays in Christology for Karl Barth*, edit. by T. H. L. Parker, p. 284.

sift out genuine from false knowledge by tracing its dialectical movement. Important as this is in philosophy, this is not what is meant by scientific inquiry, for its central point of reference lies in the thinker himself rather than in the object under investigation. Socratic thinking must also have its place in scientific discipline, but it is not inquiry after new knowledge and does not yield discovery.[1]

Inquiry that is open to new knowledge takes the form of questioning in which we allow what we already know or hold to be knowledge to be called in question by the object. We must submit ourselves modestly, with our questions, to the object in order that it and not we ourselves may be the pivotal point in the inquiry. Therefore even the way in which we shape the questions must finally be determined from beyond us, if we are really to pass beyond the stock of previously acquired knowledge. Of course it is true that in every inquiry question and answer are correlated and that a measure of independence as well as mutual dependence is involved, as Tillich has pointed out. It is also true that in the last resort 'the question, asked by man, is man himself',[2] but far from meaning that it is man who finally determines and shapes the answers in accordance with his stipulations, it means that man with his questions must be questioned down to the roots of his existence before the object. It is only through the unremitting questioning of our questions and of ourselves the questioners, that true questions are put into our mouths to be directed to the object for its disclosure to us. Formally it is we who put the question, but the material constituent of our question is radically altered through the impress of the object upon our questioning.[3]

Therefore we cannot let out of sight the fact that the question, while directed by us toward the object, always has a backward reference to us as questioners. Indeed the question is not designed properly or primarily as criticism directed to the

[1] This was the point seen so clearly by Bacon but not by Descartes whose method of inquiry remained essentially Socratic.

[2] *Systematic Theology*, Vol. II, pp. 14 f.

[3] Tillich remarks that man cannot receive an answer to a question that he has not asked—a decisive principle of religious education (op. cit. p. 15), but it must also be said that he never really learns anything new, beyond what he somehow already knows, unless new questions are put into his mouth from the side of the object which he can never think up on his own out of his religious predicament. Tillich's principle describes the initial step, but the decisive step forward is only taken in the radically novel question. Cf. *Theology in Reconstruction*, p. 123 f.

object but as criticism directed toward our knowing of it, and therefore toward ourselves. It is not normally the object that is responsible for our failure to observe or cognize it aright but we ourselves. In the field of natural science, of course, knowledge has to be wrested from nature, but nature does not intend to deceive us, so that if we are to be successful in our inquiry we must be humble before nature and let it impose itself upon us. Scientific questions thus pivoted upon the object are intended, therefore, to uncover all deception or unreality in ourselves in order to open us up to learn what is new, and to make our thinking as real as possible, that is, in accordance with the reality of the object.[1] Normally the unreality lies not in the object but in ourselves, and therefore true questions are a form of self-criticism. But where human beings come under our investigation, as in psychology or sociology or history, for example, we have to reckon with unreality in the object, and then we must be particularly careful not to let criticism of the object displace or depreciate self-criticism, for that would inevitably lead to the imposition of ourselves upon the object and so to the betrayal of scientific objectivity.

To achieve their end scientific questions must be ruthless and unrelenting, probing down into the deepest depths of our knowing in order to uncover and cut away all that hinders us from behaving in terms of the nature of the object, and in order to allow ourselves to be 'told' by the object what we cannot tell ourselves about it, and so genuinely to learn what is beyond what we already know or think we know. Questions are certainly directed toward the object as it *appears* to us. That is something we have learned from Kant in a way that we can never forget, but a false understanding of it can be very harmful, for it may lead the autonomous reason to assume such a masterful role that it insists on shaping what it seeks to know, and so becomes often its own greatest obstacle. Properly, however, the questions are designed to uncover the object to our view, by removing the covering which we lay over it by our preconceptions and distorted habits of observation. It is one of the most difficult things in the world to observe what is actually there, and especially to observe it for the first

---

[1] See the clear discussion on 'the sources of unreality' and 'on being real in our thinking' by Macmurray in *Freedom in the Modern World*, pp. 121 ff., and 130 ff. to which these paragraphs are indebted.

time. In order to achieve that we have above all to struggle with ourselves, i.e. to *repent*. As Oppenheimer has put it, 'We learn to throw away those instruments of action and those modes of description which are not appropriate to the reality we are trying to discern, and in this most painful discipline, find ourselves modest before the world.'[1]

The importance of this backward or self-critical reference of scientific questioning is very obvious when we study the history of science, which in all its great stages of advance has entailed radical revision of its premisses and methods.[2] Advances can be made only through new ways of looking at things, through asking daring new questions, but new questions require corresponding changes in language and representation; they require changes in the framework of our concepts and in the logical structure of science itself.[3] They may even call for a new meaning of the word 'understanding'.[4] But all that is part of the pain and awe and excitement of radically new knowledge. The refusal to be bound by the rigid framework of our previous attainments, the capacity to wonder and be open for the radically new, the courage to adapt ourselves to the frighteningly novel, are all involved in the forward leap of scientific research, but in the heart of it lies the readiness to revise the canons of our inquiry, to renounce cherished ideas, to change our mind, to be wide open to question, to repent.

Scientific questioning is not the same thing as *doubt*.[5] Doubt rests upon a form of self-certainty, whereas scientific questioning

[1] *Great Essays in Science* (edit. by M. Gardner), p. 198. Cf. here what A. Farrer has to say about the metaphysician's method, *The Glass of Vision*, p. 68: "The metaphysician's method is to keep breaking his yardsticks against the requirements of real truth. The method which thus aims at the comprehension of the reality of things is that method of which Plato said that it and it alone proceeded by smashing the suggestions it put forward. By continually breaking and bettering and breaking his descriptions the metaphysician refines his understanding of that which he tries to describe."

[2] Cf. E. Grisebach, *Gegenwart*, p. 50 f.; M. Polanyi, *Personal Knowledge*, p. 170.

[3] The importance of new questions and new ways of looking at things is a recurring theme in S. Toulmin's work, *The Philosophy of Science*, e.g. pp. 36, 43, 64.

[4] Cf. Heisenberg, op. cit. p. 201.

[5] See the analysis of theological doubt by F. W. Camfield, *The Collapse of Doubt*, 1945. Cf. also M. Polanyi, *Science, Faith and Society*, p. 62, where he shows that complete methodological doubt would destroy all belief in natural science and lead to metaphysical nihilism. Cartesian scepticism as a scientific method had already been brilliantly examined and refuted by Bolzano, *Wissenschaftslehre*, 1, sections 34–44, and *Lehrbuch der Religionswissenschaft*, i, sect. 62. See the analysis of his argument by H. Scholz, *Mathesis Universalis*, pp. 236 ff.

rests upon the certainty of the object before which we are open to question in ourselves. That is very apparent in the programme of Descartes where the dualism already posited in the Platonic method of inquiry becomes so extreme in the division between the ego and the world, mind and matter, that the halting of sophisticated doubt upon self-certainty (*cogito, ergo sum*), makes self-certainty the starting point and basis for methodological doubt.[1] That is the very reverse of scientific procedure. There is always a deep-seated element of false subjectivity in doubt, so that doubting questions are fundamentally unreal for they are posed in self-isolation from the object, whereas scientific questions are directed toward objectivity in which we open ourselves up to face whatever the object may disclose to us. It is supremely important to distinguish questioning that is genuinely scientific from the systematic doubting or scepticism that so often claims to take its cue from Descartes,[2] for unless we learn to put our questions openly and without ulterior motives, they will be directed past the object; they will be blind questions.

What, then, are the requirements for scientific questioning?

A primary requirement is that scientific questions must be genuine, questions aimed at reality. Questions are not genuine if we already know the answer; they are only poses that do not get us anywhere but rather hold us back.

Nor are they genuine if they are simply inquisitive, that is, questions that we do not mean to follow up.[3] Genuine questions

---

[1] Contrast the phenomenological ἐποχή of Husserl which he substituted for Descartes' attempt at universal doubt—i.e. the bracketing off or disconnecting of phenomena from questions as to its reality, in order to acquire clear grasp of it. Ἐποχή is a refraining from judgement which allows the matter under investigation to be treated as a *supposition* without implying like the Cartesian doubt a negative *position* in regard to it. Cf. *Ideas*, pp. 80 f., 109 ff. Even in Augustine (*De vera religione*, 39. 73, the passage used by Descartes) the negative position is opposed to the positive in the truth of being, i.e. that truth is what it is by truth.

[2] Cf. the trenchant words of M. Polanyi in his Gifford Lectures: 'The test of proof or disproof is in fact irrelevant for the acceptance or rejection of fundamental beliefs and to claim that you strictly refrain from believing anything that could be disproved is merely to cloak your own will to believe your beliefs behind a false pretence of self-critical severity.' (*Personal Knowledge*, p. 271.) And with reference to Bertrand Russell's 'rational doubt': 'Since the sceptic does not consider it rational to doubt what he himself believes, the advocacy of 'rational doubt', is merely the sceptic's way of advocating his own beliefs' (p. 298). See also J. Macmurray, *The Self as Agent*, p. 76.

[3] Such, for example, are often the questions we ask in the ecumenical movement, for we are afraid of the changes they will involve.

must be governed by a purpose which directs the question with the intention of listening to its answer honestly and relating it to the rest of our knowledge by acting in terms of it. In other words, they must be meaningful or significant and must be open and not closed to the object. Nothing is more unreal than a question that methodologically excludes the reality under investigation, or is merely 'disinterested'.

Further requirement for scientific questions is that they must be of the right kind, that is to say, questions appropriate to the nature of the object. 'If we ask the wrong question the logical correctness of our answer is of little consequence.'[1] If we ask only anthropological questions we will get only anthropological answers. Theological thinking is concerned scientifically to ask theological questions. The question must be in the mode of the reality under inquiry and be expressed in an idiom congruent with it. This means that scientific questions can never be asked singly, but only in a series of questions, in which the questions themselves come under question, as we learn more and more about the nature of the object and learn more and more therefore how to put them properly in accordance with the nature of the object. It is not always easy in this inquiry to reject questions that further knowledge discredits, or to see when a question can no longer be asked, or to refuse to push a question beyond its relevance. But all this belongs to disciplined investigation. Scientific questioning is thus a progressively self-critical operation as well as an unceasing and unrelenting inquiry.

Another fundamental requirement is that scientific questions must group around and reflect the one supreme question that arises from the side of the object as it confronts us, the question as to its nature and ground. Our questions are genuine, truthful questions when they are rooted in this basic question, that is, when they are controlled by the sheer pressure which the objective reality exerts upon us. Our scientific questions are then to be regarded as the many counter-questions put into our mouth as we allow ourselves to be questioned by the impact of the given—its supreme question to us. The decisive test here is whether our questions are questions which we merely think up, or whether they are aroused and directed from beyond ourselves.

[1] John Macmurray, *The Self as Agent*, p. 21.

The supreme formal requirement in scientific questioning is that we look for the central point of reference, and then in relation to it order all our questions. This is partly, at any rate, the significance of the logical economy so stressed by Einstein, in which we press for increasing simplicity in the logical basis of our thought. It is only through questioning that this basis or central point will become evident to us, but as it becomes evident, we must correct our questions by reference to it, for it is through that reference that they have their legitimation or verification, that they become significant or meaningful, and can therefore be employed as trustworthy instruments for the disclosure of truth from the side of the object.

Now in theology the object is the Lord God, and the supreme question that is directed to us from the side of the object is in the form of a Person within our creaturely and human existence, the Lord Jesus Christ. That means that scientific questioning in theology is necessarily given a mode in accordance with the unique nature of its object, which differentiates it from the mode in which questioning arises in other fields of knowledge. Theological questioning is of the acutely personal and historical kind that we see in the Gospels taking place between Jesus and the Jews or the disciples.

It is in theological science that the *interrogative* form of inquiry is scientifically justified to a degree it is nowhere else, so that it is here that we learn what questioning really means. But here, too, as nowhere else, the questioner is questioned before ever he begins even to think of asking questions of his own. The question directed to him is the supreme question that takes precedence over every other, and by reference to which every other question has its supreme significance and justification. Here the human questioner is essentially a questioned man, a man addressed from beyond in such a way that the whole of his being is determined by the summons to answer the question put to him from above and beyond himself. It is only in answer to that supreme question that he can truthfully ask his questions. He can ask them responsibly only as he listens and lets himself be questioned by the Truth down to the very roots of his being until he is set free from himself, from his own preconceptions and self-deception, from self-willed and arbitrary thinking, from pride of reason and desire to control the questioning of God. It is in theological questioning of this kind that we may really learn the meaning of scientific questioning as questioning controlled by the nature of the given objective reality and so learn that the truth or falsity of our questions is determined by whether they arise ultimately from the side of the object or not.

(e) A further aspect of scientific method calls for consideration, the *problematic* form of thinking,[1] which is cognate to the aspect we have just discussed. This is the activity in which we throw forward (προβάλλω, πρόβλημα) our questions and answers into an ordered sequence which enables us to penetrate intuitively into the order in the nature of the object. It is in this 'economic reduction' of our indicative statements into a skeletal form, which represents the actual probing into the truth which we have undertaken in obedient conformity to the given reality, that its nature and structure become more evident to us. That is, to borrow some words from Collingwood, we have to dispose our questions into such an order that they form a 'series of thoughts in which thinking the thoughts is at the same time thinking the connections between them'.[2]

The value of this is very obvious in empirical science where the hypothetical process (if *a*, *b*, *c*, ... then *x*) is the most accurate form of argument because it gives a clear account of the steps taken in discovery and required in verification.[3] This hypothetical form of argument is governed by the nature of the determinate objects investigated by empirical science and the applicability of mathematical thinking to it, i.e. by the kind of serial order it involves, but it will necessarily take another form with an object of a different nature such as a subject who talks back to us and questions us and whom we cannot compel to reveal himself.[4] Here the suppositions with which we work are of quite a different kind from those which

[1] For a valuable discussion of this in theological thought see Heinrich Vogel, *Grundfragen des Studiums der Theologie*, 1957, pp. 43 ff. (E. T. *Consider Your Calling*, 1962, p. 27 f)., and his article '*Wann ist ein theologischer Satz wahr?*' in *Kerygma und Dogma*, 4. 3, 1958, pp. 176 ff.

[2] R. G. Collingwood, *Metaphysics*, pp. 23, 63. This is the idea which, as we noted earlier, stems from Descartes.

[3] Cf. the account of this given by Cook Wilson, *Statement and Inference*, pp. 525 ff., and 560.

[4] Even in the passage from classical physics to quantum mechanics the hypothetical form of thought has to undergo a measure of modification—cf. von Weizsäcker, *The World View of Physics*, pp. 100 f., and 200.

we freely assume in mathematical argument, and the truth about the other does not become evident to us through experimental manipulation or compulsory conclusions, and yet scientific clarification of our knowledge requires it to be set out in an orderly form in which the processes of thought are laid bare and can be verified in terms of the object.

Now when we come to theological thinking this is peculiarly difficult—to translate the indicative mode of speech into the problematic where it can be formally tested and verified. The difficulty here is not so much in bringing the processes of our rational thinking into conformity with the nature of the object, as the setting out of our theological thinking in such a way that it represents our probing into the nature of the Truth and yet faithfully reflects its nature in the form of our statements and especially in their inter-connections. The difficulty is that in setting out our theological thinking in this way we are tempted to replace the kind of connection truths have in their Object, Jesus Christ, with another kind of connection, i.e. a dialectical or logical connection. Therefore in order to set out our theological thinking in a coherent sequence that faithfully reflects the nature and the pattern of the Truth itself, we have to re-live encounter with the Object, allowing ourselves to be re-addressed by Him, re-thinking His Word to us, and responding to His action upon us, and at the same time translate that into our statements in such a way that their necessity does not lie in themselves but in the Object, and their inter-connection reflects the order or action of the Object. Therefore in theology the problematic form does not necessarily, perhaps only rarely, represent the actual way in which conviction arises.

We can see this problematic form, operating in various ways, in the pages of the New Testament in the original protocol statements as they are co-ordinated to the Word and Action of Christ—'Ought not Christ to have suffered these things?';[1] 'that it might be fulfilled';[2] 'it behoved him to be made like unto his brethren';[3] 'if Christ be not risen, ye are yet in your sins',[4] etc. In such statements the New Testament witnesses are both reporting and thinking inside the inner movement of

[1] Luke 4. 26   [2] Matt. 1. 22, 2. 15 etc.
[3] Heb. 2. 17.   [4] I Cor. 15. 14.

the Truth, yielding their thought, and therefore their speech, to its inner compulsion or election, for it is only through penetrating into the coherent structure or pattern of the Truth in that way that they are able faithfully to translate what they hear and understand, and genuinely to report.[1] Scientific theological thinking is not simply kerygmatic, but thinking that probes deeply into the intellectual processes formulating knowledge of God in Christ, tracing out the order reflected in the given reality and so allowing it to shine through, i.e. *the logic of Grace.* This refers not only to the condescension in which God has humbled Himself to enter within our existence, to adapt Himself to us and our forms of thought and speech (which for that very reason we must learn to respect), but to the whole motion of Grace in the overflowing of the divine Love upon men in Jesus Christ and to His own inner compulsion in saving purpose, i.e., to His election. Authentic theological thinking must carry its inquiry into the very heart of that purpose (πρόθεσις) and from that centre think out the 'had to' of Grace.[2]

It is very easy to do this in a wrong way, by breaking off our conversation with God, or conducting it, as it were, behind His back, as if He were not actually party to it. This would mean the transmutation of dialogical theology into dialectical theology, that is, to be more concerned with working out a system of ideas or thinking out a series of theoretical problems, than with real communion with the living God. What happens is that theological speech is abstracted from the idiom of its proper object, and becomes incomplete and therefore 'problematical' (in the other sense of the term) because it is estranged from its rooting in reality and so from its ultimate meaning. Then a new meaning has to be found on the ideological level. This is often achieved through examining the functions which the various terms and statements come to assume within a

[1] Failure to see this makes the usual form-critical analysis of the Gospel material appear superficial. Contrast in this respect the argumentation of Hoskyns and Davey in *The Riddle of the New Testament*, e.g. p. 158 f.

[2] This is apparent in the kerygmatic passages of the Acts of the Apostles in which the proclamation of the 'mighty Acts' is theologically geared into the electing purposes of God and its fulfilment; cf. Acts 2, 16 f., 23 f.; 4. 28, etc. The temptation of theology is to convert this living predetermining and co-ordinating movement of election into a necessary relation through assimilating it to a logical nexus which gives rise to a deterministic predestinationism alien to the New Testament.

chosen context or system. In that event their necessity is purely logical and no reduction of them by analysis can lead to the object, for they are essentially unreal, no matter how 'true' they may be in relation to one another. Another way of finding meaning is attempted through phenomenological analysis and description of recurring features of conception and speech with the hope that they may yield fundamental motifs revealing an underlying essence through which religious experience can be interpreted in some systematic way.

In proper theological thinking, however, we have to break through the surface to the depths of intelligible reality and engage with orderly relations lodged in it that reach out far beyond our experience and understanding, that is to say, with patterns that have objective depth and which cannot be identified with the surface patterns of our formal logic or phenomenal motifs. It is only when we penetrate behind phenomena in this way that we can understand the reality of which they are phenomena and so understand the phenomena themselves. Moreover, in proper theological thinking we have to act within the boundary imposed upon us by the nature of the object, and think within its inner compulsion, for example, arguing from the inner ground of the divine act in Christ to the possibility of knowledge and reconciliation. When we set that out problematically, we not only show the steps taken in the order of knowing but show how these steps correspond to the order of being and acting in the Truth Himself. And this must be done if theology is to keep faith with its object. Scientific theology does not arise until that takes place.

Two main reasons may be offered then, why scientific theology requires this problematic form. (i) It is through this procedure that theological thinking is tested so that in every step it takes it may be able to say on what grounds or with respect to what basic presuppositions and with what consistency or coherence, it does it. That means that theological activity must be regarded as a whole in accordance with our intuitive apprehension of the whole pattern of Truth.[1] (ii) It is necessary to grasp the elements of a coherent sequence in order to perceive the shape or order of the given reality, for our

---

[1] Cf. Otto Weber, *Grundlagen der Dogmatik*, Bd. 1, p. 64.

principal clue to the reality of an object is its possession of a coherent outline.[1] Only when we can see this coherence in its dimension of depth, and only when we can bring the sequence of our thinking into line with it, can we advance to new knowledge or come to know more about what we already know.

Before we pass on we must pause to compare the two forms of inquiry we have just discussed, the interrogative and the problematic. In the interrogative form of inquiry our questions are directed ultimately toward the self-disclosure of the object and should lead to the confrontation and revealing of the Truth in its objective reality which can only be intuited. In the last resort we are cast upon the object, for what is disclosed to us of itself cannot be inferred by a chain of inferences carried forward by the progressive questioning. Or to put it the other way round, the progressive series of questions in which we engage is designed to break a way through to a point where we have to engage in an act of heuristic discernment, in a forward leap of apprehension or discovery.

The problematic form of inquiry, however, is not concerned with new knowledge so much as with clarifying what we already know or elucidating what we know by bringing out into the open its hidden implications or steps. Here we are concerned with digging out of our apprehension elements which we are unable to specify very clearly, and this we can do only by recasting our knowledge in a series of questions and answers which through its chain of implication reveals the interior logic of our knowledge and so brings out into the open unsuspected or dimly discerned forms of truth. The problematic form of inquiry seeks to order the knowledge we have already attained so that no distortion in the framework of what we know may hinder or misdirect the acquisition of further knowledge. The interrogative form of inquiry is a means of opening up the way to apprehend what is new, and therefore is not a procedure that can altogether be formally anticipated, just because it must always involve the leap forward to be obedient to the new as it is allowed to disclose itself. The

[1] Cf. Michael Polanyi, *Personal Knowledge*, chs. 1, 3, 4. Compare here what Whitehead called 'the method of imaginative rationalisation', *Process and Reality*, pp. 5 ff.

interrogative form of inquiry must always reckon with the fact that in the last analysis it cannot say just how it has come to learn the truth. In natural science this is spoken of as *discovery*, in theology this is spoken of as *revelation;* the difference between discovery and revelation being determined by the nature of the object with which each has to do.

3. *The Scientific Requirements of Theology*

Inevitably we have already had to discuss some of the specific requirements of theology as a science in order to distinguish the way in which general scientific activity takes place in theology from ways appropriate to other sciences, but we have now to examine more closely the distinctive characteristics of theological activity. Some repetition is therefore inevitable. All of these specific requirements arise directly out of respect for and devotion to this unique Object, *God in His Revelation*, or rather all are required of us from the side of the Object, as adaptations of our rationality in modes of activity congruent with it.

(a) The primary thing we have to note is the utter lordship of the Object, its absolute precedence, for that is the one all-determining presupposition of theology. Theological activity would not be scientific if it did not yield to it its rightful place. This prescribes for theology a unique form of inquiry in which we ourselves altogether and always stand in question before the Object. We know only as we are known, and we conduct our research only as we are searched through and through by God. The main point we have to single out here is that knowledge of God entails an *epistemological inversion* in the order of our knowing, corresponding to the order of the divine action in revealing Himself to us.

In all our knowing it is we who know, we observe, we examine, we inquire, but in the presence of God we are in a situation in which He knows, He observes, He examines, He inquires and in which He is 'indissoluble Subject'.[1] He is the Lord of our knowing even when it is we who know, so that our knowing is taken under command of the lordship of the Object, the

---

[1] Karl Barth, *Church Dogmatics*, I. 1, p. 438; II. 1, pp. 21 ff. See the excellent discussion of this by F. W. Camfield, *Reformation Old and New*, p. 37 ff., and James Brown, *Subject and Object in Modern Theology*, pp. 140 ff.

Creator Himself.[1] We can only follow through the determination of our knowing by the Object known who yet remains pure Subject. This relation, in which the ultimate control passes from the knower, who yet remains free, to God who is known in His knowing of us, is an important aspect of what we call *faith*. Faith entails the opening up of our subjectivity to the Subjectivity of God through His Objectivity. Faith is the relation of our minds to the Object who through His unconditional claims upon us establishes the centre of our knowing in Himself and not in us, so that the whole epistemological relation is turned round—we know in that we are known by Him.[2] His Objectivity encounters our objectivity and our objectivity is subordinated to His and grounded in His. But it is precisely in knowing us, in making us the objects of His knowledge, that He constitutes us subjects over against Him, the lordly Subject, and therefore gives us freedom to know Him even while in our knowing we are unconditionally bound to Him as the Object of our knowledge. Here our effort to subdue everything to our knowledge is halted and obstructed by God, for He is the one Object we cannot subdue. We can know Him only as we are subdued by Him, that is, as we obediently rely upon His Grace.

Now God gives Himself to us where we are in an existing subject-object relationship, where we are involved in a whole complex of ideas and conceptions and categories and analogies. But when God the Lord gives Himself to be known by us in that situation He accredits Himself to us, and far from throwing us back upon ourselves, upon our own frailty and inadequacy and incapacity, to accredit Him, He comes in Grace to draw us out of our frailty, to lift us above ourselves, and create

[1] 'When we ask about the Creator', says Karl Heim, 'we have in so doing passed beyond all possibility of human knowledge. The question could never even arise in our mind by our own evocation, it comes by the act of the Creator Himself.' *God Transcendent*, p. 195.

[2] Cf. P. T. Forsyth, *The Principle of Authority*, p. 167 f. 'In religious knowledge the object is God, it is not the world, it is not man, and that object differs from every other in being for us far more than an object of knowledge. He is the absolute Subject of it. . . . That is to say, the main thing, the unique thing, in religion is not a God whom we know but a God who knows us. Religion turns not on knowing but on being known. . . . In Religion we know what knows us back again, and not only so, but His knowledge of us is the source of our knowledge of Him.'

within us the capacity to know Him, and in this action He acts critically and creatively upon our ideas, conceptions, categories, analogies, giving them an orientation and a possibility beyond any power they have in themselves. They thus become the instruments of His Grace to reveal Himself to us and establish Himself within our knowing as the object of our knowledge. In this way there takes place in our actual knowledge of God a radical conversion of all our analogies, so that wherever we are tempted to use them as archetypal analogies they are restored to their true ectypal function in our knowing of Him. This reorientation in the subject-object relationship, and in the analogical relations that arise within it, is an indispensable scientific requirement for faithful theological thinking.

(b) A second requirement derives from respect for the *personal nature* of the Object of theological knowledge, Jesus Christ. He is at once Person and Word, who communicates Himself to us as the Word addressing us, and who communicates His Word to us in the form of His own personal Being. This means that if theological inquiry is really to break through to its Object it must get inside and operate from within a dialogical relation to the Object, or rather it must allow the Object to break through the monologue of reason with itself,[1] where it only asks questions and answers them itself, where it only asks questions requiring answers acceptable to its own presuppositions,[2] and force it into real dialogue. Therefore it must cease putting its question in such a way as to prevent the question as to the Truth from really being put to it by the Object, and only put its question in such a way as to be open to conversation with the Truth and to communication from Him. In the language of Karl Heim, this is a question that has to be put in

---

[1] This is one of the recurring themes in several of Emil Brunner's works, *God and Man*, *The Divine-Human Encounter*, etc. So long as I am simultaneously questioner and answerer I cannot know personal Truth, for I am acting in such a way as to cut myself off from the mode appropriate to knowing it.

[2] This is why the hypothetical form of thinking that obtains in the mathematical sciences is inapplicable to theology. So long as we argue in the form 'If A, then B' or 'Let us assume X = Y, then . . .', all valid thinking must take place within the bracket imposed by the hypothesis or the supposition entertained. Thus as Collingwood has pointed out, "the hypothesis forms a barrier to all further thought in that direction; . . . it (mathematics) is a way of thinking, but it is also a way of refusing to think"! *Philosophical Method*, p. 13.

the dimensional mode of the *I* and *Thou*, and yet it must be put in such a way that it lets the intramundane form of our knowing be called into question in order that it may look for an answer from beyond the frame of intramundane possibilities and intuitions. But how can such a question be put unless a transcendent *Thou* invades the form of our experience from which we cannot emancipate ourselves and turns us to Him to listen to His Word and converse with Him?[1]

As we have seen, the very putting of a proper theological question presupposes that we are already under question by the Word of God, but to the communicating and questioning of the Word we have to yield the obedient response of faith. Thus dialogical theology is essentially the theology of the Word, which operates through the conformity of thought with its object, but an Object who is God revealing Himself in His Word, encountering us as Subject, addressing us as subjects over against Him, and drawing us into free and spontaneous communion with Him. Dialogical theology of this kind carries with it certain scientific demands for its faithful fulfillment.

(i) It proceeds by constant reference to its source in the Word of God, so that the content of theological knowledge is derived from the Word. It is this derivation that becomes the criterion of its formulations, for they must constantly be brought back to the bar of the Word for criticism and creative re-interpretation.

(ii) Theological activity must not seek to step outside the dialogical relationship, for that would be to attempt to step outside its own reality, or seek for some kind of justification or vindication on alien ground, that is, on ground where as a matter of fact dialogue with the Word does not take place. Theology cannot retreat from its own ground without becoming unreal, without falsifying its terms and statements and its whole structure. Theological inquiry can be conducted only in direct encounter with the Word and in the mode of activity set up within that encounter.

(iii) Dialogical theology requires a personal medium in which it is to be continued and maintained, that is, a community of persons. Or rather, it is properly conducted in the community of persons created by the self-communication of the

[1] See *God Transcendent*, especially §§29 and 33, pp. 173 ff., and 209 ff.

Word. Here too we see where the scientific requirements of theology correspond *mutatis mutandis* with those of other sciences. Thus Professor A. D. Ritchie has written:

To form part of scientific account observations must be vouched for by somebody and available to anybody; they must be public in both these senses. All this means that the apparently simple single observation, if it is to be used, is part only of something very complex, not simple or single. There is no science at all without a society of scientifically interested and competent persons, making, checking and recording, and their instruments for doing these things.[1]

Similarly theological science posits a community in which the Word of God which has assumed personal and historical form in the Incarnation requires personal and historical communication, for the Word of God is communicated to us not only singly but to each of us in a community of people in conversation with the Word where no one can tell himself the Word but requires it to be spoken to him by another.[2] The Word of God encounters us in such a way that it creates for itself a sphere of human and personal conversation in which the Word is addressed to each and all, but in which each helps the other both in hearing and in speaking it. It is thus that dialogical theology has its essential place in the Church as the sphere of a two-fold conversation between God and His people and between the different members of the Church in the presence of the Word Himself. Perhaps the truest example of dialogical theology of this kind is to be found in the catechetical theology of the Reformation pursued within the worshipping community gathered to listen to the Word of God.[3]

(c) A third scientific requirement for theological activity derives from the nature of the *objectivity* of the Object. Dialogical theology arises in a community of conversation created by the Word, but that conversation takes place on earth, in the midst of the earthly objectivities. When He does that God is not intruding into the world, for it is His world that He has made to reflect His divine glory and to be the sphere within which He reveals Himself to man and shares with man His own divine life and glory. It is then, within our creaturely existence that God has

[1] A. D. Ritchie, *Studies in the History and Methods of the Sciences*, 1958, p. 20.
[2] Cf. *The School of Faith*, 1959, pp. xxx ff.
[3] Op. cit. pp. xxi ff.,

condescended to objectify Himself for us. Just where our objectivity encounters His divine Objectivity and His divine Objectivity encounters our human objectivity He has made His divine Objectivity overlap with ours, assuming our objectivity into union with His own, and within that overlap created by His Grace, He stands before us in Jesus Christ. In Him God meets us as on our own plane and as one of us in order to give Himself as the Object of our knowledge and to lift us up, as it were, on to His plane where we may converse with Him.

Here, then, the Object of theological knowledge has a two-fold objectivity, a primary objectivity which is God's giving of Himself the Lord, a secondary objectivity in which He gives Himself to us in human form within our space and time.[1] This means that dialogical theology is concerned with historical and earthly conversation with God. It is dialogue which God conducts historically and dynamically with His people, but only through the media of creaturely and earthly forms which He uses as the signs and instruments of His self-communication, as tools of His Word. It takes place within the sphere marked out by His Covenant in which He has gathered His people into communion with Himself. Now that the Covenant has been wholly fulfilled in Jesus Christ, it is in Him that the his-torical conversation continues. The time element in that we shall consider in a later chapter. What we are concerned with here is that God's Word assumes and makes use of and comes to us through creaturely objectivity so that it is in and through that creaturely objectivity alone that we meet His divine objectivity. This double objectivity distinguishes theological knowledge sharply from any other kind of knowledge (and gives rise to some of its difficult problems), but theological knowledge must act in terms of this double objectivity if it is to be scientifically faithful.[2]

[1] This distinction between God's primary and secondary objectivity is Barth's, *Church Dogmatics*, II. 1, p. 16 f.
[2] A very imperfect analogy to this may be found in psychology in which we seek to understand people in their wholeness and duality as bodies and minds, that is in their double objectivity as subjects and organs of behaviour. Cf. also the dual nature of the 'objects' of quantum physics, and the two-fold character of statements involved in describing a nuclear experiment, statements still grounded in classical physics, and statements in quantum physics.

We may note three important implications from this double objectivity.

(i) The object of theological knowledge is creaturely objectivity bound to divine objectivity, not just creaturely objectivity in general but that specific creaturely objectivity which the divine objectivity has assumed, adapted and bound to Himself, Jesus. Thus theological activity is concerned with that special creaturely objectivity *in its relation* to divine objectivity, and therefore with that creaturely objectivity as it is given ultimate objectivity over against all other objectivity within the created universe. We shall see how this distinguishes theological science from other sciences.

(ii) In the nature of the case we cannot break through to ultimate objectivity, to the sheer reality of God, simply by an examination of this creaturely objectivity, for of itself it can only yield knowledge of the empirical world of nature.

(iii) Nevertheless we are bound unconditionally to the creaturely objectivity of God in the Incarnation of His Word in Jesus Christ. What scandalizes rationalist man is that in his search for ultimate objectivity he is bound unconditionally to contingent and creaturely objectivity, in fact to the weakness of the historical Jesus.[1] To try to get behind this creaturely objectivity, to go behind the back of the historical Jesus in whom God has forever given Himself as the Object of our knowledge, and so to seek to deal directly with ultimate and bare divine objectivity, is not only scientifically false, but the *hybris* of man who seeks to establish himself by getting a footing in ultimate reality. Scientific theology can only take the humble road in unconditional obedience to the Object as He has given Himself to be known within our creaturely and earthly and historical existence, in the Lord Jesus Christ.

(d) A fourth scientific requirement for theology arises from the *centrality* of Jesus Christ as the self-objectification of God for us in our humanity, that is, from the supremacy of Christology

[1] On the other hand as D. M. MacKinnon (op. cit. p. 269) reminds us, the Incarnation has 'radicalised and transformed the notion of the contingent'. 'The sheer contingency of Christ provides a new sort of use for the logical ontological notion, a new standard for its employment, for in the Incarnation there is contingency so sheer and unequivocal that inevitably at all levels we shrink from it, preferring 'necessary absolutes,' whether abstract values, or institutions, or even spiritual experiences.'

in our knowledge of God. All scientific knowledge has a systematic interest, for it must attempt to order the material content of its knowledge as far as possible into a coherent whole. It would be unscientific, however, to systematize knowledge in any field according to an alien principle, for the nature of the truth involved must be allowed to prescribe how knowledge of it shall be ordered. In other words, the systematic interest must be the servant of objective knowledge and never allowed to become its master. The order is in the Object before it is in our minds, and therefore it is as we allow the Object to impose itself upon our minds that our knowledge of it gains coherence. In theological knowledge the Object is God in Christ whom we know as we allow Him to impose Himself upon our minds or as we allow His Word to shape our knowing in conformity to Him. Scientific theology is therefore the systematic presentation of its knowledge through consistent faithfulness to the divine, creaturely objectivity of God in Christ.

It is the centrality of Christ that is all-determinative here, for He is the norm and criterion of our knowing and it is out of correspondence to Him that theological coherence grows. Scientific theology is systematic, therefore, only through relation to Christ, but its relation to Christ cannot be abstracted and turned into an independent systematic principle by means of which we can force the whole of theology into one definite and fixed pattern. Some use of formal Christology is necessary in systematic theology for the way that the Word of God has taken in the Incarnation, life, death, and resurrection of Christ is the way in which God has revealed Himself to us and the way in which He continues to do so, but we cannot abstract it from direct dialogical encounter with God in Christ for it is only through sharing in the knowledge of the Son by the Father and the knowledge of the Father by the Son, that we can know God as He has given Himself to us in Jesus Christ.

Thus the organic unity of theology goes back in Christ to the unity of the Godhead, but in the nature of the case theology cannot, and must not try to seek knowledge of God apart from His whole objectivity, divine and human, in Jesus Christ. Therefore the modes and forms of our theological knowledge must exhibit an inner structural coherence reflecting the nature of Christ. Moreover, it is because mystery belongs to the nature of Christ as God and Man in one Person that it would be unfaithful of us not to respect that mystery in our knowing of Him and therefore in our systematic presentation of our knowledge. It is upon this fact that every attempt to reduce knowledge of God to a logical system of ideas must always suffer shipwreck.

(e) The kind of demonstration. which a scientific theology requires is one in strict accord with the nature of its Object. We need not say much about this here as we shall have to handle it more fully in the next chapter, but this much must be said right away. Theology cannot demonstrate its reality in any way except a theological way, for only a unique demonstration is scientifically permissible in accordance with the unique nature of the Object. It is the Object that must prescribe the mode of activity of the reason directed toward it. Hence what is expected of theology is that it should exhibit the kind of rationality which corresponds with the Object of its thought and therein reveal the appropriate demonstration.[1] In the nature of the case, the divine Object requires a divine demonstration, that is, the demonstration of the Spirit (ἀπόδειξις τοῦ πνεύματος) as St. Paul called it,[2] for it is only in that way that the demonstration can be controlled throughout by the divine Object.

But the Object has earthly, human, and historical objectivity and therefore theological statements sharing that kind of objectivity, which they invariably do, require the kind of verification appropriate to these fields. But what we are concerned with is not divine Truth and human truth, but divine–human Truth, and we are concerned with only one of its kind—deus non est in genere. This confronts us, therefore, with the problem of relating the truthfulness of theological statements to divine–human Truth, and also with the problem of proof for what by its very nature is not open to verification through comparison in the same way that other scientific observations are verifiable. This does not mean that the Object of theological knowledge is accessible only to a few. It is accessible to all, for the Object is God Himself who makes Himself known to all in Jesus Christ, but it does mean that only

[1] Cf. F. W. Camfield, op. cit. p. 38 f.   [2] I Cor. 2. 4.

those who take the way in which God reveals Himself in the contingent particularity and sheer singularity of Jesus Christ may know Him and bring themselves within the area where the Object provides His own demonstration of His reality and authenticates Himself to men. 'He that hath ears to hear, let him hear.'[1]

[1] Matt. 11. 15.

4

The Nature of Truth

What is truth? In early Greek thought, before Socrates, truth seems to have been regarded as the unveiling of what is hidden, the disclosure of being, or the manifestation of the reality of things that are. But when thinking became more dialectical the emphasis changed and truth was more closely associated with the intellect since it is only through the mind that we contemplate the reality of things and discern truth and falsity. In Hebraic thought truth seems to have been understood in relation to God as the source and standard of all truth, for He is Himself the Truth. There is no darkness or deception in God. He is toward men what He is in Himself. He keeps truth for ever. The Truth of God is His steadfastness and consistency, His reliability in being and action, but it is Truth that presses upon us for acknowledgement and for responsible activity on our part that we may keep faith and truth with God and with one another. In the Christian tradition Greek and Hebraic strands were woven together in the understanding of Truth as Personal Being revealed to us in Jesus Christ, for in Him God is known to be in Himself what He is in His Word and Grace toward us, while the Spirit of Truth is understood as the presence of God to us in His own Being who enlightens us and leads us into all truth. It is through this relation to God that the onto-logical and intellectual aspects of truth, the truth of being and the truth of understanding, are held inherently together.

In theological formulation as it developed in Augustinian and Anselmic thought, truth came to be defined as that which shows that which is, for the truth of a thing is that it is what it is and not something else, and so the truth reveals the being of each thing.[1] To this truth of being there corresponds a truth or necessity in knowing, namely, the impossibility of conceiving of something as being other than it is, for behind all truth of being and knowing there stands the Supreme Truth of God who is immutably what He is. Truth as we know it consists in the conformity of things to their reason in the eternal Word of God, so that the truth of every created thing is evident only in the light of God Himself. Truth, then, is the reality of things as they necessarily are, and as they ought to be known and expressed by us. This is what Anselm called *rectitudo*, the relation in which a thing *is right* and *is as it ought to be*.

Now because the Truth of God is apprehended by the mind we are tempted constantly to take a purely intellectual view of truth, and when we do it affects the whole of our theology. This is something that one can trace through patristic, medieval, Reformation and modern thought, although it takes on a different form and comes to expression in rather different idiom in different times. St. Thomas Aquinas, for example, for all his undoubted realism, appears ultimately to take an intellectual view of truth, for even when the notion of ontological truth is broached it is traced back to the divine *mind* as the *prima Veritas*. There can be all the world of difference between *veritas* as the *adaequatio rei et intellectus* and *veritas* as the *adaequatio intellectus ad rem ad extra*, or to put it otherwise, between the *veritas propositionis* and a *vera propositio*. If we make use of a three-fold way of looking at truth as *veritas essentiae rerum*, *veritas significationis*, and *veritas compositionis*, advanced by some medieval thinkers, we may say that there was a persistent tendency to pass from the truth of being to the truth of signification and then to the truth of composition. The problem posed here is whether truth is primarily concerned with the reference of statements to the reality of things beyond them, or whether it is concerned rather with the logico-syntactical relations of statements to one another and therefore to be discerned in ideological complexes. A double error appears to lurk here: (a) the reduction of truth to ideas, which rests on the mistaken notion that we can express in ideas how ideas

[1] See especially Augustine, *Soliloquia*, II. 5.8, *De vera religione*, 36, 66, and Anselm, *De veritate*, 2, 7, 10. Behind this lies a Christian development of Aristotle's teaching, *Metaphysica*, Γ 7, 1011 b 25; *De interpretatione*, 18b; but cf. *Metaphysica* E4, 1027 b 25.

are related to being; (b) the reduction of truth to statements, which rests on the mistaken notion that we can state in statements how statements are related to what is stated.[1] The one implies the 'conversion' of universals into abstract entities, and the other implies that in the last resort science is about propositions. This represents a mutation from intuitive knowledge of the real to abstractive knowledge either of the ideal or the symbolic, and in both instances a lapse from the truth of being.

So far as theology is concerned, fuller place must be given to the truth in the form of personal Being. This is Truth which has taken the form of active life and being in our historical existence and is revealed in Jesus Christ. He has come not only to communicate the Truth to men but to be the Truth amongst us, for in the whole course of His human life He was the Being and Word of God's Truth incarnated in our creaturely being, the Truth enacted in the midst of our untruth, the Truth fulfilled from within man and from the side of man and issuing out of human life in faithful and obedient response to the Truth of the Father. As such He is the source and standard of truth, the one Truth of God for all men. In Him God turns in Grace toward us and makes Himself open to us, summoning us to be open toward Him and to keep faith and truth with Him in Jesus, so that we may be true as God is true, and learn to do the truth as He does the truth.

It is in this Man that we come up against God's own personal Being in which He bears directly upon us with the presence and impact of ultimate Truth. We know Him truly as we know under the compulsion of His divine Being, that is, of His being what He is and by His nature must be, and under the light of His Truth which is His divine Being coming to view and becoming in our understanding and knowledge of Him what He is consistently in Himself and in all His relations with us. This is Truth which we can meet and know in our concrete existence through personal encounter and rational cognition, yet Truth who retains His own Majesty and Authority, Truth who so bears witness to Himself through His Spirit that we may

---

[1] That is to say, as A. E. Taylor would have expressed it, there was a failure to see that actual thought necessarily involves an aspect of discrepancy between its content and reference, 'for thought, to remain thought, must always be something less than the whole reality which it knows.' *Elements of Metaphysics*, p. 410 f.

testify to Him and reiterate His witness, Truth who makes Himself the object of our statements and the truth of their reference, and yet who transcends all our speaking of Him.

There is no way to demonstrate this Truth outside of the Truth; the only way for the ultimate Truth to prove Himself is to be the Truth, and the only way for us to prove the ultimate Truth is to let Him be what He is before us, in His αὐτουσία and αὐτεξουσία. That is the majesty and prerogative of the Truth of God as it is in Jesus, Truth who is ultimate in identity with the Being and Act of God, Truth who is and cannot be established by us, Truth who will not be mastered and yet will not remain closed to us, Truth who unveils Himself for us and who is known only through Word and Grace on God's part and faith and thankfulness on our part. It is He who says 'I am the way, the truth and the life; no man cometh to the Father but by me.'[1]

Hence a faithful theological inquiry operates with concrete positive reference to Jesus, for it is in Him that we are put in the right with the Truth, and in Him that the Reality of God becomes truth for us and therefore in Him that we are released from ourselves and become free for God. All our questions as to the Truth of God have to follow the way which Jesus took and which He has forever laid down in the course of His life and death and resurrection for our sake, and all our statements about the Truth will have validity or truthfulness only through their derivation from and correspondence to Him as their source and norm, that is, through the Grace of His justification and reconciliation.

On this ground and in this light we have now to consider principally two things, the nature of the Truth of God with its ultimate authority and ultimate objectivity (which we seek to do in this first section), and our statements concerning it with their authority and truthfulness (which we will attempt in the second section). To set the field for that discussion we may note the relevant problems right away.

(a) Because theology is occupied here with the highest Authority or with ultimate Objectivity, that is, with an ultimate term of reference, it has a corresponding conception of Truth,

[1] John 14. 6.

Truth that is not provisional or relative, but final and ultimate.

(b) Our statements of this Truth, however, are not ultimate or final, precisely because they refer away from themselves and beyond to the ultimate Truth. The statements belong to our world of contingency and relativity, and therefore we cannot claim for them ultimate or final validity. Nevertheless they have their truthfulness by reference to the ultimate Truth, and they are true so far as that reference is appropriate. To keep faith with that Truth they have to be absolutely related to it, but because it is the absolute Truth to which they are related, they are relative only to that truth and are relativized by it. On the other hand, because they belong as human statements to this world of contingency and relativity they are to be related also to relative truth within this world. However, it is only because they are to be absolutely related to the absolute Truth that they may be related to relative truth only relatively. Falsity would thus arise through their relative relation to the absolute Truth or their absolute relation to the relative.[1]

(c) There is still a basic problem to be faced. Because our theological statements are on this side of ultimate Truth and belong to the world of relativity, is there not an unbridgeable gulf between them and the ultimate Truth to which they claim to refer?[2] By claiming to refer to the ultimate Truth are they not thereby positing a discrepancy between themselves as statements and the ultimate Truth, which if taken seriously, as is intended, would actually mean the end of all theology? How can this-worldly or intra-mundane statements actually refer to what is utterly beyond them? The difficulty about that question, of course, is that it is asked in abstraction from our actual knowledge and runs into contradictions. The question cannot be answered, therefore, in that form, but there is a problem here that is not to be avoided. What our actual knowledge does tell us is that ultimate Truth meets us on this side of that chasm within our mundane experience, where it is accessible to us and amenable to our statements. Therefore we have to think theological Truth, and think it out from its

---

[1] Cf. Kierkegaard, *Concluding Unscientific Postscript*, pp. 364 ff., and *Fear and Trembling*, p. 75 ff.

[2] Cf. H. D. Lewis' judicious discussion of this in *Philosophy of Religion*, on 'The limits and lessons of empiricism.'

own real centre on this side where it has established itself. It is impossible for us on our own to find a way of thinking the infinite in conjunction with the finite for we cannot bring that conjunction about. The question as to the truthfulness of our statements cannot be answered, therefore, in abstraction from the Truth and its activity toward us, for everything depends upon the nature and activity of the Truth itself and not simply upon how it is conceived in our thinking. Knowledge of it can be verified only on its own ground.

We have now to consider more specifically the nature of this Truth as it is in Jesus, as the Truth of God which we are summoned to revere and adore in His infinite transcendence over all our experience of Him and as the Truth who meets us in the midst of our human existence asking of us our inquiry and our response.

(a) We begin with the majestic claim of Jesus, 'I am the Truth'. He is the Truth in the form of His Personal and Lordly Being. But these words 'I am the Truth' are a statement, and as such are a communication of the Truth, part of Christ's self-communication. It is not something that He is communicating in these words, but Himself in and through them. This is not just someone speaking about the Truth, but the Truth uttering Himself in human words. In Him, we encounter the Truth of God, but the Truth as a Person. He is not Word because we understand Him, or in so far as we interpret Him, but He is Word in His own right, in His own nature, Word in so far as He is Person and Person in so far as He is Word. As such He is the Truth.

Calvin used to express this by saying that Christ was *clothed with His promises* or *clothed with His Gospel*.[1] By that he meant that Christ does not come to us apart from His own self-revelation in Word and Deed, apart from His promises of salvation which He fulfilled in His life and death. He cannot be separated from all that, and therefore we cannot know Him 'naked', as it were, without His 'clothing'. The only Christ we know is the Christ who is what He is in His teaching and healing, in His Life and Death and Resurrection. He encounters us as One whose Word and Act belong to the constitution of His Person.

---

[1] *Institute*, 2. 9. 3. See a discussion of this by Hans-Joachim Iwand in *Antwort. Karl Barth zum siebzigsten Geburtstag am 10. Mai, 1956*, p. 183 f.

Now admittedly this is difficult for us to grasp, not to say to describe, for we have to stretch our thought and speech here beyond anything we are cognisant of elsewhere. We only know persons whose words are in addition to what they are and whose words in themselves are impersonal acts separate and distinct from their persons.[1] With God this is not so. His Word is His Person in communication, for in His speaking He Himself is personally present communicating Himself. That is the Word of God who became flesh in Jesus Christ in whose self-communication God communicates Himself in Person and confronts us with His Person as Word. He is not less personal because He is in Person identical with His Word, and His Word is not less Word because He is in Word identical with His Person. On the contrary, His Word is truly and properly Word and His Person is truly and properly Person in this identification. In the strict sense, as Barth has said, it is God who is properly and really Person, not we, for He only is Person in His own right.[2] We are persons only through derivation from Him and dependence upon Him, persons in a very real but a secondary sense. He alone is personalizing Person, and it is ultimately from His Word that all that is truly personal among us derives. We cannot understand His unique Person by explaining it from our persons, but only through the fact that His Person explains ours.

This identity of Word and Person, then, is a primary characteristic of the Truth of God as it is in Jesus. It belongs to the nature of this Truth to be at once Person and Message, to be personal Being and yet communicable Truth. If it were only a communicated truth we would be thrown back upon ourselves to authenticate it, but if it were only a Person we would be thrown back upon ourselves to interpret Him.[3] But because He is Person and Message in One, He is the Truth who both authenticates and interprets Himself. He is the Truth truthfully communicating Himself, and enabling us truthfully to receive Him. He is the Truth communicating Himself in and through truths, who does not communicate Himself apart from truths, and who does not communicate truths apart from Himself. It is a communication of truths, but of truths that

[1] But cf. G. Gusdorf, *La Parole*, 1953, for the relation of word to personal existence in this world.
[2] *Church Dogmatics*, II. 1, p. 272.
[3] See F. W. Camfield, *The Collapse of Doubt*, p. 52 f.

cohere in the one unique Person of the Incarnate Word of God, and it is a personal encounter in life and being with Christ, but not in abstraction from a Message. It is personal Truth that not only comes to us in the form of Word, and therefore in and through words, but has Word in its very content.

In other language, this is Truth that is both personal and propositional, but uniquely personal and uniquely propositional in the unique nature of Christ. As Person and Message in one this Truth communicates and interprets Himself; He accredits Himself to us and draws us out of our autonomous efforts to penetrate into the Truth and establish it, by confronting us with Himself as the Truth and establishing us in relation to Himself as the Truth. Reception and understanding of this Truth, participation in and interpretation of it on our part, must be analogous to this two-fold nature of the Truth. The Message is not received except in personal relation to the Truth, and personal communion with the Truth does not take place apart from the reception of the Message. Therefore our theological statements have a truthful reference to this Truth when that reference is at once personal and propositional, that is, dialogical.

(b) 'I am the truth.' He who spoke these words is acknowledged and worshipped as God and Man. The Truth which He is, is both divine and human. The Word which He communicates is Word of God and Word of Man. These words were spoken with a human voice, but the speaker was the incarnate Son or *Logos* of God who discloses and imparts Himself in and through them. While our words are distinct and separate from our persons, His words have an essential relation to His Person, and, to use a technical theological term, partake of the hypostatic relation between His humanity and His deity. In and through His words He the *Logos*, the Word of God, is hypostatically present to men. Moreover, in the Hebrew idiom, His human utterance within our historical existence is an event that corresponds faithfully to the Word uttered, and is to be credited as Truth, but here the correspondence in the human event is to the divine Word, and the Truth credited and acknowledged is divine Truth actualizing itself in our humanity and communicating itself through human speech. On the other hand the human speech (λαλιά) does not cease to be human when used in this way, for if it had only the appearance of human speech it would not be a real correspondence in the human to the reality of the divine Word (λόγος)—it would not be truth.[1]

Here we are faced with another fundamental characteristic of the Truth of God as it is in Jesus; it is both divine and human. Knowledge of it, accordingly, is essentially bi-polar. This bi-polarity corresponds to the two-fold objectivity of the Word we have already noted. Knowledge of *God* is given to us in this *Man*, Jesus, but that knowledge does not allow us to leave the *Man* Jesus behind when we know Him in His divine nature. There is an indivisible unity in the ultimate Fact of Christ, true God and true Man. Theological knowledge rests upon and partakes of that duality-in-unity in the Person of Christ. In Him we know God in terms of what God is not, namely, man, for in Christ God, who is God and not man, has become Man and comes as Man, but in such a way that what God is in Christ He is antecedently and eternally in Himself. We know God is indissoluble unity with Jesus as we encounter Him through the witness of men, and we know Jesus in His human and historical actuality in indissoluble unity with God.

Such knowledge we may describe as *sacramental*, for it is knowledge in which visible and invisible, audible and inaudible, earthly and heavenly, the human and the divine, are held together in the unity of the self-communication of the Truth of God to us and of our communion with that Truth. To use other New Testament language, the Truth is communicated to us in the form of mystery (μυστήριον), that is, in the form of a concrete fact or particular event to which nevertheless the Truth is infinitely transcendent. It is the revelation of Truth so full and rich and inexhaustible that the more we know of it the more we realize the ineffable and infinite fulness of its reality which defies complete disclosure within the limits of our experience.[2] On the other hand, this is not arbitrary mystery,

[1] Cf. here the relation between the *lalia* and the *logos* of Jesus, John 8.43, *Theology in Reconstruction*, p. 141.

[2] As A. E. Taylor expressed it, mystery is a direct consequence of the individuality of the real which when given to our knowledge cannot be reduced to our 'constructions' of it, *The Faith of a Moralist*, vol. 1. 2, pp. 211 ff. See also the healthy treatment given to the notion of 'mystery' by H. D. Lewis, *Our Experience of God*, p. 38 f., and *Philosophy of Religion*, pp. 141 ff.

for while it reaches out indefinitely beyond our apprehension it throws an increasing light upon ever wider areas of our experience. 'Mystery' of this kind expresses the objective depth of rationality. Thus from the point of view of our experience of the Truth, mystery means that our knowledge contains far more than we can ever specify or reduce to clear-cut, that is, delimited, notions or conceptions, and is concerned with a fullness of meaning which by its very nature resists and eludes all attempts to reduce it without remainder, as it were, to what we can formulate or systematize. Or, to put it otherwise, mystery means that behind the objectivities in which the Truth discloses itself to us there is an infinite depth of reality calling for our recognition and reverence, openness of mind and wonder toward it. There is an ultimate objectivity which cannot be inclosed within the creaturely objectivities through which we encounter it, but the creaturely objectivities have their meaning through this relation in depth to that objectivity that indefinitely transcends them.

In the full sense Jesus Christ is Himself the Sacrament (μυστήριον, sacramentum) for it is in Him that the One Truth of God comes to us in creaturely form and existence, so that in the objectivity of His particular and historical humanity we encounter the eternal objectivity of God Himself. The Word made flesh is the concrete embodiment of the Truth, and is the source and basis and norm of all God's revelation of Himself, so that relation to Him constitutes the sacramental area where human knowledge of God may actually and truthfully correspond to God's revelation of Himself. It is in Jesus that God's Word has so communicated Himself to us in our humanity that human words are taken to speak for God, and therefore it is in Jesus also that our human words may rightly and properly speak of God. Thus theological knowledge and theological statements participate sacramentally in the mystery of Christ as the Truth to whom they refer and upon which they rely for their reality. They must derive from, and be grounded in, the human nature and existence of Jesus, for it is in Him that the Word has become flesh and the Truth is embodied in our humanity.

It is this two-fold nature of theological truth that lays it wide open to misinterpretation by those who will only examine the human speech (λαλιά) without listening for the divine

Word (λόγος). We may see an imperfect analogy to that in a
telephone conversation. Part of it is open to our hearing and
examination; the part of it at the other end of the line is not
open to public hearing and listening, but only the private
hearing of the man in touch with it. It is of course open to
everyone to enter into that private hearing if he listens to the
voice at the other end of the line in the way in which it comes
over, by putting his ear to the telephone. Hence the knowledge
mediated is open to universal recognition. In theology we are
concerned with a conversation between man and God which
involves the bi-polarity of *lalia* and *logos*, the speech at this end
and the Word at the other end. The *lalia* is the aspect of it
which is open to general acknowledgement and investigation,
and as a historical happening partaking of natural events, it
requires an investigation corresponding to its nature. Therefore
we must direct to the *lalia* our historico-critical questions for its
elucidation. But the *lalia* does not stand alone, for it is bound
up with the *logos* that stands behind it. Thus in and through
the *lalia* we apprehend a rationality that transcends that of
the mere speech, so that we can only apprehend the *lalia*
properly by listening through it and beyond it, and do not stop
short at it. We allow the *lalia* to direct us beyond itself or
rather allow the *logos* to reach us through the *lalia*. Unless we
hear that divine Voice from the other end of the line, as it were,
unless we are carried through into the objective depth behind
the *lalia*, genuine theology does not arise. Genuine theology
arises when we meet with *divine revelation* in the midst of the
objectivities of this world, and so see the objectivities of this
world in accordance with the infinite scope of the divine
objectivity that reaches out above and behind them.

Bi-polarity of this kind is particularly baffling to those who
have acquired uniform habits of observation in accordance with
determinate natural objects. While the object of knowledge
is accessible to sensory-empirical investigation in proportion
as it overlaps with natural objects, in proportion as it transcends
them it is beyond the reach of exploration by merely experimental devices. Indeed it is that two-fold nature of the Truth
that constitutes a great difficulty for the theologian, for he
must acquire habits of discernment and interpretation appropriate to the two-fold nature of the Truth. But his knowledge
is scientifically faithful only as it is in strict accord with the

two-fold nature of the Object, and his theological statements are truthful only through participation in the double reference required of them from the side of the Truth.

(c) 'I am the truth.' The speaking of these words was reported as a historical happening, but He who spoke them and still speaks them is the eternal Son of God.[1] 'In the beginning was the Word, and the Word was with God and the Word was God. . . . And the Word became flesh and dwelt among us, full of grace and truth.'[2] This Truth is both eternal and historical, Truth who is not timeless, for He so participates in time-relations and assumes time into Himself that time is an inalienable element in His nature as Incarnate Truth. Far from the historical being but the outward symbolic draping of the Truth, it belongs to His very substance. And yet Jesus is not simply historical as other men or events are historical, for He is the Eternal become historical and is historical only as He remains the Eternal. He is really historical because in Him time is redeemed of its decaying and illusory tendencies and made fully and permanently real, resisting corruption and vanity. Therefore this Truth remains and continues as real historical happening throughout history, which, just because it is real, moves against the stream of all that decays and crumbles away into the dust of the past, or vanishes into unreality.[3] He is not dead, but living Truth.

How is this Truth known? It is not known timelessly as the necessary truths of reason are known, nor is it known only historically as other historical events are known, but known according to its two-fold nature as eternal and historical, as the movement of the eternal in time, a movement that takes our time seriously, and has for ever taken it up, sanctified and healed, into union with itself. There is, therefore, a two-fold movement here, the movement of the Eternal becoming temporal, without ceasing to be Eternal, and the movement of the temporal in inseparable union with the Eternal without ceasing

[1] Those who hesitate to agree that the speaking of these words was a historical happening, can substitute, for the purposes of the argument, the words of Jesus "Follow me" which are their Synoptic counterpart.

[2] John 1. 1, 14.

[3] See the article by E. Brunner on 'The Christian Understanding of Time' in the *Scottish Journal of Theology*, vol. 4., pp. 1–12; the long discussion by Karl Barth in *Church Dogmatics*, III. 2, Section 47. 1, 'Jesus the Lord of Time'; and *Royal Priesthood*, Ch. 3, pp. 43 ff.

to be temporal. Knowledge of this Truth must be analogous to that two-fold involution of movement in the Truth. To behave in terms of it the reason of man must act or move, not just sit back and think in repose, and actually participate in the movement it seeks to know.

Our traditional mode of thinking is confronted here with a very difficult problem, for when we think movement we inevitably abstract the relation involved in actual transition and transpose it into a still, formal relation, that is into a logical relation, and so really fail to think movement after all. This problem seems to have been raised first by Trendelenburg in his critique of Kant and Hegel in which he sought to give movement (κίνησις) a fundamental place in the derivation of the categories as the vehicle or mediating activity of all thinking in space and time.[1] According to Kierkegaard's estimation of Trendelenburg, 'his merit consists among other things in having apprehended movement as the inexplicable presupposition and common factor of thinking and being and as their continued reciprocity'.[2] But it was Kierkegaard himself who carried this thinking further in seeking to go beyond logical connections and to develop a mode of thought adequate and appropriate to real movement or transition, that is, a mode of thinking that is itself a free movement inseparable from real becoming.[3] This called for serious attention to objective movement in the object of knowledge and to subjective movement in the subject, but it also meant a refusal to isolate pure thinking from the whole activity of the empirical subject, particularly from his acts of *will*. Thinking of this kind takes place in the medium of the historical and involves *decision*. This is the element that has no place in traditional logic, for logic is concerned only with *is*, not with *becoming*. So long as we remain within the limits of logical connection we make the serious blunder of converting becoming into necessity. Real thinking, thinking that moves from the known to the unknown, thinking that involves transition, moves across a 'breach' in the processes of logic in order to act in accordance with objective

---

[1] See *Logische Untersuchungen*, especially Chs. iv-vii, and *Geschichte der Kategorienlehre*.

[2] S. Kierkegaard, *Unscientific Postscript*, p. 150; cf. *The Journals of S. Kierkegaard* (selected, edited and translated by Alexander Dru), 1938.

[3] See especially *Philosophical Fragments*, pp. 59 ff.; and *Unscientific Postscript* pp. 86 ff.; 99 ff.; 267 ff.; 306 f.

movement in the object of its knowledge.[1] This is what Kierkegaard characteristically called the *leap* and when he had theology in mind, *the leap of faith*.[2] By this Kierkegaard did not mean at all a leap in the dark, an irrational act, as is often supposed, but on the contrary, the activity of the *reason* in obedient reaction to the action of the Truth, an activity analogous to the Truth in time, or to the Truth in action.

The significance of this can be brought out by comparing it to the achievement of Einstein who made such an immense advance through abandoning the conception of space and time reached from a point of absolute rest, an achievement which has lent a new dynamism to the whole of modern science. That was Kierkegaard's achievement roughly a century earlier in the realm of philosophy and theology. But in so doing he was deliberately wrestling with the fact that knowledge of Jesus Christ as Eternal Truth in the form of historical being involves a modification in our theory of knowledge, in fact a change in the logical structure of our consciousness.

We cannot enter further into that here, but must note carefully that eternal Truth encounters us also as *temporal fact*, requiring of us in our knowing relationship to it in time. This time-element, or movement, cannot be eliminated from our knowledge without falsification. Theological statements require to be related to the Truth in time if they are to be truthful, but they require to be continuously upheld in that temporal relationship through living participation in the movement of the Truth, if they are to remain true. Real theological thinking is thus alive and on the move under the control of the Truth that makes it free from imprisonment in timeless logical connections. At no point can a genuine theology allow this temporal relation to be confounded with logical relation, for if it cannot despise the latter, as indeed it cannot, it cannot exist without the former. Theological thinking is historical thinking; it is more than that, not by leaving the historical behind, but through participation in the eternal which has entered into the historical and gathered it into inalienable relation to the Truth in Jesus Christ.

(d) 'I am the way, the truth, and the life.' Our concern in this chapter has led us to concentrate upon the middle term

---

[1] *Philosophical Fragments*, p. 66 f.; *Unscientific Postscript*, p. 103.
[2] *Unscientific Postscript*, pp. 91 ff.; 96, 236, 306, 327, 240 ff.

in that statement of Jesus in which He claimed to be the Truth, but we would be misunderstanding Him if we did not see the relationship of 'truth' to what He called 'way' and 'life', for He is not the Truth apart from the whole course of His life and acts, in which He lived His life as one of us for our sake that in Him we may share in the Life of God, and in which He actively took our lost cause upon Himself in order to redeem us and open up a Way to communion with the Father. In the whole of His Life Jesus is the bodily presence of the Truth of God for us. This is what we mean by saying that the Truth of God in Jesus Christ is *Grace*. Grace is the turning of God toward us in His mercy and love, His self-giving to us and His action for us, whereby He establishes us in union and communion with Himself and so gives us a true place in relation to the Reality of God. As such Grace is identical with Jesus Christ. He is Grace and Truth in Himself, and therefore Grace and Truth for us.

In order to elucidate that we shall consider the relation of God's Action to His Person, as earlier we considered the relation of His Word to His Person. With us action and person are different. We are persons who act, but our acts are not personal in themselves. We have power to act, power to decide and power to fulfil the act. The latter follows from the former but it is itself impersonal, and physical. Thus we think of a person *and* his action.

I have power to will and power to do; but the power to do is, for me, a different kind of power from the power to will. With God, however, the situation is wholly other. His power is always and altogether the power of His person, the power by which He lives His own life. What He wills takes place; there is no need of the exercise of some power, different from the power of His decision, to turn the willing into doing; willing and doing are with Him identical. 'He spake and it was done, He commanded and it stood fast.' And that means that we may not think of the power of God as something which He has, to put it crudely, continually on tap, something which is wholly distinct from the power by which He lives His life as God.[1]

It is essentially in that way that we are to think of the Person and the Life of Jesus, the Son of God on earth. In Him we have the power of the Life of God in human form, but though it is

[1] F. W. Camfield, *The Collapse of Doubt*, p. 43.

translated into a fully and perfectly human life that human life is hypostatically united to the life of God. His human and divine natures are united inseparably in one Person. The miracle of the Incarnation is not simply that God has come *in* Jesus, but that in Jesus God has come *as* Man, and that the human life and action of Jesus are unique in their oneness with the life and action of God. Thus His power to act is not other than the power of His Person, the power by which He lives His own personal Life. His Action and His personal Being are inseparably one, for His power is personal in itself for in His actions the *hypostasis* of Jesus is fully present. Thus He is not known apart from His Acts, nor His Acts apart from His Person. His power is the Life which He lives as God, and His Life is His Person in Action, but as the incarnate Son, a Life *and* a History, and it is in and through the power of that Life and History that He acts upon us, as the Lord and Saviour of our life. It is in that sense that the incarnate Son says, 'I am the way, the truth, and the life, no man cometh unto the Father but by me.' He is 'the Way', the way in which He lives His Life and uses His Action, and as such is the way in which He turns to us in the overflowing of His divine Life and Love and gathers us into communion with Himself. The way in which God lives His Life toward us in Jesus, and in which He acts toward us in Him, is His Grace. Because His power is His Life, His own personal Being and Living, He makes Himself known to us and available to us, redeems and saves us by condescending to bring His own divine Life within our life and living it within our life as a human life and a human history, and yet He who lives this human life and has this human history is none other than the living and eternal God, who by joining His Life to our life has come to stand in for us, to be the Life of our life. As such He is the Way and the Truth *for us* and therefore also the *Life*. In all that He does, He is Truth for us, the living Truth, who makes Himself present and accessible to us, who meets us and gives Himself to us, and yet does not come under our control, for He does not cease to live His own divine Life. The Truth of God is He who has turned to us in the Life, Actions and Words of Jesus Christ in order to reconcile us to God and redeem us into communion with the divine Life. The Truth of God is Jesus Christ in the whole of

His Life and History, the Truth for us as the Way and the Life in and through which alone we may go to the Father.

We must now consider the relation of His Truth to the Way and the Life more concretely and relate it to our theological knowledge.

(i) The *Way*. God's Truth is His Person turning to us and condescending to become one with us that He may turn us to God in revelation and reconciliation. God does not have to do this. He is entirely free to live His own Life apart from us, but in His freedom He chooses to turn to us and give Himself to us to be known and loved. God does not have to be the object of our knowledge like the natural objects with which we are bound together inseparably in the structure of our crea- turely existence, for when we know them they have to be known. With God it is quite different.[1] It is out of pure Grace that He gives Himself to us to know and think as the Truth, so that our knowing and thinking Him presuppose and repose upon His prior decision or movement in Grace to be the object of our knowing and thinking. This communicating of the Truth in Jesus is not for God's sake, but for our sake, and is therefore the communicating of Truth as Truth adapted for us and amenable to our human thinking and speaking and communicating. And yet while the Truth as it is in Jesus is rationally communicated Truth, it is Truth that remains identical with His Personal Life and History, and therefore does not come under our manipulation or coercion or under the power of our questioning, far less under the power of our dialectical dividing and compounding. It is therefore not merely objective, but supremely Subject. It is not only given, it is self-given. He who gives Himself to us to be known does not cease for one moment to be He who gives, so that all through the giving and receiving He draws near, He propitiates Him- self, and by giving the Truth to us, reconciles us to Himself and puts us in the right with the Truth. He gives Himself to be our Truth and so to be Truth for us. This is Truth from beyond us, Truth upon which we have no claim, but Truth nevertheless which in sheer Grace gives Himself to us and establishes us in fellowship with the Ultimate Truth beyond ourselves. There- fore in all our knowledge of the Truth we have to look beyond

[1] Cf. K. Barth, *Church Dogmatics*, II. 1, p. 205 f.

ourselves, to appeal to what transcends us for justification. By entering like this into our life from beyond and sharing in it, the Truth reveals that we are not in the Truth and delivers us from the vicious circle of our own untruth, reconciling us to the Truth and putting us in the right with it beyond us. That is the movement of God's Truth as Grace, and therefore it is the Grace of God which is the ultimate secret of the truth of our knowledge of God. It is because the Truth of God is His Grace that justification by Grace alone belongs to true knowledge of God—that is to say, the verification of theological statements is to be undertaken in terms of justification by Grace alone.

(ii) The *Life*. God's Truth is His Life which He has chosen to live, not for Himself or in Himself alone, but for us, and within our human life in Jesus Christ, and so to be the very Life of our life. God's Truth is not dead Truth, but Truth that really lives and operates and gives Himself to be known through giving us to share in His Life. This is Truth that makes alive, creative Truth, quickening Spirit. To know this Truth we have to be assimilated to His quickening Life, so that in knowing the Truth we are made free, renewed, regenerated, born again, resurrected out of our 'dead truth' and 'untruth' and given to share in the living Truth of God. Because God's Truth is His Life, we cannot know the Truth without sharing in that Life, and hence without living the truth, doing the truth, without becoming true. True knowing is inseparable from true living and true living is living in the Truth of God as it is in Jesus.

Thus the communicating of the Truth and our understanding and receiving of it are accomplished through the Incarnation in which the Life of God is translated into our creaturely life and history, into our human knowing and thinking and speaking and communicating in Jesus, and so becomes the power and the content of our knowing and thinking and speaking and communicating as we through the Spirit of Christ are assimilated to His Life and History. In and through His incarnate Life and History the Truth is both communicated Truth and received Truth, spoken Truth and heard Truth, given Truth and answered Truth, Truth from the side of God but also Truth from the side of Man. Hence knowledge of the

Truth is fully communicated knowledge in which revelation and response, question and answer, are brought together and fulfilled in the Life and History of Jesus Christ, regarded not only as the Life and History of true God in the flesh, but as the Life and History of True Man in apprehending, believing, living and doing the Truth. That whole Truth is the Truth as it is in Jesus Christ who has thus become the Life of our life and the Truth of our truth. In Him the Truth is already translated into human life, uttered in human form, declared in our speech and enunciated in human statements, but inseparably from the divine-human Life and History of Jesus, for the Humanity and Life of Jesus belong to the essential content and substance of the Truth.

This is a fact of fundamental importance: in Jesus the human hearer and respondent and knower has a place in the material content of the Truth, so that the Truth with which we are concerned in theology is Truth not only as pronounced in the mouth of God but as pronounced in the mouth of Man, Truth that is already articulated and made communicable for us in human form. We do not have to incarnate the Truth; we do not have first to translate it into human audits and concepts and words, and so to fashion it in communicable human form; that has already been done for us in the human Life and History and Activity and Teaching of Jesus.[1] It is therefore in that Truth already intelligibly articulated in our human forms of activity and life, of knowing and thinking and speaking, that we participate in our knowing and thinking and speaking of the Truth and our truth-statements are made only through assimilation to and derivation from His Truth-statements.

This assimilation to and derivation from the Truth as it is in Jesus involves, as we have already noted, both justification and reconciliation. The Truth meets us in its divine-human wholeness as Truth for us, as Truth that displaces us and calls in question all our claims to truth, Truth that calls us to look for it not within what we already are or have derived from a source or starting point of our own determining, but beyond

---

[1] As MacLeod Campbell put it, 'God has already in Christ connected us in the very truth of things'. We know the truth through union with Him who is in Himself the perfect response to the truth. Hence our faith in Christ 'is subjectively the fellowship of Christ's own faith'. *The Nature of the Atonement*, pp. 146, 337, etc.

us in Jesus Christ, for it is only through reconciliation with Him and participation in Him that our knowing can be assimilated to the Truth and our statements of the Truth be themselves true or truthfully related to it.

This means that we do not only look at Jesus Christ as the Way, the Truth and the Life, but that through assimilation to Him we look *with* Him, so that *by* Him and *through* Him we are directed to the Father. Jesus is not the Way, the Truth and the Life in abstraction from the Father, but is the Way, the Truth and the Life who brings us to the *Father*. Therefore our knowing has to be assimilated to Jesus' knowing of the Father, and our thinking has to be informed by His thinking of the Father and our statements have to be conformed to His statements of the Father. Thus theological activity and theological statements derive their basic form from the life and obedience of Jesus as the incarnate Son toward the Father in heaven, from His prayer and praise, His worship, adoration, and His glorification of the Father. Theological statements as responses to the Truth as it is in Jesus are through assimilation to His Life and History given a basic doxological orientation in their reference away from ourselves to the Glory of the Father.[1] They are at their very root statements of inquiry, prayer and praise to God made in the Name of Jesus.

We conclude that this positive reference of our theological statements to Jesus has a two-fold importance in respect of their *matter* and *form*.

(i) It attests, and tests, their material derivation from the one Truth of God as it is in Jesus. Not all statements about God are theological statements and not all theological statements are true statements. They are truly theological and they are true in so far as they conform to the way in which the Truth of God has come to us, and are assimilated to the life of God as it has been translated into our life and history, in the human nature and activity of Jesus. Theological truth has, therefore, its essential *basis* in the kerygmatic and didactic material of the New Testament Scriptures through which the self-revelation and self-communication of the Truth as it is in Jesus are mediated

---

[1] See the remarkable essay by Edmund Schlink, 'Die Struktur der dogmatischen Aussage als oekumenisches Problem' in *Kerygma und Dogma* 3. 4 pp. 251, 306, especially p. 253 f.

to us. It is by critical reference to that material source that we test whether our theological statements are statements of the Truth uttered and heard in Jesus, whether they comprise authentic audits deriving from the Word of God or are simply concepts that we have thought up on our own. Unless they derive from the Truth that is heard and uttered again, understood and repeated in the self-communicating and self-authenticating Witness of Jesus they cannot be accepted as true theological statements.

(ii) It shapes and clarifies their conformity to the Truth of God as it is in Jesus. Theological statements by their very nature cannot be abstracted from the Life and History of Jesus, and therefore they are truly theological in so far as they are faithfully Christological, that is, in so far as they take their living shape from assimilation to the obedience and prayer, the praise and adoration of Jesus which He offered to the Glory of the heavenly Father. Theological truth, therefore, has its essential *form* in the Life of Jesus in which He laid hold upon our mind and will and bent them back in Himself to perfect love and confidence in the Father, to joyful acquiescence in the Truth and to glad submission to the will of God. Unless theological statements participate in that glorification of the Father in Jesus, and so take on the form of humble inquiry, of reverence for the Majesty of God, of witness and service to the Truth, they cannot be credited or sealed with a genuine *Amen*.

2 THE TRUTHFULNESS OF THEOLOGICAL STATEMENTS

Some remarks on terminology seem to be required at this point. We shall use the word 'statement' in a general sense to refer to a positive or declarative communication, and to refer to what is stated as well as the stating of it, since language significantly used in communication should not be abstracted from that to which it is made to refer. A statement may be oral or written but it is always the act of a subject. This use of 'statement' will become clearer through comparison with that of 'judgement' and 'proposition'. A judgement is what we do in thinking, what takes place within the mind. Even if it is in question and answer form, it is 'the meeting of question and answer within the mind. The ultimate decision is given from within'.[1] A proposition is different, for it refers to a communication from one subject to another about something. In question and answer form it is given in answer to a question, but in such a way that it offers something for acceptance, or decision, and may therefore be the propounding of a further question. In this case 'question and answer meet from opposite directions.'[2] Propositions take place within the relation of objectivity between two subjects where the objectivity of one encounters the objectivity of another and where the ultimate decisions are not taken in the isolation of one mind but in dependence on another or other minds. Of course no such encounter takes place *in vacuo*, but only in relation to a reality objective to both subjects and in a medium from which they draw their signs for communication with one another. Propositions have their place, therefore, in a triadic relationship in which some 'object' is pointed out or put forward by one person for the attention of another who is meant to apprehend it under the direction of the proposing statement and through a judgement on his part in agreement with that of the proposer.[3]

When we look at it in this way, we must admit that propositional relations are basic and that judgements depend on them and arise within them. That is another way of saying that our subjectivity requires the objectivity of other subjects, and our thinking depends upon encounter with other minds, as we are directed to what is other than ourselves. Judgements arise out of our meeting with objective reality, not least that of other subjects. On the other hand, although a judgement presumes a proposition, the proposition calls for a decision, and so refers us back for our own judgement. It is not simply forced upon us, but calls for a response, i.e. an *act* of judgement on

---

[1] A. R. Whateley, *The Focus of Belief*, p. 41. See the whole of the note on p. 40 f.
[2] Ibid.
[3] There is another way of using 'proposition' which we shall take up later, where propositions are statements within a logical calculus where we are concerned with the relations of ideas.

This distinction must be observed if we are to avoid the confusion that arises when, for example, revelation as the communication of propositional ideas is contrasted with revelation through experienced events engendering reflection. This contrast is distortingly sharp and excludes direct cognitive experiences that are propositional in the sense noted above. Cf. here John Baillie, *The Idea of Revelation in Recent Thought, passim*, but cf. pp. 36 ff., 62 ff. Also John Hick, *Philosophy of Religion*, pp. 61 ff.

our part. In the language of the ancient epistemologists, it involves a willing assent of the mind, a συγκατάθεσις διανοίας that is ἑκούσιος, or an act of judgement on the ground of persuasion, a κρίμα that implies πίστις.

This inter-connection between proposition and judgement is of considerable importance, for it means that our thinking presupposes the structure of our active personal inter-relations and takes place within them. Even the activity of natural science is inextricably involved in the structure of society, and would be impossible without a community of empirical subjects in which mutual questioning and criticism and communication provide the necessary condition for verification and progress in knowledge.[1]

Theological statements take place within such a community, for they involve the meeting of subjects, the dialogue in which propositions and decisions and judgements are essential, and in which there is articulated inquiry and articulated communication. A statement involves an act of personal judgement and an act of communication, but everything depends on the nature of that which gives rise to it. Even statements about impersonal realities cannot be appreciated properly by forgetting the subject who pronounces them, or by abstracting his existence, or that of the hearer, from the structure of communication and society in which the propositions and judgements take place. That holds in greater measure of statements about personal subjects, for here we are concerned not primarily with judgements but with propositions, that is with the communication of a 'position', or the propounding of a question, or with an articulate word, requiring personal response and decision and judgement. This is especially the case with statements about God, for they are not statements that we think up or that arise from the activity of question and answer within one mind; they are not logical constructions out of experience, inferences which we make from other items of knowledge; they are statements made in response to a Word that is heard, a Truth that is communicated, or an Act that is done to us, a propositional question or rational communication that is directed to us from God

---

[1] This is one of the main theses sustained with great power by Michael Polanyi in several of his works, *Science, Faith and Society, The Logic of Liberty, Personal Knowledge.* Cf. also the contribution of Michael Foster to *Faith and Logic* (ed. Basil Mitchell), "'We' in Modern Philosophy," pp. 194 ff.

Himself by His Son, the Word made flesh, requiring recognition, response, decision for their articulation on our part. They arise out of real dialogue initiated by God and not out of some irrational monologue we carry on with ourselves. God is not the answer to our question or the conclusion of our reasoning. He is before all. He is. He questions us, and utters His Word, directing it, not to our judgements and inferences but to our hearing and understanding and for our judgements and decisions, that we on our part may pronounce recognition, enunciate propositions, and make statements appropriate to the Word spoken and the Truth revealed. Because these statements all have propositional relation to the Word and Truth of God and all involve judgements which we make in our responsive rational activity, they are also inter-related with one another i.e. 'propositions' in the logical sense of the term. If they were not or if they implied contradictions among themselves, that would indicate that they were not all truthfully related to the Word and Truth of God which gave rise to them. Theological statements thus have a double reference, a responsive, denotative reference in correspondence with the Word and Truth of God, and a formal, morphological reference in coherence with one another.

i. *Existence-statements and Coherence-statements*

In order to deal with this more fully we may take up the old distinction made by David Hume between two kinds of propositions, as he called them (we shall call them statements), those about *relations of ideas* and those about *matters of fact*.[1] The former, Hume held, are reached through *demonstrative or abstract reasoning*, and 'are discoverable by the mere operation of thought, without dependence on what is anywhere existent in the universe'; the latter are reached through *experimental* or *moral reasoning* and knowledge of them 'arises entirely from experience'. We shall speak of the latter as *existence-statements*

---

[1] *Enquiry concerning the Human Understanding*, section IV, 20 f. Cf. the similar distinction by Joseph Butler between *abstract truth* (or *the abstract relations of things*) and *matter of fact*, *The Works of Bishop Butler* (ed. by J. H. Bernard), vol. 1, p. 4 f and vol. 2, p. 265. Corresponding to this is the distinction widely current in recent philosophy between analytic statements or tautologies, and empirical statements or hypotheses. See A. J. Ayer, *Language, Truth and Logic*, preface to the first edition.

and of the former as *coherence-statements*, and in that order as existence-statements are undoubtedly the basic statements.[1]

Hume also pointed out that the evidence for the truth of matters of fact and existence is of a very different nature from the evidence for the truth of relations of ideas. In the latter case there are demonstrative arguments giving demonstrative certainty, but not in the former. No theoretical proof can be offered for the validity of existence-statements. Thus, as G. E. Moore has expressed it in a famous essay on Hume's Philosophy: 'It is quite impossible for anyone to prove, in one strict sense of the term, that he does not know any external facts. I can only prove that I do, by assuming that in some particular instance, I actually do know one. That is to say, the so-called proof must assume the very thing it pretends to prove. The only proof that we do know external facts lies in the simple fact that we know them.'[2]

This means that we can only 'convince' others of the truth of our existence-statements if we can get them to see or hear the reality they refer to as we see or hear it. It can never be forced upon them. They must be brought to share our *intuition* of the object given.[3] That does not mean that by describing or explaining to others our intuition we can induce them to have a similar experience, for no act of knowledge is explainable from the side of the knowing subject (i.e., psychologically) but only from the side of the object known, for true knowledge arises in proportion as the subject allows his knowing to be determined by the nature of the object before him. Therefore

---

[1] It should be noted that we are speaking here of *sentences* which are of many different kinds and are to be distinguished in different ways. This distinction between *statements*, however, holds good when we are looking at statements in a certain way with a particular end in view, but when looked at in other ways with other ends in view similar distinctions may validly be drawn, e.g., the distinction made by I. A. Richards between the *scientific* use of language in which statements are made for the references they promote, and the *emotive* use of language in which statements are made for the attitudes they evoke, *Principles of Literary Criticism*, 2nd edit. ch. XXXIII. Other useful distinctions are between statements intending to impart information and statements intending to express more clearly what is already known, ontological and ideological statements, or contingent and necessary statements.

[2] G. E. Moore, *Philosophical Studies*, 1922, p. 160.

[3] We shall use the term 'intuition' to speak of our apprehension of a reality in its objectivity and unity, as a whole.

the nature of our intuition will depend upon the nature of the object. The intuition of a personal object, or a subject, will be different from our intuition of an impersonal object, but in neither case are we able to prove to another the validity of our intuition; that is, we cannot demonstrate to him its existence or external reality. The best that we can do is to try to get him to ask the right question, or to open himself up in an attitude or in an orientation toward the given reality in a way that we believe to be appropriate to its nature or in accord with the way in which it presents itself. To intuit an object in a way appropriate to its nature and to be convinced of its external reality coincide, and therefore the question of truth is inseparable from the question of existence.

Another characteristic of our basic existence-statements must be noted: they are never complete for by their very nature they reach out beyond themselves. Considered in themselves they are defective and necessarily incomplete. They are essentially denotative. Their meaning does not lie in themselves but in that which they denote, and therefore they are themselves meaningful only through their relation to the thing meant. Thus behind existence-statements there are acts of intuition in which the mind is always open to the reality beyond and cannot, if it is to be faithful and truthful, foreclose its cognition of the existent and so delimit its meaning to what can be expressed in clear-cut ideas or abstract concepts. Existence-statements have thus always an indefinite quality for they refer to a reality that cannot by its very nature be reduced to pure thought or be enclosed within the brackets of mere ideas and so be made entirely transparent to our reasoning.

This is a matter upon which von Hügel laid great and even startling emphasis in his distinction between two kinds of apprehension, knowledge of real existence and of real qualities attaching to them, which are indefinitely apprehensible, and knowledge of abstract ideas and numerical and spatial relations which is always, or ought always to be, clear and distinct and readily demonstrable. Things that are real in themselves, he held, and distinct from our minds must be dim and difficult for our minds, for our analysis and reasoning, but 'to require clearness in proportion to the concreteness, to the depth of reality, of the subject matter is an impossible position,

I mean a thoroughly unreasonable, self-contradictory habit of mind'.[1]

There are two points to be distinguished here. First, existence-statements are necessarily open and to that extent indefinite because they refer beyond themselves to a reality which by its very nature cannot be expressed in the language of abstraction. Therefore existence-statements cannot without change of significance, i.e., without falsifying them, be translated into purely formal statements. To attempt to bring them within the clear-cut ideas of our thought is to ignore precisely what is concrete and definite and to be most imprecise—it only gives the illusion of precision by transferring thought from existence into the realm of pure possibility or from the particular to the universal. Knowledge of existence that is true and adequate to it must resist such a μετάβασις εἰς ἄλλο γένος. Secondly, everything depends upon the nature of the existent. Some existents are themselves limited and clear-cut and corresponding statements can be made about them, for knowledge of them is easily transferable, but others are of a different nature for they have a richness and fulness that reach out far beyond what we can specify and delimit in our thought of them, so that the incompleteness of our statements about them is the measure of their superiority over us or their depth in reality. Thus openness or indefiniteness in existence-statements is part of their adequacy to the object or of their truthfulness in relation to it.

A third observation must be made about existence-statements. We must beware of limiting their reference to existents of one kind only, that which is amenable to sense-experience. To restrict 'matters of fact' to that which is explicable to the senses only is as unverifiable as it is unwarrantable.[2] It is upon this piece of false metaphysical dogmatism that ultimately the particular theory of verification advocated by philosophers like Ayer rests when they employ a criterion of literal significance or factual meaning, arbitrarily laying it down that nothing has significance or meaning of this kind except that which falls within the range of spatio-temporal sense-experience,

[1] F. von Hügel, *Essays and Addresses*, First Series, p. 100. Cf. also Whitehead's claim that what we can easily discriminate in clear-cut ways and think in clear-cut connections belongs to what is comparatively superficial, *The Function of Reason*, p. 62 f., *Adventures of Ideas*, pp. 209, 225, 283 f, etc.

[2] See John Baillie, *The Sense of the Presence of God*, pp. 61 ff.

and then claiming that statements that fail to pass this test are senseless. It is very difficult to avoid the conclusion that this is mere sophistry. As Karl Popper has said, nothing is easier than to brand something as 'meaningless' in this way. 'All you have to do is to fix upon a conveniently narrow meaning for "meaning" and you will soon be bound to say of any inconvenient question that you are unable to detect any meaning in it.'[1] That is what Ayer has done—everything follows from his own home-made convention or definition (which he makes strong or weak to suit his own desires) for his conclusions are already contained in his presuppositions although he can offer no proof of them that satisfies his own principle of verification, so that the whole argument is ultimately meaningless. Thus to cite Popper again, 'If you admit as meaningful none except problems in natural science, any debate about the concept of "meaning" will also turn out to be meaningless.'[2]

Let it be agreed that existence-statements are basic and can be tested only empirically by returning to the ground of actual and primary cognitions, or, if the language will be admitted, that they are statements about matters of fact which can be known only through direct experience, but let us not make the unscientific assumption that all matters of fact are of one kind, and so assimilate all knowledge to sense-perception. The important thing to remember is that matters of fact are known in accordance with their own nature, and if their nature is such that they cannot be sensed or directly observed, or therefore remembered as a result of previous sense-experience or observation, or deduced from them, then they cannot be challenged by submitting them to a test of empirical perception or observation that does not apply, for that would not be genuinely empirical because it would not be a test in the mode of the realities concerned. In other words, the nature of the empirical reference is always (we do not say entirely) determined by the nature of that to which empirical reference is actually being made, and cannot rationally be limited or

[1] *The Logic of Scientific Discovery*, p. 51.

[2] Ibid. The adoption of Ayer's verification principle would stultify nuclear physics for it can proceed only through renouncing the criterion of perceptibility, not to speak of engaging in metaphysics. In any case, as Margenau points out, physics requires more than empirical verification, F. Heinemann, *Die Philosophie im 20. Jahrhundert*, p. 396.

fixed beforehand in accordance with certain natures only, or some restricted areas of experience, or to selected modes of perception or intuition. We insist that this cannot be done rationally, since to prescribe beforehand how something shall be known before we know it, or to limit empirical experience and knowledge in this way, is to imply that our own experience and knowledge do not come under this prescription or limitation. Moreover it kills empirical discovery through substituting terminological decisions for hard thinking. Hence we would conclude with John Baillie: 'The formal pattern of the verificatory procedure is thus the same in theology as in physical science, the difference being that in the latter case the appeal is to what is "revealed" to ordinary sense perception, but in the former to what is revealed to the "eye" of faith.'[1]

One further observation must be made concerning propositions about matters of fact and relations of ideas, or existence- and coherence-statements: to posit a radical dichotomy between them is to open up an abyss of sheer unmeaning, e.g. by abstracting coherence-statements from all ontological import. In empirical science no statements are purely analytic or devoid of factual reference, while even mathematical statements cannot consistently be treated as tautologies. Existence-statements and coherence-statements require one another if they are to be significant, for, to adapt a sentence of Kant about the relation between sensibility and understanding, coherence-statements without existence-statements are empty, existence-statements without coherence-statements are blind.[2] Or to put the matter quite differently, coherence-statements are properly made, as it were, at right-angles to existence-statements for that angular relation is the hinge of their meaning. If they are entirely detached as pure abstractions, self-sufficient and self-contained, and do not even have a general ontological reference, they lose real meaning.[3] Existence-statements, on the other hand, are shot through and through with conceptual

---

[1] *The Sense of the Presence of God*, p. 68.   [2] *Critique of Pure Reason*, B. 75.
[3] It is possible of course to abstract the pattern of meaning entirely and develop its merely formal possibilities, e.g. in pure Euclidean geometry, and on that analogy to invent other purely formal geometries out of a set of initial relations. This can reduce it to a mere game which we play according to arbitrarily fixed rules. Then it has ultimately no meaning, or perhaps we should say, its meaning consists merely in 'playing', in an enjoyable exercise. Nevertheless it was 'play' of this kind by Lobachevsky and others that led to the discovery of four-dimensional geometries which were subsequently found to reveal actual properties in nature itself.

interpretation, so that unless they yield coherence-statements they are incapable of significance. It must be noted, however, that the relation between coherence-statements and existence-statements is not theoretical but practical. But if there is no logical continuity between them this does not mean that they are disconnected—even at the minimal point their connection is apparent in that both make use of ordinary language that 'depends on matter as well as form because the assertions are material.'[1] They overlap in function and reference. This means that our statements, whether existence-statements or coherence-statements, have an ambiguous nature, a primary and a secondary reference; the truth-reference of existence-statements is primarily to existents, the truth-reference of coherence-statements is primarily to other statements.

We may express this differently by saying that no meaningful existence-statements can be made except in correspondence, consistency and integration with others in a pattern of meaning; but the pattern of meaning does not hang in the air, as it were; for it is grounded upon the existence-statements. Now the pattern itself is two-fold. On the one hand, we are concerned with a pattern in the existent or object which consists of relations of fact, but on the other hand we have a pattern in our cognition which consists of relations of ideas—the first we may call the material pattern, and the second the formal pattern. We never discern anything as an absolute particular, but only in real relations which may be internal to it or external. We intuit it as a whole with these relations, and therefore not apart from a pattern discerned in the object. Our existence-statements refer to this and in that reference have their meaning.[2] But when we seek to express this meaning we represent it in the relations of ideas and so coherence-statements arise which must be consistent with one another in reference to the existent and in that consistency they offer a formal pattern of meaning.

[1] A. D. Ritchie, *Essays in Philosophy*, p. 72.

[2] It is important to take note of Frege's warning that 'the reference and sense of a sign are to be distinguished from the associated idea' (*Translations from the Philosophical Writings of Gottlob Frege*, edit. by Peter Geach and Max Black, p. 50) for the idea is subjective and differs from man to man. Hence the need to test the reference every time to make sure that we are talking about the same thing, that which we intend to designate.

This interrelation of existence- and coherence-statements has not been sufficiently realized by some writers who appear to misunderstand or misuse what is called 'ostensive definition'. Consider the case of the primitive person who had a large watch put into his hand with the words 'that is a watch'. He looked at it, saw the minute hand moving and heard the watch ticking, and then dropped it with the word 'animal'. He interpreted it quite properly and intelligibly within the structure of his previous knowledge. He offered an intelligent sign to stand for and express what he perceived. His perception was shot through and through with an implicit pattern of meaning, and therefore he acted significantly. He happened to be wrong, for he was lacking in information, but he was rational, for he related the facts of movement and noise in the object as particulars in a perceived whole which formed a significant pattern in the only way that was apparently possible for him. To that corresponded, therefore, the relation of ideas expressed in the word 'animal' by which he sought to express in speech the pattern he used in interpretation. The next step in understanding would have involved a considerable change in the structure of his previous knowledge, for only through such a change could there take place a true perception of what was new to him, the discovery of its meaning, and the acquiring of a new sign in speech to stand for the new fact and express its meaning. An ostensive definition is meaningless apart from a coherent and indeed developing pattern of meaning.

Existence-statements and coherence-statements are mutually dependent. To make use of older philosophical language, matter and form are not to be separated or sharply divided, for it is only through the form that the matter becomes comprehensible to us. This is not to say that we have to operate with the priority of forms as independent entities, for form is relative to that of which it is the form and has no meaning apart from it. Form and matter belong together. That certainly holds good with what I have called the material pattern and the object or existent. Now when we come to express the formal pattern, what we do is to represent in ideas the form through which we cognize the object, but unless we distinguish the formal pattern of our knowing (relations of ideas) from the material in what we know (relations in matters of fact) we confound our knowing with what we know or mistake our logical constructs for existents. In other words, the formal pattern is to be used as a sign which we recognize as standing for the thing signified, and therefore we use it, not in order that through analysis of the sign we can construct knowledge of the thing signified,[1] but that by means of it we may be put into such a relation to the thing signified that we may intuit it again through the appropriate sign, and so be thrown back upon the objective reality. In that way we renew and revise our intuition and verify our cognition.

We have maintained that genuine knowledge involves the recognition of a distinction between the formal pattern intrinsic to our coherence-statements and the material pattern in the referent of our existence-statements. All this implies that there is a close relation between the formal pattern and the material pattern, or that there is a certain *propriety* between our coherence-statements and that which is denoted by our existence-statements. But because our existence-statements are basic, there is an irreversible relation between them and our coherence-statements. Thus while we must say that the formal pattern and the distinctions it involves *ought* to correspond to the material pattern and the distinctions it involves in the existent, we cannot argue that to the pattern and distinctions in our coherence-statements there *must* correspond a pattern and distinctions in the existent itself.[2] At no point is it valid to determine the nature of objective reality by beginning at the human end, with the analysis of the patterns of our speech or forms of thought; rather ought these to be the media through which we apprehend objective reality. Thus while our coherence-statements ought to have an *ectypal* relation to existents, they can never be used validly as providing *archetypal* patterns for determining the structure of reality.[3] Existence-statements remain basic and primary.

[1] This is the fault of those who confuse the analysis of language with the analysis of propositions. See the vigorous protest against this mistake by G. E. Moore, *The Philosophy of G. E. Moore* (ed. by P. A. Schilpp), pp. 660 ff.

[2] This is a difficulty, epistemologically, with 'natural theology', viz. argumentation *from* a formal pattern to existence, which in the nature of the case, is not open to empirical verification.

[3] This is one of the important points brought home with such force by David Hume in *Dialogues concerning Natural Religion* (edit. by N. Kemp Smith), p. 229.

ii. Theological Statements: Their Nature and Justification

We now turn to examine specifically *theological* statements. But let it be clear that we have not sought to build up a philosophical basis first in order to do that. Statements must always be matched to the grounds on which they are based. What we have tried to do is to clear some of the ground in order that we may go on to consider theological statements in their own right, for while as statements they overlap with other statements, what is materially determinative is their objective reference in respect of which their validity stands or falls. Nevertheless, because they are our statements a distinction between the reference of existence-statements and the reference of coherence-statements holds good for them also.

Theological statements may be divided into two sorts.[1]

(1) Statements which refer to an objective reality above and beyond them, and which are true in terms of that reference. They are essentially denotative and signitive, pointing beyond themselves, so that they do not have their meaning in themselves, but in that which is intended. They are statements with extrinsic meaning, and are to be discriminated from other similar statements by the nature and content of that which is meant. Of course, each statement is not just a jumble of denotative symbols but comprises words which are arranged to make sense (i.e. its subjective meaning) and that arrangement in sense has a denotative function; it is used to point articulately to a reality beyond it (i.e. its objective meaning).

(2) Statements which are related to one another in a coherent framework of knowledge, and which have their truth in their inter-relations or with reference to a system of ideas, within which they have an appropriate place. They are statements with intrinsic meaning, and are to be discriminated from speculative statements that are independently thought out and systematized. This is not to say that each statement is to be construed merely according to its sense or the formal arrangement of its words but is to be read, or listened to, in the light

---

[1] Richards' distinction between the *scientific* use and the *emotive* use of language is specially applicable to theology. But we must not forget that there are many kinds of statements, descriptive, biographical, speculative, doxological, hortative, performative, etc. even though they may be grouped within these wider distinctions

of what it intends to communicate, that is, as a proposition in an orderly sequence of communication.

Theological statements are fundamentally of the first sort, for they are basically existence-statements in the sense that they refer to the Being and Existence of God as the given Reality. As such theological statements are theo-nomous, theo-logical, not just statements about God and divine things, but statements of God, having their reference from a centre in God and not in ourselves; they are derived from God, and have their truth from Him and not in themselves. This is not a truth that is specifiable or producible by us at will. But they are empirical statements, in the sense that they arise *a posteriori* out of an actual encounter with objective reality, while the nature of that reality determines the kind and mode of empirical reference they involve. They do not arise from inference, nor are they produced by analogical reasoning, for the logic of their reference is not explicable from this side of that reference but only from the side of God's activity in self-disclosure. They are essentially analogical, but their analogical character arises through submission to Reality, through conformity to the Word and Truth of God. If God is really God, He comes first, and is the ground of their truth, the determinant in our knowledge of Him as well as its referent.

In this kind of statement, to borrow a way of speaking from John Macmurray,[1] its truth is its reality, the objective world beyond the statement. Reality does not depend on its truth but its truth on reality. Truth depends on the externally real so that true thinking is real thinking. Real statements are statements that are forced upon us by the pressure of objective reality. Apart from that reference or derivation the statements are without 'truth', they are dead, merely 'letter' and not 'spirit'. To be true statements they have to have a reality to which they point, and actually point to it. They can be justified only from the ground of that to which they refer and can be refuted only if that ground should disappear or fail.

Theological statements of this kind have to be distinguished from other statements, for example, from the statements of natural theology in which 'reality' is derived from ideas or inferred from observations, and in which everything depends upon the truthfulness of that act of derivation or inference.

[1] *Freedom in the Modern World*, pp. 130 ff.

But here 'reality' depends upon 'truth', for this 'god' or 'reality' is posited in and with my ideas and coexists with the world out of which the ideas arise and to which they belong—the world and he are relative to each other. He is not independent reality. As Camfield has expressed it:

He never meets us, and we never meet him. He is not a fact. The world of our actual life and experience is the fact. We take this world as a datum, the given thing, the one thing to be accepted; and from this datum the idea of this god arises. It is clear that this god has no independent life or being of his own, none at any rate that we can know about. The world is as necessary to him as he is to the world; indeed, more so. Since we know about him only from the world, since he is just its cause, or the ground and principle of its existence, he is quite inconceivable without it.[1]

Theological statements have to be distinguished from other statements also in that their empirical relation is to the active, living and speaking God, and in that they derive from and so refer to the Word and Truth of God—Truth that is already articulate Word as it comes from God. Thus what distinguishes genuine theological statements from those of natural theology is that their reference to God is real and articulate in its own right, for at every point they are determined by the activity of the living God in His self-impartation and self-communication to man from above and beyond him.

On the other hand, theological statements are always our statements. They express our hearing of God's Word, our knowing of God, and are statements that we make. While they derive from God's own articulate self-revelation, our hearing and knowing and stating are not set aside and simply displaced. God does not speak instead of us. He speaks in order that we may respond and speak with Him and after Him, and so be fully responsible for our own statements. In so far as they are statements of ours, human statements, they cannot escape being statements of the second kind, i.e. statements which claim to be true propositions within a chosen set of symbols and within a certain system of ideas. They have their truth in relation or inter-relation to certain other statements, and they are formally correct or logical as they are consistent with these other statements.

In theology, however, statements of this kind depend entirely upon the basic statements, and are themselves never devoid

[1] *The Collapse of Doubt*, p. 40.

of reference (direct or indirect) to existents, or of material content.[1] They continue to be theonomous statements which have their primary norm or law beyond them, and not simply in a system of ideas and certainly not in any immanent truths of reason. Theological statements are not logically necessary statements; they are not tautological and therefore are not true in every possible case and in every situation, timelessly and spacelessly true or universally true in an abstract sense. Their truth depends on the actuality and the reality of their reference, and by their necessary relation to it.

Several further observations require to be made about these theological statements.

In the first place, it is to be noted that no radical dichotomy can be posited between existence-statements and coherence-statements, or, to use more theological language, *kerygmatic* statements and *didactic* statements. They are much more closely interwoven than existence- and coherence-statements in other spheres, e.g. in natural science, for the existence-statements derive from the Truth of God who is not only Truth in the form of Being but articulate Word addressed to man in Jesus Christ. Thus existence-statements are already laden with Word and are propositional and conceptual in their own right, while coherence-statements are by no means abstractions or just systematic statements consisting merely of formal relations of ideas, but are statements within a dialogical relation with the Truth where they are propositionally assimilated to the self-impartation and self-communication of the Word made flesh. Thus while they do involve relations of ideas or relations of truths they are inseparable from a personal and 'existential' mode of communication grounded in the personal Being or Existence of the Truth as it is in Jesus.

To use other language, we may speak of the existence-statements as having a vertical reference, and the coherence-statements as having as horizontal reference, but the basic point at which the vertical and horizontal meet is in Jesus Christ—on earth, in history, in Israel, that is, within the space and time of our world where they have an observational and

[1] This is not to claim that *all* theological *sentences* must be statements, for we have to reckon also with indicative, imperative, subjunctive and optative sentences that are forms of action or of self-expression rather than assertions.

historical reference. That is the hinge of their meaning, for it is in and through Jesus Christ that the existence-statements have their reference above and beyond themselves, to the Father (their extrinsic meaning), and it is through conformity with Jesus Christ that the coherence-statements have their interior reference in a coherent whole (their intrinsic meaning). Thus in Jesus Christ all theological statements are made within the concrete forms of time and space, within the medium of historical thinking and action, where they involve commitment to the Truth in historical life and action and an appropriate mode of verification. In existence-statements verification will involve concrete reference to Jesus Christ and in Him a fulness of light and a richness of illumination for their reference to the Reality of the Father. In coherence-statements verification will involve concrete reference to Jesus Christ and in Him a basic 'logical simplicity' through which all coherence-statements will have their orientation and inner perfection.

This brings us to the point where we must note, in the second place, that all theological statements have a two-level reference corresponding to the primary and secondary objectivity we discussed earlier. Existence-statements have a reference to the historical Jesus Christ as the objective reality beyond them, but in and through Jesus Christ they refer to God Himself as the ultimate objectivity. They are thus incomplete statements in a double sense. They are incomplete like other existence-statements in that they denote an existent or reality beyond them and which they refuse to translate into pure thought or ideality, but they are also incomplete because in Jesus Christ they are opened above and beyond themselves toward the eternal God: they cannot stop short at the historical Jesus. The audits and concepts they carry are thus open, grounded upon the concrete reality of the historical Jesus Christ, but in and through Him they are opened out to eternity. In accordance with the nature of the reality they denote they are statements that derive from the action of the eternal God upon us in and through Jesus Christ, and are by way of response to His revealing and redeeming activity. Theologically speaking, existence-statements of this sort are essentially *kerygmatic*, for they bear *witness* to the saving Act and Word of God that encounters us in Jesus Christ.

Now it is just because we are concerned here with a two-fold objectivity in this way that the two-fold reference of existence-statements is characterized by a historical relation to the historical fact of Christ and a personal relation in faith toward Him as Lord and Saviour. The existence-statement expresses the act whereby we seek to be obedient to the whole fact of Christ, as God and Man. We cannot act toward Him as if He were only a simple historical fact like any other historical fact (person or event) for He is God become Man, the Eternal acting in history. He is a unique Fact in History, the absolute Fact become historical fact,[1] and therefore our knowing of Him and our speaking of Him must be in a mode corresponding to His historical and His divine nature. We are thus unable to report the historical fact of Christ truthfully without reporting in the mode of faith, in which we seek to behave rationally in accordance with the whole fact; but nor can we speak of Him only in purely 'spiritual' terms without involving concrete and actual reference to Him as historical fact. A 'merely spiritual' or 'merely historical' reference would be an abstraction and would be untruthful. Thus existence-statements, in so far as they are truthfully related to Jesus Christ, necessarily involve a historical and a spiritual relation to Him. This whole relation is the relation of faith—let it be quite clear, a faith-relation which involves a historical reference to historical fact in its very essence, but in the nature of the case this is such a historical reference that it is open toward the sheer Reality of God who comes to meet us in the historical Jesus Christ.

Because existence-statements are *kerygmatic* in this way, they necessarily involve didactic elements—they do not just point to 'bare facts' stripping away from facts their rationality, but in faithful witness to them, point to them in a mode of rationality appropriate to them, and thus in the act and understanding of faith in which kerygmatic and didactic statements share in the revealing and reconciling activity of God in Christ. Those who make them, point to Christ in such a way that they are committed to historical thinking and action in response to Him and only report within that historical thinking and action, and so in reporting the facts communicate to others what has been communicated to them by the facts or rather by Christ

[1] See Kierkegaard, *Philosophical Fragments*, p. 83 f.

Himself through His Word and Acts. It is through this didactic constituent that kerygmatic statements are bent out horizontally to overlap with systematic or coherence-statements. This results in *dogmatic* statements.[1]

Coherence-statements, on the other hand, are predominantly *didactic* for they are statements of the Truth in an articulated form that can be transmitted clearly from person to person and are in fact acts of rational communication. They are dogmatic in character for they involve the communication of a framework of knowledge in and through which witness to the reality of Christ can take place meaningfully and effectively. As such, however, they are rooted in the concrete reality of Christ and are never without kerygmatic reference themselves. In this sense they are also incomplete in that they are rooted beyond themselves in Christ and are always open to modification and enlargement for they indicate more than they can express in communication to others. In another sense, however, they are not incomplete—that is, they cannot be treated like the incomplete symbols of logic where the forms are handled without respect to content. The systematic statements of theology are not simply relations of ideas or symbols to one another in an abstract system, for they cannot be made in abstraction from their rooting in Jesus Christ, or therefore from space and time. By abstracting theological statements from their factual content or from the idiom of the existence and being of the Truth as it is in Jesus, they are bereft of their meaning and are falsified.

We may express this otherwise, by saying that theological statements even in their systematic or coherent form are not devoid of ontological import; they have a dimension in depth so that their meaning cannot be discerned when they are read in the flat or only on one level. When they are ironed out by the rigorous application of formal logic they become paradoxical and contradictory and nonsensical even if somehow the aura of their origin still clings to them and invites wonder and inquiry.[2] But the perplexity will remain so long as we turn our backs upon the very conditions which give theological

---

[1] For the specific character of dogmatic statements see below pp. 341f., 349ff.
[2] A significant example of this approach is Professor R. W. Hepburn's able study, *Christianity and Paradox*, written from the point of view of 'reverent agnosticism'.

statements their meaning, or persist in interpreting the nature and function of theological forms on a false analogy derived from some other field of experience or habit of expression, for that can only mythologize them.[1]

The whole focus of attention has to be changed in order to see theological statements in their dimension of depth; then they are not simply looked at but looked through toward the Reality which they indicate; they are seen to be the didactic means through which we encounter and intuit Truth in the form of personal Being and hear God's Word incarnate in Jesus Christ. In this perspective the so-called 'paradoxical' or even 'absurd' character of theological statements is not evidence that they lack meaning but that they are being subjected to an inadequate and inappropriate method of interpretation.[2] They only appear paradoxical to a false approach or to interpretation with an alien framework, much as nuclear processes can only appear contradictory and absurd when an attempt is made to interpret them by dragging them back within the limited range of classical physics.

A third characteristic of theological statements must now be noted, the fact that they collide with our natural forms of knowing and speaking. Surprising as it may appear to those approaching them from the outside, this is not an accidental feature of theological statements, for it is essential to them. In one sense, of course, they are continuous with our ordinary language and like it make use of syntax and logic, for they are human statements employing rational human means of communication. If the conflict they involve is intended and unavoidable, the ultimate intention they embody is reconciliation. The reason for this is that they are statements in the mode of the Word and Truth of God as it is in Jesus and in accordance with His activity of justification and reconciliation. In Jesus Christ the Truth of God has broken into our human life and history in such a way as to involve crucifixion on

[1] Cf. G. Ryle's definition of myth as 'the presentation of facts belonging to one category in the idioms appropriate to another'. *The Concept of Mind*, p. 8.

[2] See Ian Crombie's essay in *Faith and Logic* (ed. by Basil Mitchell), p. 48 ff., where he argues against the assimilation of theology to anything else, and that the anomalous formal properties of theological statements help to 'fix the reference' of these statements.

His part as He endures the contradiction of sinners against Himself, and 'crucifixion' on our part as we take up the Cross and follow Him in an act of obedience in which we repent of our untruth and are changed in adaptation to the Truth of God. Theological statements thus correspond in form and content to the Truth of God in His revealing and reconciling activity, and are to be enunciated in a material mode appropriate to that correspondence.

This is the reason for the baffling character of theological statements when they use ordinary language in an extraordinary way for they have to stretch it beyond its natural use in which it is adapted to natural existents and merely creaturely communication. Theological understanding, as we have seen, involves a serious change in the logical structure of our knowledge, as is inevitable where something new is to be cognized and assimilated. It should not be surprising therefore if theological statements entail a structural shift in our ordinary language in order that it may be adequate to the nature of the Truth it is employed to convey—indeed, apart from such a mutation in language theological statements could not be truthful in their reference to the Word and Truth of God. It must be emphasized that the essential meaning of theological statements includes the structural changes within which they are made,[1] just as our knowledge of the Truth includes the reconciliation and reorientation of the very conditions under which it takes place. It would be irrational to seek to understand theological language by transposing it back to ordinary usage where it is only adequate to ordinary knowledge and suited to a range of experience limited entirely by the boundaries of our spatio-temporal universe. Theology is bound to use ordinary language in a theological way in accordance with its material content, or rather in accordance with the nature of the object proper to theological knowledge. But this does not allow theologians to depreciate the place and importance of logical forms, if only because all theological statements include a this-worldly reference through their fundamental relation to

[1] It is because they fail to see this that in the present debate philosophers and theologians tend to talk past each other, but many theologians failing to understand the true nature of the theological statements talk past their own subject.

the historical Jesus Christ, and therefore they must beware of stretching ordinary language to the point where it becomes guilty, as it were, of a 'linguistic docetism'.

To speak of Jesus Christ as 'a concrete universal' or rather as 'the concrete universal' brings us to the very brink where theological language may appear contradictory and even absurd to the philosopher, but this is a point that is fundamental to theological statements. Jesus Christ is not only the eternal Word and universal Truth of God but He is a concrete individual existent in human history, combining in Himself the universal and the particular, truth and existence, God and creaturely man. It is in Him that all theological statements, kerygmatic or dogmatic, have direct or indirect rootage, and it is through Him that they are linked together in a coherent pattern of truth and meaning. He is the source of their basic and positive 'logical economy' or 'inner perfection' as He is apprehended in His own wholeness and unity in the total pattern of His Life and Work. In the last resort it is our intuition of the universal Truth of God in this one Man that gives depth and meaning to all our theological statements, while that Truth is only fully grasped in coherent apprehension and articulation of Him, as it derives from His articulate self-revelation and self-communication that opens up for us full and real knowledge of God the Father.

We maintain, then, that theological statements are true in virtue of having a real term of reference beyond to which they point. Their truth lies in having a reality from which they derive and to which they respond. They are true not merely as human statements about God but, in a fundamental sense, as God's statements, as God's communication of His own Truth—that is, they are true only as they are true from the side of God and correspondingly true from the side of man, true in so far as they repose upon the self-statements of God and in so far as they are 'hearing-statements'[1] deriving from God's Word. The truthfulness of that derivation and response has to be tested in the appropriate modes. The verification of their reference will involve examination of the structure of kerygmatic statements to make sure that they really are kerygmatic,

---

[1] 'Hearing-statements', or 'heard statements' in theological science correspond to the 'observation statements' in natural science, as 'audits' correspond to 'percepts'.

that is, that they arise as 'hearing-statements' in response to the Word of God and it will involve examination of the structure of dogmatic statements to make sure they conform to the material pattern of the Truth, that is, that they derive analogically from the Truth of God—and this, in turn, raises again the problem of the relation between the interior logic of theological statements and the formal logic in which they must participate as they share forms of thought and speech with other human statements.

Meantime let us return to the fact that theological statements have a reference beyond and above themselves, and are not true in themselves but have their truth beyond them. Here critical philosophers have several things to say, to which we must listen.

(a) If we make this claim for theological statements that means that there is a real discrepancy between the statements themselves which are human and this-worldly and that to which they intend ultimately to refer which is divine and other-worldly. How can statements truthfully refer to what is utterly transcendent and beyond them, infinitely beyond the limits of all 'experience' in this world?[1]

(b) We may say that theological statements refer to an eternal world and are related to it, but even if they did relate to it, we could not say how they are related to it, for what we cannot represent in language is the relation of language to the external facts—that is, in the language of Wittgenstein, we cannot produce a picture of the relation of a picture to that which is pictured.[2]

(c) Bound up and overlapping with both of these critical observations is another. If we claim that theological statements are analogical, do we not need an objective standard by which to measure them, and if we are to claim that all theological statements are analogical, how are we to get the required objective standard? We cannot get outside our own thinking or speak outside of our own human language.[3]

These critical observations are to be taken seriously, and, we believe, admitted from the side of the critical reason. Indeed they are to be reinforced from the side of the theological

[1] Cf. A. J. Ayer, *Language, Truth and Logic*, chs. i and vi.

[2] L. Wittgenstein, *Tractatus Logico-philosophicus*, 4.01f, 4.12f. Cf. the discussion of this by J. O. Urmson, *Philosophical Analysis*, pp. 87 ff., 127 f., 141 ff.

[3] Ayer, op. cit. p. 128 f.

reason. We grant that considered entirely and only *in themselves* theological statements have no *real* truth and we admit that we cannot just say how they are related to the reality which they indicate, for they have no claim on God that He must be their object or their content. It is, however, the very nature of the Truth that demands of us these acknowledgements, while it is because the Truth comes to us that we are delivered out of the circle of our own autonomous thinking, and are given a relation to what is outside of it and beyond what we can say to ourselves or think out for ourselves.

In regard to these observations it should be noted that they do not apply to theological statements only, that is, to the case where the referent is infinitely beyond the statement itself, but also to the basic statements of empirical science where the referent is an existent or a process and not an idea, that is, where it is quite another thing than the statement itself. If the critical observations are meant to demolish theology, they also demolish empirical science and lead to pure scepticism. If they are meant to be sceptical, they involve a serious error, in presuming that thinking of a thing is identical with making actual contact with it. Or to put it otherwise, as sceptical observations they assert the primacy of bare thought, they abstract thinking from existence, disconnecting mind from matter, and so create a gap which it is impossible to bridge by thinking alone.[1] Then to question the reality of an existent beyond the gap would be a contradictory movement of thought. But the observations need not be taken in a sceptical sense, for their truth lies in the fact that they reveal that in our knowledge of external reality, creaturely or divine, we cannot account for its comprehensibility; there is no purely theoretical bridge between our thinking and the objective reality of existence. Rightly taken, then, this does not produce scepticism but what Einstein called 'awe' before a mystery which we shall never understand.[2] That is no less applicable to the mystery of the knowledge of God by human creatures.

The problem raised by the critical observations is relevant not only to our knowledge of existents but also to our knowledge

[1] That is to say they are guilty of the mistake Ryle denounces as 'Descartes' Myth'. *The Concept of Mind*, pp. 11 ff.
[2] Albert Einstein, *Out of My Later Years*, p. 60.

of new facts, for we are unable to reduce to forms of thought, far less express it, just how we discover new facts. To do this would involve operating with an unbroken continuity in our thinking which would not allow us to advance beyond what we already know or can derive out of what we already know, whereas the learning of what is really new involves knowing what is not, or is not fully, in continuity with what we already know, and can only be assimilated to it through a reconstruction of the framework of our knowing. Now this is the very fact that faces us in all knowledge of God who is quite other than ourselves and whom we cannot know by beginning with ourselves or the creaturely world, but only by beginning with God Himself. Knowledge of Him is only explicable from His side—and by His act.

Not for one moment can we separate knowledge from the nature of what is known. That would be to introduce what Whitehead called 'incoherence' or even 'arbitrary disconnection'.[1] It is an error, therefore, to seek to understand theological knowledge through abstracting it from the Reality of God Himself. But when we take this Reality seriously as the Reality of *God* who gives Himself to us to be known, who reveals to us what we could never know of ourselves, and who enables us to apprehend what is altogether beyond us, then we must also take seriously the fact that the relation our knowing involves is not one that can be established by us but only by Him. That is why our theological statements cannot claim that God *must be* their object or their content; if He is their object or content it is only by His Grace.

By claiming to refer to the ultimate Truth of God our theological statements are thereby positing or acknowledging a discrepancy (N.B. *not* an *incoherence*), from their side, between themselves as statements and the ultimate Truth, just because they rely upon a relation which God, from His side, established between Himself and our knowing. That relationship God has established finally in Jesus Christ, for in the Incarnation the ultimate Truth meets us on this side of the discrepancy, actually within our mundane experience, in the midst of our

[1] Cf. A. N. Whitehead, *Process and Reality*, p. 8 f. Whitehead was concerned particularly with the abstractions of positivist physics or indeed with positivism in any area of science and philosophy. *Modes of Thought*, p. 202 f.

contingency and relativity, and there makes Himself accessible and amenable to our thinking and our statements. Therefore we have to think theological Truth and think Him out from His own real centre on this side where He has established Himself in the midst of our existence and established rational connection between us and Himself, respecting at once the 'hard fact' of His deity and the 'hard fact' of His historical humanity.

In other words, if we are to think scientifically in theology, that is, *a posteriori* and realistically, we have to think out the problem of our theological statements from within our actual knowledge of God in Jesus Christ on the ground of its own real and intrinsic coherence. We cannot abstract our statements from the centre to which they refer and where they have their Truth, namely in Jesus Christ, and then try to answer these critical questions from a standpoint foreign to them—that would be artificial and unreal, not to say irrational. We go, therefore, to Jesus Christ Himself as the Truth of God who has come to us on this side, meeting us where we are within our world. The Truth of God has become Man, so that while He is the Truth from the side of God toward man, because in Jesus Christ man has perfectly responded to that Truth, He is the Truth also from the side of Man toward God. He is both the Truth uttering Himself and Man hearing and receiving that Truth. In Jesus Christ the discrepancy between theological statements and the reality to which they refer has been overcome, and in Him that relation between human statements and the objective facts to which they refer, which cannot be put into words, nevertheless shows itself. Here we are up against an objective and essential interconnectedness in the nature of things which we are forced to recognize and which can only be judged by the self-evidence of its issues. Theologically speaking, there becomes evident in His language that which language itself cannot express, the Communion of the Spirit, the personal presence of the very Being of God bearing upon us and establishing relations with us. It is because in Jesus Christ we meet with God, the ultimate Truth, for Jesus Christ is Himself the embodiment of the Truth, that in Christ we have the sole objective standard by which to measure the truth of our analogical statements. Therefore it is in and through Christological thinking that we can probe deeply into the referring back (i.e. the ana-logic) of our statements to the Reality of God.

Before we go further, however, let us pause to note some false ways that are undertaken to answer the critical questions as to the truthfulness of our theological statements.

(1) The humanistic theologian tends to answer the critical questions by identifying the Truth of God with this-worldly truth.[1] That is to say, he denies that theological statements are empty of truth by claiming that they do not refer to a transcendent reality but only to realities within our mundane experience, of which they are symbolic expressions.[2] To use the dimensional mode of speech, the vertical reference is set aside altogether in favour of a purely horizontal reference. Thus, for example, the statement, 'God so loved the world that he gave his only begotten Son that whosoever believes in him should not perish, but have everlasting life',[3] may be interpreted to mean only: 'A true father loves his children and gives them the best he has'; or the statement, 'God was in Christ reconciling the world unto Himself',[4] may be interpreted to mean simply, 'In Jesus we learn to love even our enemies as ourselves.' True as these statements may be in themselves, as reinterpretations they will have to reckon with the obvious fact that this is to twist the meaning of Jesus in the first statement and the meaning of Paul in the second, and will have to face the charge of unfaithfulness or evasion in hermeneutical procedure[5]—but we do not raise that here.

We must never forget that theological statements are worldly statements and have this-worldly reference. Therefore they can be interpreted from several points of view, the historical, the psychological, the ideological, the ethical, the aesthetic,

---

[1] Cf. E. Troeltsch, *Glaubenslehre*, 1925, and *Gesammelte Schriften*, II, pp. 386 ff, 500 ff. The influence of this upon Bultmann's reductionism is very obvious.

[2] Cf. Braithwaite's Eddington Memorial Lecture, *An Empiricist's View of the Nature of Religious Belief*, though of course Braithwaite cannot in any sense be spoken of as a theologian.

[3] John 3. 16.   [4] 2 Cor. 5. 19.

[5] See the relevant critical questioning advanced by R. W. Hepburn who wants to make sure that theology is not being transformed into a kind of literary criticism, *Metaphysical Beliefs*, p. 85 ff. That is to say, in Richards' language, theology is in danger here of jettisoning the 'scientific use of language' to promote a reference for a 'poetic use' to evoke emotive responses.

etc. and as such come under the demands for verification according to the criteria that operate in these various realms of experience and use of language. We cannot deny that theological statements have this reference and therefore have a meaning and truthfulness in relation to other intra-mundane statements that have to be examined and set forth. Just because the Truth of God has come into this world, is on this side, we have to respect its earthly and worldly form and its this-worldly objectivity—on earth, in history, in Israel, in the Church. To deny that would be disrespect to God's Truth as it is in Jesus. But to identify God's Truth with the truth of the worldly forms into which it enters, would not only mean the identification of theology with mere phenomenology and therefore the rejection of theo-logical thinking, but would bring 'God' under the compulsion of our observation and thinking, and make 'Him' a prisoner of mere historical happening and relativity. This kind of 'God' could only be the apotheosis of man.[1] If the objective reference and material content of theological statements are eliminated so that they are converted into purely ideological statements, then they have to submit to being examined and tested only on that level where there would be little difficulty in showing that they are nonsensical and contradictory.[2]

(2) The other extreme answer is that of the mystic who discounts the worldly involvement of the Truth and seeks to transcend it all by a sharp division between the transcendent Truth of God and all this-worldly truth. This is to seek a truth in sheer detachment from all that is finite—spaceless, timeless, ecstatic truth. That is to say, it seeks to elude the actual way in which the Truth of God comes to us within the objectivities of this world, within historical happening, or perhaps to deny that the Truth of God actually condescends to us at all or that He stoops down in pity and mercy to reveal Himself to us in our lowliness and brokenness and earthiness.[3] Such a way would provoke all the more the challenge of the first critical question we noted and would induce it to become

---

[1] See Heinrich Vogel, op. cit. p. 79 f.

[2] Cf. *New Essays in Philosophical Theology*, edited by A. Flew and A. MacIntyre, or R. W. Hepburn, *Christianity and Paradox*.

[3] See H. Vogel, op. cit, p. 78 f.

a sceptical as well as a critical question. As against that, we cannot but submit to thinking as humble creatures on earth refusing at any point to try and think 'as God', above and beyond all our contingency and earth-bound relativities. Certainly the New Testament insists on pulling us down to earth and will not allow us to take off into realms of timeless truth, for it is on earth and in history that the Truth of God has chosen to meet us and to speak to us, within the limits of our lowly human speech and our earth-bound ways of thinking.[1]

(3) Between these two extremes is a third way that is often sought—and this has a Roman form and a Protestant form. In the Roman form, this is the way that brings in the *analogia entis* (like a *deus ex machina*) and seeks to ground and justify theological statements in a movement that rises by analogical reasoning from the creaturely and the contingent to the Divine, positing unlikeness as well as likeness between man and God, thus giving it resilience as well as resistance in face of critical and sceptical attacks. An outstanding example of this in modern times is to be found in the writing of Erich Przywara.[2] This derives from the Neo-Platonic idea mediated through Augustine that 'in the mind itself, even before it is a partaker of God, His image is found'.[3] It is the doctrine of an inherent kinship between divine and human being, or of a pre-established harmony between ultimate Truth and human truth. In its distinctive Protestant form, this is the way taken not only by the romantic-idealist theologians of the nineteenth century but even by thinkers like Albert Schweitzer who look upon 'the historical Jesus' not as giving us any direct knowledge of God but as providing us with an impressionistic picture (cf. the art of van Gogh) painted with strong apocalpytic

---

[1] This has been stated deliberately in an extreme form. I would not like to discount genuine mystical experience, but an experience in which the mystic is said to take leave of his senses is to be discounted, that is, an experience in which cognition is not *rationally* mediated through the senses or which uses sense-experience merely as a spring-board to enter a realm that transcends it altogether. That is a form of *docetism*.

[2] *Religionsphilosophie* (E. T. *Polarity*). The term *analogia entis* brought into prominence by Przywara does not go back to St. Thomas as some of its advocates appear to assume, and cannot truthfully be used to express his cautious and subtle conceptions of analogy for which there is much more justification, certainly within his own orbit of thought, than many of its Protestant critics admit or some of its Roman supporters allow to come through their 'Thomism'.

[3] *De Trinitate*, 14. 8.

strokes through which somehow we 'tune in' (it is Schweitzer who changes the metaphor) to the truth in the anonymous spirit of 'Jesus'.[1] Another version of this is found in the teaching of Rudolf Bultmann who treats the whole framework of the Gospel as 'myth' but uses it as the occasion for an existential decision in which we reinterpret the substance of the Gospel and find truth and 'authentic existence' beyond.[2] Both of these are fundamentally subjectivist for they do not succeed in breaking through their anthropological starting-point, but Schweitzer's at least is not characterized by a 'double-think', and has the merit of acknowledging that if no theoretical justification can be offered for the Truth of God as it is in Jesus, it is incumbent upon us to seek 'verification' by commitment to action.[3]

All these ways ultimately fail to wrestle seriously with the basic fact upon which the Christian Gospel rests and with which it stands or falls, the condescension of God to enter our lowly and creaturely existence in Jesus Christ, to break through the discrepancy between us and God, to enter into the midst of our hostility to the Truth and restore man to union with God, and so to be the Truth of God to man and the Truth of man toward God, and as such to be the Truth for man.

In contrast to the three ways mentioned we maintain that our theological statements are true only in reference, direct or indirect, to Jesus Christ. They stand or fall with the fact that they are statements proceeding from this centre of the Truth in Christ who is the source, basis, support, fulfilment and master of them all. But because they have to respect this centre they have to respect the majesty of the Truth that confronts us in Him, that is, its ultimate objectivity, and they have to respect the kind of truth we have in the modes of our this-worldly experience, that is, its secondary objectivity.

In so far as our theological statements refer to ultimate Truth they have their truthfulness in that reference, and their justification in what is true from the side of the objective reality, but in so far as they are human statements and have their meaning also in reference to other statements of this-worldly

---

[1] See especially *The Mystery of the Kingdom of God. The Secret of Jesus' Messiahship and Passion*, tr. with introduction by Walter Lowrie.

[2] *History and Eschatology, Jesus Christ and Mythology*, and the essays in *Kerygma und Muthos*, edited by H. W. Bartsch.

[3] Cf. John Macmurray, *The Self as Agent*, p. 202.

experience they have a truthfulness in the realm where human criteria claim to be applicable, e.g. historical facticity, logical consistency, ethical validity, etc. To despise this is only to open up a chasm of unmeaning. Thus the truthfulness of theological statements has to be considered from their double orientation: in relation to the ultimate Truth which is their primary reference, and in relation to their consistency with other human statements which is their secondary reference. The latter involves the whole question of the distinctive logic of theological statements[1] which will be taken up later.

We are now to consider the truthfulness of theological statements by asking the questions, How are theological statements related to the Truth? What kind of orientation must they have to be truthful? Here a formal relation and a material relation to the Truth come up for consideration.

Formally considered, our theological statements are true in so far as they are faithful responses to the self-communication of the Truth of God in the way in which He reveals Himself in and through the witness of the Holy Scripture, in the historical life of the Church, for it is there in the Holy Scripture that we actually hear God's Word. A theological statement is truthful only as answer to God's Word, as a reflex of the Truth addressing us as Word and claiming from us obedient and faithful response. It does not have its truth in itself but in that to which it is orientated and therefore can be truthful only in so far as that Truth is heard and received and answered. Here we have to remember the dialogical nature of theology and the nature of the Truth who summons us to dialogue with Him. It is precisely in that dialogical relation to the Truth that our statements have their truth, while they are emptied and falsified immediately they are divorced from it, for within it alone are they valid as statements that derive from the Truth and are obediently related to the Truth in the way the Truth comes to us. Concretely, it is in Christ Himself that our theological statements have their central and supreme term of reference, by which they are to be judged true or false, for He is the basis, the support, the content, the Truth of all our

---

[1] Cf. here the call by Edmund Schlink, citing G. Söhngen, for a *theologische Aussagenlogik* in Evangelical and Roman theology, *Kerygma u. Dogma*, 3.4, p. 291 ff., reprinted in *Der Kommende Christus und die Kirchlichen Traditionen*, p. 64 f.

theological statements. Some of them repose directly upon Him, and some are derived from Him indirectly but all have their proper place within the frame of reference which He creates and sets up in and through Himself and His Life and Work, and through which He directs them to the Father.

It is important, however, to consider how they are related to this frame of reference: to Christ speaking and revealing Himself and establishing a community around Him of those who hear and believe and obey Him and as such are used by Him as the medium of His continued revelation and communication. We cannot enter here into the whole doctrine of the Church in its apostolic foundation or into the doctrine of Holy Scripture bound up with that, although the formal relation that engages our concern at the moment cannot be separated from that material content.[1] The point we are concerned to make now is that our theological statements are related to the Truth as it is in Jesus in the way in which He relates Himself to us, comes to meet us, and addresses us, in and through the witness of the Holy Scriptures in the midst of the Church. He does not come to us apart from our modes of existence in space and time, or apart from the mode of being which He assumed in our space and time, and therefore He comes to us through the personal and historical communication of His Word deriving from the protocol reports and statements immediately in touch with Him in the apostolic witness and Scriptures. Hence we are thrown back upon Holy Scripture as the source and norm of all our theological statements. They are formally correct statements, accurately related to the Truth, as they are in obedient conformity to the Word of God addressing us in Christ through the Scriptures. That is the reference that tests whether they are *heard* or simply thought up, whether they are genuine audits corresponding to the Word of God or speculative constructs out of our own spirituality. Only 'heard statements' are true, that is, statements that repose upon or derive from the self-statements of God in Christ, and are therefore true from the side of God and correspondingly true from our side. Thus theological statements must be made within the sphere of Biblical revelation, as statements answering the Word heard in and through them.

[1] See *Theology in Reconstruction*, pp. 134 ff., 202 ff.

Now in the nature of the case we are unable to offer a purely theoretical justification for our hearing of the Word of God in Holy Scripture in the midst of the Church, for that is fundamentally an *empirical* reference, albeit an empirical reference in accordance with the nature of the unique referent and therefore not to be judged merely by the nature of other empirical references. But if we cannot explain how we are cast upon God in this way or state in language how the Word of God can come through to us (that is part of the meaning of the doctrine of the Holy Spirit), we can say something of the actual way in which we have come to know it, and so offer some account of the formal reference of theological thinking and stating which allows the inner logic of it to show through and in this way let the Truth become evident or come to view. A full account of this cannot be separated from an exposition of the content of Christian theology in its wholeness and inner coherence, but formally it will involve an examination of scientific inquiry as applied to Holy Scripture in order to ensure genuine hearing, and an examination of the interior or material logic of theological knowledge. We are now isolating the formal requirement for testing the truth of theological statements as obedient conformity to the way in which the Word of God actually comes to us and is heard within the Church through the witness of the Holy Scriptures.

We maintain, then, that the formal method of verification of theological statements is in accordance with the steps actually taken in learning and knowing the Truth, that is, through conformity to the Biblical revelation as it has reached us in the Church and within it through conformity to Jesus Christ Himself as the Truth of God for us. The *real* text with which we are concerned is not the letter of the Scriptures as such but the Humanity of Christ including His historical Life and Work, that is, the actual way in which the Word of God has objectified Himself for us within our human modes of existence in space and time, and has revealed Himself within our human speech and thought. It is because this is the Truth of God in all His majesty and lordship who comes to us in this way that we have to respect the way in which He has come and through which He still encounters us, and therefore we have to respect the accurate and correct conformity of our statements to that way.

That, as Heinrich Vogel has reminded us,[1] is the part of humility before the lordship of the Truth, and respect for its majesty in rejecting all ways that are inaccurate and incorrect and therefore 'unorthodox'.[2] Any theology that has not the courage to distinguish between true and false statements, has not the humility to submit to the majesty of the Truth and so betrays Him.[3]

But where our theological statements are truthfully related to the Truth in this way, they point away from themselves altogether to the Truth above and beyond them. As human statements they are to be subordinated to the Truth and related absolutely and therefore self-critically to it. They acknowledge thereby that in themselves they are inadequate and without truth. They have their truthfulness by reference to ultimate Truth and they are true in so far as they are absolutely related to the absolute Truth. Yet precisely because it is the absolute Truth to which they are related they are relative only to that Truth and are relativized by that Truth. On the other hand, because they belong as human statements to this world of contingency and relativity they are to be related also to relative truth within this world. It is only because they are absolutely related to the absolute Truth that they may be related to relative truth only relatively. Falsity would thus arise through a relative relation to the absolute Truth or through absolute relation to the relative.

We conclude that no matter how accurate or correct our theological statements are, they do not *possess* their truth in themselves. By being related to the ultimate Truth they are relativized in themselves and only in acknowledging their own poverty and relativity as statements can they truthfully refer to the ultimate Truth, and cling to that Truth as ultimate and final and as the sole source of their justification and legitimation. They are not true in virtue simply of *our* efforts to make them true, by bringing them into conformity to the Holy Scriptures, or even to Jesus Christ Himself, (that would be a

[1] H. Vogel, op. cit., p. 73 f.

[2] Properly 'orthodox' means *rightly related to the truth* in accordance with the truth itself, *not* (necessarily) in accordance with official or accepted opinion.

[3] Cf. here what D. Bonhoeffer is reported to have said about positive and critical Christology and the catastrophic loss of the concept of 'heresy'. *Christology*, tr. by J. Bowden, p. 77 f.

false conception of 'orthodoxy'), but true only in virtue ultimately of the Truth Himself, who is pleased to authenticate Himself to us and in spite of the poverty and inadequacy of our words and statements to be Himself their Truth, by Grace. Thus the final decision about the question of the truth does not depend on how it is conceived in our thinking or on how correct we can make our statements of it, but on the living Truth Himself. There is always a point before the face of the Truth of God as it is in Jesus where we break off speaking and are silent in order that God may declare Himself to us and the Truth be His own witness.

Materially considered, our theological statements are true through a content in the Truth which God alone gives them by His Grace. We cannot insist that God *must be* the content of our statements about Him.[1] It does not belong to our power or competence to say whether our statements have to be accepted as true and faithful to God. We cannot command the Truth or conjure up His real presence or compel His validation by our correct formulations of the Truth. This inability on our part is the obverse of the power of the Holy Spirit, the Spirit of Truth, as Jesus expressed it. We can but wait upon the Truth, listen to His Word, receive His communication into our minds, seek faithfully to express it in our statements, but at no point can we claim that God must be their actual content, that the Truth of God is enclosed in or is forcibly related to our statements of it, and therefore that God must acknowledge them.

Where our statements have to do with the ultimate Truth of God true verification must be through appeal to the judgement of God Himself. It is to be sought in a way that guards the true Majesty of God and preserves the true limits of the creature and so does not allow the creature to exalt himself above God, and thus to falsify himself or to turn the truth of God into a lie. We cannot anticipate or arrogate to ourselves the decision as to the truth but can only cast ourselves upon God, offering ourselves with our statements for His criticism and correction, for His approval or disapproval, and praying that through His judgement they may receive justification and truth.

---

[1] I have adapted this way of speaking from Barth, *Church Dogmatics* II.-1, p. 229. See the whole section on 'The veracity of man's knowledge of God', pp. 204–254.

In this submission to the judgement and Grace of God we rely upon the Incarnation, upon the condescension of the Truth to enter within our weakness in order to make Himself accessible and communicable to us (i.e. upon its own objective effectuality), and by the Grace of His revelation and reconciliation to be the object of our knowledge in spite of the limitations and inadequacy and poverty of our words and thoughts, for far from allowing His power to be limited or halted by them, He sanctifies and elevates them in His assumption of our humanity, and gives them a content in His Truth which they are utterly unable in themselves to hold or possess. Thus in Jesus Christ God has not only revealed Himself, objectified Himself, given Himself to be known but has actualized understanding and knowledge and speech of Himself within our humanity and its creaturely forms. It is that Truth spoken and heard, given and received, communicated and understood, and therefore spoken and given and communicated again within the idiom of our existence in space and time, that comes to us and claims from us understanding and thought and speech. Therefore as we hear and receive and understand the Truth of God and think it out and communicate it again in statements, we cast ourselves upon the reliability of God behind it all, by resting as Augustine used to say, upon the same Grace by which the Truth became incarnate, praying that our words and statements which we seek to utter in faithful conformity to the Truth of God as it is in Jesus may by Grace be given actual content in the Truth to which they humbly and obediently claim to refer. And we believe that according to His promise and in accordance with the judgements of His Grace, He will adopt them and give them their Truth in Himself, as it pleases Him.

'As it pleases Him', for He may reject our statements, putting us in the right with His Truth precisely by convicting us of error and by correcting us as we lay ourselves on the scales of the divine judgement. Therefore there can be no talk of verification except, as Barth has expressed it,[1] in a readiness to have our knowledge or our statements tested and revised with reference to the criterion whether they take place under the claims of our own majesty or under the claims of the Majesty

[1] *Church Dogmatics*, III. 2, p. 191.

of God, whether they are put forward as our own work or with the humility of those who are ready to receive justification from Him who alone is capable of justifying them. For verification we can only cast ourselves ultimately upon the justifying Grace of God, since in the last resort verification of our knowledge of God must come to us from without from God Himself.[1]

This two-fold way of answering the question as to the truthfulness of theological statements corresponds strictly to what we earlier considered as the twofold objectivity of the Truth, and the bi-polarity of our theological knowledge. We cannot break through into knowledge and understanding of the *Logos* simply by linguistic analysis and interpretation of the *lalia*; we cannot bring ultimate Objectivity of the Truth within our perception or apprehension by manipulation of its secondary objectivity. Yet it is only within the *lalia* that we may hear the *Logos*, and only through faithful conformity to the secondary objectivity of the Truth that we may meet the ultimate Objectivity of God Himself. The way of verification cannot be other than the way of actual knowledge; therefore the meaning and truthfulness of our theological statements will be in accordance with the steps we took in reaching knowledge or rather in accordance with the way in which the Truth has come to us and claimed us for its understanding and communication.

It is the actual content of our knowledge that tells us how it is known and prescribes how it is to be verified. Because the content of our knowledge cannot be separated from the activity of the Truth in objectifying Himself, in fulfilling revelation and reconciliation, it is the way that the Truth has taken with us, and therefore the way of our knowing of the Truth, that prescribes how our knowing of it and our statements about it are to be verified. Thus the discovery of the material form and mode of our knowing is a *sine qua non* of verification. A difficulty is constantly presented here by those who seek to

---

[1] To this, *mutatis mutandis*, corresponds the fact that in natural science verification requires in the last resort a personal judgement in assessment of the evidence. No theoretical demonstration will ever give final certainty in the realm of the empirical, so that the scientist must judge whether he will commit himself to the pressure of the facts upon him. Cf. M. Polanyi, *Personal Knowledge*, pp. 17, 59 f., 63 f., 202, 264, 299 ff. etc.

abstract a theoretical verifying from the actual way of learning. This is to assert the primacy of what is purely formal and to confound the analytical explanation of symbols and operating with them.[1] We can see this outside the realm of theology in the conflict between the critical verification inseparable from the process of scientific discovery, and the abstract steps of demonstration laid down by some empiricist philosophers as the only valid method of verification. But since the abstract steps laid down by these philosophers are not in accord with the actual steps taken in positive learning and discovery they can only eliminate the very movement they are intended to verify and so convict themselves of futility. It is not otherwise with those who would seek to abstract out of theological activity a method of verification which is 'dead' from the very start because it is torn away from the living movement of actual learning and knowing the Truth, and in particular is divorced from the way the Truth acts upon us and makes Himself accessible and knowable for us.

Knowledge is real only as it is in accordance with the nature of the object, but the nature of the object prescribes the mode of rationality we have to adopt towards it in our knowing, and also the nature of the demonstration appropriate to it. The object of theological knowledge is the Truth of God as it is in Jesus, Truth that is certainly in human form, and therefore human forms of thought and speech have all to be taken seriously and strictly honoured, but Truth who is by His very nature Grace and Spirit, and therefore His nature must be taken seriously and strictly honoured. What the nature of this Truth requires, then, is *justification by Grace*, and *demonstration of the Spirit*, that is, verification and action by the Truth Himself. At this point we recall our previous discussion about the nature of the incarnate Truth of God and all that it requires of us in true and faithful knowledge of Jesus Christ. That may be summarized by saying that justification by the Grace of God in Jesus Christ applies not only to our life and action, but to our knowledge, and is essentially relevant to epistemology.

When St. Paul taught the doctrine of justification by Grace alone he was opposed by those who thought he was encouraging

---

[1] Cf. here Gilbert Ryle's distinction between using concepts and talking about them, *The Concept of Mind*, p. 8 f. However we must also learn not to mistake thinking concepts and *thinking things through them*.

moral irresponsibility, and in fact undermining the law, but Paul insisted that on the contrary he was establishing the law. Similarly when Luther reasserted the same doctrine at the Reformation he was met with the charge of fostering anti-nomianism, but he showed that the contrary was the case, for out of justification flowed the life ruled by the law of love, and that far from subverting moral responsibility justification by Grace alone established it upon a profound and unshakeable foundation.

Likewise, when justification or verification by the Grace of God is applied to the realm of knowledge it is met with the charge of antinomianism or irrationalism, that is, with under-mining the laws and norms of responsible thought and the requirements for orderly and controlled knowledge, but, once again, it is the contrary that must be maintained. It is justi-fication that really establishes our knowledge rationally upon the Truth of God as its *real* ground and by putting it in the right with the Truth establishes it with appropriate laws and norms according to which it is formally testable and verifiable.[1] It is through such an integration of form and matter, thought and action, knowledge and life, that meaning, rationality and responsibility are firmly grounded. It is in the establish-ment of such a framework of knowledge with its own interior logic that we may achieve the clarification within which the validation of theological knowledge may take place in the continued prosecution of theological inquiry.

Now it is through this combination in justification by Grace of the formal and material methods of verification that we have a continuous unfolding of the inner rationality of theological knowledge which is not only fertile in illuminating further inquiry and in shedding light on a great manifold of other questions, but involves the development of a living structure of human life in commitment to the Truth of God. Formally considered, the verification of our theological statements

[1] From this point of view traditional 'theism' appears too abstract, and to be operating only with ideological truth rather than with the truth of being. Since ultimately the proof of an unknown reality is its own evidence and the evident assent it calls forth from us, theistic arguments can have power only if they persuade us to allow our minds to fall under the compulsive self-evidence of the divine Reality, otherwise we merely lapse back into our own manipulation of ideas. If I judge him correctly, it is in this direction that E. L. Mascall's thought has been moving over the years.

consists, as we saw, in their reference to Jesus Christ in the way in which knowledge of Him reaches us through the Church and through the witness to Him in the Scriptures in the midst of the Church. Materially considered, the verification of theological statements is found only in the Grace of God in Jesus Christ, as He actively gives Himself in His own Being through the power of the Spirit to be the object of our knowledge (*per modum entis*) and the justification of our human modes of knowing and speaking of Him as we seek to act in conformity to His Word and Truth in Jesus Christ. This is a justification so total in its claim over us and all our knowing and being that we cast ourselves upon it, submitting to its judgement and justification alone, but in abandoning ourselves to its control and operation we find that we are assimilated to the Truth and established in conformity to the Word of God as it is in Jesus. Thus in Him our knowing and our learning and our living are brought together through a living and personal union with the Truth, and that in turn becomes the medium in which we continue to have dialogue with God in Christ and continue to think and speak of the Truth in a mode of life in which we live the truth and do the truth.

Hence if it is true from the side of the ultimate Truth of God in Jesus that the only way to prove the Truth is to be the Truth, it becomes correspondingly true from our side that there is no proof of the truth or of our knowing and speaking of Him apart from actual engagement with the Truth, in doing the truth and being true. Theoretically, this means an assimilation of our knowing of the Truth to the Truth Himself, so that verification involves the clarification of the real or analogical relation involved; practically, this means an assimilation of our life and history to the life and history of the Truth of God as it is in Jesus, so that justification issues in the obedience and conformity of our life to the normative Life of Christ.[1] But the theoretical and the practical cannot be separated from one another for they are like soul and body, faith and works, and one is wanting without the other.

We may state this question in another way, by saying that justification by the Grace of God alone has as its correlative

---

[1] For the relation between the cognitive and the practical in verification see again John Baillie, op. cit., p. 68 and pp. 130 ff.

commitment to the Truth in action. This does not mean that in addition to verification by the Grace of God theology operates also with another subsidiary test, but it does mean that any mode of verification that cuts off action from knowledge, or knowledge from action, is not a true test, for it does not correspond to the nature of the Truth as it is in Jesus. Commitment in action *by itself* cannot be used as a pragmatic test of truth precisely because it is correlative to justification by Grace alone which insists that the true is the *real*, and which therefore summons us to cast ourselves entirely upon God, to reject reliance upon ourselves or our own works and to live constantly and entirely, not from a centre in ourselves, but from a centre in Christ. It is only by being justified in Christ like that, that the Christian can live in the truth, for when he is thrown back on himself he is thrown back into a situation of unreality where there is a contradiction between the statements which he makes concerning the truth and his actual existence as a sinner. Thus to live from a centre in himself is to live in untruth; only if he lives from a centre in the Truth can he be assimilated to it, live in the truth and do the truth.

On the other hand, then, justification by putting us in the right with the Truth of God calls in question all that claims to be knowledge of the truth on our part and calls into question our theological statements in so far as they claim to have truth in themselves, and directs them away from themselves to Christ as the one Truth of God. And yet in so doing justification establishes us in certainty through grounding and pivoting all our knowing and thinking and acting objectively upon the divine Reality in Christ. On the other hand, however, justification summons us to live no longer unto ourselves but unto Christ and therefore unto one another in Him as those whom He loves, and so to bear fruit in our life and action. 'By their fruit', said Jesus, 'ye shall know them.'[1] Justification has thus the profoundest consequences for our life and thought and action for in it we are committed to a way of acting and thinking that affects the whole structure of our existence as human beings. This difference would appear to offer some *prima facie* evidence for the truth of our theological statements, but Christian theology will not have it so, and cannot have it so,

[1] Matt. 7.16.

for to rest upon it as evidence would be, thus far, to withdraw from reliance upon justification by Grace alone and therefore to undermine the very commitment which gives rise to such 'evidence'. Hence justification involves such a commitment in action to the Truth as it is in Jesus that in the nature of the case we cannot rely upon that action but only upon Christ, but it also insists that only through such commitment to Christ, through obedient conformity to Him, may we know Him and that only through doing the will of God can we know His doctrine, whether it is of God.[1]

[1] John 7. 17.

5

Problems of Logic

In an earlier chapter we made use of the old distinction between *scientia generalis* and *scientia specialis* to show that while in theological knowledge we are concerned with forms of disciplined rational activity common to all scientific knowledge, nevertheless we are also concerned with a specific mode of rational activity in strict accordance with the nature of the given Reality, namely, Jesus Christ as the incarnate Word of God, full of Grace and Truth. In Him the eternal God has condescended to objectify Himself for us in time and within our own humanity, freely giving Himself to us as the Object of our knowledge, reconciling and assimilating us to Himself as the Truth. This specific mode of rational activity set up between us and the Truth is *faith*, i.e. the theological reason in which our knowing is adapted to the manifold nature of the incarnate Truth as divine, personal, human, historical. This is in no sense ecstatic activity for in faith we do not stand outside our rational activity but stand within it where the Truth of God has assumed human form and where our human knowing attains an inner conformity to the Truth of God in Christ. It is through this conformity that theological knowledge and in and through it that theological statements can have truthfulness. Thus theology does not and cannot, by its own scientific operation, step outside of faith and conformity to Christ in faith: rather is it a disciplined and accurate handling of the forms of rational reflection that arise in faith under the creative impact of the Word or Truth of God. Because we are concerned in theology with ultimate Truth, ultimate Authority, and ultimate Objectivity, these forms must be accorded a precedence and supremacy in accordance with the ultimate nature of their Object, and yet because the Object has assumed the kind of objectivity we have in the space and time of our world (i.e. human and historical form), we must respect the forms of rational reflection that arise in the knowledge of human and historical and this-worldly realities. Because its proper Object is personal, human, historical, etc., theological knowledge overlaps with other kinds of knowledge which involve the personal, human, historical, etc., but because it is knowledge of *divine* Truth in personal, human, historical forms, theological knowledge cannot be reduced or resolved into these other kinds of knowledge. It has a fundamental mode of rational activity that transcends them all and yet never leaves them behind. What is the relation between specifically theological forms of thought and forms of thought common to theology and other rational knowledge? This is the question that must now engage our attention. It is not the question as to the relation between the thought-forms of theological science and the thought-forms of other special sciences, such as historical science or natural science, but as to the relation between theological thought-forms and the general thought-forms employed in all knowledge.

We recall the distinction between statements that have their truth not in themselves but in a reality beyond them to which they refer, and statements which have their truth in themselves in their orderly or consistent inter-relations. Theological statements have both characteristics but they are basically statements which refer beyond themselves altogether to the Truth of God. They are, to speak rather naively, statements with a vertical reference which must have its own specific logic, yet they are also statements with a horizontal reference and have their formal logic on that level. But how can we consider the Truth of God, to which our statements have vertical reference, on the horizontal plane? Can we think out to the end within the linear modes of formal logic the living and eternal Truth who condescends to us and meets us in Jesus Christ, and interacts with our world?

A double problem is involved here. There is the constant difficulty of relating knowledge or speech to being, for being always breaks through the limits of our statements and outruns their logical forms; it will not be cramped within the structures we contrive in order to determine apprehension of it, even when we do apprehend it through them. This is something that every science has to face more acutely the further it advances, how to relate the logic of abstract form to the logic of objective reference—it is the problem of *ontologic*. But theology has an added difficulty, for the way in which statements refer to God is rather different from the way in which they refer to anything else. God Himself is different and cannot be conceived in the same way in which other things are conceived, and so we have to reckon with a change in the habits of mind and the meanings of terms, with a different type of concept and indeed with a different use of language and form in regard to Him. How are we to relate the *logos* of man to the *Logos* of God, formal logic to the Logic of God? In addition to the problem of ontologic, this is, so to speak, the problem of *theologic*. Since it is evident that the logic of theological statements cannot be treated through any logical abstraction from their ontological reference, we shall first consider the basic forms of theological thought that arise in virtue of their reference to the real, then try to clarify the bearing within theological discourse of the logic of coherence-statements to the logic of existence-statements.

I THE LOGIC OF GOD

By speaking of 'the Logic of God' we must not think that we can climb up to God and pry into His Mind or understand His secret judgements. 'My thoughts are not your thoughts, neither are your ways my ways, saith the Lord. For as the heavens are higher than the earth, so are my ways higher than your ways, and my thoughts than your thoughts' (Isaiah 55, 8–9). The Logic of God is the way His Truth has taken in His self-giving and self-objectification for us, and therefore the forms of reflexion that arise in our knowledge corresponding to the form of the Truth. God who is infinitely greater than our words or logic has stooped down to speak with us in our poor creaturely words and human logic, and thus to give them a Truth beyond any power or capacity they can have in themselves. By 'the Logic of God' we can only mean Jesus Christ, for He and no other is the eternal *Logos* of God become flesh. He is the incarnate *Logic* of God, the Logic of God's Grace and Truth toward us, and therefore we are bound to think in terms of this incarnate Logic in Christ. The Logic is in Christ before it is in us; it is in the given Reality before it is in our knowledge of Him. What we have to do is to lay bare the organic meaning or structural coherence of theological knowledge as it takes form and order in accordance with the living unity and order of the Truth in Jesus Christ.

Several aspects of the nature of Christ the Truth, which we have already considered, are nomothetic for our understanding of the essential framework of theological knowledge and the kind of relations that obtain within it.

(a) We begin with the Grace of Jesus Christ—that is, with the condescension of the Truth of God to become incarnate and freely to give Himself to us. The whole movement of the Truth of God from beginning to end is one of pure Grace toward us and it never ceases to be Grace even in our knowing of the Truth. This means that we must acknowledge the unconditional priority of the Truth and the irreversibility of the relation He establishes with us. For example 'the Word became flesh' cannot be reversed as 'the flesh became the Word' without falsification. The action of the Truth belongs to its nature as the Truth and can be truly known only in accordance with that action. When God gives Himself to us as the object of our knowledge He does not thereby cease to be Subject or hand over the control in that knowledge to the human knower—He remains throughout the Lord. The God—man, Lord—servant relationship is not reversible in fact, even when formal statement in human speech may require grammatical reversal. We may well say, 'We know God', but when on the ground of this actual knowledge we go on to make the further statement, 'therefore we are able to know God', we cannot truthfully detach this 'knowability of God' from the actual fact that God in the freedom of His Grace gives us knowledge of Himself, and so predicate it of ourselves. Strictly speaking the knowability of God can be predicated only of God, for it is grounded in His divine freedom and nature, but it may be predicated of man on the ground of the divine Grace and as reflexive of the self-giving of the Truth in Grace. This unconditional priority of the Truth and the irreversibility of His relationship to us may be called *the Logic of Grace*, that is the way in which we are bound to think the Truth in accordance with His nature and action as Grace.

(b) This incarnate Truth confronts us in Jesus Christ as true God and true Man united in one Person. He makes Himself known to us as One who has already established in Himself relation between God and man and man and God, and therefore is truly known only in accordance with this *union* in His nature. It is this relationship within the Person of Christ between His divine and human natures (called the *hypostatic union*) that provides the normative relationship for every theological statement where the relationship between God and man is involved. Thus whenever our knowledge of the Truth is properly ordered it will reveal a structure in its material content that reflects the Christological pattern of the hypostatic union. This is the *interior logic* of theological thought, logic that arises under the impact of the Object, that is impressed upon our knowledge of God from its basic frame of reference in Jesus Christ, logic that informs and guides all scientific thinking in this field.

(c) We cannot forget here that the divine and human natures of Christ are united in *One Person* and that this Person is the *One Word* of God. He is the Truth of God in the form of Personal Being, Word of God identical with His Person. Since He is Person and Word the forms of knowledge that arise in us are correspondingly personal and verbal (or propositional). Since He is Person of God, the personalising Person, personal forms of reflection are begotten in us as we are obedient to Him. Since He is Word of God, the Creator Word, thought-forms are created in us as we yield our minds to His self-communication. Since He is Person and Word in One, conformity to Him in Person and conformity to Him in Word are one and indivisible in us. Therefore we do not just learn of Christ, we learn Christ. Nor do we just think about Christ, we think Christ. We think a Person, the Person, and in doing that we are adapted to personal thinking and gain true subjectivity. He certainly communicates truths to us, but they are truths that inhere in His Personal being and are not detachable from Him. They are truths that cohere together through inhering in Him and are truly known only in that cohering and inhering in His Person. Understanding of them is gained in dialogue, in what we might call 'personalogical' relation with Him. Because these truths are essentially of a personal kind, they are related to one another in an inter-personal way, that is, in *love*, for love is the inter-personal mode of relation. This is not love as emotion but love as the form of personal union. It is this personal logic, the *logic of love* inhering in the Truth that comes to view in our theological knowledge as we learn to behave according to the nature of the Object, Jesus Christ, that is, as we learn to love Him objectively.[1]

(d) We have now to consider a fourth aspect of the incarnate Truth of God which is nomothetic for our understanding of theological logic—its permanent and essential form in space and time. Because the Truth has entered into our creaturely existence and has become historical, because He lives and acts in space and time, He is only known in active, living, temporal relation to Him. This is living Truth, Truth that has come into our human life and has taken up our time and life into Himself, Truth that is identical with the whole life and activity of Jesus Christ. He does not first become living and active by entering into our space and time and sharing in our human life, but in and through doing that He reveals that living and acting belong to His being as the Truth of God. What He is toward us He is eternally and antecedently in Himself, but what He is in Himself He is toward us within our life in space and time. In Himself and toward us He is the Way, the Truth, and the Life. The Truth of God is what He is in the whole of His incarnate life and work, in His self-communicating to us and His self-giving for us. We cannot know this Truth unhistorically or statically, therefore, by seeking to pass behind or beyond His action and life *in time* to what we may imagine to be the Truth in Himself, for there is no other Truth of God for us than this Truth in life and action who decisively intervenes in our human existence and pours Himself out in love to redeem us from our plight. He is not to be found or known except as He *gives* Himself to be known in space and time, that is, as He *becomes* flesh, as He *lives* His life in time and action on earth for our

---

[1] Cf. John Macmurray, *Reason and Emotion*, p. 32: 'The capacity to love objectively is the capacity which makes us persons. It is the ultimate source of our capacity to behave in terms of the object. It is the core of rationality'.

sake, as He *dies* upon the Cross for our salvation, and as He *rises again* from the dead for our justification. The Truth of God cannot be separated from the whole historical Jesus Christ, for time, decision, action, history belong to the essential nature of this Truth. Therefore we cannot apprehend or consider the Truth in detachment from relations in space and time without downright falsification. The Truth of God in Jesus cannot be known except in a way analogous to His nature, that is through relation to the Truth in time and space, in history and action.[1] Knowing the Truth involves on our part a corresponding movement in space and time, a dynamic, living, active relationship, a constant historical communion with the Truth, in which we grow in the Truth and learn the Truth increasingly, so that there can be no genuine knowing the Truth or speaking the Truth without *doing the Truth*. The living Truth requires a *kinetic* mode of knowledge and thought.

We maintain, then, that knowledge of the Truth of God demands relation to the Truth *in time* and *in action*, that is, a *verbal relation*, one described by verbs and adverbs. This is a relation that is not still, timeless and necessary, like the relations we express in pure mathematics or in symbolic logic, but a relation involving movement in time and freedom in decision, rather akin to a resolution of the will or a decisive action. Here the theological reason functions in a transitive, historical way corresponding to the living, transitive nature of the Truth, and therefore it operates with a rational nexus between the truths that make up the content of its knowledge that is correspondingly transitive and historical. In order to express this adequately theology requires something like a *four-dimensional logic* or a *logic of verbs* in which the all-important relation to the Truth in time and in action is preserved, whereas that is precisely what is eliminated by symbolic or mathematical logic.[2] Logical relation (in the traditional sense) and temporal relation cannot be confounded without error, but it is just with such falsifying abstractions of actual

[1] Cf. the idea of O. Cullmann that faith involves incorporation into saving history, *Heil als Geschichte*, pp. 97 ff.

[2] Perhaps the nearest thing we have to what is required is 'quantum logic', the logic of the profound connection between the geometrical and dynamical aspects of things—see the way in which this is expressed by de Broglie, *Physics and Microphysics*, pp. 100, 126.

knowledge that theology has constantly to struggle if it is to be faithful to the nature of the Truth or genuinely objective and scientific.

Before we can discuss this and draw out its implications for theological thinking, we have to examine a little more the way in which the Truth of God in Christ is received and communicated. True knowledge of Him is not isolated or individualist. To a certain extent that is true of all knowledge, which is never finally the activity of single individuals. It arises in community and requires community for its full and proper operation, and can never escape from it. The thinking of all of us is conditioned by history, by previous thinking and the communication of knowledge already acquired; but it is also conditioned by our personal relations in the present, for even our basic rationality requires the objectivity of other minds. This is particularly the case in theological knowledge where the object of our thinking is the Person of Christ, the Personalising Person, for to think Him is an acutely personal function and in thinking Him we are adapted to personal thinking. Jesus Christ does not come to me alone but as He comes to others, and so comes to me in such a way that He requires of me personal relations with others. Hence we cannot think Christ without thinking Him together with others in a community of persons. If I isolate myself from my brother for whom Christ has given Himself, I thereby call in question my own relationship to Christ and so isolate myself from Him who is the Truth. Thus in so far as theological thinking is Christological it is also communal thinking. It is only *with all saints* that we may comprehend what is the breadth and length and depth and height, and know the love of Christ which passes knowledge (Eph. 3. 18 f.).

Moreover this communal thinking is part of a historical movement and is conditioned by previous thinking in the community. That is indeed one of the fundamental results of the Incarnation, for with the Incarnation, as we have seen, Truth in the form of Personal Being came into time, assumed and lived a historical life, and by His very nature established a historical Community in personal and historical communion with Him. The Truth is the Person of the historical Jesus, who is both known and communicated only in personal and historical relations. The Truth is of such a nature that He must be communicated to us by other persons in time. The Truth is not something we can tell ourselves or to whom we can relate ourselves timelessly. Thus the receiving and communicating of this Truth are continuously creative of the Church as the community in and through which the Truth communicates Himself, i.e. in and through the inter-personal and historical relations which obtain between the members of the Community. Theological knowledge is found just there within the historical Church where both individual and corporate reception and communication of the Truth take place from generation to generation. This is not to deny that the Truth comes to each of us and to the community directly through the Word and Spirit of Christ. He does come to us directly but not apart from His coming personally and historically through the Word communicated by other historical persons. Christ communicates Himself to us personally in and through the historical Church where the Word is mediated to us in temporal acts by others, and where through that Word He comes immediately in direct address and personal meeting. Thus the Truth is received and communicated, and therefore known from generation to generation, within the Church as the Community of the Word, the Community of Christ revealing Himself through His Word, and of those who conjointly hear and receive it, in short, within the Church as the Body of Christ.

We are now in a position to state two things.

(1) Because of the personal and historical nature of the Truth of God in Jesus Christ theological knowledge arises within a certain delimited sphere, where the Truth is personally and historically received and communicated. Theological thinking takes place within that sphere of actual knowledge—it is not free thinking that strays wherever it likes beyond the bounds laid down by the nature of the Object.[1] Theological thinking is in no sense arbitrary, but is unconditionally bound to its proper Object, in orderly correspondence with His nature. It does not run ahead of its Object through *a priori* speculation; it does not lag behind its Object through attachment to static

---

[1] This is what distinguishes theological science from philosophy, for philosophical thinking is a form of thinking beyond set bounds, undetermined by concrete subject-matter and therefore transcendent of any particular methods. Yet philosophy is not arbitrary or free-thinking for it is limited by the conditions and possibilities and necessities of thought-forms.

forms of thought, but it follows Christ in ardent discipleship, in self-denial and repentance, obedient to the limitations and restraints and necessities imposed upon it by the nature and work of Christ, and therefore within the personal and historical relations of the Church as the given sphere of union and communion with Christ. Genuine theology is thus an important function of the Church as the Body of Christ in history. That aspect of theology is pursued in dogmatics, that is (from this point of view) the disciplined thinking of the Church in which it clarifies knowledge of the Truth in the historical succession of its understanding from generation to generation. Faithful theology cannot but be dogmatics, just because it cannot divorce itself from historical conversation with Christ the Truth and cannot abstract its content from organic relation to the Church as the sphere of reconciliation and communion with Christ. It is partly from the living continuity of the Church that theology derives its dynamic and teleological character as well as the organic pattern of its understanding that struggles for articulation in the historical decisions and formulations of the mind of the Church. That is not the aspect of theological thinking that is our immediate concern here, although we cannot leave it out of sight altogether. Behind this outward organic pattern of theology we are concerned with the inner Christological pattern of the Church's understanding of the Truth.

(2) If the Church as the Body of Christ constitutes the sphere where actual knowledge of the Truth is to be found, within that sphere the understanding of the Truth is articulated in a body of truths that derive from and ultimately cohere in the Person of Christ who is Himself the one Truth of God. It is because these truths are personal and historical in their very nature that they require to be known in the Church, but because they are personal and historical they have inter-connections of a unique kind which require articulation. How are we to describe this interior constitution of the body of personal truth? What is the *interior logic* of theological knowledge? And what is its relation to the exterior or formal logic which consistent theological statements cannot but employ? How is doctrine to be related to doctrine, and truth related to truth, in such a way that we are entirely faithful to the nature

of the One Truth from whom they derive and to whom they point?

When we try to express theological truths in statements, and in particular when we put them down on paper, we are aware of an element of abstraction in our thinking. The living, personal, historical truths tend to be refracted in the process and abstracted from their source and ground. They lose touch with reality and become incomplete symbols. Once they are detached they become idea-truths which can be given rigorous presentation in a coherent system. To be treated as real or to have the semblance of reality they must inhere in something as its ideological articulation. This is the constant temptation of theology: to allow its doctrines and truths to become abstract and then, since we cannot remain content with mere ideas, to graft them on to something, the Church, or society, or the State, or the nature of man himself, as the ground of their reality. In that process theology is resolved into something else, sociology or anthropology, for example. It ceases to be genuine *theo*-logy, to be concerned with truths that derive from and inhere in the One Truth of *God*, and which are thought only *theo*-logically. When theological truths inhere in something other than their proper object they become an ideology which attains its power, sometimes incredible power, from the natural forces latent in that in which they inhere and for which they act in ideological interpretation. The temptation of the Roman Church is to turn its theology into an ecclesiastical ideology and the temptation of the Protestant Church is to turn its theology into an anthropological ideology. In this way both can betray the Truth and the basic nature of theology. Theology can be genuine *theo*-logy if it is Christologically orientated toward God. Important as the place of the Church may be, and important as the place of man may be, for true theological thinking, neither can usurp the place of Jesus Christ as the given Reality in whom all theological truths inhere and through whom alone they cohere with each other. In our world where our relation to God is damaged and where all things await the consummation of their redemption, we cannot avoid elements of refraction and abstraction in theological knowledge, but we must be constantly on our guard against handling theological truths merely in their form as incomplete symbols or as idea-truths. We must seek at every point to trace the reference of our theological statements to their given Reality, and learn to see their truth not in themselves but in Jesus Christ and in His relation to the Father. In the last analysis it will be in and through that Christological reference that we can discern the true logic of their relation to one another.

We may now attempt to describe the logic of God from two different but related points of view, and at the same time gather up our discussion so far.

(1) It is *the Logic of Grace*. This is what we have spoken of as the unconditional priority of the Truth as Grace and the irreversibility of the relationship established between the Truth and us. The Logic of Grace is the way the Truth has taken in His disclosure to us. Because He does not cease to be Grace in our knowing of Him, all our thoughts and their interrelations must reflect the movement of Grace.

Let us return to the fact that knowledge of the Truth requires acts of obedience on our part, and that it is only through these acts of obedience that we can see how the truths are related to one another. The act of obedience we may describe as *decision*. No decision is required when we state that $2 \times 2 = 4$. We are concerned there with what is timeless and necessary. No time-element is involved in truth of this kind; it is not something that becomes true, and has to operate in order to be true. No choice, no decision is involved. The conclusion is necessary; it is not reached through a free act.[1] In theology, however, we cannot discern the truth except through decision. It is he who does the will of God who knows of the doctrine, and he who does the truth who comes to the light. Thus there is no necessary, timeless, and no formal-logical relation between the death of Jesus Christ on the Cross and the forgiveness of

---

[1] 'If religious belief was the kind of thing that could be presented as the conclusion of an argument, we should either have too much certitude or too little for the belief in question to be a religious belief. For if we could produce logically cogent arguments we should produce the kind of certitude that leaves no room for decision; where proof is in place, decision is not. We do not decide to accept Euclid's conclusions; we merely look to the rigour of his arguments . . .' Alasdair MacIntyre, *Metaphysical Beliefs*, p. 179. MacIntyre's mistake, however, is to equate the 'objective justification' of belief with this kind of proof, p. 209. In his whole approach to theological concepts and language he fails, like R. W. Hepburn, to work within the scientific necessity of different *levels* of thought.

our sins. There is indeed a relation but it is only established by divine action and discerned through faith.

However, it would be a serious mistake to think of faith or decision as an organ for perception or as a means of 'making real' the truths of the Gospel. Personal decision or the act of believing by itself tells us nothing. The act of faith reposes upon the prior act of Christ, a final decision made by Him on our behalf. Our decision for Christ answers to His decision for us, and relies upon it as its objective ground. "Ye have not chosen me, but I have chosen you". "Herein is love, not that we loved God but that he loved us". "Ye know God, or rather are known of God". We have already had occasion to note that epistemological inversion of our relation to God. Here it can be stated by saying that our act of faith is grounded on God's decision of Grace to give Himself to us and to choose us for Himself. In other words, our personal decision is rooted in *election*, the prevenient movement of God's love that is so incarnated in Jesus Christ that in Him we have both the pure act of divine Grace toward man and the perfect act of man in obedient response toward God's Grace. It is because Jesus Christ has offered a perfect obedience in our place to the Father, because He has appropriated God's Grace for us, because from beginning to the end of His incarnate Life He stood in for us and not only gave an account to God for us, offering our response to the Father, but actualised in Himself the Truth of God translating it into His human life, that we may know the Truth in and through Jesus Christ. Thus in His total obedience of mind and body, in the whole logic of His perfect human life, He has already realised and provided the inner relation between the truths that cohere in His incarnate Person. The way that the Grace of God has taken in the assumption of our humanity in Christ and in the whole of His incarnate life and death and resurrection is the decisive action upon which our personal decision reposes, and which it reflects in its corresponding action. We do not relate the truths of the Gospel to one another by our decision, but in and through our faith we discern how the truths are already related in the decisive movements of the Grace of God in Jesus Christ. Every theological doctrine must reflect in its way, directly or indirectly, the unconditional priority of the

Grace of God if it is to be faithful to the Truth—it is that relation that is revealed and established in the relation of the incarnate Son to the Father, in the relation and union of the human nature and the divine nature of Christ. It is in that light alone that we can reach a genuine understanding of how our human decision is related to the election of Grace actualised in Christ. The way that the Grace of God has taken in the whole life and work of Christ belongs to the essential pattern of the body of theological truth. It is the logic of Grace that shapes the inner form of every true theological statement.

(2) It is *the Logic of Christ*. This is the other side of the Logic of Grace, for it is the logic of the Grace of the Lord Jesus Christ that is the manifestation of the Logic of God. It is in considering it from this angle that we may discuss the actual pattern of that logic, not only its movement and action.

Here we may begin in a different way, by thinking of all the truths or doctrines of the faith as forming an organic whole, cohering in one body in the unity of the faith, with its own essential pattern. We do not seek to impose a pattern upon theological knowledge but rather to discern the pattern inhering in its material content, or to let it reveal itself to us as we direct our questions toward it to find out its central frame of reference. When we do that we are directed to Jesus Christ, to the Incarnation, to the hypostatic union, the unique to-getherness of God and man in Christ which is normative for every other relationship between man and God. By the hypostatic union we must not think of some static relation but rather of the union between God and man in the one Person of the Son running throughout all His historical life from His birth to His resurrection. It is the whole life of the incarnate Son, the historical, crucified and risen Jesus Christ that forms the core or the axis of the body of Christian theology. It is from that centre that we take our bearings as we consider the doctrine of the Trinity, of the Father and of the Holy Spirit as well as of the Son, and therefore of creation as well as of redemption—for this is the mystery hidden from the ages and now revealed in the Gospel, that in Jesus Christ all things consist and are gathered up. The other doctrines of the faith, the Church, the Sacraments, man and the last things, etc., all have their place and their truthfulness by reference to this central point in Jesus Christ. The one supreme personal relation is the hypostatic union, the unique relation of divine and human natures in the One Person of the Son, but by reference to that personal relation, all other personal relations are to be understood in their likeness and in their difference to it. It is here then in the inner life and being of Jesus Christ, in the hypostatic union, that we discern the interior logic of theological thinking, the logic of Christ, the logic that is in Christ before it is in our knowledge of Him, the logic that inheres ontologically and personally in Him but which is reflected noetically and sacramentally in us in the conformity of our life and thought to Him and in the directing of them through Him to God the Father.

A word of warning is now in place: we cannot turn the doctrine of the hypostatic union into ideological truth, and use it as the masterful idea of a system of thought. The notion of the hypostatic union is nothing in itself, for it does not have its truth in itself. Its function is to point us to the reality, Jesus Christ who meets us as very God and very Man in one Person, who is Lord over all our knowing of Him, and must remain Lord over all our articulation and formulation of the truths He communicates to us. Here we must hold together 'the logic of Grace' and 'the logic of Christ', for it is only in the freedom of His Grace that God's Truth has come into our midst and assumed human nature into union with Himself, thus establishing the hypostatic union. Hence the doctrine of the hypostatic union can be handled aright only as the expression of the act of divine Grace and the irreversible relation between God's Grace and man. To use severely technical terms, we may say that the logic of Grace and the Logic of Christ are to be related to one another as the doctrines of *anhypostasia* and *enhypostasia*. In this way we can say two very important things with theological accuracy. *Anhypostasia* asserts the unconditional priority of Grace, that everything in theological knowledge derives from God's Grace, while all truths and their relations within our thinking must reflect the movement of Grace. But *enhypostasia* asserts that God's Grace acts only as Grace. God does not override us but makes us free. In merciful and loving condescension He gathers us into union with Himself, constituting us as His dear children who share His life and love.

In this way He sets us on our feet as persons in personal relation with Him, affirming and recreating our humanity in ccmmunion with Him; He bestows His love freely upon us and asks of us the free love of our hearts; He takes our cause upon Himself and makes provision for true response on our part as we are allowed to share in the human life and response of Jesus to the Father. Just as the doctrine of *enhypostasia* asserts the full unimpaired reality of the humanity of the historical Jesus as the humanity of the Son of God, so it affirms in our theological knowledge full and unimpaired place for human decision, human response, and human thinking in relation to the Truth of God's Grace.

That two-fold truth of the doctrine of *anhypostasia* and *enhypostasia* is what we have to keep clearly in mind in thinking out the interior logic of theological thought. The primary and determinative relation in all our knowing and thinking is prescribed by Grace, but that Grace is translated into a discernible pattern within our humanity in the incarnate Son, and it is only through conformity to that pattern which is the fruit of Grace, and therefore only in conformity to the movement of Grace in Jesus Christ as the Way, the Truth and the Life, that we may discern the interior logic of theological knowledge. Because it is Grace from beginning to end, it is Christ the Truth who adapts us to Himself, but it is precisely in that adaptation, through assimilation to His own perfect humanity, that He both affirms our humanity and imprints upon it the pattern of His own life. That is the logic that is in Christ before it is in our knowing. As we are faithful in our knowing to the nature of the Truth as Grace, and what He reveals about Himself as God and Man in one Person, there arise analogical forms of personal life and understanding within us—that is what we call the interior logic of theology, a logic that inheres in the material content of our knowledge. It is a material as opposed to a formal logic, for it cannot be abstracted from the objective reality and attached to our own 'reasons', even although our knowledge of that objective reality is also a subjective or mental experience. It is, then, as we examine the way which the Grace of God has taken in the Incarnation, in the whole birth, life, ministry, death and resurrection of Jesus Christ, as we examine the person and nature of Jesus Christ, and are faithful to all that He reveals to us, that we discern the central frame of reference for all the other doctrines of the faith in Christ Himself, and may therefore work out the logic of it in the different doctrines in the way appropriate to each and in their consistent relation to one another in Christ.

Now all this has to be done in human thought-forms, human words, human speech and human sentences, since we who know are human and the object of our knowledge is also human—the Eternal Truth of God in human form. It is because God has taken our humanity and creaturehood seriously, because He respects it by entering into it and by revealing Himself from within it, that we too must respect it, that is to say, respect the creaturely word and the logic that are required in the correct and orderly arrangement of our human statements and are therefore necessary to set forth our knowledge of the Truth and its own order or form. The interior or material logic of theological knowledge does not allow us to neglect the external or formal logic of our human modes of thought and speech.

On the other hand, it is evident that we cannot express the interior logic of theological knowledge merely within the framework of the external logic of our human speech and thought, or at any rate in such a way as to yield to this external logic the normative power and control.[1] Formal logic does not tell us how we actually learn the truth, although it does have its rightful place in clarifying the way in which we are to order our speech in correct non-contradictory statements. Thus we must respect the importance and indeed the necessity of formal logic, but we cannot allow it to usurp the authoritative place occupied by the Truth Himself or be a substitute for the material logic that inheres in what He reveals to us of Himself. The problem becomes acute immediately we put our theological thought down on paper in an orderly consistent way, and make use of verbs, nouns, adjectives, grammar and syntax and therefore of formal logic. But is this 'paper-logic' to be the master of the Truth? Is the Truth to be domesticated and tamed and put into the strait-jacket of grammar and logic? Surely the Truth of God is so great in majesty and grace that

[1] This is why, in the nature of the case, we cannot give a logical account of how we know God or the reality of the God we know, in answer to the kind of question posed by Ronald Hepburn within the framework of formal logic. *Christianity and Paradox*, pp. 56 ff. But no more can we give a logical account justifying our awareness of the world or of its reality.

He breaks through the framework which we use in order to set forth our knowledge of Him? Is that not why, for example, in the pages of the New Testament the grammar appears to break down again and again before the great truths of the Gospel which in our very knowing of them we know are more to be adored than expressed? How can we describe in neat and tidy syllogisms or in clear-cut, prescinded concepts, the transcendent Majesty of the risen Christ? The poverty of our grammar and the inadequacy of all human statement is revealed again and again before the ineffable Holiness and Love of God. Is that not why so frequently St. Paul's sentences about the exceeding abundance of the riches of the Grace and Glory of God just break off, since the subject itself will not let him round them off grammatically and have a period put at the end of them? There are times when it is utterly impossible to finish our sentences, for if they really do what is required of them in referring to the transcendent reality of Grace they so point beyond themselves that they acknowledge that in themselves they are only broken stammering indications of the Truth. The fact is that the majesty and the freedom of the Truth resist the rigid framework of our thought-forms, the Grace and the personal Being of the Truth break through the logical necessity we seek to impose upon Him. He cannot be captured and imprisoned in human statements and compelled to be their content. It is this transcendent quality of the Truth that we have to respect, even when we have to respect at the same time the creaturely modes of thought and speech within which alone the Truth communicates Himself to us.

There is a deep-going tension here between the material content of our thought with its ontologic and the forms we abstract and work out in their interconnections in order to control our statements and check the argumentation. This is a tension with which every science has to reckon especially in its need to express abstract thought. The tension arises, however, not only because the processes of theorization require the elaboration of symbolic forms detached from their ontological reference but because these forms then become attached to our mental and psychical processes and develop into a masterful system on their own which we are constantly tempted to impose upon the matter we are investigating, but this threatens to undermine the basic principles of scientific objectivity. There is of course a very important element of truth here, for science is not a passive activity but one in which the movements of discovery involve acts of intervention in the processes of nature and of imaginative invention. It is important to realize that the logical structure of human thought grows out of the way in which the inner ordering of our consciousness interacts with the external order inhering in the world around us, and is not unaffected by the psychological and social structures of our history and culture, but this means that the logical reconstruction which scientific theories require in every forward advance must involve reconstruction also in the social and psychological patterns of the community in which we live, and indeed change and reconstruction in ourselves as those who are engaged in scientific inquiry and who have to be questioned and changed along with the revision of our questions.[1]

This is the kind of tension and change in which we are involved in theological science when we have to be faithful to 'the relation of transcendent reference'[2] on the one hand, and to the development of coherent formulation in the interest of precision and accuracy on the other hand. In theology, however, this is inevitably accentuated for the Truth of God in Jesus Christ challenges the logical structures of our thought at their very roots in calling for a radical reconstruction of human existence. Here there is revealed not only an abstraction of form from matter but in it all an alienation of man from his proper bond with reality. This is why forward steps in Christian living and theological thinking can take place only through deep changes in man's natural habits of mind, i.e. in the social and psychological patterns of his historical and cultural existence within which his logical and symbolic thinking operates. This is the far-reaching import of the incarnation of the divine *Logos* in our humanity, the activity of the divine Grace within the estranged conditions of our nature reconciling us to the Truth, and the activity of the divine Truth within the servitude of our existence under law making

[1] See here *Theology in Reconstruction*, pp. 117 ff.; T. S. Kuhn, *The Structure of Scientific Revolutions*, especially chs. V, VI, and IX; and E. H. Hutten, *The Origins of Science*, chs. IX and XIII.

[2] This is A. D. Ritchie's expression, *Essays in Philosophy*, p. 106.

us free for God. It is therefore out of the Christological content of our knowledge that we must seek a final answer to the question as to the relation between the Logic of God and the logic of man, but just because we find there more fully than anywhere else the divine purpose for the renewal and rehabilitation of man in the heart of the creation, we are bound to respect the interaction between the human mind and world in which God has placed us, and seek to understand as far as we may the relation between the formal structures which human thought is compelled to employ and the objective forms manifested by the Truth of God in making Himself known to us.

2 THE LOGIC OF MAN

If by 'the logic of God' we mean the logic of God's self-revelation to man that took place in the incarnation of the *Logos* in our human form evoking from us organic forms of knowledge in conformity with it, by 'the logic of man' we mean the logic of man's activity in formulating understanding of that divine *Logos*, i.e. the logical structure of our knowledge of God as it employs human forms of thought and speech. There is no knowledge or speech apart from form, for that which is without form cannot be intelligibly grasped and that to which we can give no form in our understanding we cannot reproduce and communicate to others in an intelligible form for them to grasp. It is this specifically *formal* aspect of knowledge that we seek now to clarify.

In conceptual and linguistic forms we are concerned not with the actual shape of things or with their images in our minds but with connections or inter-relations, for we conceive of things in their relationship to other things and we articulate what we conceive in orderly connections and patterns of relation. To think is to think relations and to speak is to express in a connected way what we think, so that form forces itself upon us in the basic activity of our thought and speech about what we experience.[1] Form arises, however, in two different ways, as we reflect upon external relations in the world, and as we seek to correlate what we apprehend in reducing the internal

[1] 'The task of science is both to extend the range of our experience and to reduce it to order'—Niels Bohr, *Atomic Theory and the Descriptions of Nature*, p. 1.

relations of our thought into orderly patterns. It may even be right to speak of two different kinds of form, *empirical form* deriving from objective relations in states of affairs, and *systematic form* deriving from the combination of our thoughts in consistent sequences, but if so they are found only in a polar relation to each other.[1] Indeed it is precisely within this polarity of form that our thought operates, e.g. within the empirical and systematic forms that polarize physics and mathematics.

These two aspects or kinds of form constantly tend to be confused because we have to use the one medium of language in which to express our understanding of them. Our conceiving and expressing are so deeply intertwined that we cannot disentangle them. We are aware of more than we can express but we inevitably use language to designate things and present them to our minds as objects of thought and to shape and organise our reflections about them. But since language itself through its use of symbolic signs and grammatical structures forces us at once into formalism we are constantly tempted to reduce all form, whether empirical or systematic, to linguistic form. The latter, of course, is an elementary mistake for it assumes that we can state in statements how statements are related to what is stated, and so reduces all relations to linguistic relations.[2] The real difficulty, however, lies at a deeper level, in the proper demand for precision in statement and consistency in working out relations.

Our natural language is rooted in being, so that the ordinary forms which it employs have an open reference to what is contingent and factual, but this makes it difficult to control and

[1] This distinction corresponds to that between primary and secondary intention or between signification and supposition made by medieval logicians who came under the influence of Peter of Spain and later of William of Ockham, and in modern times to the distinction between semantic and syntactic meaning made by Carnap, or to the two sorts of concept in modern science (see Mary B. Hesse, *Science and the Human Imagination*, pp. 132–134).

[2] It is equally a mistake to reduce all relations to symbolic relations as Tillich seems to do, especially in *Systematic Theology*, vol. III, in which he sets out to overcome the 'cleavage between subject and object' through developing an aesthetic relation in which the conceptual distortion of reality is eliminated, and *sapientia* is substituted for *scientia*. This carries with it a highly expressionistic notion of language (see pp. 68 ff., 253 f.) but at the expense of losing *referential relation* on the one hand and by-passing the problem of *logical relation* on the other hand. Yet this is certainly the most fascinating and exciting of all Tillich's works.

connect up our statements in a coherent way. This is what gave rise to traditional formal logic as the instrument whereby we recast our statements into forms which we can combine in valid argumentation without falling into contradictions, but this concentration on the form or structure of statements is at the cost of abstraction from their material content. Similarly our normal scientific language presupposes an inherent rationality in nature, so that it makes use of basic forms that refer to states of affairs and patterns of events in the external world, but the contingent and factual elements in these forms impede strict theoretic demonstration. Hence the need for mathematics, that is, for the transposition of scientific statements into notations in which their form or structure can be worked up in a calculus that enables us to clarify the argument and develop the proof.

Both in formal logic and in mathematics the material content is subsumed in the form of a condition for inferential operations, so that the implications in our trains of thought can be worked out in the same class or calculus: If x, then y. However, both traditional logic and traditional mathematics make use of ordinary language in which form and matter are not easily distinguished and in which logical and psychological elements are deeply intertwined.[1] As a result the argumentation is apt to be obscured or made ambiguous or even distorted through the obtrusion into it of influential overtones, irrelevant notions and misleading images from the natural and subjective habits that have grown up in our historical and national modes of thought and speech. Hence in modern times in the interest of rigour and precision there have been elaborated in logic and mathematics symbolic techniques to eliminate the distorting effects of personal and subjective elements lurking in the idiom and to bring to view the basic connections that ordinary forms so often conceal. This represents such an

---

[1] It is one of the interesting features of Bernard Bolzano's logic that he rejected the disjunction of form from matter while sharply distinguishing the logical from the psychological, in order to lay a realistic foundation for exact scientific thought (cf. here Leibniz, *Dialogus de connexione inter res et verba et veritatis realitate*, which seems to have influenced him). This gave rise to the difficult idea of truths in themselves (*Wahrheiten an sich*) that have propositional form and that are 'objectively grounded' in the logical sense—that is, as structured logical facts. *Wissenschaftslehre* (edit. by Alois Höfler), vol. I, *passim*, espec. pp. 77, 111 ff. Cf. Husserl's note in which he detects a basic ambiguity between the 'noetic' and 'noematic' in Bolzano's notions, *Ideas*, p. 274 f.

extension of the processes of abstraction and generalisation already at work in logic and mathematics that logical and mathematical forms are treated in complete detachment from their empirical reference or material content, that is, as purely analytic statements (frequently but strangely called 'tautologies' to express the fact that they do not lead to new or deeper truth).

It must be pointed out that purely abstract symbolic statements of this kind state nothing about the world of reality and therefore mean nothing, even though they have an important role to play as technical instruments for testing chains of inference. The difficulty that we are concerned with at the moment, however, is that when we allow our thoughts to run the course of such a symbolic system they are apt to become trapped and confined within it, for by its abstract formal nature a symbolic system is so rigid that we have difficulty in freeing our mind from it.[1] It is in this way that we find ourselves replacing empirical form by systematic form, and transposing the referring function of statements into purely formal-logical or symbolic-logical terms. A double error would appear to be present here. On the one hand, it appears to restrict relations, and therefore form and order, to the world of mind while positing things and existents in nature or the real world, which not only denies to the latter any inherent rationality or knowability but implies that the more we think it in terms of relations the more we misrepresent it.[2] On the other hand, it seems to confound the logic of reference with the logic of syntax whereas referring statements and systematic statements, e.g. existence-statements and the generic formulae of mathematics, belong to different logical systems, even though they require each other in our scientific constructions and theories.[3]

We must keep steadily in front of us the distinction between the logic of empirical reference which is directed to material relations in objective reality, and the logic of systematic

---

[1] Cf. the remark of Sir Arthur Eddington: 'For strict expressions of physical knowledge a mathematical form is essential, because that is the only way in which we can confine its assertions to structural knowledge. Every path to knowledge of what lies beneath the structure is then blocked by an impenetrable mathematical symbol'. *The Philosophy of Physical Science*, 1958 edit., p. 142.

[2] Cf. M. R. Cohen, *A Preface to Logic*, 1958 edit., pp. 8 ff., 38 ff., 85, 192 ff.

[3] Cf. F. Waismann, *Introduction to Mathematical Thinking*, p. 98.

correlation which has to do with formal relations in our theoretic demonstrations, and at the same time see how they are coordinated with each other, but it must be clearly recognised that we are using 'logic' in two different ways relative to the acts of reasoning involved. In the former case we are concerned with the logic of active inquiry (what the Germans call *Sachlogik*) or the art of carrying out inductive processes of reasoning in the attempt to acquire material knowledge which cannot be inferred from what we already know, while in the latter case we are concerned with the logic of formal argument (*Sprachlogik*) or the technique of testing the deductive sequences of thought in order to exhibit their validity or invalidity. This is the old distinction between logic as the *ars inveniendi* and logic as the *ars diiudicandi*, although that has broken down again and again under the quite mistaken attempt to recast the processes of induction into formal-logical relations and thus to substitute systematic form in the place of empirical form instead of respecting their polarity and operating within it. But this was also quite futile for it assumed that advance in knowledge is always only advance into clarity from a prior but confused form of apprehension or indeed that genuinely new knowledge can be gained merely by a rearrangement of our previous ideas.

Our task, then, is to discern and exhibit the diverse *types of order* that reasoning takes in accordance with the objective and the kind of evidence which it has in view, one in the field of actuality and the other in the field of possibility. We have to clarify the material structures that are imposed upon our knowing in the *interrogative* mode of inquiry, and the formal structures that necessarily arise for connected thinking in the *problematic* mode of inquiry, and to bring to view their bearing upon each other. We shall discuss this first under *the logic of existence-statements* and then under *the logic of coherence-statements*, in the conviction that since these require one another in scientific knowledge the different logical systems they involve must somehow penetrate each other, for otherwise coherence-statements would be quite irrelevant to the real world.

(i) *The Logic of existence-statements*

Existence-statements are acts of reference in which we experience and cognise something other than ourselves. They express our intuitive apprehension of the external world in its own forms, and thus have their meaning not in themselves but in the things they denote.[1] They direct us to objective realities as they are and as they show themselves and so serve to open out the relations of disclosure between being and thought. Obversely, they serve to reflect the adaptation of our minds to those objective realities and so contribute to the establishment of significant relations between thought and being. But since our speech plays its own part in designating things and focussing our attention upon them, thus enabling them to become manifest to us, we inevitably think of things through the forms of our speech, so that in referring to things existence-statements form part of our actual connection with empirical reality. Acts of reference are temporal processes. They are, as it were, practical or dramatic statements for they do something as well as say something, and when they are employed in scientific inquiry they are in their own way experimental and heuristic operations in which we probe into the nature of things as they are constituted in themselves, helping us to maintain contact with them and presenting them to us as subject-matter for our understanding and reflection as it is shown in itself.

Existence-statements are not singular acts but complex operations for they are enunciated in clusters or groups and manifest patterns of signification through their correspondence with each other. They function in semantic systems and so help to delimit or describe a universe of discourse. They presuppose, point to, and fall in with, the objective order in the nature of things which we experience, give it distinction and shape in our minds (i.e. descriptively, not prescriptively), and by bringing our minds up against the transcendent aspects of form they mediate to us the basic concepts we require in

[1] Cf. here Bolzano's attempt to relate our statements and concepts to their objective ground in truths independent of our thought and speech. Thus he distinguished between 'a spoken statement' (*ein ausgesprochener Satz*) and our expression of it (*Aussprache*), and between 'a 'thought statement' (*ein gedachter Satz*) and our thought of it (*Gedanke*). This led to the notion of 'statements in themselves' (parallel to the 'truths in themselves' already noted) which gave one of the earliest leads to modern mathematical logic. See *Wissenschaftslehre*, I. pp. 77, 86 etc. See also B. Bolzano, *Rein analytischer Beweiss des Lehrsatzes, dass zwischen je zwey Werthen, die ein entgegengesetztes Resultat gewähren, wenigstens eine reelle Wurzel der Gleichung liege* (cf. the discussion of Bolzano's contribution by H. Scholz, *Mathesis Universalis*, pp. 219–267).

interpretation and explanation. They establish themselves in our grasp and acceptance in so far as the objective order they serve to reveal is discerned to be independent of our knowing of it and to reach out in the depth and range of its power of enlightenment, or its instrumentality in the disclosure of reality, far beyond anything we could determine or anticipate. But how do we arrive at these existence-statements—not the naive existence-statements of our common, uncritical knowledge, but the basic existence-statements of scientific knowledge? How do they take shape in our understanding and how do we organise them? How do we clarify them and test them for their truth? In short, what is their logic?

The logic of existence-statements is the logic of their referential relations, of their pointing to and their deriving from their proper objects. It is unfolded through *interrogative operations* leading to the uncovering of evidence and structure from the side of objective realities, and it is developed through *analogical operations* leading to the establishing of relevance and the checking of application in respect of those realities. In neither direction, from them or toward them, is it a logic of fixed forms or prescribed rules but one that arises with and inheres in heuristic and diacritical activity, i.e. an operational logic.

In the *first* place, then, this is a 'logic of question and answer'[1] designed to uncover the relation of transcendent reference and to let our minds fall under the compulsion of 'the transcendent aspect of form' where we have to struggle with ourselves in order to let our minds be informed with basic and revolutionary concepts. It is through questioning that we set out to explore entirely new territory. We have already had occasion to discuss fully these interrogative processes in which the questions together with the questioner himself must ever be questioned so that the inquiry proceeds through a perpetual revision of our position and a logical reconstruction of prior knowledge. There is no need to go over that ground again but there are several aspects of this interrogative mode of scientific inquiry to which we must now give special heed. The primary question for empirical knowledge, as A. D. Ritchie has said, is of the form 'What have we here?'[2] That is not easy to put or to answer

---

[1] This way of putting it is taken from A. D. Ritchie, *Essays in Philosophy*, ch. VIII, 'The Logic of Question and Answer'. Cf. also Hans-Georg Gadamer, *Wahrheit und Methode*, 351 ff. for a useful discussion of Collingwood on this logic.

[2] Op. cit., p. 109. This is the question, *quale sit*, as distinct from *quid sit*.

for we have to engage in an *activa inquisitio* in which we interfere with things as we find them and struggle with our own hardened habits until we can see things as they really are.[1] This is the difficulty of learning to ask really *new questions* when we have to break free from the comfortable frame-works in which we are already set and achieve a measure of self-renunciation and self-transcendence—new questions being questions to which no answer can be given on the ground we already occupy because they are forced upon us from new ground beyond it.[2]

Although questioning of this kind is guided by an objective and is purposive, not blind or random, the radicalization that it involves, in the ruthless questioning of our questions and of ourselves the questioners, means that we are more and more cast upon the object of inquiry as it comes to view under our questioning and are submissive to it as it shows itself to us for what it actually is. This means further that although it is we who have to frame the questions and the answers to them, so far as the words or symbols are concerned, nevertheless it is not we ourselves who are finally determinative but the object itself, for all that we do presupposes that it is so constituted that we can think it, that it is what it is and not another thing and that it shows itself as it is and therefore as it must be in our conceiving of it and acting toward it. Thus in interrogative operations of this kind we trace back the referential relation through chains of questions to the reality itself, penetrating through the false and distorting forms with which we have obscured its self-disclosure, until it stands clear before us in the overmastering power of what it actually is, and our understanding is transformed in face of it.

It is only as we are thus determined from beyond ourselves and our knowledge is radically reconstructed in face of the object that we can pass beyond what we already know and advance to radically new knowledge which we could not tell ourselves or infer from what we already claim to know. Now as in this way the object of our inquiry becomes more and more disclosed to us and our questioning takes new shape under the impress of the object, new form and order enter into our

---

[1] Cf. the examples of this given by A. Mercier, *Thought and Being*, p. 34 f.
[2] Cf. F. Waismann, *The Principles of Linguistic Philosophy*, ch.XX, 'Towards a Logic of Questions', p. 413.

conceiving of it which are reflexions in us of transcendent form and independent order in the reality itself. Moreover since it remains what it is transcendent of our knowing of it and remains in its own being an inexhaustible source of conceptual knowledge, the forms that arise in our conceiving of it cannot be defined apart from the interrogative operations and the constant reconstruction they involve, so that by their nature they are open and dynamic.

This is the logic of reference, the logic of heuristic induction or discovery that we are concerned with in existence-statements,[1] but it is a logic that receives its structure not from behind, as it were, from prescriptions or axioms, but from in front of it, from objective, transcendent aspects of form. It operates with open conceptual forms which direct us beyond themselves to higher levels reflecting different types of order, and which are kept open through transcendent reference and involvement in objective order. Hence they cannot be treated like the abstract forms of formal or symbolic logic which are largely (but not entirely, as we shall see) closed at both ends in so far as they constitute a system or a calculus on one and the same level. Moreover this logic operates with a mode of transition from one form to another by steps that cannot be specified in advance according to fixed rules as in formal or symbolic logic,[2] but that are taken in the process of radical change in which one form gives place to another in natural sequence as the range of reference is opened out in accordance with a seried advance in the disclosure of being. The logical operation which this involves does not yield theoretic demonstration on the ground of given principles and from accepted premisses, but it is an active form of induction that clears the ground and puts us on the way to proof, for it directs us finally to the realities themselves which are their own factual demonstration.[3] The difficulty is that the kind of evidence they provide for themselves is not immediately evident to us, and it has to be disclosed to

[1] Cf. the *Heuristik* or *Erfindungskunst* of B. Bolzano, *Wissenschaftslehre*, Bd. III, §§ 269–391.

[2] Behind this lies what Eddington has called the 'irreversible relation to observation', *The Philosophy of Physical Science*, 1958 edit. p. 93 f, 102 f.

[3] Cf. the helpful discussions of induction by F. Waismann, in connection with the discovery of mathematical periodicity, *Introduction to Mathematical Thinking*, 1959 edit., pp. 88–99, and of M. Polanyi, *Personal Knowledge*, pp. 120 ff, where he speaks of discovery as ' a heuristic act which leaps across a logical gap' (p. 125).

us through operations that we find very arduous for our minds have to be stretched, our thinking transferred to a different level, and our conceptual forms prized open in order to take it in. But it is important to note that it is the open and flexible character of these forms, taken together with our recognition of their limitations, or what we may call their 'logical suspension of form', that makes it possible for our reasoning to take in new knowledge as realities become disclosed to us, and when taking in new knowledge not to redact it to a form of what is already known. We return to the fact, then, that it is in and through the operation of interrogating realities that conceptual forms are forced upon our minds from the side of the objects interrogated, but so powerfully that they demand a logical reconstruction of earlier forms and a revolutionary shift in the whole structure of meaning.

In order to see how far this holds good for theological statements we have to give close attention to the inherent claims of the subject-matter of theology upon them.[1] A great many of the existence-statements in theology refer to events and states in human life in this world of space and time, but the distinctive thing about them, of course, is their reference to the presence and activity of the divine Being in these events and states. And since these existence-statements are contingent upon their object, the divine element must determine the nature of their reference. Here their description as 'contingent' and 'transcendent' is wholly in character, to a degree that is evident nowhere else. In the nature of the case there must take place an adaptation of existence-statements in accordance with the creative, revealing, and saving acts of God among men. The logic of their reference must therefore *correspond* to the logic of God's self-communication to men—and *correspond* is here the appropriate term, as it is not always the case in other sciences, since strictly speaking, as A. D. Ritchie has pointed out, 'words correspond only to words, thoughts to thoughts, sensations to sensations, things to things.'[2] Thus the mathematical description of natural events does not often correspond to them, although clearly certain geometrical patterns correspond to crystalline formations, and certain numerical ratios

[1] See the earlier discussion of existence-statements in theology, pp. 173 ff.
[2] A. D. Ritchie, *Essays in Philosophy*, p. 106.

correspond to musical vibrations, etc. But here in theology we are concerned not simply with the reference of human forms to divine Being but with the correspondence of human word to divine Word and human act to divine Act. We have been thinking of scientific *discovery* as the disclosure of reality that takes place in the process of question and answer which we initiate and carry through, but in theology we are concerned with an active self-disclosure of Reality before whom we are called in question and to whom we must make answer as question compellingly follows question of itself, so that we have to think of theological knowledge in terms of response to divine *revelation*.

This does not do away with theological science, for disciplined interrogation, interpretation and justification must continue in accordance with the nature of the divine Object of our knowledge. It is because He is who He is and cannot be known as other than He is that out of love and respect for Him we must discipline and test our thoughts and statements about Him that they may be worthy of Him. Scientific inquiry for its part requires us to be rigorously faithful and to beware of making 'category-mistakes' (to borrow an apt expression from Ryle) in connection with Him.[1] Hence as we make proper allowance for the difference in nature of the object and for all that this implies for the reference of our statements, then all that has been said of the nature and logic of existence-statements applies, *mutatis mutandis*, in theological science. In the course of inquiry in this field existence-statements are made by way of rational answer to the address of God toward us and by way of living response to the work of God for us, and their truth is found to lie not in themselves but in Him to whom they gladly and humbly refer. In the nature of the case existence-statements in theology are far more than linguistic and ostensive formulations; they are empirical operations performed in obedient conformity to the divine Will, and their logic is the logic of their correspondence in word and act to the Word and Act of God. Hence they have to be tested for the mode and propriety of that correspondence.

[1] G. Ryle, *The Concept of Mind*, p. 16 f.; *Proceedings of the Aristotelian Society* 1937–38, pp. 189 ff.

Let us take, for example, the statement 'God is love' which we read in the Holy Scriptures and through them hear as the Word of God to us, that is, as a statement which God Himself addresses to us in the act of His own self-revelation.[1] In this statement the 'is' is determined by the nature of its subject 'God', and is only therefore the kind of 'is' that God is. When it is said that 'God is love' the love in question is thus not any kind of love but divine love, love that issues from God and is in accordance with the nature of God. Now when we use this as an existence-statement in theological formulation we must test our use of it to see that it is used in accordance with its proper reference and source and in the true mode of its correspondence—that is as a 'heard statement', an 'audit' which we have reached through listening to the Word of God, and not as a statement which we have thought up on our own and projected descriptively of God. It is a statement the truth of which lies in God Himself who makes it, and is true as His Word and Act for what He speaks as God and His speaking of it to us are inseparable. It is the kind of statement which cannot be detached from the fact that it is spoken by a Subject and addressed to another for his hearing. It is, so to speak, a proposition that is operationally defined at both ends.

In the passage in which the biblical form of this statement is found, 1 John 4.8, it is added: 'In this was manifested the love of God toward us, because God sent His only begotten Son into the world, that we might have life through Him. Herein is love, not that we loved God, but that He loved us and sent His Son to be the propitiation for our sins' (vv. 9–10). That is to say, that God is love is defined in terms of God's activity in the incarnation of His Son and in His atoning work for us. Hence the theological form of the statement must correspond to it in mode and reference—the logic of our existence-statement must correspond to the logic of God, the logic of Grace and the logic of Christ. We cannot use it truly, therefore, as a statement detached from its ontological source and considered abstractly and timelessly as a general statement in relation to other general statements, without specifying at the same time when and under what conditions

---

[1] Cf. the admirable discussion of this by Heinrich Vogel, *Kerygma und Dogma*, 4.3, 1957, pp. 185 ff.

it is true, for then its basic nature and meaning would change. It would become a reversible statement, a mere tautology, when 'God is love' would be the equivalent of and could be defined as 'love is God'. This would not only be a confusion of logical types, a μετάβασις εἰς ἄλλο γένος but would in fact turn the statement into a lie, in which we would be absolutizing and divinizing our human love and perverting into untruth the love of God by defining it in terms of this hypostatized love of ours. Similarly, it would make 'God is love' into a timeless statement,[1] treating the 'is' as merely a syntactical sign of equivalence, thus detaching it from the way in which God is what He is both in Himself and from what He is toward us in Jesus Christ. The statement would thus be uprooted from its ground in the Incarnation, detached from historical factuality in Jesus Christ, and abstracted from the operation of the divine love in His sacrifice, as if it were necessarily and universally true without reference to the activity in which God makes it true for us, and therefore apart altogether from the relevant question, as to when and in what conditions this statement is true. That God is love is certainly universally true, but it is not a necessary truth, for He does not have to love us, nor does He owe it to Himself or to us to love us. He loves us out of His love, in the transcendent freedom of His Grace, but we know it because He has come among us in Jesus Christ and revealed that what He is toward us in Christ He is eternally and antecedently in Himself, but here the 'premiss' that God is love is, in a way, like the premisses of empirical science which are not known in advance, but are known only *a posteriori* and therefore not apart from the whole process of scientific inquiry and verification, and so cannot be treated like a formal-logical premiss. Put otherwise, that God is love is not an analytic statement, any more indeed than 'God is God' is merely an analytic statement for Christians, for it can only mean that God is Father, Son and Holy Ghost, God is He who He is in His historical self-revelation to Israel, and in the

---

[1] Cf. Waismann's discussion of Augustine's problem in relation to the question *Quid est ergo tempus?* (*Conf.* XI. 15), in which we are apt to be led astray by a wrong approach to 'is' in this context, *Introduction to Mathematical Thinking*, p. 116 f., and *The Principles of Linguistic Philosophy*, pp. 40 ff, 172 ff, 412.

Incarnation of His Word in Jesus Christ.[1] All this means that we must find ways of stating that God is love that are appropriate to it and do not turn it into another thing. Let it be granted that the statement 'God is love' may, for certain restricted purposes, be cast into a formal-logical sequence, but if so we must keep the restricted purpose in mind and not imagine that here where we are concerned only with rules for valid implication on a syntactical level we can learn anything about the *truth* of the statement concerned, which is quite a different thing.

In the *second* place, the forms which we reach in this way through question and answer require to be tested for their relevance to reality and developed in their correspondence with each other through analogical operations if they are to be confirmed in our understanding. That is to say, existence-statements have to be analysed to see whether they are what Frege called 'recognition-statements', objectively derived and orientated, coordinated with a transcendent level of order, or whether they are but psychological constructs of our own.[2] This we do by tracing back the conceptual forms that emerge to their source to see whether they really derive from and repose upon the realities they claim to indicate, and how far subjective elements through our own forceful thinking have entered into them. At the same time this should help us to formulate existence-statements with a greater degree of propriety.

We recall that existence-statements occur in meaningful connections or chains of referential relation—otherwise they are blind. Hence it is not the reference of singular statements but a whole pattern of statements that we have to investigate, thus determining their ontological as well as their analogical import. This does not mean that we are to read the patterns embedded in the forms of our thought and speech back into being, as if there were a reversible or necessary relation between

---

[1] Cf. again H. Vogel, op. cit., p. 187 f. who contrasts 'God is God' with 'Allah il Allah'.

[2] G. Frege, *The Foundations of Arithmetic*, section 106, p. 106. My use of 'recognition-statement' would, however, be more realist than Frege's. See in this connection A. E. Taylor's definition of a true proposition as that which has an *unconditional claim on our recognition*, 'Truth and Practice', *Philosophical Review*, XIV. 3, 1905, p. 271 f.

those patterns and ontic structures, nevertheless we have to examine those patterns in the light of the realities and their structures which they serve to point out to us, and form a judgement as to their relevance and adequacy to them. We have to decide how far they help and how far they hinder the disclosure of those realities, and what must be done by way of purifying and clarifying them in order that they may be better media *through* which fuller disclosure can take place.[1] Statements that fail to function in this way will have to be rejected as spurious, or as objectifications of subjective states which can only obscure and overlay the realities we seek to bring to view.

On the other hand, because existence-statements are made in groups, they have to be connected together through other statements, not all of which will show an objective reference, directly at any rate. This holds good for all the established theories of natural science, for they cannot be formulated simply through 'physical concepts', far less expressed merely in 'object-language'. The more abstract they become, the fewer will be the statements that have empirical referents, but what is important is that the whole theory should be applicable to the real world. Hence it must be put to the test through a deductive analysis of its component statements to see whether they lead to results that can be empirically verified or falsified. Formal and material implication cannot be separated sharply in any scientific activity, so that all statements for which ontological status is claimed must be investigated to see whether they have immediate objective reference or, if not, whether they fit in with other statements that do, and whether the pattern of reference in which they share in that way is as a whole ontologically relevant. However, since the various statements that are connected together in a pattern of reference all tend to lend evidential support for each other, it is necessary to penetrate down to the really basic existence-statements and the conceptual forms they embody through which we let our minds fall under the logic in the realities to which they refer, in order that we may come to a decision as to their truth

[1] It is interesting to note that Eddington could speak in the same way about 'seeing through' the forms of thought (op. cit. pp. 66, 117) even though he held that scientific theory administers 'Procrustean treatment' to nature, forcing observational knowledge into our conceptual forms of thought by our method of formulating it (op. cit., pp. 104, 109 f., 123, 134 f.).

or falsity under the compulsion of the realities themselves. What sustains and fortifies us at this point is the discovery of a rationality in the nature of things that goes far beyond our understanding and that transcends the clues on which we have relied in attaining vision of it.[1] Of course from a purely logical point of view, as Karl Popper has pointed out, we do not have to stop at any particular basic statement rather than another, but if we do not stop somewhere and accept some basic statement, the testing of a theory falls through.[2] Thus in the last resort we are cast upon the objective reality itself and have to decide in the light of it whether the ontological status of our basic existence-statements is acceptable or not. There are no formal-logical operations which can undertake this for us—in the last resort we are thrown back upon the judgement of our own reason.

In the more abstract sciences which work not only with a frame of experimental interpretation but with a highly formal calculus, the testing of statements in their interconnection in the same theory is carried out through strictly deductive reasoning, although even then it is only experiment which, to cite Popper again, 'saves us from a track that leads nowhere',[3] for even false theories can be made completely consistent internally. But in the more concrete sciences where existence-statements are specially prominent, it is a form of analogical reasoning that is required to establish whether existence-statements contingent upon the same object correspond with one another properly or not. Here we are not analysing, comparing and generalising in the same way as in the sciences amenable to mathematization, for what we compare are contingent referential relations which combine in a different sort of nexus from that of necessary statements. We work out their correspondence with each other *mediately* in respect of their referents and not *immediately* in respect of each other or in proportion to one another. This is a complex and difficult operation in which we have to attend constantly to the polarity of empirical and systematic form in the reference and conference

[1] This is M. Polanyi's way of stating the personal commitment involved at the basis of scientific constructions, *Personal Knowledge*, pp. 63 ff.

[2] K. Popper, *The Logic of Scientific Discovery*, p. 104 f.

[3] K. Popper, op. cit., p. 268.

of our statements. On the one hand, we work with a relation reaching out through a series of referential forms at different levels to the realities they denote; and on the other hand, we determine the bearing of several such relations to one another at different levels of reference and in the light of the pattern of reference they build as they all converge in agreement upon their common object. Because we are comparing relation with relation, behaviour with behaviour, form with form, at different levels of reference, we cannot flatten them out into the same formal calculus without eliminating their ontological import and destroying their meaning by breaking it up into formal-logical paradoxes and contradictions. Nor—and this may well amount to the same thing in the end—can we bring the referring form and the reality referred to, the contingent sign and the object signified, within the same conceptual framework as though there were a common measure of being between them, assimilating existence-statements to the same logical structure as coherence-statements, thus rationalizing away their specific meaning. This seems to be the problem with certain Thomist-Aristotelian notions of analogy when they are transposed into mathematical *proportiones* (direct similarities), although admittedly the concept of analogical *proportionalitas* (equality of proportions) attempts to get round the difficulty by keeping the thought at different levels. This is unsuccessful, however, whenever the logicalization of analogy transposes reference into predication and attribution and so rationalizes the meaning by converting contingent into necessary form. Analogy by its very nature must be inadequate, for it points out far more than it can specify, but when analogy is cast into a logical structure of adequation between being and thought, its nature is changed and its depth of significance vanishes.

The *analogic* of existence-statements must be conceived in terms of analogical 'correspondence' rather than analogical proportionality. Vertically, so to speak, it is the logic of their *transcendent reference* which comes to view as we trace existence-statements back (ἀνά) to the reality upon which they rest. Unlike formal-logical relation this is not reversible, but one-directional. Thus in pointing out the reality referring forms are to be understood ectypally in the light of it and cannot be read archetypally into it. Since analogous forms of this kind are by their nature contingent no conclusions can be drawn from them as such. Horizontally, as it were, the analogic of existence-statements is the logic of their *orderly conference* which comes to view as we trace the way in which they correspond to one another through referring to repeatable patterns in the same reality, i.e. on the ground of a correspondence between its disclosures to us. Existence-statements are thus linked to one another through their conjoint function in transcendent reference, and are to be compared with each other in a triadic relationship in which their conference of reference yields a conceptual pattern or epistemological harmony *through* which the objective pattern in the denoted reality discloses itself.[1]

It must be emphasized that the component forms of this conceptual pattern are *paradeigmatic* in character.[2] That is to say, as forms contingent upon their objective realities they direct our minds to apprehend them and provide us with some means, however slender, of holding them in the grasp of our apprehension, yet without giving us any conceptual control over those realities, since as forms they are open and limited at the same time. 'By the nature of their transcendent and contingent reference they indicate that the realities to which they point range far beyond their demonstrative capacity, so that it belongs to their peculiar 'adequacy' to fall short of them. The conceptual structures of scientific theory can never have a one-to-one correspondence with the ontic structures of reality, far less be identified with them.

This analogic may become clearer if we consider it the other way round, from the side of our scientific activity in discovery. In the process of question and answer in some field, we find imposed upon us a new and enlightening form which we judge to be an important intimation or essential clue to the reality we are investigating. We make it central and organize the other forms round it in a harmonious pattern of reference. Then we imaginatively and tentatively project that as a hypothesis and put it as a complex question to the reality we are investigating in such a way that the answer is clearly intuited, and so once again in the light of what is revealed we proceed to

[1] Cf. E. L. Mascall's exposition of models or theories as *objecta quibus*, *Christian Theology and Natural Science*, pp. 80 ff. See also p. 174 ff.

[2] 'Paradeigmatic' is used here in the Patristic, not in the Platonic, Aristotelian or Kantian, senses of the term—see *Theology in Reconstruction*, pp. 44, 49 ff.

reconstruct it. We clarify and sharpen its focus as an act of interrogation, we simplify and unify its conceptual form, in the hope that it will become such a transparent medium for our apprehension that our thoughts will fall under the power of the logic or the interior connection in the components of reality itself. This is the theory or 'mechanism', what we now call a 'model', or better still an 'analogue' (especially for the more concrete and less mechanical sciences),[1] but it remains only an instrument of reference in the successive advances of our cognitive interrogation, a kinetic model or analogue that is to be 'operationally defined' (in Einstein's sense), and must never be allowed to become fixed or rigid for that would suppress its intended function in discovery.

We may now draw together this discussion of the analogical character of existence-statements in several paragraphs.

(a) Because existence-statements retain their referring function even when they are correlated through analogical reasoning into organic patterns for scientific knowledge they work with open concepts and what E. H. Hutten has called 'open systems'.[2] They are open in front because they indicate far more than they can specify at any time and must constantly be stretched out and adapted to new disclosures, but in order to be sufficiently subtle and flexible they cannot be closed from behind, and so must be prepared for a critical re-examination and reconstruction of already acquired and formulated knowledge.

(b) The analogues into which existence-statements are built through their correspondences with each other are forced upon us through a correspondence in the disclosures of the real world, but they are not replicas or transcripts of

---

[1] 'The word *analogue* is generally preferable to *model*, because the latter may seem to imply something mechanical or at least pictureable'—Mary B. Hesse, op. cit., p. 138. This seems to me to be a sound remark but the analogue must be thought of as comprising not iconic but paradeigmatic forms or signs, for it is not a picturing but a disclosure analogue. Much of the difficulty we still have with the concept of analogy is due to the residual influence upon it of Greek notions of 'correspondence' or 'imitation' through 'imaging' or 'picturing'.

[2] E. H. Hutten, *The Origins of Science*, p. 209. 'Scientific theories are open systems, not closed off as are pseudo-scientific theories, which resemble the closed systems of thought characteristic of the infant or of the paranoid patient.' See also p. 220 where he speaks of these systems as '*open at both ends*—not only towards new developments, but, equally, with regard to old achievements.'

objective structures far less categorial patterns of order which we impose through our thought upon the real world. They are *perspicuous forms* through which (though without discarding them) we discern the real world and allow it to manifest itself to us in its own inherent rationality and order, and as such they become the means through which we are given, however scantily, a unitary vision of reality in some field of experience. On the other hand, since it is conceptual (and linguistic) form and structure that are communicable and not the realities themselves, we must beware of using them merely as tools for forcing epistemological unity in the scientific drive from the many to the one. They have their proper place in our knowledge in a triadic relation with reality, knowledge of which is communicated only indirectly as we follow through the referring operations of our analogues.

(c) Since analogues built out of existence-statements are compound recognition-statements their proof must involve at its heart a repetition of the original intuitive experiences that gave rise to them, when an acknowledgement of their truth is evoked from us in the 'shock of recognition'.[1] In the experimental and mechanical sciences this happens when a prediction proves true as we follow through the directions of a theory or a model and come immediately up against the object that first gave rise to it, but in other sciences where we do not work with physical experimentation it is nevertheless much the same sort of thing that takes place as we are led through the analogues to a direct cognition and recognition of the denoted realities and so discern the relevance of the analogues to them. In all sciences this element of judgement or appraisal is unavoidable and necessary for proof. Let us note once again that while in some sciences this is preceded by strictly deductive reasoning in order to make consistent and to draw out the formal implications of the statements that construct our theories, the conclusions have still to be compared and their correspondences elucidated if we are to discern their material implications, and use them as fruitful disclosure-models of the real world.

One of the essential ingredients in this kind of demonstration is particularly powerful, and it is this which, it would appear, finally clinches our conviction as to the validity of the theories

[1] Cf. again, E. H. Hutten, op. cit., p. 226 f.

we advance or at least commits us to their acceptance. It can be described in various ways, as the *applicability* of a model to the real world, which in some sciences is empirically verifiable in determinate ways, or as the persistent *relevance* of an analogue to the nature of the reality into which we inquire, as we experience it or intuit it with increasing understanding through the analogue, or as the *fertility* of a theory in throwing light upon a set of stubborn problems and at the same time revealing new facts, but in whatever form it may be stated it is the discovery of a far-reaching rationality in the nature of things which we are forced to distinguish from our knowing of it, and to which we give authority in working our conception of it. It is the discerning of an objective structure of this kind that so often opens up the way for the great new advances.[1] This is what Michael Polanyi has called 'the indeterminate scope' of the true implications of some theory which constantly surprises us as it continues to reveal more than we had anticipated or indeed could anticipate at the time of its formulation. It is just this that makes it evident to us that our theoretical explanations of experience are on the right track and have established contact with a reality that reaches out behind them in such a depth of objectivity that we are confirmed not only in the early intimations around which the theory was built but in the knowledge we have subsequently gained through it.[2]

(d) In the organisation of existence-statements through analogical reasoning they are made to overlap with coherence-statements, for both are required in a scientific theory which must be consistent in itself as well as applicable to the real world. It is not simply two kinds of statement that we have here but two sorts of reference penetrating each other, the reference of statements empirically to things and the reference of the same statements formally or systematically to other

[1] Cf. C. F. von Weizsäcker, *The World View of Physics*, pp. 21 f., 179 f., 193 f.

[2] M. Polanyi, op. cit., ch. I on 'Objectivity' *passim*, especially p. 5 f., and also pp. 15 f., 37, 43, 64 f., 104, 116 etc. Karl Popper, in his opposition to all attempts to operate with ideas of 'inductive logic' (i.e. in our language, to reduce inductive acts to formal-logical sequences) and in his insistence on the theory of *the deductive method of testing*, appears to hold much the same view, e.g. when he points out the only way to argue in support of his own proposals, *The Logic of Scientific Discovery*, p. 38.

statements, and therefore the distinction between the two kinds of statements can never be drawn very sharply. Since we are concerned with two different logical systems, existence-statements cannot be reduced to coherence-statements—although those sciences which are amenable to severe formalization through mathematical calculi go a long way in this direction.[1] How are they, then, coordinated with each other, especially in their compound forms? They are, of course, already coordinated in our ordinary language where semantic and syntactical functions overlap in what we have called 'the hinge of their meaning'. Our concern at the moment, however, is to understand how to relate the *general patterns* that are built up through analogical reasoning with existence-statements and the *general patterns* that are built up through deductive reasoning with coherence-statements. This is the question of what may be called 'the concrete universal'. In the exact sciences we proceed by analysing particulars, abstracting their common forms, comparing and universalizing them—that is, we work with and by means of the *general:* only what can be seen in the light of the general and is judged to be an instance of the general is accepted for only it can fit into the formal system. That is, as it were, the 'abstract universal'. But with the 'concrete universal' we proceed the other way round. We apprehend it not through abstraction for it is not a generic formulation, but through a focal awareness of it in its own power and wholeness, aided by analogical reasoning that directs us away from symbolical formality to what is concretely real and self-evidencing. It is known as it throws light on other things and gains acceptance in our understanding the wider and more universal we discern the range of its enlightenment to be. But it does not take light from other things, for it is known only through the power of its own illumination not through the power of other things to illumine it. This is why it is so difficult to understand when our minds are engaged with abstract universals: we have to step up to a different level of apprehension or vision. Yet something like it is necessary for the exact sciences, for in spite of their

---

[1] That we cannot carry through a complete reduction of empirical statements to systematic statements without total loss of meaning is one of clear implications of Gödel's theorem.

abstraction and generalization they must seek to grasp their logical or mathematical sequences as a whole by penetrating down to a profound 'logical simplicity' which will throw a unifying light upon the whole universe of their discourse, but the abstract universal by its very nature and origin is finally unable to do justice to the concrete particularities of the real world. Whenever we fail to allow for this kind of limitation in the abstract universal we are tempted to let invention and a masterful technology supersede patient interpretation and discovery as the norms of pure science.

How does all this apply to theology and especially to the organic forms of dogmatic construction? In much the same way, it must be said, *mutatis mutandis*, as to other sciences if we remember the scientific requirement at all times to conform to the nature of the object. Indeed the kind of analogic we have been discussing is particularly relevant to theological existence-statements for in them, as we have seen, we are concerned with correspondence to the Word and Act of God, so that the correspondences of their referential relations to one another are or should be clearly rooted in the correspondences between the divine acts of communication. But because referential relations remain utterly contingent, their analogical patterns direct us back to a divine source infinitely transcendent over them.

Vertically, the *analogia fidei*, to use the theological expression, operates in such a way that we refer everything to God and nothing to ourselves, that the Truth of God may retain His own weight and majesty.[1] That is to say, the analogical reference of existence-statements back to their ultimate source in God Himself carries with it a radical questioning of the forms through which that reference is made, which helps to ensure that our theological statements really serve the self-communication of the Word of God and are not erected as substitutes for it. It is through repentant rethinking in this kind of operation that theological statements may be maintained in their paradeigmatic character and in their open conceptual forms, and so direct our minds beyond themselves to apprehend something of the divine revelation in its own inner connection and logic.

[1] For a clear, sensitive account of the *analogia fidei*, see the preface to Calvin's *Institute*, Eng. edit. by J. T. McNeil and F. L. Battles, vol. I, p. 12 f.

Horizontally, this applies no less to compound existence-statements or what we may call dogmatic formulations, for the organizing of referential relations into analogous patterns must make clear its own limitations through self-correcting operations if those patterns are to serve their purpose in directing our minds to objective structure and order which we can distinguish from our knowing of them. Since this is something that must be discussed in the last chapter we may limit our consideration of it here, by way of example only, to the famous 'Chalcedonian Definition' in regard to the divine and human natures in the one Person of Jesus Christ.

This is a compound existence-statement derived by tracing certain basic existence-statements back to their biblical sources and through them to an empirical relation, in worship and faith, to Christ Himself. In this a rigorous attempt was made to be faithful in thought and statement to encounter with divine and human nature in the unity of His Person, but it was organized through analogical reasoning into a form that has proved remarkably fertile in illuminating many other theological questions, far beyond the expectations of the Chalcedonian fathers. In this statement the analogic is clear in both ways that we have discussed. On the one hand it makes clear its own limitations in the light of the reality to which it refers, and so speaks only in negative terms in order that the transcendent fact of Christ Himself may continually disclose itself, in its own structure and mystery, unobstructed by statements that pretend to be able to reduce to a positive formula that which is more to be adored than expressed. On the other hand, the formulation that is offered clearly makes use of the traditional logical distinction between statements of identity and statements of difference, or statements of likeness and statements of unlikeness, with appropriate modifications, to express in an analogical manner the Christian understanding of the relation between the divine and human natures in Christ, as *without confusion or conversion* and *without division or separation*. It is made evident that the analogical form into which the understanding is cast is not itself important—it is in fact expendable—but what does matter is Christ Himself, truly divine and truly human in His one incarnate Person. The form itself is employed as a *transparent medium* through which we may continue to discern the self-disclosure of Christ in His own reality, and as a *paradeigmatic help* to our minds in holding what is disclosed of Him in the grasp of their cognition. As such the Chalcedonian Definition is a subtle and flexible analogue, provided with the means of its own correction, so that when used rightly it invites reconstruction in view of the fuller disclosure of the reality it serves and proclaims its own inadequacy and limitation by a logical suspension of form so that it cannot be made a substitute for the truth of the divine Word.

(ii) *The Logic of Coherence-statements*

Singular existence-statements referring to particular events cannot manifest their proper meaning in isolation, but require to be associated in a consequential way if they are to refer to connected events in the real world and if they are to fulfil their function in a consistent manner.[1] Even for this semantic purpose they require coherence-statements. Coherence-statements are themselves of two sorts, existence-statements considered obliquely in their syntactical relations with other statements, and systematic statements which have no direct empirical reference of their own but which fulfil a conjunctive purpose in the general combination of statements in rational discourse. Thus the purpose of coherence-statements is to serve the deployment of statements in orderly sequences which will bring out their full meaning, and throw into relief at the same time the structure of the argument. It presupposes therefore that coherence is ultimately grounded in the nature of things referred to. This is akin to the procedure we discussed at an earlier stage in regard to the problematic form of inquiry in which we throw forward our questions and answers into a serial order designed to lay bare, as it were, the bone-structure of the demonstration so that joints and connections can be analysed.[2]

This is the task of *formal* logic, not to be concerned, however, with the active processes of inquiry, but to be the formal science of coherent statements that sets out their conditions

---

[1] Statements may be associated meaningfully in various ways (cf. F. Waismann *The Principles of Linguistic Philosophy*, pp. 364 ff.), but ontic necessity, that a thing is not other than it is, calls for a consequential necessity in the relations of our statements if they are to express relations in being. Nevertheless ontic and noetic necessity may not be confused.

[2] See above, pp. 126 ff.

and formulates their principles. It investigates and enunciates the general rules of valid implication between propositions in which certain propositions (the conclusions) follow necessarily from other propositions (the premisses), so that unless the conclusions are true the premisses are not. This is of particular interest to a special science in establishing its axioms or theoretic premisses through testing the factual truth of their conclusions by their applicability to the real world, but formal logic treats these statements not in their semantic but in their syntactical aspect, and so has to do not with material or factual truth but with formal truth or validity, i.e. with entailment, necessary connection and inferential consistency. Formal logic does not claim to accumulate truths but only to lay down a clear system of rules for formal validity that are applicable in every science irrespective of their factual truth or content—that is, it tests the validity of arguments from true or false premisses, and leaves the question of factual truth to each special science to determine in its own field and in its own appropriate way.

Aristotelian logic was essentially classificatory, for it sought to set out valid (and invalid) connections between statements through recasting them into the subject-predicate form, and developed the syllogism as a calculus of class inclusion and exclusion. Hence unlike Stoic logic this was a logic of predications rather than of propositions. Although it did not give specific attention to the problem of existence-statements it was concerned with significant propositions, i.e. statements whose meaning is lodged in their objective relation to things or states of affairs but which are used in a logical calculus. Thus Aristotelian logic was not unconnected with and not undetermined by physics because it was concerned with the connection of things in the real world through their conceptual representations.[1] But this fundamental logic, which has a long tradition, with significant developments in the work of Stoic, Medieval and even some modern thinkers (Bolzano[2] or Trendelenburg[3] or Lukasiewicz,[4] for instance), was bound

---

[1] Cf. A. D. Ritchie's defence of Aristotle's logic, op. cit. pp. 120 ff.
[2] See his major work, *Wissenschaftslehre*, and the discussion of it by H. Scholz, *Mathesis Universalis*, pp. 219–267.
[3] Adolf Trendelenburg, *Logische Untersuchungen*.
[4] Jan Lukasiewicz, *Aristotle's Syllogistic from the Standpoint of Modern Formal Logic*.

to change with the transformation of physics in its concern
for events and processes, relations and operations, in which
the 'what' and the 'how' have merged together.[1] Logic has
in fact become relational and operational, which fits in better
with the dynamic style of modern thought and the active
character of modern science. On the other hand, it functions
through a logical suspension of the ontological import of
existence-statements, throwing them into hypothetical forms
of possibility in order to consider them in a calculus of propositions on the same logical level as mere coherence-statements
where their connection can be determined with the utmost
exactitude.[2] The ignoring altogether of the referring element
in ordinary speech,[3] and therefore the total abstraction of
form from matter, have naturally shifted the emphasis from
the factual to the linguistic and tended to restrict the function
of logic to a technique for the control of our words and statements in their syntactical structures. But since this in turn
throws logic into closer connection with grammar and syntax,
it has been forced to clarify its relation with ordinary language
more carefully in the development of an artificial 'logical
language' (*Begriffsschrift* as Frege called it)[4] that will be free
from object-words (in Russell's sense) or any interpreted words,
and so be applicable to any and every science. This is the reason
for the development of formal logic into symbolic logic,

[1] It is a distinctive character of modern physics that we cannot formulate
statements without defining at the same time how we have come to make them, i.e.
scientific propositions are operationally defined. But for this very reason modern
logic has not taken sufficient account of Bolzano's idea that logic must be concerned
with the ways in which we reach knowledge, *Wissenschaftslehre*, ed. by A. Höfler,
Bd. I, p. 8.

[2] This had already been anticipated by 'terminist logic' in the later Middle
ages, in which forms suppositing for statements of direct meaning enabled them
to be correlated with other statements with an oblique meaning. But the essential
idea is also found in Leibniz (see H. Scholz, *Abriss der Geschichte der Logik*, p. 52 ff.)
and in E. Husserl's principles of phenomenological ἐποχή or bracketing off of the
external world in order to consider eidetic forms by themselves in a science of
pure possibility (*Ideas, A General Introduction to Pure Phenomenology*, 31 f, 56–69).

[3] See P. F. Strawson, *Introduction to Logical Theory*, p. 215. The relation of
modern logic to Aristotelian logic is rather like that of projective geometry to
Euclidean geometry in its ignoring of unnecessary information in order to preserve
and maintain the essential relations in their sharpest and clearest form. Cf.
W. W. Sawyer, *Prelude to Mathematics*, ch. 10.

[4] G. Frege, *Begriffsschrift, eine der arithmetischen nachgebildete Formalsprache des
reinen Denkens*. For a full account of Frege's views and an estimation of their
importance, see W. and M. Kneale, *The Development of Logic*, ch. viii, pp. 478–512.

which is not finally a difference in kind but in degree (it is purely or completely formal), designed to strip away from the rational structures of argumentation everything that detracts from the perfection and sharpness of their form and so from the precision and exactness of their inner sequences—for this purpose they have to be treated apart altogether from their content. This is done through the analysis of the fundamental units of language into 'constants' and 'variables' and the construction of a technical vocabulary of arbitrary signs, having no semantic significance whatsoever, to represent them, so that they can be used in an axiomatic logical calculus[1] for the elaboration of complicated inferences in complete consistency. While this logic is entirely formal, it provides us with a cognitive apparatus which vastly increases the range and power of our inferential thought. A similar development, owing its earliest impulse to Leibniz,[2] has taken place from the side of mathematics, and indeed it is largely to the mathematicians themselves (Hamilton, de Morgan, Boole, Hilbert, Dedekind, Cantor, Frege, Peano, Schröder etc. and in a different way to Poincaré and Brouwer) that modern logic owes so much, but the result has been a massive attempt to assimilate pure mathematics and symbolic logic together into a basic logico-mathematical calculus on an axiomatic basis, or a *logistic*, that can be used as the universal scientific language in the deductive testing of argument (Whitehead, Russell, Peirce, etc.). This calculus is constructed out of what are called 'second-order' symbols, that is, not symbols that are signs of things, but symbols that are signs suppositing for other signs representing things, and which therefore function only as symbols. Not only are these symbols cut off from the real world but they are cut off by definition from symbolic linkage with the real world and bracketed off for linkage only with each other. Their significance is entirely exhausted by logistical definition within the calculus in which they are used.

The value of modern formal or symbolic logic lies in the extreme rigour and generality with which it can function as a

[1] That is, a calculus in which the *premisses* are replaced by axioms regarded as part of the rules of inference.

[2] See again H. Scholz for an appreciative account of the part of Leibniz in this development, *Abriss der Geschichte der Logik*, pp. 48 ff., and *Mathesis Universalis*, pp. 128 ff.

sort of *scientia scientiarum* in Peter of Spain's sense,[1] as 'laws of the laws of nature' in Frege's sense,[2] or as the logic of *scientia generalis* in Leibniz's sense,[3] in which the conditions of valid implication can be completely controlled. Somehow also it appears to have an aesthetic and speculative value in itself, for the sheer beauty of internal consistency which it idealizes, like that of pure mathematics, can apparently enhance scientific vision and guide speculation, as seems to have been the case with Einstein in his formulation of the theory of relativity or de Broglie in the formulation of his theory ascribing wave nature to particles of matter.[4] But the particular value of modern logic is that in a computer-like way it enables us to formulate very complex statements and to perform feats of elaborate and sophisticated deduction which we would not be capable of otherwise, just as the casting of scientific results into a mathematical notation may not only give them consistency, making them precise and clear, but, as it were, do some difficult thinking for us by unfolding the implications of our scientific work beyond what we could determine with our empirical statements alone.[5] This is evident, for example, in the two-way relation possible between geometry and algebra, where the translation of algebraic equations into geometrical form and of geometrical theorems into algebraic form reveals and clarifies what each really implies. But how far is logico-mathematics or mathematico-logic relevant or applicable to every science, to those concerned with the real world of space and time, to the human sciences, and not least to theological science? Clearly the logic of *scientia generalis* will be of value for any *scientia specialis* only if it can be brought to work in polarity with the logic interior to it, establishing with it a rapport similar to that between algebra and geometry.

It can hardly be denied that this modern logic raises some very intractable problems which we are a long way from clearing up and certainly cannot attempt here, but there are several difficulties that we must note for they bear upon our discussion.

[1] Petrus Hispanus, *Summulae Logicales*.
[2] G. Frege, *The Foundations of Arithmetic*, section 87, tr. by J. L. Austin, p. 99.
[3] G. W. F. von Leibniz, *Préface à la Science Générale* (1677), *Opuscules et fragments inédits de Leibniz* (L. Couturat, Paris, 1903), pp. 153 ff.
[4] These examples are given by M. Polanyi, op. cit. p. 148 f.
[5] Cf. G. Frege, op. cit., Introduction, p. xvi.

(a) The bringing together of logic and mathematics, even on the axiomatic basis (suggested by the discovery of non-Euclidean geometry), which does not involve the reduction of one to the other, appears to ignore the fact that they belong to different types of order. Verbal relations and numerical relations are not isomorphic, for they belong to diverse logical systems or rather diverse sets of logical systems.[1] In fact the kind of rationality we have in *logos* (word or statement) is different from the kind of rationality we have in *number*, although it must be granted that they overlap in the conceptual forms in which we think out their internal relations. Number and word are both forms of rationality, but if we ignore their inherent differences we will be led to impose an artificial and monotonous uniformity upon the world of our manifold experience, and will make serious 'category-mistakes' with very far-reaching consequences in meaninglessness and in irrationality. There is undoubtedly important truth in the view that a close relation obtains between mathematical equations and existence-statements of a certain kind, but even so mathematical models stand only in an analogous relation to the patterns of nature. There is no justification for the idea that there is a preestablished and universal harmony between being and number, so that to think being we *have to* think mathematically, as seems to be implied frequently in the application of statistical principles to psychological and social states of affairs.

(b) Along with this must be raised the question as to the applicability of patterns of thought developed through second-order symbols to the real world, for once we start freely generating formal possibilities in total disregard of our intuitive or empirical contact with the world of actuality (i.e. bare possibilities as distinct from the possibilities of things) we are bound not only to develop artificial patterns of thought that are incompatible with the real world but to give rise to serious discrepancies bringing our thought into conflict with it. Practically, the problem with these rigorous symbolic systems is that

[1] Contrast the way in which we use a logical calculus, as a system of rules, with the way in which we use a geometrical calculus, as theory. Cf. F. Waismann, *The Principles of Linguistic Philosophy*, ch. XIX, 'The Logical Calculus', pp. 377 ff.

to get any advantage from them we have to let our thought travel through them to the end, only to find that it is so schematized to them that it cannot break free. Symbolic logic may set our minds free in one sense by lifting them up into a world where they are not tied down to the nature of the object,[1] but only too often it is to cramp them in realms of abstract possibility and artificiality where they are not free for the real world. This carries at its heart the old problem of the divorce of *nomos* from *physis* or *logos* from *physis*, to which Martin Heidegger has been drawing our attention again; when our thought becomes detached from being it develops imperious and legislative habits in seeking to impose nomistic structures upon being. It must be granted, of course, that our statements (like number apart from a calculus) become indistinct and vague, unless they are correlated in a well regulated system, but the system itself must have some authentic and natural coordination with existence if the statements within it are not to be forced away from their real meaning or truth. This is why, as Waismann insists so much, stress must be laid upon the applicability of our systems, for applicability is the criterion of existence.[2]

(c) In spite of the sharp bifurcation between form and matter assumed by symbolic logic, it is extremely difficult to maintain the investigation and manipulation of pure form as a logical device, i.e. simply for the technical purpose of acquiring consistency. Forms are what they are as forms of something, and when detached from matter, they become attached to something else as their form.[3] This tends to happen in one of two different ways. Either ideal forms are posited and projected into an objectified realm of pure form which is the Platonic tradition, or forms become attached to intra-mental or psychological states as their symbolic representations, which is the tendency that has so often prevailed since the Renaissance. In the latter event, as we have already had occasion to note, even our logical structures get caught up in the developing patterns of consciousness and in the determinations of human and social growth. This is the reason why it is

---

[1] See H. Weyl, *Philosophy of Mathematics and Natural Science*, 1949.

[2] F. Waismann, *Introduction to Mathematical Thinking*, p. 242—see the whole chapter on 'Inventing and Discovering?', pp. 235 ff.

[3] Cf. the discussion of E. H. Hutten, *The Origins of Science*, p. 117 f.

such a struggle to achieve the new logical concepts that are necessary for scientific advance, for we are never so tied down as when we are tied to ourselves, and never so incapable of new thinking as when we are unable to forget our own old ideas. It is as difficult to repent or change our minds as it is to grow young again, but unless we repent and become like little children we cannot enter the kingdom.[1]

How are we, then, to assess the importance of formal or symbolic logic in scientific activity? As the logic of coherence-statements its value will be in proportion to its effectiveness in the service of strict consistency, but logic will ultimately prove of little actual help unless at the same time it can be harnessed to the objectives of the special sciences in the attainment of material knowledge of the universe, for in every such science it is quite essential that statements be applicable to the real world. If logic is to be as serviceable as it is necessary it must operate within relations of *detachment* and *attachment* to actuality, or within the polarity of *systematic form* which is the chief concern of *scientia generalis* and *empirical form* which is the special concern of each *scientia specialis*. On the one hand this is held to mean that logic needs to be detached not only from physics, biology, psychology, etc., but from all ontological ties such as a metaphysics of being understood in the old classical sense, if it is to be free to develop the exact forms of thought and expression which are required in the construction of systems, but on the other hand if it is to fulfil a function at all relevant to the purpose of the sciences it must be open to being which is the conceptual source of our thought-forms and therefore open to the kind of metaphysical thinking that is unavoidable in the achievement of new conceptions and that marks the great forward advances of scientific knowledge and method.

The *detachment* of logic from ontological reference is perhaps best seen in its application to test materially false hypotheses by working out deductively their logical consequences. As Cohen has expressed it, 'Logic cannot be confined to the world of existence—meaning by the latter, actual existence—for

[1] Undoubtedly it was one of Wittgenstein's most important contributions to devise ways of thought which would help to break up the rigid and cramping structures of our thought and make us free for real thinking, weaned of preconception. Cf. David Pole, *The Later Philosophy of Wittgenstein*, p. 28.

science is concerned with the weighing of evidence and that means with the weighing of rival hypotheses. We must, therefore, be able to deduce the consequences of false propositions, that is, of propositions which assert either the non-existence of what does exist, or the existence of what does not exist'.[1] Hence if logic could not be detached in some way from ontological reference, science could not carry on.

Another way in which the detachment of logic becomes apparent is in its abstraction of logical order from temporal order which is apparent in the way in which formal logic recasts statements into forms in which a timeless copula is substituted for the active verb in order to consider them in relation to the general or universal. This represents a substitution of bare syntactical relation for real relation.[2] That is to say, logic works out the implications of statements by ignoring the temporal activity of referring and so treats both the statements and the events that they are about as if they were timeless, but as a formal science it must do so since here formality itself is a-temporal.

This detachment of logic from space and time is more severe the more highly formalized it becomes in the transformation from traditional logic to logistic as words are replaced by uninterpreted symbols and they become counters manipulated in accordance with the notations of a stringent mathematical calculus, but the fact that there is a similar ratio of detachment in the serial structure of the sciences from descriptive formalism to mathematization and from mathematization to axiomatization indicates that logical abstraction plays not a little part in their development. To cite Polanyi again, 'It is a sequence of increasing formalization and symbolic manipulation, combined with decreasing contact with experience. Higher degrees of formalization make statements of science more precise, its inferences more impersonal and correspondingly more "reversible", but every step toward this idea is achieved by a progressive sacrifice of content.'[3] From this we may gather that logic is serviceable in the cause of science when we appreciate its relativity and employ it in accordance with its strictly limited

---

[1] M. R. Cohen, *A Preface to Logic*, p. 193.
[2] Cf., for example, Bertrand Russell's treatment of 'is', *An Inquiry into Meaning and Truth*, Pelican edit. pp. 59–73.
[3] M. Polanyi, op. cit. p. 86

technical objective, namely, to make our statements clearer within a restricted context. As Mary Hesse has written, 'A clear understanding of the relativity of logic and mathematics is a great gain, since we require a healthy distrust of logic when it is applied to the real world.'[1]

Perhaps the *attachment* of rigorous logic to existence or at least its openness toward existence is best seen today in the light of Gödel's famous theorem to the effect that every system of arithmetic is necessarily incomplete since it contains within it propositions or sequences that are not definable or demonstrable within the system, so that no system of arithmetic is complete if it is entirely consistent. If the consistency of a system is to be demonstrated it must be from beyond the system in question.[2] This is a discovery of immense significance for it holds good for every logical or mathematical deductive system, for every such system must contain in it undecidable or extrasystematic propositions (i.e. statements which so far as consistency within the system is concerned appear irrational), if it is to be meaningful.[3] Thus Gödel's discovery serves to reveal the limits of logical formalization or of axiomatization, since it shows that the structure of a formal system by its very nature must be open, and can therefore be free for new discoveries, while a closed system, one entirely consistent, and demonstrably so within itself, would not be true for it could have no relation to reality.

This means again that the complete logicalization of a special science is impossible, and obversely that a logical system must be relevant at essential points to experience and intuition if it

---

[1] M. B. Hesse, op. cit. p. 88

[2] K. Gödel, *On Formally Undecidable Propositions of Principia Mathematica and Related Systems*, tr. by B. Meltzer, with an introduction by R. B. Braithwaite, pp. 37 ff. For a clear, brief exposition of Gödel's thought see F. Waismann, *Introduction to Mathematical Thinking*, p. 100 ff, and for an estimation of its significance for logic see R. Freys, in F. Heinemann, *Die Philosophie im 20. Jahrhundert*, p. 327 f. Also E. Nagel and J. R. Newman, *Gödel's Proof*.

[3] Something like this was of course known in a general way already, for it was realized that while logical propositions in a system can be demonstrated through their implications with one another, this is only possible if some of them cannot be demonstrated in this way, since what is required in every demonstration cannot be demonstrated in it, yet propositions which are indemonstrable in one system may be demonstrated in another. See M. R. Cohen and E. Nagel, *Introduction to Logic and Scientific Method*, pp. 133, 187. This point was already made with reference to the *Principia Mathematica* of Whitehead and Russell by A. E. Taylor, *The Faith of a Moralist*, vol. 2, p. 73 f.

is to be significant or even possible. It must correspond therefore more or less to ordinary language.[1] In the final analysis it cannot be detached from the real world but will be relative to the purpose of science, for it retains semantic function as a system, directing our attention to realities that outrun its logical form. Expressed in terms of scientific theory this asserts that the concepts comprised by a model, and coherently combined within it, do not for the most part have to have empirical or objective reference, but what is necessary is that the organic system which they build together must bear upon the real world here and there contingently at decisive points, for that ontological orientation is the very hinge of their meaning and the base on which they are constructed into the system or theory. These are the points where coordination takes place between the logic of existence-statements and the logic of coherence-statements, on the one side through empirical operations to determine relations within the real world, and on the other side through the employment of a logical calculus to combine the significant relations of our thought into an integrated concept which enables us to grasp the sequence of the demonstration as a whole and which thus enables us to see more clearly the objective relations in the real world, but in so far as it engages in a compound semantic act it often opens up for us the door to new knowledge. In this way it must be granted that the great advances of modern logic do not refute Aristotelian logic, though they often correct it, for they consolidate it more securely on its own proper basis where it is orientated to the nature of things, but within a limited range of usefulness.

It should be noted that the coordination between the logic of existence-statements and the logic of coherence-statements may be understood in two diverse ways, and indeed is sometimes carried out in diverse ways—it is this that lies behind the tension between 'invention' and 'discovery'.

When the logico-mathematical calculus is clamped down

---

[1] See F. Waismann, *The Principles of Linguistic Philosophy*, p. 368. This is the point made by Frege in *Basic Laws of Arithmetic*, Vol. II, section 91 f., in which he argued that if we consider arithmetic without its application, thus detaching it from our word language altogether, we turn it into a mere game.

upon empirical form it fosters and is used to justify the attitude of mind that regards science only as a means of doing things, that is, as an instrument of power in man's mastery over nature, so that creative invention and technology are extolled as the characteristics *par excellence* of modern science. This in turn involves, retroactively, a revision of the fundamental nature of logic which becomes a purely axiomatic or postulatory system, suggested by the success of non-Euclidean geometry, in which it is thought that the calculus is a free-floating invention of our own, built on the basis of arbitrary conventions and entirely independent of the nature of things. Yet this is the complete axiomatization that has been shattered by the Gödelian theorems, for any such system could only be meaningful or useful if it were not complete in itself and were given a meaning by a relation of some of its own postulates to another system providing them with definition and demonstration. It would seem, therefore, that this line of thought could in the end only lead to the stultification of empirical science since it would turn it finally only into a system of propositions defined by a particular calculus, thus substituting rationalization for rationality.

However, when the logico-mathematical calculus is co-ordinated with scientific exploration and interpretation in such a way that the systematic form serves the empirical form as a necessary instrument of special science, then it builds together with it the interpretative frame-work through which we look at nature and are engaged in actual discovery. This does not mean that discovery is a merely passive process. On the contrary, it is an extremely active mode of inquiry in which we are engaged in the creation and construction of models and analogues of great subtlety and in the invention of very sophisticated cognitive tools, such as four-dimensional geometry, yet all this is in the service of material knowledge, for the creations and inventions must not be empty possibilities, mere toys of the mind, which are utterly useless in the real world and are pure fictions, but real possibilities, e.g. Hamilton's famous quaternions, which are seen, it may be after their invention, to apply to the real world through the light they cast upon it. That is to say, even in our 'creative' and 'inventive' activity we are engaged in strenuous obedience to the nature of the real world for we retain in our scientific knowledge only what submits to its requirements. This is what is meant by 'discovery', authentic knowledge in which we assent to reality beyond ourselves: we distinguish what we know from our knowing of it, acknowledging that far from being exhausted in our formulations it remains utterly transcendent to the order in which we have tried to reduce our knowledge of it, and acknowledging that it is only through subjecting ourselves to its authority that we have attained the knowledge we have.

It is in the very success of our scientific achievements that we know how limited science is, not that reality or being is limited as a source of conceptual knowledge for us but that we are limited in the power to conceive forms of knowledge adequate to it. The element of invention in the construction of theories and calculi shares in the limitation of science and even axiomatization must be regarded in this light. Knowledge is given in the interaction of subject and object, and scientific knowledge cannot escape being a compromise between thought and being.[1] Nevertheless, although we cannot finally transcend our own selves and limitations, we use theories, models or analogues as means or instruments through which we discern and cognize objective reality as far as we may, relying upon a rationality embedded in the nature of things and independent of our knowing of it, since it is this that makes science possible at all.[2]

How then are we to understand the coordination of the logic of coherence-statements with the logic of existence-statements, for the assimilation of existence-statements to coherence-statements on the same level would undoubtedly land us in logical contradictions? Clearly we have to work with different *logical levels* and what one might call a 'trans-logical' relation between them. Here we return to the point exhibited so clearly by Gödel to the effect that it is not possible within a single

---

[1] This aspect of scientific knowledge is very clearly expounded by C. F. von Weizsäcker, *The World View of Physics*, and André Mercier, *Thought and Being*.

[2] See A. N. Whitehead, *Science and the Modern World*, p. 23; *Adventures of Ideas*, p. 292.

all-embracing system to define and demonstrate all its essential propositions, so that we have to have recourse to a further system beyond. This would appear to be the principle behind the graduated extensions of logical abstraction that we have noted in the development of formal logic. That is to say, in the formalization of a 'primary' or 'basic' language (in Russell's sense) we require another language beyond it, a 'secondary', logical language, sometimes called the 'meta-language', and if we are to be completely rigorous we require still another beyond that, a 'meta-meta-language'.[1] We begin with the natural logic of our ordinary speech, then we have a formal logic which is a system of rigid rules to help us determine the connection of our statements and make their meaning exact, but within a restricted context that only touches ordinary speech at decisive points, and finally a logistic system or a radically symbolized logic entirely detached from ordinary speech with its concealed assumptions, and devoted solely to deduction.

The application of this to the special sciences, however, particularly the empirical and human sciences, raises some problems, since we have to take into account the nature and claims of the object in each field of inquiry. They vary in their amenability to this kind of treatment for they are not so open to formalization as the essentially deductive sciences. Even an exact science like physics would appear to resist complete formalization, while in the study of language we run the risk of confusing two different types of order, the logico-verbal and the logico-mathematical. On the whole, however, we operate with three logical levels distinguished in the following way:
(i) the fundamental level of our actual knowledge of things in accordance with what they are, (ii) the level where we test and formalize this knowledge through some sort of calculus into a coherent system, and (iii) the level at which we interpret the formulations of this system and determine its mode of connection and consistency. Thus in theological science we operate with the actual knowledge which we have through rational assent or faith (συγκατάθεσις, πίστις), the orderly and coherent

---

[1] This is the notion of a 'hierarchy of languages' suggested in different ways by Tarski, Carnap and Russell. Wittgenstein, however, remained an opponent to the notion of 'meta-languages'.

account of this in dogmatics, the pure science of theology, and the philosophy of theology or its meta-science, including its logic and epistemology (e.g. the concern of the present work).

Several observations may be made about these logical levels in the special sciences.

(a) Theoretically the hierarchy of levels may extend indefinitely for when we reflect upon the language at one level we treat it as an object-language relative to another meta-language, and may do the same to that meta-language and so on, but actually this indefinite sequence does not arise—and it may well be that some sciences need no more than two logical levels. It is the nature of the subject-matter that will determine this for us.

(b) The different levels extend upwards, as Russell, says, not downwards since if they did we could never get started.[1] Each level, then, is open at the top, but its purpose is to serve the level below. Thus the meta-meta-language serves the meta-language and through it the basic language which is orientated toward the realities through ostensive designations. The whole hierarchy of levels is meant to serve scientific knowledge by making it a more adequate and effective semantic system for the attainment of clear and exact knowledge of the real world.

(c) The logical formalization of a science takes place only after we have reached organic patterns of reference in the processes of question and answer, that is, in the formulation of an analogue or model through analogical reasoning. But since that is then projected tentatively in the form of a compound question to the object of investigation, its logicalization can only be provisional. As more facts come to be disclosed from the side of the object, the model or analogue will suffer a change through the inclusion of new basic statements. This calls for a logical reconstruction of the whole theoretic framework, but at the same time it becomes clear that the science in question cannot be treated merely like a logico-deductive

[1] Bertrand Russell, *An Inquiry into Meaning and Truth*, p. 59. The difficulty with Russell's discussion all through this work is that he runs together knowing and expressing knowledge, and so does not escape the tyranny of linguistic formalism.

system, since the kind of 'premisses' with which it operates come to be known only in and through the processes of inter-rogation and discovery and not beforehand.[1] Thus since we must always expect the entry of new existence-statements into the basic structure of a science the logicalization of a theory can be only a tentative and provisional undertaking at each successful stage or definite level in the advance of empirical inquiry. Considered purely logically the 'trans-logical' step from one level to another (which Polanyi calls the 'crossing of a logical gap')[2] is like that revealed by the Gödelian theorems, the transition to a wider syntactical connection, which can be effected by the inclusion of a single new proposition, but considered empirically the 'trans-logical' step may involve a forward advance of such a character that it staggers us as it appears to call for a breaking of logical form and a step into absurdity. Nevertheless we have to break free from the for-malism with which we have been operating if we are to appre-hend what is really new. This is what happened to Bohr and Heisenberg when they found themselves having to take a step forward beyond the rationality of classical physics in their attempt to reduce to order what was being learned of nuclear activity. Looked at from the perspective of logical formalism such a step appears to be definitely *in-formal*, yet in point of fact it is a step into a deeper and fuller rational form, but into a different type of order. At the new level, however, logical reconstruction must take place to clarify the forms imposed on our understanding to make sure that they contain no intrinsic incoherence which would obstruct us in taking further steps to increase our hold on the real world.

(d) It is worth emphasizing again that there are different types of order comprising different types of concept which must not be elided even if they are to be correlated with one

[1] If the premisses are known beforehand, we are operating only within the formalization of what we already know. Cf. M. Polanyi, *Personal Knowledge*, p. 163: 'The logical antecedents of an informal mental process like fact finding, or more particularly, the finding of a fact of science, come to be known subsidiarily in the very act of their application; but they can become known focally only later, from an analysis of their application, and, once focally known, they can be applied by re-integration to guide subsidiarily improved performances of the process'. Cf. also E. H. Hutten, *The Language of Modern Physics*, p. 38.

[2] M. Polanyi, op. cit. pp. 123, 125, 143, 151, etc.

another. It is one thing to step from one calculus to another of the same logical type, as in multiple algebras or geometries, but it is another thing to step into a new calculus that cannot be logically related to the other, even by the kind of trans-logical relation posited in the Gödelian theorems between one system and another. Thus it can be quite nonsensical to step out of one family of concepts into a very different one with a different mode of connection between the concepts, as from mathematics to history. As Waismann has said, "no one would dream of joining a historical statement and a mathematical statement by 'and' ".[1] Of course when we seek to explain something about music, for example, we use our ordinary language as a meta-language for this purpose, and we do the same with regard to any art or science, so that there is bound to be a 'logical overlap' so far as the formulation of our knowledge of them is concerned, but we would not confuse the orderly sequence of statements with the sequence of sound in a piece of music. Now when we consider music apart from this ordinary language used to speak about it, we find that there is nothing beyond it to which its order is contingent, and even if we do think that there are real objective forms of some sort behind music, the transition from one level to the other would still be within the same kind of order. But when we turn to the natural sciences where we have to coordinate systematic form with empirical form, if we are to have science at all, we must respect the empirical form in its own right and use the logical form of our systematic thinking to help us to develop our understanding of it in accordance with its own 'inner logic' which arises not from the calculus we are using but from the systematic connection of things or a 'material logic' in the real world. In each special science we have to do with this kind of logic that is interior to it and that becomes evident as we cognize things in accordance with their own natures and their material implications. This is why a positive science like physics, for example, came to be thought of in its pure form as a *dogmatic science*, that is, the science in which we are not free to think as we may want but think what we are forced to think by the facts themselves, the science in which the *basic forms* of our thought are determined for us by the subject-matter

[1] F. Waismann, *The Principles of Linguistic Philosophy*, p. 367.

itself.[1] It is indeed the discerning and exhibiting of this material logic through the referring and ostensive operation of our models or analogues, together with the working out of its own inner logic answering to it, that is the major work of each science. Until this is done it has not achieved any significant 'breakthrough' in its understanding of what it investigates, and it is this that the other levels of logic must serve if they are to have a relevant place in scientific activity. Husserl has suggested that logic offers its help to science not by giving method, for method cannot be brought to any field from beyond its boundaries, but by giving 'the *form* of possible method' within the appropriate generality.[2]

They have at the same time an important critical service to offer in the rigorous formalization of scientific theory, by distinguishing those statements which are basic and absolutely necessary, upon which everything depends and around which the theory is organized, so that we may see how far we really are thinking as we are compelled to think and how far we are arbitrarily assuming as part of our dogmatic thinking ideas and propositions for which we have no proper reason in the connection of things. In this way logical formalization can help to deliver us from false dogmatisms, and so make us freer to submit our minds again to what the facts themselves have to teach us.[3]

(iii) *Logical Formalization in Theological Thinking*

So far as theology is concerned it must be admitted that logical and mathematical formalization is not a relevant form of accuracy, as we can see in the grave doubts of faith over the stringent applications of logical precision to religious experience—nevertheless theological science, like any other science, cannot do without verbal and logical machinery if only in the interest of methodical habits and tidy thoughts. Moreover,

---

[1] It is for this reason that in fundamental scientific activity there is an inner necessity to press beyond the tentative to what is basic and complete within its own limits—see A. D. Ritchie, *Studies in the History and Methods of the Sciences*, p. 3.

[2] E. Husserl, *Ideas: General Introduction to Pure Phenomenology*, pp. 95 f., 214 ff.

[3] The two senses of 'dogmatic' may be distinguished thus: one referring to the way in which we think as we are compelled to think by the facts and are cataleptically indoctrined, as it were, by them, and one referring to the arbitrary way in which we force our opinions on the facts in accordance with our untested assumptions and preconceptions, a doctrinaire way of thinking.

at ground level, even in the knowledge of faith, theology works with a principle of *reliability* similar to that with which we work in our ordinary natural logic when we presuppose that in the real world around us things fit together in the same sort of way as our thoughts do. There is a systematic connection in the nature of things, a regularity upon which we can rely that makes it possible to live a planned and rational life. But then from time to time we are jerked out of our assumptions by experiences which reveal a discrepancy between our customary forms of thought and what actually happens in the world. We are forced to reflect upon things at a deeper level for we have evidently been working with too superficial a view of uniformity, and have clamped down abortively, as it were, upon nature a form of unity which it rejects. Yet we still presume that form and order are endemic to nature and so we set about the task of laying bare its inner form and proper unity, and we try to reduce our understanding of it to order. We could not live rationally if the appearances could not be 'saved', if we could not reduce the phenomena to intelligibility, for we cannot but believe that things are so constituted that they are capable of rational treatment.

In religious experience and knowledge we work with the principle of the *faithfulness* of God, and we live and plan our lives accordingly. But we keep meeting evil and suffering which rise up before us as manifestations of disconnection and disorder in the nature of things and we are shocked at their deformity, i.e. their contradiction of rational form. And so we are driven to meditate upon them more profoundly for even disorder argues for order, seeking to reduce our understanding of experience to fuller intelligibility. We still believe that God is reliable and faithful, and that form and order belong to the fabric of the universe, and that behind creation and fall there remains God eternally and infinitely loving and wise. From the point of view of logical form there is a grave disconnection between the goodness and power of God and the facts of evil and suffering in the creation; for faith this element of incoherence is a problem only vis-à-vis ultimate coherence; faith insists on asking whether this is not to work with a superficial notion of uniformity, in which our formalization of things has been allowed to run ahead of the facts and to impose a false and illusory unity on them, e.g. by deriving a notion of 'omnipotence' through a logical construction out of the kind of power that we find in nature, brute force, formalizing its abstract possibility to the nth degree, and then setting beside it a notion of 'infinite goodness' derived in a similar way through logical construction and projection out of our common human ideas, only to find that they contradict each other in the face of the evil and suffering of our world. It is in the Cross of Christ, however, that faith penetrates deeply into its understanding of the faithfulness of God, for there He is found at work in the depth of measureless evil and the unappeasable agony of mankind overcoming contradiction, achieving reconciliation and bringing unity through atonement. Hence theology is forced to reconstruct the notions of power and goodness as applied to God, from what *God* has done and does do, instead of from hypothetical possibilities that are logically detached from the facts of existence and have run us into perilous error through their formalization.

In other words, here we are operating with *a posteriori* science in which the 'premisses' are properly revealed only at the end and in which we work with an operational logic at different levels. If we flattened everything out into a complete system at one level it could not but be self-contradictory, but we operate at different logical levels and discern the form and order we seek in a dimension of depth. This is not to reject a proper place for formal logic in theological discourse, but we are faced here with a situation not unlike that of the physicists when they have to relate quantum mechanics to classical physics and develop a logic of nuclear activity that will not reject but be on a different level from the logic of classical dynamics and mechanics as its 'limiting case', as von Weizsäcker speaks of it.[1] The difficulty modern physics has with classical physics is that the latter is built up from a knowledge of nature as it is commonly perceived, and works with an interior logic that corresponds to that. The difficulty theology has with our common knowledge is somewhat similar, for the latter works with a logic formed by abstraction from thinking of things as they are commonly observed, but the

[1] C. F. von Weizsäcker, *The World View of Physics*, pp. 104, 124. Cf. also at this point, M. Polanyi, *Personal Knowledge*, p. 282.

conceptual framework, as well as the vocabulary that this involves, is not always appropriate to the subject-matter of theology and when applied to it can even make it meaningless. What is required is a transition to another level of thought in which we develop an appropriate conceptual framework and an apposite vocabulary, and this involves a process of logical and linguistic reconstruction.

It is thus apparent that theological science cannot avoid the questions of detachment and attachment, of abstraction and application, which we have already discussed. Otto Neugebauer has pointed out in a remarkable book that the development of mathematical concepts and systems is closely connected with the structure of a language, in its speech and writing, through which it may be hindered or helped.[1] The reason for this is that different languages embody different cultural traditions and so carry forward different conceptual frameworks. It is with this that every science has to struggle, and as Frege has shown, often it is only after immense intellectual effort, which may have continued over centuries, that humanity at last succeeds in achieving knowledge of a concept in its pure form, in stripping off the irrelevant accretions which veil it from the eyes of the mind.[2] In this respect logical thinking can contribute not a little to theology in pruning its statements and arguments of the many associated notions that grow up in our common language and find a lodging in popular theology but which cannot be logically integrated with the basic existence-statements around which coherent formulation is built. It is when unwarranted preconceptions and ideas enter unnoticed into the body of knowledge that they are most damaging, but it is the function of logic to clear them from the ground in order that the real structure may stand out clearly.

A rigorous formalization of theological language can also play an important positive role, when the reference of the terms is clarified and their usage is reshaped in accordance with the nature of the object to which they direct our attention, for then their hold upon it is more apparent and as we use them they extend our apprehension of the object. This is what Polanyi

[1] Otto Neugebauer, *The Exact Sciences in Antiquity*, 2nd edit. Cf. ch. II on Babylonian Mathematics.
[2] G. Frege, *The Foundations of Arithmetic*, Introduction.

has called the 'indeterminate anticipatory powers of an apposite vocabulary' due to its contact with reality.[1] But this requires behind it and along with it a logical recasting of our concepts and the elaboration of a theoretic notation relevant to reality. This is the discovery and development of the interior logic of theology which proceeds together with the elucidation of its basic thought-forms and the construction of dogmatic forms and analogues in correspondence with their realities. As we noted earlier, *correspondence* is in place here for we are concerned with forms of *response* to the divine Word. It is this Word above all that makes theology an autonomous science with its own appropriate methods in the establishing and checking of its knowledge. It is under the address and claims of the Word that we have to mint an apposite vocabulary and through thinking out what the Word communicates to us that we have to reform our conceptual instruments and reconstruct the framework of our knowledge.

This does involve logical and metaphysical thinking, but it is important to see that they cannot be undertaken apart from actual theological inquiry. There is an interesting passage in a recent work of John Wisdom that relates to this.[2] 'The pure logician', he says, 'is not concerned with whether or how far a religious, moral, physical, or psychological, statement is true but with how one would know the truth of one of these statements given another of the same type. The pure metaphysician goes further. He is concerned with how one could know the truth of a statement of a given type, say the moral type, not from other statements of the same type but from the sort of thing which in the end is the ground for any statement of the type in question. We might say he is concerned not with the "domestic" logic of statements of a given type but with the ultimate logic of statements of a given type. Such a study is not ordinarily called logic but epistemology. The epistemologist, the metaphysician, traces further than does the orthodox logician the justification-refutation procedure proper to statements of a given type. But, like the pure logician, the pure metaphysician is not engaged in the physical, psychological, historical, religious inquiry.' This appears to pose

---

[1] M. Polanyi, op. cit. p. 116.
[2] John Wisdom, *Paradox and Discovery*, p. 120.

a double difficulty for theology. Theological statements are so closely bound up with the Word to which they refer and from which they derive (i.e. as 'heard statements') that they do not have their truth in themselves but in their referents. Hence a logician who would consider them by ignoring their reference altogether would not only fail to discern their truth but fail properly to discern their typical character— theological statements are not morphologically different from others, moral and social statements, for example, for what distinguishes them is precisely the uniqueness of their object, which is logically ignored. Once theological statements are detached from their referring function they are merely carica- tures of themselves, with at best an ordinary this-worldly mean- ing, but they may be non-sensical.[1]

On the other hand, it is quite right that we should be con- cerned, in Wisdom's language, with the ultimate as well as the domestic logic of theological statements, but how is it possible to determine how we are to relate their truth to their ultimate ground without actually engaging in theological inquiry and 'inhabiting its framework'?[2] What we are con- cerned with in the making and testing of theological statements as distinguished from other statements, as well as in the arduous heuristic endeavour to reach, assimilate and understand a *new conception*, with all that it entails in the repentant re- thinking of our prior knowledge, is certainly a form of *metaphysical* thinking, but it is similar to the metaphysical thinking (*mutatis mutandis*, of course) in which the pure scientist is engaged, and like that cannot be undertaken apart from actual scientific inquiry. It is difficult to understand how the pure metaphysician, detached from theological inquiry, can do what Wisdom claims, any more than he can through pure metaphysics trace mathematical statements to their ultimate ground.

[1] Of course once the reference of theological statements is set aside, another alternative open is to interpret them for the attitude they evoke, i.e. as poetical or aesthetic statements, but this would certainly force them into a different logical type.

[2] Contrast the discussion of Polanyi, op. cit., pp. 279 ff., where he insists that theological statements cannot be understood or treated aright except by those who engage in and dwell in worship ('heuristic vision') and theological inquiry.

Nevertheless, the disconnection of theological statements from their living source, and consideration of them on their own as formal statements of a certain kind, is one of the persistent temptations of the systematic theologian. He must engage in logical, as well as metaphysical, thinking to unfold the *inner logic* of his subject-matter and to construct the kind of 'calculus' he needs for this end, that is, a rigorous theological notation which will enable him not only to lay bare the essential structure of theological knowledge in its dogmatic integration but which will enable him to work out its implications beyond the range of his immediate experience or his power to determine on the ground of the protocol-statements from which he took his start. The pure theologian cannot do without this formal notation any more than the physicist can do without his algebra, but the theologian is constantly tempted to dwell too much in his 'theological algebra' and to let it do all his thinking for him, when it is only by translating it back into the actual forms and conditions of existence that he can grow in his knowledge and understand its material implications.

A striking example of this 'theological algebra' is the compound conception of *anhypostasia and enhypostasia* which, taken together with the doctrine of the hypostatic union, serves to bring out the essential logic of Grace and logic of Christ, not only in our understanding of Christ Himself but in the other doctrines that are organized round the Incarnation as their centre of reference. Used in this way the conception of anhypostasia and enhypostasia is remarkably fertile in its power to throw light on many difficulties and to reveal the true form in which many relations are to be conceived. But like all formalizations it can become dangerous for it inevitably detaches theological statement from its hold on reality if it is turned into a basic statement rather than a cognitive tool. Regarded in itself the conception is merely a sort of 'algebraic formula' and therefore must be transposed back into the living and actual forms of personal being if we are to think theologically and not just 'theologistically', so to speak.

What we are concerned with here is the *applicability* of our formalized conceptions to reality, for apart from that applicability theological science can easily be as much of a mere game as any arithmetic similarly bereft of applicability.[1] Now this means that in the process of detachment and attachment in theology we have to commute, as it were, back and forth between highly formal and incomplete modes of thought that are abstracted from the idiom of their proper objects and have no truth in themselves but only an epistemological function in their relations to one another, and real modes of thought that are congruent with the nature of their proper objects and have truth in so far as the structure of those objects becomes manifest through their reference to them. Hence in our theological statements (to borrow some apt expressions from Carnap) we have to operate with a *formal mode of speech* and a *material mode of speech*,[2] for our decisive statements must be allowed to maintain their hold upon reality even when we must purify and perfect their form for coherent discourse, but it also means that we cannot work with a complete detachment of form from matter.[3]

This takes us back once more to the necessity of thinking at different logical levels. Unless our thought takes this way, as we have seen, it will be led into impossible paradoxes and contradictions. We have to think in a dimension of depth at different levels of reference, and at each level clarify our thought through logical formalization, but the difficulty that we face in theology particularly is that this rubs out of our patterns of reference at each level their structure in space and time. To take a geometrical analogy, it is not simply a transition from plane to solid geometry that we need to effect in the focus of our apprehension but a transition to four dimensional geometry of space and time. In theology however we have never constructed a cognitive tool of this subtlety and usefulness, but have traditionally relied on formal logic, with the result that when we apply it to our thought we find that our concepts become dehistoricized and dematerialized. We require something like a logic of verbs, a logical instrument of a unique kind that will enable us to formalize our levels of

---

[1] See the sections of Frege's *Grundgesetze der Arithmetic*, vol. ii, 86 ff., in *Translations from the Philosophical Writings of Gottlob Frege*, edit. by P. Geach and M. Black, pp. 182 ff.

[2] R. Carnap, *Logical Syntax of Language*.

[3] A similar point is made by B. Bolzano in his *Wissenschaftslehre*, 11.§186, doubtless due to his theological interest.

reference without mutilating or destroying the essential forms of our thought and without flattening out our statements each time in such a way that their ontologic is damaged.

The problem that theologians face is not unlike that which confronts natural scientists in grappling with the quantum of action or with the form of biological development, where new concepts have arisen or are in process of arising but where no cognitive or linguistic tools exist which will enable them to think and speak consistently of them.[1] In these situations the scientific mind must learn to think in terms of quite new kinds of connection and to work with different kinds of precision. This would seem to be the significance of quantum logic which is concerned to express the profound connection between the geometrical and dynamical aspects of things which cannot be expressed merely through an extension and modification of the formalizations in language and logic that are already to hand. At the same time it would appear to involve setting quantum logic in relation to traditional logic in a way corresponding to the relation between quantum theory and classical physics. Biological science has not yet advanced as far as this but it is struggling with the same sort of thing in determining the kind of connection between subsisting form and movement or between permanence and change, which cannot be construed at all in terms of the a-temporal notions of form that we gain through processes of abstraction. We are concerned here with stability of form in the midst of organic movement or with what one might call the logic of kinetic form.

The logic of theology shares with quantum logic and the logic of biological development the difficulty that arises from the fact that traditional logical forms and connections are too narrow and restricted to express the kind of reality that comes to light in our inquiry while any modification of those forms can only extend further the abstraction of those very features in thought and speech which must be brought into play if the orderly forms of our thought and speech are to match the realities cognized. Like quantum physics and biology theology lacks the particular kind of precision that is demanded in the field of classical physics and its corresponding logic, and rightly

[1] See W. Heisenberg, *Physics and Philosophy*, pp. 154 f., 173 f., 177 ff., and Louis de Broglie, *Physics and Microphysics*, pp. 109 ff, 124 ff., 212 f.

so, for to cast the statements of any of these sciences into the limited mould of classical formalization could only lead to inaccuracy and imprecision, but since this is so it is incumbent on theology, as it is on those other sciences, to show its own kind of precision in accordance with the kind of connection forced upon its thought from the nature of the realities being investigated. But this means that it must forge for itself a logical instrument that fits the apprehension of those realities. Failing that the least that we can do is to keep constantly before us the fact that logical formalization in the traditional way oversimplifies and seriously distorts our statements and most of all where they express action, movement and change, and therefore where we are concerned with creation, fall, incarnation and atonement, conversion and regeneration, history and eschatology. It is through being cast into static formalization even at different logical levels that theological statements are laid wide open to the misinterpretation in which they are regarded as merely temporal and transient expressions of timeless and necessary truth.

It is of the utmost importance, therefore, to bear in mind the *limitations* of formal or symbolic logic, its abstraction from existence and actuality and its restriction to timeless and motionless involution. In logical thinking of this kind we are shut up to the world of pure *possibility* and thereby excluded from the world of *reality*. Abstraction is a never-ending process in which we soon outrun all possibility of the real into bare and empty possibilities, but since we begin by abstracting forms from reality and considering their formal possibilities, they may well keep within the range of real possibilities for some time, but even so we have to break off this logical thinking if we are to let *real* thinking take place, i.e. thinking of what actually happens in the real world, of material and dynamic relation, of movement, change and activity, and of being itself in all this.[1] As it is impossible to state in statements the relation of statements to being, so it is impossible to logicalize the relation of different logical levels to actual existence: all that linguistic and logical forms can do is to indicate where they come to an

---

[1] This point is made with great power by Kierkegaard in *Concluding Unscientific Postscript*, E. T. pp. 99 ff., 267 ff. See H. Diem, *Kierkegaard's Dialectic of Existence*, E. T., pp. 15 ff.

end, to show their boundary by breaking off the process of formalization in order that actual existence may be allowed to thrust itself upon our thought. This means that we are not concerned simply with different logical levels and with the 'logical gap' between them, but with a relation at right-angles, so to speak, to some logical level, like that made by an axle thrust through the centre of a wheel which gives it its usefulness and significance. The converging spokes must be cut short to leave a hole in the centre, for if they were actually to converge everything would be useless. Thus the converging lines of our thought must be broken through and be brought to an abrupt end, not by some undecidable proposition that can be demonstrated at another logical level, but by a different sort of relation altogether, in a transition to being and act. Formal logical levels become meaningful only at the point where they renounce their completeness and limit their processes of formalization, in order that room may be left for ontologic.

In theological thinking it is the Incarnation that does this, for it is the great axis thrust through the organic structures of our life and thought to give them purpose and significance. It is by relation to the Incarnation that our statements have their fundamental *ontologic* for it is in the Incarnation that our forms of thought and speech are grounded in God and yet earthed in the sphere of actuality where we live and move and have our existence. It is because of the Incarnation that the different logical levels in which we have to think do not run out into a meaningless and endless stratification of systems of bare possibility, but are made to start somewhere and to lead somewhere, so that man upon earth can think appropriately about God and his thinking about God can be applicable to his daily being and life in this world.

How are we, then, working with our inadequate cognitive tools to think out the trans-logical relation between the different levels of theological thought? Let us take the teaching of Jesus as reported in the fourth chapter of St. Mark's Gospel and consider its logical form in the light of what we learn from Frege and Gödel.[1] If we take a simple arithmetical statement like $2 \times 2 = 4$, it is not easy to explain even though we regard

[1] Cf. also Waismann, *Introduction to Mathematical Thinking*, especially ch. 16.

its significance as obvious. We have to use word-language to say what the symbols '2', '4', ' × ' and ' =' mean and at the same time we try to apply it to the real world by demonstrating it as we do, for example, to children, with two sets of two apples. It is impossible to teach children without using at least two levels, but it is also true that if we want to make it clear and precise even for those who well understand what $2 \times 2 = 4$ means we still have to use word-language. This is Frege's point that when arithmetic is torn away completely from its connection with ordinary language and from its application it becomes a meaningless game. But there is also Gödel's point that the system of arithmetic is not complete in itself, and if it is to be consistent and clear we require to bring it into relation with another syntactical system where at least one of its primary propositions can be demonstrated. Now the teaching of Jesus in Mark 4 is given on two levels, that of parable in one form and that of interpretation in another form. In spite of the obviousness of the parable and indeed the analogical coherence of its form, it becomes meaningful only in its application to existence on the one hand and only if on the other there is supplied a conceptual framework on a different level, while the latter is necessary if genuine application is to take place (which is again one of the points that Frege makes in regard to arithmetic). Thus considered from the point of view of their logical form, the interpretations of the parables are essential to the discourse and are not extraneous adjuncts or accretions, as some form-critics regard them.

There is undoubtedly a difficult hermeneutical problem here where we have also to operate on several levels. We are interpreting a written text by St. Mark which reports on the teaching of Jesus. Thus the object of our investigation contains two levels in itself: (i) the written text of the Evangelist embodying his understanding and statements, and (ii) the Evangelist's own original text, the teaching of Jesus which he reports to us. In order to understand the latter we have to look at it through Mark's language and understanding of Jesus, so that we have to assume as our subject-matter not only the teaching of Jesus but Mark's teaching about the teaching of Jesus. In interpreting something in nature we direct our questions to it in order that it may disclose itself to us, and as it discloses itself to us we check the form of our questions and correct them, for what hinders us in knowing the 'thing' is not the thing itself but some form of unreality with which we have overlaid it such as the presuppositions we have brought to its understanding. But when the object of our investigation is a human being we have to do with someone who is not what he ought to be, and is thus unlike a thing that just is what it is. Hence if we fail to understand a person, the fault may lie not only with us, who are not what we ought to be, but with the other who is not what he ought to be. This is always a difficulty in interpreting a human text, for even though we are not interested in the writer, primarily, at any rate, but in what he refers us to, we have to test what he says in the light of that to which he refers, to make sure, if we can, that it is as he says. Hence the form-critics have rightly raised the hermeneutical problem regarding the parables and their reported interpretation by Jesus, but when that is discussed without any attention to the logical form it cannot but risk erroneous conclusions.

Our concern at the moment, however, is only with the logical form, and from this point of view it seems clear that the connection between the parables and their interpretation reported by the Evangelist, cannot be cut without damaging the essential structure of the evangelical witness, making impossible the application, and so threatening it with meaninglessness. It may well be that the neglect of this essential logical form in which the parables are set in the biblical narratives lies at the root of some of the questions that have been baffling New Testament scholars in this connection.

Considered from the point of view of theological inquiry the parable (παραβολή) is the concrete form which Jesus throws (βάλλειν) alongside of or parallel to (παρα-) His Word in order to bring it to bear upon our understanding and to apply it to our actual human life. Taken properly parables are not so much forms that biblical and theological statements have to have in referring to transcendent realities but the instruments by means of which they are applied to our common life and maintain contact with our ordinary language. They have to be understood at two levels, an obvious moral and social level that touches us in our daily existence, but also at a deeper theological level where the meaning becomes evident in the light of the *incarnation* of the divine Word who comes to meet us in the structure of our human existence in history, speaks to us in its forms of the transcendent Kingdom of God, and establishes contact between our speech and thought and God Himself. The parable arises as the eternal *Logos* penetrates like an axis into our subject-object structures, and therefore into our human logic where we may know Him out of His own self-communicated content, and does not just impinge upon our world in a timeless and asymptotic manner without ever intersecting it in space and time, so to speak, in which case it could never become objective to our knowledge but would remain only asymptotically related to it, yet might be 'known' in a 'non-knowing' and 'paradoxical' way, as Bultmann would have it.[1] Parables thus operate in a dialogical situation in which the *Logos* of the Father mediates divine revelation to us in lowly forms appropriated from our human existence, and at the same time directs our thought through them back to the Father. On the ground of the *ontologic* established in the Incarnation the form of the parables exhibits the material mode of speech while the interpretation or explanation exhibits the formal mode of speech between which theological understanding must commute, i.e. between the empirical and the systematic form. On the other hand the conceptual content in the interpretation needs to be understood by being brought into connection with a wider syntactical system, where systematic theology plays the part of a meta-meta-language, as it were, to the ordinary language of proclamation and faith.

Logically, then, we have to work on different levels of thought, if we are not to run into non-sensical contradictions, but *theologically*, we have to understand these levels in the light of the incarnate Word, for it is the Incarnation that gives ontological import to their trans-logical relations. This is why the parables of the New Testament quickly lose their distinctive significance when they are flattened out on to one level, for their truth-value lies in their dimensional reference through the Incarnation. It is easy to see that they become not only empty of content and without any useful application but sometimes even morally revolting (e.g. the labourers in the

---

[1] See, for example, the first three essays of Rudolf Bultmann translated and published by S. M. Ogden in *Existence and Faith*.

vineyard who all received identically the same wage for quite disproportionate amounts of labour, Matt. 20. 1-16), when they are robbed of their inner trans-logical relations. The same applies to our concepts and statements in the scientific activities of theological inquiry and formulation. They must be open at both ends, to the transcendent realities to which they refer through their coherent forms or dogmatic analogues, and to the concrete actualities of our human life and existence. Severe and rigorous formalization of the knowledge of faith can render an important analytic service in helping us to discern the full implications of our basic statements and to understand their applications, and not least to deliver theological tradition from countless associated notions that creep in from popular sources to corrupt and distort it, but it has to break off in order to serve *real* thinking. Theology is not an abstraction or a game, and it is synthetic rather than analytic, for it is an advancing and positive movement of thought in response to the Word of God, which cannot be finally analysed through any system of logical formalization, far less be contained in it. Theology is a living activity of human beings in which knowledge develops through a series of constructive steps in the understanding of that which can never be exhausted in human knowing of it.

A scientific theology of any worth at all shares with rigorous logic the concern for purity of form and statement in the attempt to cut away the false assumptions and inappropriate ideas that have grown up uncritically in popular thought and have become deeply lodged in our ordinary and colloquial language, so that they may not distort the argument or deflect statements from fulfilling their proper function. Some of these associated ideas that creep in unawares from our ordinary modes of thought and speech have personal and social sources—they may be the creations of fantasies arising out of deep inner disturbances and conflicts, or the result of built-in mechanisms for defence against insecurities and anxieties, or they may be symbolic expressions of our hopes and longings and ideals, and so on, which are the deposit of the myth-making in which every society and civilisation is engaged, and which play a determinative role in the formation and development of their paradigms and rationalized self-understanding. Now so far as rigorous logic is concerned all this must be cut away from our rational thought and speech about things so that pure forms may be abstracted from them as precise moulds for the mathematically exact relations and involutions required in scientific construction, but this represents a ruthless suppression of the personal and social coefficients and therefore the radical impersonalization and objectivization of our thought. This is not something that pure theology can be content to accept, important though it is for limited technical purposes, because the kind of knowledge which theology builds up is one in which form cannot be separated from matter, and in which the material content moulds the form, i.e. in which the very structure of human and social existence is transformed. By the very nature of its object, the creating, revealing, reconciling and regenerating Word of God, theology is committed to a movement of transformation in which material modes of thought and speech are created in appropriate adaptation to the material truth they have to express. Thus instead of suppressing the personal and social coefficients of human knowledge, theology is evangelically concerned for their conversion and regeneration in accordance with the Truth of God as it is in Christ Jesus, and instead of using logically abstracted and perfected forms as empty moulds into which to pour its subject-matter, it opens up the way for the subject-matter to transform the modes of our thought and speech that they may be suitable and apposite in the service of our knowledge of God.

We may put this in another way, by saying that theology is concerned to overcome the abstraction between form and matter that has arisen in human knowledge as a result of the Fall—that is, in man's lapse from the Word of God, in his contradiction to the Truth, and in his flight from reality. It is owing to this profound estrangement in his existence, from God and from himself, that the mythological fantasies and rationalizations keep erupting in man's mental and social life, affecting everything that he thinks and does from below. The natural forms of his thought and speech have grown up within this separation of man from God and are thus adapted to a world out of harmony with its Creator. As such they cannot be used unchanged to interpret the new situation created by the Incarnation in which God has come to seek man in his estrangement, to heal him and reconcile him to Himself.

It is possible that the concentration upon visual modes of thought which we naturally develop in touch with observable realities has even affected our logic. We see and observe external form, so that when we think with our eyes it is comparatively easy to abstract forms from things and consider them apart from their material ground. Be that as it may, our natural knowledge is conditioned by a strange breach between the sign and the thing signified, the symbol and the reality it indicates, between image and idea, so that we have to struggle hard against making perceptibility the criterion of truth, not least in our knowing and thinking of God.[1] This is why theological knowledge which comes through hearing and is constructed on the basis of the Word is not at all easy for those who find themselves thinking only in pictorial images or plastic ideas. But it is just here that it becomes so evident that in theological inquiry we have to engage in a profound sort of reconstruction, for man himself must be reconstructed in his existence before God if the modes of his thought and speech are to be transformed into any kind of apposite relation to His Word and Truth.

It is in Jesus Christ where the Word of God has become man that man is restored to union and knowledge with God. It is in Christ, therefore, that there has been minted out of our human life the material mode of speech and thought that is truly adapted to God, and it is by reference to Jesus Christ, critically and constructively, that we must develop appropriate forms of thought and speech about God. That is the task of a living and constructive theology, to discover and work out the interior logic of our knowledge of God, but in the nature of the case it will not be able to avoid constant tension between the material logic thrust upon it from the side of the creative and redeeming operations of God in Christ, and the logico-verbal patterns of our thought and speech that are already schematized to this world, for the Truth of God as it is in Christ Jesus breaks through all our linguistic and logical forms. While God has made His Word audible and apprehensible with our human speech and thought, refusing to be limited by their inadequacy in making Himself known to us,

---

[1] A similar problem, of course, arises in science when we are tempted to treat our scientific theories as descriptions of reality, but as Ryle points out, they apply to but do not describe things, *Dilemmas*, p. 85 f.

He nevertheless refuses to be understood merely from within the conceptual framework of our natural thought and language but demands of that framework a logical reconstruction in accordance with His Word. Hence a theology faithful to what God has revealed and done in Jesus Christ must involve a powerful element of apocalyptic, that is epistemologically speaking, an eschatological suspension of logical form in order to keep our thought ever open to what is radically new.

If we cannot allow formal logic to dictate the forms in which we develop our understanding of God and His renewal of creation, we must nevertheless respect it and try to speak as far as we can grammatically and logically about God, for we have to carry out our work within this world where God has placed us and so within the breach between what our world actually is and what it was made to be, still ought to be, and indeed will be in the consummation of all things. But the theologian who thinks theo-logically, from a centre in God and in accordance with the logic of God, must never forget that his thought will inevitably have a novelty of form baffling to the natural thinker and that the new content which he seeks to express in grammatical and logical language may impose too heavy a strain upon it. As Jesus taught us, the new wine will burst the old wine-skins.

6

Theological Science among the
Special Sciences

Our purpose in this final chapter is to draw together certain
lines of thought from the preceding discussion in the attempt
to offer an account of theology as a dogmatic, or positive and
independent, science operating on its own ground and in
accordance with the inner law of its own being, developing
its distinctive modes of inquiry and its essential forms of thought
under the determination of its given subject-matter. Theology
is the unique science devoted to knowledge of God, differing
from other sciences by the uniqueness of its object which can
be apprehended only on its own terms and from within the
actual situation it has created in our existence in making
itself known.

We recall, therefore, that there is a theo-logical way of
thinking, not from a centre in ourselves but from a centre
in God, not from axiomatic assumptions which we make but
from a frame of reference that derives from God Himself
through His Word. This is possible only because it really is
God who is the object of our knowledge and thought, God who
is Himself the ground and possibility of all our experience and
knowledge of Him. Yet as a *science* theology is only a human
endeavour in quest of the truth, in which we seek to apprehend
God as far as we may, to understand what we apprehend, and to
speak clearly and carefully about what we understand.[1] It
takes place only within the environment of the special sciences
and only within the bounds of human learning and reasoning

---

[1] Cf. the interesting distinction drawn by Duns Scotus between *theologia in se*,
the pure science of theology as it is in God, and *theologia in nobis* or *nostra theologia*,
such knowledge as our human understanding can have of God as its primary
object, *Ordinatio*, prol. p. 3, q. 1-3, n. 4, 12.

where critical judgement and rigorous testing are required, but where in faithfulness to its ultimate term of reference beyond itself in God it cannot attempt to justify itself on the grounds occupied by the other sciences or within their frames of interpretation. As an undertaking in the service of the divine Truth, wherever it encounters it in this world, theology is dedicated to sheer truthfulness in all its processes, and therefore must always be open for self-criticism in the face of new learning and reasonable argumentation on its own ground. It is therefore the task of scientific theology to put all that claims to be theological thinking to the most severe test to make sure that it really is what it should be if it is to be knowledge of *God*.

Because it is with *God* that we have to do here theology cannot be isolated and made independent of the total claims of God upon man and of the total response of man to those claims. Theological science is not therefore a special science in the sense in which all the other special sciences are bracketed off in their own specializations. Special sciences by their very nature deal with multiplicity and are properly separated off from each other in accordance with the particular aspects of being to which they are devoted and the nature of the evidence that obtains in each field of inquiry, so that direct criss-crossing from the one to the other violates their scientific procedure. But theological science has for its primary object the one God who is the source of all being and the ground of all truth, and as such it is concerned with a wholeness and unity that does not characterize any other special science.[1] It is only within that wholeness that theology as a science has its right place, but it is no less scientific because it must operate within the total response of the believer to God, for to do anything else would mean a refusal to behave faithfully in terms of the nature of its proper object and therefore a betrayal of its true objectivity. This alone makes theological science unique among the sciences because it is more than a particular science, more than disciplined, controlled, accurate knowledge within some limited field, but it can be scientific knowledge of *God*, only

---

[1] There is an appreciable measure of overlap in content among the natural sciences, out of which there arises a mutual criticism that helps to maintain their authority. While theology has some measure of overlap with them, and even more with the human sciences, its uniqueness means that it does not overlap very much with their kind of authority, and betrays itself when it seeks to acquire it.

if it is more than scientific knowledge in the ordinary sense. That is to say, theological science is not simply explanatory in terms of itself as a special branch of knowledge among others, but is explanatory only in relation to the one Truth of God in His total claims upon us and in His ultimate purposes for us and all creation.

In view of this the claim is sometimes still advanced that theology is the queen of the sciences, not because it possessses some specially competent scientific method, but because of the nature of the one Truth of God upon which it reposes and by which all its activity is determined.[1] Certainly theology cannot and must not claim to be queen of the sciences in the old medieval sense, in which she is thought of as presiding over a hierarchy of *scientiae speciales*, and therefore as supreme over all the sciences through which man seeks to understand and rule over the natural world in which God has placed him and given him his duties and tasks. By its own nature, however, theology as a science is concerned with man and creation only in their relation to God the Creator and Redeemer. It recognizes that the investigation of what is creaturely in its contingency and utter distinctness from God is required of man in his God-given vocation to occupy and exercise do-minion over nature but that apart from knowledge of God it is ultimately without meaning.[2] As we have seen, by its doctrine of God and creation theology acknowledges the full place of the other sciences as independent branches of the knowledge of contingent realities, but whenever these special sciences seek to unify and extend their knowledge of contingent processes beyond the boundary of what is creaturely, contingent and relative, claiming to be the one and only way of penetrating into the ultimate secrets of the universe, or at least of being able to test theological knowledge for its truth or falsity, then theology cannot but come into conflict with them. It will be forced to reject these claims, on scientific grounds for such an extrapolation of technical methods would be a serious trespass

---

[1] Cf. here the conception of theology enshrined in the Gifford Foundation, 'a strictly natural science, the greatest of all possible sciences, indeed in one sense the only science, that of Infinite Being'—cited by John Baillie, *The Sense of the Presence of God*, p. 168.

[2] *Fumus est omnium scientiarum cognitio, ubi abest coelestis Christi scientia.* Calvin, *Comm. in 1 Cor. 1.20.*

upon scientific propriety, and on religious grounds for behind attempts of this kind there are Promethean attitudes giving rise to substitute symbolisms of a pseudo-religious nature in which something else is being put in the place of God.

It is indeed out of its profound respect for the ultimate majesty of the Truth that theology is forced to call in question the desire for absolutes in any human science, and therefore to remind us of the limited range of scientific inquiry and the relativity of scientific results. No science can transcend the objective that delimits and defines it as a special science, or lift the horizon of inquiry beyond the finite limitations of the human questioner. Thus in distilling among the sciences a healthy scepticism in regard to their powers of penetration and explanation, a theological science that acknowledges its own relativity before God cannot but contribute to the purity of the human sciences, but it can hardly do that unless it is prepared to enter into a genuine dialogue with them in which the limited objective and range of each science will be brought to view. This in turn should have a healthy effect upon theological science, for it will help to remind it that scientifically its dogmatic formulations are to be regarded as operationally defined through their service to the one supreme Truth that cannot be exhausted by our conceiving or speaking of Him.

When we turn to discern the relation between theology and the other sciences we concentrate upon that aspect of theological activity that is strictly scientific, rather than its setting in a total response to God, i.e. its character as rational knowledge. But we do not abstract theological knowing from what is actually known for its structural forms cannot be uprooted without alteration from their inhesion in doctrinal substance. Hence no direct comparison between theological science and the special sciences is possible, for in their case too scientific procedure is controlled by material content and the language each uses is adapted to its own subject matter. What we may do, so far as theology is concerned, is to trace the structural forms of its knowledge to their doctrinal source and show the procedure that theological thinking cannot but adopt within them if it is to be true both to the nature of its divine Object and what He reveals of Himself. The only kind of comparison that would be apt would be one of proportionality in which there is no direct transference of language or extrapolation of method but a comparison between the relations subsisting between the knower and the object in one field of knowledge and that between the knower and the object in another field of knowledge. Doubtless some direct comparison is inevitable and right in so far as the objective facts are within the same creaturely sphere of existence or on the same creaturely plane, but so far as they are not any direct comparison is illegitimate for it would involve serious category-mistakes.

This indirect comparison of theological science with the other sciences requires to be undertaken in our day, not for apologetic purposes or for the achievement of some kind of scientific security for theology within the same terms as the other sciences, for that could never be valid, but for quite a different reason, in the interest of theological purity and in the struggle to prevent theology from degenerating into an ideology. It should throw theology back, vis-à-vis the other sciences, upon its own proper ground where alone it can be true to the law of its own being, and really be a science in its own right. Subsidiary reasons also play their part here. Christian theology has not a little responsibility in the rise of modern empirical science and has thus a genuine interest in the preservation of its purity against the corrosion that threatens from the side of non-scientific factors, such as the fear of the unknown or of breaks in logical form, which can have the effect of closing the mind of the scientist to what is beyond that which can be observed and specified in certain determinate ways. But indirect comparison is also to be undertaken in the interest of theological communication which cannot succeed unless we show others that theology operates through a different interpretative framework with distinctive conceptual forms apposite to its own subject, and that apart from such a framework they cannot engage in the new way of thinking and the heuristic activity it involves. But indirect comparison must also supply those operating in the other sciences with sufficient conceptual content to guide their recognition of divine realities and give their minds some hold on what they are being asked to consider. In this way we seek both to gain the intellectual sympathy of others by showing them the rationality of theology, and to induce them to step out of their own position and into another for the purpose of apprehending divine realities in a way appropriate to them. This kind of comparison, therefore, is a form of intellectual witness and persuasion in which we convince the minds of others by directing them to intuit divine realities that are not immediately communicable but which are open to cognition through rational assent and critical judgement as people allow their minds to fall under the power of their objective logic.

(I) *Similarities and Differences Between Theology and the Other Sciences.*

i *Similarities*

(1) Perhaps the first thing to be said is that theological science shares with the special sciences in being a *human inquiry*. It presupposes, of course, as they all do, that its object is intelligible and therefore open to rational investigation along certain lines, and it assumes the existence of its object without stopping to justify its undertaking for these are questions that will be resolved in the actual process of examination and construction. As this kind of human inquiry theology involves like every genuine science both the art of learning and the art of reasoning. The same problems therefore crop up, how to grasp its own proper object without carrying over to it habits of thought that belong to other spheres of knowledge, and thus how to forget old ideas in the struggle to learn what is new, then how to reason upon what we learn by getting hold of it through its essential characteristics and organising everything round them as the basic clues, and how to develop the appropriate notation which will help to carry our thought beyond the scope of what is familiar so that the reality being investigated may be allowed to disclose itself in its own structure and order. It is in this process that we develop and progressively refine 'theoretic constructions', 'analogues', or 'models' *through* which we cognize the object.

We have discussed this sufficiently already but here it may be in place to focus our attention upon the main features of this scientific method as it is employed in empirical science. In the course of active exploration and experimentation scientific thought moves forward from its premises and its data to new understanding by means of a speculative project (*Entwurf*) to account for the data, or an imaginatively advanced sketch of the reality into which it is probing, but this in turn is deductively tested by empirical reference to the data, and if it is corroborated it involves a revision of the premises and a new assessment of the data. In this way the whole theory gains in depth and breadth, and it is regarded as justified in accordance with the range of its richness or fertility, that is, as it is able to throw new light upon the data and other relevant material. Scientific 'finds' or 'results' are set out in these 'theoretic myths' or 'models', but ultimately they are no more than cognitive tools constructed in the process of scientific inquiry or, as it were, windows built into the structure of our thought through which the real nature of things may be discerned or even arrows pointing in the direction of real order and form in the nature of things. The scientific reason refuses to confuse its own noetic constructions and formulations with the ontic structures of reality, but regards its formulated 'laws of nature' only as attempts within the framework of our creaturely experience and existence, and the possibilities and necessities of our thought, to attest the fact that there are ontic laws.[1]

The interpretative method adopted in scientific theology and the kind of formulation which it yields are not unlike these in empirical science. Even though we are concerned in theology, not metaphorically but literally, with a self-declaring and self-communicating Object where 'recognition-statements' are more in place than in natural science since they are 'heard statements', it still remains true that theological science is a form of human inquiry in which we can only seek to grasp as far as we can what is communicated to us through orderly constructions of our own forming, and in which we have to distinguish the substance of the truth from our scientific formulations of it, so that all dogmas must be regarded as relative to and relativized by that which we seek to cognize through them. We can no longer formulate Christian dogmas without at the same time showing how they are known and expressing the purpose that lies behind them. It would be a grave error to identify them as such with the transcendent form

[1] This is Karl Barth's way of putting it. See *Church Dogmatics*, III. 3, p. 141 ff.

and being of the divine Truth, but it would also be a grave error to treat them as symbolic expressions of our encounter with reality with no ultimate *fundamentum in re*.[1]

(2) The second basic similarity we note between theological science and the special sciences, has come before us frequently—respect for the objectivity of facts, or, in other words, for real thinking that proceeds only by way of reference to the externally given reality. In the methodological procedure of the sciences we have just been discussing active and passive elements are always involved. The reason is actively at work in constructing the model or developing the analogue as it puts its questions to nature and elicits its answers, but throughout the reason submits itself to the objective realities and seeks to cognize them passively through its theoretic constructions. The model or the analogue is only ectypal, and not archetypal, and therefore is subject to criticism and revision at every fresh moment of disclosure in order to allow reality itself to retain its own authority and majesty over our knowing of it. Far from being otherwise with theology ' this is a primary characteristic of theological thinking. Because the Truth of God encounters us within the world of creaturely objects theology is inevitably concerned with all sorts of 'objects' which it must respect, for it cannot otherwise know and speak of the Truth of God truthfully. But theology is bound to respect this objectivity in an unprecedented way, precisely because ultimate Objectivity encounters us within the realm of contingent objectivity. It is respect for the objectivity of contingent facts that characterizes every authentic empirical science, but theology makes that respect a religious as well as a scientific obligation.

(3) Neither theological science nor any other special science operates with a *preconceived* metaphysics. Without any doubt the language we use in physics or mathematics, for example, and certainly in theology, is already laden with metaphysical ideas, for it is shaped through centuries of history and culture and is impregnated with previously adopted attitudes to life or views of the world, but scientific procedure through sheer respect for objectivity must allow all this to be called into

[1] This would appear to be the line finally taken by Tillich in the third vol. of his *Systematic Theology*, in which the conceptual forms of Christian faith are replaced by symbolic forms—see the very revealing sections on the Trinity and Immortality, pp. 283 ff., and 409 ff.

question. That is why in modern physics or mathematics and in modern theology the ontological presuppositions inherent in traditional logic, which derive from ancient Greek physics and metaphysics, have to be brought to the light and detached from our formal constructions lest they should obstruct our reasoning and intrude upon our apprehension of things as they are revealed in themselves under our questioning. Here the criticism of natural law and older conceptions of causation in physics is remarkably parallel to the criticism in modern theology of traditional natural theology. This is why some modern physicists find in the theology of Karl Barth ground for real dialogue and rapprochement in understanding between theology and physics.[1] This arises out of the understanding of theology as a science in its own right rather than as a form of religious philosophy, and out of the dedication of science in each field to its proper object and method, together with its determination to work positively on its own ground, without dreaming, romancing or speculating. This is not to say that a special science or theological science is without metaphysical import, for all the basic concepts of positive science are concerned with aspects of being and include epistemological relation to being, as we have seen, but it does mean that metaphysical presuppositions have to be renounced in order that we may be free for the authentic metaphysical thinking that arises as we struggle to grasp and assimilate new conceptions that are thrust upon us from the side of objective reality.[2] Theological science is more deeply concerned with this sort of metaphysical thinking than any other science because it has for its primary object not this or that being, but the Source of all being or the ultimate Ground beyond the ground of being.

Like modern science theology must develop and use appropriate metaphysical conceptions, for it must clarify the nature and the status of the realities to which its statements refer and therefore engage constructively in a proper ontology. It can no more escape this than it can escape what Gollwitzer has

[1] See the discussion of Professor Günter Howe, one of 'the Goettingen circle' of physicists and theologians, in *Antwort*, 'Parallelen zwischen der Theologie Karl Barths und der heutigen Physik', pp. 409 ff.

[2] Cf. A. D. Ritchie, *The Scientific Method*, p. 6, who points out that scientific thinking cannot escape from metaphysics; if the scientific man thinks he can he is simple repressing it.

called 'is propositions'.[1] But again, theology, like modern science, must develop its own distinctive methods which it cannot do without developing its own epistemology and cannot avoid engaging in serious philosophical thinking to clarify the necessities and possibilities of its own thought and to determine their rational status. Hence it is not enough for the theologian simply to disengage his thinking from philosophy in order to concentrate it scientifically upon its own special subject-matter,[2] for he must engage in his own meta-science and in his own form of meta-meta-science both to carry through distinctive thought about the material content of his knowledge and to acquire the appropriate cognitive tools, logical and metaphysical conceptions, by means of which to articulate his knowledge. Here philosophical and scientific thinking are locked together as the theologian seeks to allow the nature of what he knows to determine the forms of his thought and speech about God and His saving acts. But in all this activity theology as a pure science makes use of metaphysical thinking solely in the service of its own distinctive ends.

(4) The other special sciences also offer a parallel to theological science in recognizing that their investigations come up against a line beyond which they cannot penetrate and cannot even attempt to pass without inconsistency and error. In theology this is the distinction between earth and heaven or between the visible and expressible and the invisible and ineffable, but in the natural and human sciences this is the distinction between what is within the range of observation or reasonable inference based on observation and what is beyond it altogether, and in quantum physics particularly it is the distinction between determinacy and indeterminacy. This is not

---

[1] H. Gollwitzer, *The Existence of God*, pp. 202 ff.

[2] Disengagement of theology from philosophy is certainly necessary for the proper development of scientific theology, just as physics had to disengage itself from natural philosophy in order to be itself and then engage in inter-thinking with it (cf. Margenau, on '*Naturphilosophie*', F. Heinemann, *Die Philosophie im 20 Jahrhundert*, pp. 381 ff.). As Karl Barth has shown, this is very necessary for theology, and for its proper dialogue with the other sciences. But in order to engage in dialogue with philosophy theology must engage more positively in strenuous metaphysical and logical work *on its own ground*. Unless it does this it will find its positive results corroded through unconscious, and therefore bad, philosophical preconceptions. That is, in part, at least, the problem in the present situation between the thought of Barth and Bultmann.

simply the acknowledgement of ignorance which we must make since the more we learn the more we know how much there is still to be learned. It is the forced acceptance of a limit when, in spite of the endless process of scientific inquiry in which we unceasingly question our questions, we cannot break free from the finite or begin to form a conception of the infinite without being involved in contradictions,[1] or it is the finding of a barrier over which we cannot force our knowledge since we are confronted by what is indeterminate either because we cannot transcend the limitations inherent in our scientific methods of observation and conception or because an element of indeterminacy belongs to the nature of things independently of our observing and conceiving of them.[2] As de Broglie says '. . . some theoretical picture is always necessary for the clear statement of the results of an experiment. Nuclear physics, in running up against the limits of resistance of matter, could, therefore, also run up against the limits of the comprehension of our mind'.[3] Hence this natural science finds itself in a difficult position which von Weizsäcker has described thus: 'We do not know what lies beyond that limit, or else it would not be the limit of our knowledge. Still, we assume that something does lie beyond it. And this alone is already an assumption about something that we do not know'.[4] Thus in actual fact natural science, and physics in particular, limits itself to what is determinable on a phenomenological basis and thereby brackets itself off from all unassessable aspects of reality.[5] It thus recognises that its investigations have a frontier and that it can only accept the sphere beyond it as outside the bounds of exact science, into which it cannot scientifically intrude and about which it must scientifically maintain a respectful silence.[6]

There can be no direct comparison between the spheres of the knowable and the unknowable in natural science and

---

[1] This does not mean that we can avoid operating with a notational idea of infinity, e.g. in mathematics; cf. W. Heisenberg, *Physics and Philosophy*, p. 124 f., 201.

[2] See particularly N. Bohr, *Atomic Physics and Human Knowledge*, and W. Heisenberg, op. cit.

[3] L. de Broglie, op. cit., p. 234.

[4] C. F. von Weizsäcker, *The History of Nature*, p. 61.

[5] Cf. L. de Broglie, *Physics and Microphysics*, p. 79 ff.

[6] C. F. von Weizsäcker, *The World View of Physics*, p. 177 f.

the two realms with which theology operates, but there is a distinct parallel between the relation of the determinable and the indeterminable in exact science and the relation of earth to heaven in theology. By the latter is intended the relation between the realm of objectivity and intelligible intuition and the realm where theological knowledge is given objective but not specifiable reality but where it can only suspend judgement and maintain a respectful silence before the depth and majesty of the objectivity. This is the eschatological frontier which a scientific theology that is faithful to the nature of its given Object is bound to acknowledge in refusing to trespass beyond the limits imposed upon it by the self-revelation of God in His Word as well as by His transcendent Glory and Holiness. It is however only out of positive objective knowledge of God that we know this, and therefore cannot speak of this transcendent aspect of knowledge of God as non-objective.[1]

(5) Not unconnected with this is a further similarity between theological science and the special sciences that should be noted, in respect of the problem in relating scientific language to ordinary language. If we consider again what happens in physics, for example, we find that the problem arises out of a situation in which scientific thought reaches quite new concepts that cannot be expressed in any ordinary or natural language and develops systems of concepts that reach out far beyond what can be observed or even related to our measurements and therefore can be related only ambiguously to our ordinary concepts.[2] The more profound and precise physics becomes the more difficult it is to correlate unambiguously the new

---

[1] Cf. here Dietrich Bonhoeffer, *Act and Being*, pp. 79–116. There is a distinct element of epistemological Apollinarianism in Bonhoeffer's thought when in his desire to maintain the independence and Lordship of God as Subject in His revelation to us and our knowing of Him he insists that knowledge of God as God is possible 'only if God is also the subject of the knowing of revelation since, if *man* knew, then it was not God that he knew' (p. 92). This is the error that Barth has sought to correct by making the *humanity* of Christ so central to theological epistemology.

[2] See Heisenberg's discussion of 'Language and Reality in Modern Physics', op. cit. pp. 167–186. This very important point is one that R. W. Hepburn (*Christianity and Paradox*, e.g. p. 84) fails to appreciate adequately in his claim that theological language must be continuous with ordinary language—his argument against the theologian's use of language would also rule out what Heisenberg has to say here and reject the proper shift in language that must take place in all scientific thought.

technical language it must devise with the terms of our common language. Correlation becomes possible only at the points of empirical interaction between the sophisticated system of scientific conceptions and the system of ordinary conceptions derived from direct relation to experience. This interaction is of course all-important for it is at that point in our experience of what is observable and measurable that we can exercise some control over the systems that outrun the conceptions of ordinary language.

Similar problems arise in theology, for example in the doctrine of Christ where we are concerned with an overlap of what is accessible to historical determination and of what is not determinable in some way. In our encounter with Christ we meet new realities that cannot be explained in terms of our previous knowledge and reach new conceptions forced upon us by those new realities which require new language in which to express them. Moreover as we inquire into knowledge of God in Christ we find that Christology directs us beyond itself to a doctrine of the Holy Trinity and so to greatly enlarged and deepened conceptions that reveal far more than we can specify. In this process scientific theology develops a system of theological conceptions that reaches indefinitely beyond the system in which the observer has a part and which he construes within the limits of his ordinary notions of space and time, but the more this takes place the more impossible it is to correlate unambiguously the severely theological language that is created with the ordinary language of our every day experience.[1] But since it cannot be construed in the observer's system (i.e. objectivistically) it makes those points of interaction with it all the more important, that is, in the historical Jesus Christ, for apart from that overlap in Him between the divine and the human, the heavenly and the earthly realms, not only would our knowledge be without the indispensable relevance or applicability to our existence, but we could not distinguish

---

[1] Cf. here the difficulty Alasdair MacIntyre finds with religious language in his essay 'Is religious language so idiosyncratic that we can hope for no philosophical account of it?' in *Metaphysical Beliefs*, p. 175 f. In this connection it is helpful to reconsider the sustained insistence of Spinoza 'that no term when applied to God can possibly bear the meaning which it has when applied to human beings' (Stuart Hampshire, *Spinoza*, p. 49). Cf. also H. D. Lewis, *Philosophy of Religion*, in criticism of J. L. Austin, p. 152; and *Prospect for Metaphysics*, p. 225.

what claimed to be knowledge from free-floating imagination and invention. Apart from such an overlap or interaction the divine realities could not be apprehended at all, but in the nature of the case this relation between the different systems cannot be construed in terms of ambiguity or univocity or even analogy for we are concerned here with a relationship that is translogical and cannot be logicalized, corresponding to a relation between language and reality that cannot be resolved into language alone. It might be right to think of this in terms of an analogy, however, provided that we understand by that something more than what is conceptual and linguistic.

Here we are up against something that has no counterpart in the natural or human sciences, the direct and personal action of the divine Being upon us through the Holy Spirit. Nevertheless invocation of the Holy Spirit does not allow us to make light of human experience or dispense with its natural language since it is after all only with human knowledge and human speech that we can be concerned. The Holy Spirit does not take us out of the subject-object relations; He does not make us *ecstatic*! Unless the most refined theological conceptions interact with our ordinary knowledge at decisive points and our theological terms bear some relation to ordinary language, if only as the tool by which they are constructed, it is impossible for us as men on earth and in history to have any understanding of God or to say anything about Him.[1] It remains a fact, however, that in theological science as in any other science it is impossible to correlate scientific language with ordinary language all along the line in any one-to-one way, otherwise we could never get off the ground of naive understanding or break through the surface of common knowledge. We must be content with correlation at certain points, but those points are of crucial and critical importance. This is why it is impossible for a scientific theology to regard as

---

[1] Cf. in this connection what Heisenberg has to say about this question in physics. 'We know that any understanding must be based finally upon the natural language because it is only there that we can be certain to touch reality, and hence we must be sceptical about any scepticism with regard to this natural language and its essential concepts. Therefore we must use these concepts as they have been used at all times.' (op. cit. p. 201 f.). That is to say common sense concepts can and must be retained when we discern their interaction with the refined concepts of advanced physics—they are not to be demythologised.

dispensable its historical roots in the historical Jesus, even though it means that the historical foundation of our knowledge in Him must be laid open to rigorous historico-critical investigation.[1]

ii *Differences*

What then are the differences between theological science and the other sciences? There are of course essential differences between every special science, and it is upon those differences that they depend as separate sciences in their own right. In spite of the overlap of concepts that they may involve it is unscientific to force the application of concepts from one field of investigation into another where they do not belong, for that is to corrode the propriety and integrity of the science concerned. While this certainly applies to the place of theology among the special sciences, there are differences between theological science and every other science due to the fact that theology has for its proper and primary object God Himself in His speaking and acting. All the other sciences deal with creaturely realities and only with aspects of being, whereas in theology we have to do also with the creative Source of all being.

There are differences here in regard to *objectivity*.

In all the sciences we refer our thought to what is external to ourselves and are devoted to objectivity: scientific knowledge and objective knowledge are one and the same thing. But there are differences in objectivity among the various sciences and even at different levels in the same science that have to be taken into account. In classical physics, for example, objectivity appears to be bound up with a strong causality or determinism and tends to be descriptive and objectivist in character. This holds good to a limited extent in modern microphysics, but as we now know objectivity of this kind obtains only when we look at things in the large and therefore imprecisely, and concern ourselves only with generalities and averages. In modern microphysics, however, especially since the rise of quantum mechanics, we are aware that what we do in science is to reduce to knowledge the relations between ourselves and the

---

[1] See Hepburn's two trenchant chapters on 'Historicity and Risk', op. cit. pp. 91 ff., 112 ff., especially his critique of Gogarten and Macquarrie.

external world, relations that are active on our part as well as passive. We do not describe the realities we know as they are merely in themselves, for we cannot separate them entirely by themselves apart from the processes in our knowing of them, but if so this does not allow us to argue that it is finally we who impose form and order upon things and that we have no really objective kvowledge of them in accordance with their own nature and rationality. What it does teach us is that the rigorous formalizations of our knowledge are not to be treated like transcripts of reality but precisely as scientific instruments and demonstrative indications referring us away from ourselves to the things we seek to know, so that by their nature they are engaged in the relentless service of objectivity. The relativity of our knowledge to external reality and its objectivity are but the obverse of each other. It is this deeper and profounder objectivity that has become paramount in modern science in which we are constantly committed to the critical revision of our premisses in the light of what we learn, and in which our theoretic models with their operational concepts manifest their objectivity through their power to carry our thought beyond what we can anticipate in the illumination of further aspects of reality. It is sometimes said that this is a 'weak objectivity', but this appears to imply the equation of really objective knowledge with a deterministic description of things, which the advance of science has forced us to reject.[1] This is, however, a kind of objectivity that does not rest upon anything hard or final, for the open, and thus limited, character of our formulations through which we cognize and maintain contact with reality means that objectivity forces itself upon us precisely through the relativity of our knowledge to what is beyond. This is why for Einstein the advance to relativity theory did not undermine but only served to strengthen dogmatic realism

[1] It is unfortunate that so many continental theologians seem so innocent of what scientific objectivity really means, and that their regular equation of objectivity with descriptive objectivism forces them to confine God to their own subjectivities. On the other hand, when they are charged with this (e.g. Bultmann by Barth) they sometimes claim an 'objectivity' for God to indicate that He is a reality apart from our subjective experience, but this 'objectivity' is the equivalent of His transcendent unknowability, the fact that He cannot be intercepted by our consciousness as its 'object', that He is beyond our subjective experience. How then do we *know* this of God? This 'objectivity' is only an empty movement of thought.

in scientific knowledge, although the way in which it had been conceived had to be changed. For any natural science, then, to claim finality for the reference of its theories would be tantamount to rejecting objectivity.

In theological science we operate with a similar kind of objectivity in all our systematic formulations for here too we have to let our questions be questioned and allow a dogmatic realism to prevent us from being dogmatic about our formulations, but there is a radical difference. In theology our thought does terminate upon what is final and ultimate, the Lord God Himself, who is implacably resistant and objective to our formulations in that He cannot be confined to them. It is because we come to know God in His transcendent Majesty and Truth, and know Him to be greater than we can ever conceive or express, that we acknowledge the limitation and relativity of all our forms of thought and speech about Him. Theological knowledge is thus profoundly relative because it is relative to the Absolute, and profoundly objective because it has for its primary Object God who can be known only through Himself and not by reference beyond Him. Here too in theological science, as in natural science, relativity and objectivity fall together, but they are differently grounded. In the natural sciences, by their nature and method we do not come up against anything that is in terms of itself, and so must always refer facts to other facts behind them in an endless regress and operate with an essentially relative conception of truth,[1] but in theological science we do come up against ultimate objectivity and our thought is given a final term of reference. Its relativity is derived from the fact that knowledge is relativized from above, as well as from below, and its objectivity is imposed upon it from the very nature of God as well as through its self-critical method of inquiry. In theological knowledge it is the finality of God that is the real source of relativity and the ultimacy of God that is the true ground of objectivity, for before God humility and certainty go inseparably together.

[1] This must be held along with the other aspect of scientific thought in which we are forced to make definite judgements and in which tentative theories give way to what Margenau calls 'verifacts' (F. Heinemann, *Die Philosophie in 20 Jahrhundert*, p. 399 f.). Apart from these we would have no solid foundations upon which to build and from which to advance.

In theological science, however, we have to reckon with a two-fold objectivity, with the ultimate objectivity of God who comes to us clothed, as it were, with proximate objectivity, for He makes Himself known to us only as He objectifies Himself for us within the structured objectivities of our world, while distinguishing Himself from them. To such a two-fold objectivity there may be adduced certain very imperfect analogies in other sciences, notably in psychology where the really objective factor, the other subject, encounters us from within and never apart from a physical body and physical relationships in space and time, and perhaps in physics where we have to reckon with a two-fold relation between the macroscopic and the microscopic, but nowhere in any of these other sciences are we concerned, as in theology, with the conjunction of ultimate objectivity and contingent objectivity. This is the baffling element in theological knowledge, the bi-polarity or bi-focality of its truth-reference, but it arises from the unique nature of the Object and the way He has taken in making Himself the object of our knowledge. It would be a failure in scientific exactitude to ignore this or to assimilate theological science to any of the other sciences as if it were of no essential significance.

The problem can be stated in the following way. In all the other sciences the human knower and the object known are both creaturely realities: they co-exist on the same creaturely plane and within the same framework of space and time. In these sciences we presuppose some sort of agreement between our minds and external realities in virtue of which our thought and language may be open to the nature of those realities and be transparent media through which they can be brought to rational disclosure. Even if we hold that man can do no more in science than reduce to order his relations with nature, we cannot exclude man from nature, for he is related to nature as nature's prophet and priest, as it were, whose function it is to bring nature to articulate and intelligible expression. Man and nature belong to the same order of rationality so that when we bring to scientific formalization human relations with nature we are laying bare the natural order and structure of created existence. But can we presume upon an agreement of this kind between ourselves and that which infinitely transcends all creaturely reality even when we are brought to apprehend it? In our natural science we operate with sequences in which precedence and subsequence belong to the same series on the same level of existence, but does this connection obtain between contingent realities that are dependent on what lies beyond them and the ultimate Reality that is only in and through itself? Even when we argue that it is the contingence of creaturely realities upon the Ultimate that gives them their meaning and enables us to grasp their natural and inherent connections, does it follow that we can project these connections univocally to take in the Ultimate as if He could be known through an infinite extension of our natural sequences?[1] But if we do not know God except in His utter difference from us and yet only know Him where He encounters us within the sphere of our contingent existence, then we must be careful to clarify our knowledge of Him both in terms of the creaturely objectivity which His self-revelation to us has assumed in our world of space and time and in terms of the transcendent objectivity of His own eternal Being. Everything will depend upon the way in which God in His transcendent objectivity makes Himself the object of our knowledge within the objectivities of our creaturely existence.

This is the way of Grace, for we know God only through His sovereign and unconditionally free self-giving. Natural objects, as we have seen, have to be the objects of our cognition when we know them, but it is only out of pure Grace that God gives Himself to be the object of our knowing and thinking. It is upon this that there rests the essential difference between the kind of inquiry apposite in theology and that apposite in the other sciences, and also upon the kind of verification or demonstration required. The experimental investigation through man-made controls, and the corresponding demonstration offered by making things work as we stipulate, are scientifically inappropriate to the living God, for it would not be the Lord God but an idol that could come under our power like that, and it would not be theology but magic that could conjure up and manipulate 'the divine' like that. Moreover, as Michael Polanyi has pointed out, if the resuscitation of the

[1] This is the question raised by Duns Scotus when he insists that natural knowledge of God as 'First Cause' does not allow us to reach a 'God' above and beyond the causal series to which we ourselves belong—we know God properly as 'First Being' rather than as 'First Cause', in the utter uniqueness of God—*Deus et creatura in nullo genere sunt. Lectura* I.d. 8. pars. 1.q.3.1.C.1.

dead could be experimentally verified, this would strictly disprove its miraculous nature, for 'to the extent that any event can be established in terms of natural science, it belongs to the natural order of things. However monstrous and surprising it may be, once it has been fully established as an observable fact, the event ceases to be regarded as super-natural . . . . It is illogical to attempt the proof of the super-natural by natural tests, for these can only establish the natural aspects of an event and can never represent it as supernatural'.[1]

To return to the point we are discussing, namely the deter-minative significance of Grace, we may say that what dis-tinguishes the objectivity of God for us in this respect is that He presents Himself to us, (a) not as a natural object which we cannot but know in a determinate way but as a voluntary object which we know only through response to His uncon-ditional self-giving, and (b) not as a mere object which we know only through our control of it but as the Lordly Object over whom we have no power but whom we may know only through humble service and love. In giving Himself to us as the object of our knowing and thinking the Gift is not detached from the Giver, so that God retains His own Majesty in our knowing and thinking of Him, maintaining His ultimate objectivity in the midst of all proximate objectivity and making possible genuinely objective knowledge of Him while resisting all objectifying attempts to subject Him to our natural habits of thought and forms of knowledge. This is a unique objectivity that does not fall within our dividing and compounding and eludes the generalities and abstractions with which we operate as a rule in the other sciences. Profound objectivity of this kind is the antithesis of all objectivising.[2]

To indicate the problem that faces us here we may adduce a very imperfect analogy from biological science in which we investigate living beings. In so far as they are physical they can be regarded as chemical episodes and are as such subject to the kind of analysis we employ in physics and chemistry and indeed to the kind of connections we work with in quantum mechanics, but in so far as they are living organisms with

---

[1] *Personal Knowledge*, p. 284.

[2] Hence it is difficult to understand how so many contemporary thinkers can hold the silly notion that for us to have objective knowledge of God compromises His Being and jeopardizes His independent Reality! But see H. R. Mackintosh, *Types of Modern Theology*, p. 19 ff.

directive centres of sensation or consciousness they have features such as vital dynamism, organic functions, tissues, cells, and also perception, affection, conation, etc. which have no counterparts in physics or chemistry and which cannot therefore be brought to complete account within those sciences. Moreover these biological features are of such a nature that they cannot be subjected to physico-chemical analyses without destroying them as living beings. This means that we have to go beyond the methods and laws of physics and chemistry if we are to have any truly objective knowledge of living organisms, for they have an objectivity that is determined by their nature as organisms which cannot be broken up into isolated parts but can be known only in their natural individuality, integrity and force and in accordance with their own interior connections. We are faced with a similar impasse when we carry over into theological science the selection, fragmentation, abstraction, and generalization that obtain in other sciences for their experimental and analytical methods of scrutiny and investigation preclude those sciences from perceiving the Truth of God in its wholeness and uniqueness. By their very nature as special sciences adapted to multiplicity they can only operate through analysing, comparing, classifying, generalizing, and therefore can handle only those aspects of things that are capable of being analysed, compared, classified, generalized, etc.[1] They are unable to deal with what is unique and incomparable, with individual wholeness and with the inner reality of something in its concrete objectivity. The concrete universal cannot be netted by empirical means, any more than it can be caught through the analytical methods of formal logic. That applies, of course, to all sorts of things, but it applies above all to the one Truth of God, for there is only one incomparable God. It holds good, therefore, in due measure for everything with which theology has to do, for theology is concerned not with creaturely realities in their abstract contingency but with creaturely realities as contingent upon God since it is precisely in their relation to God that they have their inner reality and wholeness.

The difference between theological science and the other sciences is thrown into sharp relief when we consider the relation of the particular to the general in each group. It

[1] Cf. J. MacMurray, *Reason and Emotion*, pp. 185 ff.

belongs to the essence of the sciences and their claim to validity that their results are open for all to investigate and verify, for their claim to truth must be universal if it is to be upheld. Likewise theology claims that its statements are true because they have reference to the one Truth of God which is valid for all men and is universally accessible. It rejects the idea that knowledge of this Truth is the prerogative only of a few.[1] But there is a real difference here that must be brought to view. In the special sciences a scientific fact is communicable because it is one of many, comparable with other facts. The particular is regarded as an instance of the general and is communicable because it is understood and interpreted only by reference to the general. Theological truth, on the other hand, is unique, and cannot be abstracted from its concrete particularity and be generalized, or interpreted as an instance of general truth. That is why Kierkegaard laid such a strong emphasis upon 'the single', that is, upon the wholeness of the concrete individual, which is apprehended only through renunciation of abstract generalization and plumbing the depth of 'the single' in its own dimension.

To those who imagine that the abstract general methods of natural science are universally valid Christian theology presents a great stumbling block in its claim that the ultimate Truth is identical with the concrete particularity of Jesus Christ. In its own understanding, however, theology claims that Jesus Christ is the Lord of the universe, that He is the Word and Truth of God for all men and is open to all men, but is accessible and communicable only through a relation of each to Him in accordance with His unique nature and absolute particularity, and therefore only by way of renouncing abstract generality and in a repentant surrender of preconceptions as supplying the frame of reference for the apprehension and acknowledgement of Him as the Truth. What Christ requires of each man is an

[1] Cf. A. N. Whitehead, *Religion in the Making*, p. 32: 'Religion claims that its concepts, though derived primarily from special experiences, are yet of universal validity, to be applied by faith to the ordering of all experience. Rational religion appeals to the direct intuition of special occasions, and to the elucidatory power of its concepts for all occasions. It arises from what is special, but it extends to what is general.' Cf. also *The Faith of a Moralist*, vol. 2, pp. 79 ff. where A. E. Taylor points out that there is permanent substance in 'revelation' which is final and universal and not just a truth for a particular time and place.

objective apprehension of Himself in His real individuality, in His uniqueness and in His Lordship, that is, in terms of Himself. It is as such that He confronts all men in the Gospel, and must be openly and freely proclaimed to all men in the clearest possible language and in the frankest and most open way, because He is the Truth for all men and extends His claim to all men without exception. 'Whosoever will may come.'

There are differences in regard to *subjectivity*.

In all scientific knowledge, including theology above all, man is unconditionally bound to his object, for to be bound and determined by what is objective is the core of rationality. But there is another side to this, as we saw earlier; although he is unconditionally bound to the object in faithful and authentic knowing of it, man is yet free, active, and spontaneous in his epistemic relations, while part of his freedom at least consists in his knowledge of his unconditional relation to the object, as well as his determination to use his knowledge of the object. At the decisive moments man is thrown back upon the exercise of his personal and rational judgement. All real knowledge has this personal-coefficient. If this were eliminated man would only be an intricate mechanical brain abstracting from things and making general propositions compounded of abstractions—he would be a prisoner of mechanical operations. When we are engaged in impartial, objective, scientific thought we are not eliminating the personal-coefficient, for that would eliminate science altogether; we are engaged in modes of thought which methodologically exclude unwarranted subjective features from influencing our observations and judgements and thus from intruding into the material content of our knowledge. This is what we mean by the 'disinterested' and sometimes 'impersonal' approach, but far from involving disinterest in the object it calls for such an attachment to the object that we become detached from all alien presuppositions and are thus genuinely objective, and far from involving the elimination of personal judgement it calls for such a profound commitment to the rationality of the object that we are able to distinguish it from our own subjective states and conditions. We are engaged in intensely personal acts when we refer our thought away from ourselves to external realities, and not least when we have to struggle hard with ourselves in breaking through habits of thought and speech forced upon us by prior experience if we are to account for new experience and grasp new conceptions. Indeed the more impersonal and rigid are the categories with which we work the more deeply rooted are the subjective factors that distort our knowledge and obstruct its advance—and yet we know more and more that we cannot exclude the subject of the thinker or the scientist from the accumulation of our scientific knowledge, for it is the knowledge attained by personal minds and is attained in such a way that, while we know only as we can distinguish what we know from our knowing of it, we are unable to set out our knowledge apart altogether from the way we reach it. It is one thing, then, to make every effort through logical and experimental devices to exclude the introduction into the object of elements derived from our own personal states, but it is another thing to imagine that we can actually cut off our knowledge of things from the fact that it is after all we who know them, or from the fact that science is a function of human minds in which spontaneity, imagination and judgement play a considerable role. It is obvious when we compare scientists at work that the most successful are those who exercise personal initiative, who engage in passionate research, who manifest distinctive original powers in selecting their facts and in contriving ingenious hypotheses and experiments as well as instruments and machines. Where would science be at all without all this personal activity in scientific thought?

Without any doubt it is methodologically correct to check all our scientific processes for the intrusion of personal factors, but we must ask how far this can be done and how far it is right to do it. Unless we recognise that complete exclusion of the personal element is impossible, will we not be at the mercy of our personal and subjective attitudes and conditions after all? And are not such unconscious determinations the most enslaving and the most damaging? There can be no denying the fact that the most rigorously objective science cannot escape from personal knowledge, or that science would be seriously lacking in objectivity if it was thought possible to effect such an escape, but since we do not escape we must learn to check and control the temptation that inevitably arises to impose ourselves on what we seek to know. This temptation is easier to detect and overcome when we are concerned with investigating impersonal and wholly determinate realities where vitiation of knowledge through personalizing the impersonal becomes so obvious, but it is more difficult when we are engaged in the realms of microphysics where we cannot ignore relation to the observer without serious inaccuracy and distortion— although it is questionable whether the subject of the scientist exercises any direct influence upon the nature of the object itself as distinct from the mental world of scientific theory which of course he does construct.[1] It is perhaps a more intricate difficulty that faces us, however, when we have to do with other subjects in the field of our investigations, where the introducing of elements from our own subjectivities into the objects of study can be so imperceptible as to be practically impossible to detect. Here there are counter-balancing factors, for objects that are other subjects can resist us, object to us, talk back to us, and so correct us—if we let them—yet since they too are involved in reciprocal relations with us it is not so easy for this corrective process to work itself out in actual fact, unless we not only take it into account but build it into our modes and operations of thought.

This takes us closer to the field of inquiry where theological science is at work, where the personal is a predicate of the object and where the object demands reciprocity from the person of the theologian. It must be remembered that the very notion of a personal subject was formed and injected into our thought through the patristic doctrines of Christ and of the Trinity, in marked contrast to the impersonal modes of thought that obtained in classical Greek philosophy. But the notion of the personal subject suffered an unfortunate change through several distinct phases of development. Through aspects of Augustine's thought, most apparent in the *Confessions*, the idea of the person began to be turned in upon itself so that the personal quest for the truth tended to be interiorized within the individual soul. This was matched by a philosophical concept of the person which was *logically* derived, as is evident

[1] See E. Schrödinger, *Mind and Matter*, p. 50. The scientist of course cannot get away from the fact that the 'objects' he deals with are not only relative to himself as 'observer' but are relative to one another—it is therefore through probing into that objective interrelatedness that he is able to pierce behind the subjective-coefficient that must have its place in reaching knowledge.

in the discussion and definition of Boethius: *persona est rationalis naturae individua substantia*.[1] Here the notion of the person is formed through assimilating the idea of substance to the logical subject. It was this view with some modification that was taken over by Thomas Aquinas and prevailed for the most part in Medieval thought—apart from Duns Scotus and certain influential trends in the Franciscan tradition. Later on in the philosophy of Descartes the logical concept of the person was cross-fertilized again with elements revived from the teaching of St. Augustine and the notion of the epistemological subject emerged, assimilating to itself the idea of self-consciousness. In this Cartesian dualism the subject became split off from the object. The dichotomy between them was accentuated through the 'Copernican revolution' in philosophy carried out by Kant, while the Romantic exploration of the depths of the self yielded the modern psychological notion of 'personality'. Along with philosophy exact science had come to accept this disjunction between subject and object and therefore operated within presuppositions that have made it difficult to advance to relativity and quantum theory. The debate now going on in these areas represents a struggle to acquire a truly objective perspective in scientific thought which does not involve the elimination of the subject but its admission to a proper and controlled relation to the object.

On the other hand, from patristic sources quite a different strain has entered into modern thought through theology. This goes back to the concept of the person developed, in opposition to Boethius, by Richard of St. Victor which he derived *ontologically* from the doctrine of the Trinity.[2] This was further developed by Duns Scotus who stressed the notion of the active agent and came to think of the subject in this sense as a 'voluntary object' of thought.[3] This was the teaching taken over by John Calvin who reconstructed it, with the help of patristic theology, in the light of our knowledge of God in Jesus Christ and the knowledge of ourselves which results from it. When therefore Calvin began his famous *Institute of the*

---

[1] Boethius, *De personis et duabus naturis*, c. iii; *P.L.* 64, 1343 C.

[2] Richard of St. Victor, *De Trinitate*, IV. 16 ff.

[3] See the account of Duns Scotus' thought given by Heribert Mühlen, *Sein und Person nach Johannes Duns Scotus*, especially chs. iii-v.

Christian Religion by clarifying the mutual relation between the knowledge of God and of ourselves he started modern theology on its most characteristic development, in which the human subject is given an integral place in the knowledge of God as he is drawn into immediate relation with Him and is opened up within his personal being for communion with God in the Spirit. The Reformation was intensely aware that the ground for this approach is provided by the fact that God speaks to us personally in His Word, for here the object of knowledge encounters us as Subject and addresses us as subjects over against Him. This had the effect of restoring theological knowledge to the field of direct intuitive knowledge of God in His Word and Spirit and of giving it an essentially dialogical character instead of the merely dialectical character it had been given in a second-order status of reflection upon abstractive and creditive ideas. At the same time this had the effect of restoring the centre of gravity to the Truth itself in its own nature and activity, for in its encounter with us the Truth retains its own majesty and objectivity, and resists every attempt on our part to subdue it to some form of our own subjectivity, even when knowledge of it becomes inward and intensely personal. It is because the Truth acts upon us and addresses us as the Word of God, calls us to account and summons us to penitent and obedient conformity to it, that here theology is not allowed to fall under the domination of philosophical preconceptions but, with the aid of critical and constructive philosphical activity, seeks to adapt and bend human thought-forms to the masterful use of revelation as tools for its articulation in our human understanding. Thus theological activity proceeds by constant reference to its source and sole norm in the Word of God, so that our theological terms and formulations are ever to be brought back to the bar of the Word for criticism and creative reorientation in direct personal dialogue between ourselves and God.

The important point for us to note here is that in theology we have to do with a divine Object that demands and creates reciprocity so that our knowledge of God involves right from the start a union and not a disjunction between subject and object, and yet a union in which God is not entangled in our subjectivity. It is precisely in distinguishing Himself from us that He posits and maintains us as personal subjects in communion with Him who can know Him only through distinguishing Him in His divine Being and Objectivity and not through confounding Him with ourselves in the depth of our own beings. The object of theological knowledge is of such a kind, the eternal and absolute Subject, that the human knower is drawn out of his isolation, for the abstract conceptions which he has gained as an observer detached from the object come under the attack of a masterful, concrete objectivity, and begin to be stripped away from him. Face to face with the divine Object the human subject is not allowed to draw back into monologue or disinterested reflection, for he himself becomes the object of the active attention and self-giving of the divine Object; rather is he drawn into responsive activity, for he is opened up to the Object in his innermost being and made capable of apprehending Him, not merely in terms of his own acts of consciousness but in terms of the Object Himself as he meets and experiences Him in His undiminished and irreducible nature as the divine Subject, the Lord God.

In this situation there takes place in certain basic respects an inversion of the subject-object relation, for even in our knowledge of Him the divine Object retains His primacy or priority and by confronting us as the divine Subject gives objectivity to us as human subjects, and thus confirms and establishes us in our subjectivity before Him.[1] Here the human knower is not just a logical or an epistemological subject but a living and active person in the most real sense, called into a reciprocal relation with God, but here too the activity of the human subject within this reciprocity does not affect or alter the Object Himself although it is essential to his relation with the Object and his knowledge of the Object. It is in this trans-subjective relation to God that the human subject is taken out of himself and made really capable of objectivity, and yet it is in this trans-subjective relation to what is objectively quite other than himself that the human knower really becomes a true subject.

This kind of subjectivity has an essential place in theological knowledge, but it also has its hazards. It is essential to its

[1] See James Brown, *Subject and Object in Modern Theology*, especially ch. vii, for a profound and convincing discussion of this.

objectivity since this is the form of rationality that the human reason must adopt if it is to be faithful to the nature of the divine Subject-Object—a merely objectivist approach could not be properly objective for it could not do justice to the divine Reality: it could only abstract from it. True objectivity is to be found only within personal communion or dialogical relation with God. According to Martin Buber it is the preservation of this that is the real significance of anthropomorphism. 'Anthropomorphism', he says, 'always reflects our need to preserve the concrete quality evidenced in the encounter; yet even this need is not its true root: it is in the encounter itself that we are confronted with something compellingly anthropomorphic, something commanding reciprocity, a primary Thou'.[1] Yet this is also the point of danger, for since the human subject is given his full place in this reciprocity he is constantly tempted to arrogate to himself a creative role by adapting the object of his knowledge to the modes of his own subjectivity and thus obtruding himself unwarrantably into its material content. This results not only in a subjectivizing of our knowledge but in the replacement of objective encounter with the divine Subject by a form of self-encounter and a reinterpretation of the divine Self-revelation in terms of our own self-understanding. There cannot be any doubt that this confinement of God to human subjectivity is the constant danger of modern Protestantism, and it can only result in what Buber has significantly called 'the eclipse of God' in which we allow ourselves to get between God and ourselves. It is our own bloated subjectivity that shuts off the divine light from the world.[2]

One of the most significant aspects of the Biblical faith is that its persistent and ineradicable element of anthropomorphism is the obverse of its immense stress upon the sublime objectivity and transcendence of God. God in His utter difference and complete otherness nevertheless turns Himself toward man and it is only as such that He gives Himself to us to be known, i.e. on the ground of His self-adaptation to our humanity which also lifts up our humanity into communion

---

[1] Martin Buber, *Eclipse of God*, 1957 edit., p. 14 f. See further the recent discussion of this by Helmut Gollwitzer, *The Existence of God*, pp. 143 ff.

[2] Op. cit. pp. 22 f., 66 f., 68, 126 ff.

with God. This is the epistemological significance of the Incarnation to which we have been forced back again and again in our discussion: we are summoned to know God strictly in accordance with the way in which He has actually objectified Himself for us in our human existence, in Jesus Christ. But this does not give us leave to read our own humanity back into God or to confine knowledge of Him within our human subjectivities. Quite the reverse is the case. Face to face with Christ our humanity is revealed to be diseased and in-turned, and our subjectivities to be rooted in self-will. It is we who require to be adapted to Him, so that we have to renounce ourselves and take up the Cross if we are to follow Him and know the Father through Him. It is in this way that the estranged human self is restored, and the damaged person of man is healed and recreated in communion with God, and thus that the disjunction in the subject—object relationship gives place to a cognitive union with God in love. The human subject is established before God by the out-going of the divine love to him, while he on his part is brought to respect the objectivity of God as he learns to love Him for His own sake.

This does not absolve theological science from its need for self-critical and self-corrective processes through which its conceptions and statements are pruned of false anthropomorphisms or illegitimate subjective features. From the objective content of its knowledge it is the assault of the pure humanity of Christ upon the theologian that exposes his self-centredness, calls in question every attempt to impose himself upon the object, and thus serves to restrain and control his subjectivity. But as a science theology must also elaborate its own forms of symbolic denotation in order to check the purity of its connections and the precision of their implications and thus to obstruct the intrusion into its trains of thought any obscuring and distorting images and analogies projected out of man's own self-analysis and self-understanding into God. However, once this has been done the symbolic denotations must be translated back again into the concrete structures of our human and personal relations with God if theology is to maintain contact with reality. Hence theological science is acutely aware that its procedures must be of such a kind that the subject of the knower cannot be kept out of genuine knowledge of God, so that far from eliminating the personal factor altogether, theological science seeks to allow the subject to be adapted to the object and controlled by it. It is through controlled subjectivity that it becomes open to real objectivity. To express it otherwise, real objectivity is not to be found except in a mutual confrontation of objectivities, as when the objectivity of the divine Subject meets the objectivity of the human subject and vice versa. And it is just in such a situation that full room is given for the proper activity of the subject whether in personal or in scientific pursuits.

In view of this theological experience it may be relevant to ask whether full objectivity is actually possible in a confrontation only with impersonal objects that cannot object to us or offer to correct us. It may well be that the kind of controlled subjectivity forced upon us by the objectivity of other subjects can be of some help in other areas of science where we may be tempted to despair of genuinely objective knowledge on the ground that we are unable finally to penetrate beyond the world we construct out of our acts of consciousness to the world itself, or beyond the effects of our observations upon the observed to the actual realities observed. This is not to suggest any transference or extension of method from theological science to natural science, but to suggest that the kind of togetherness of subject and object that obtains in theological knowledge may throw some light upon how in other fields of knowledge full justice may be done to the human subject without damage to objectivity, since true subjectivity requires as its foil something that is irreducibly objective in order to open it up for trans-subjective reference and apprehension. True subjectivity and true objectivity evoke and support each other. This is a lesson, however, that many modern theologians have yet to learn, if one is to judge from their reaction to false objectivism and their attempts to find refuge in a transcending of the subject-object relationship altogether. Far from lessening their problems this can only lead them into a progressive irrationalism, as it serves to insulate them from the healthy and critical questioning that arises from disciplined science. This is very evident in those scholars and theologians who keep on insisting on what they call 'the non-objectifiability' of God, for it is they above all who tend to convert biblical and theological statements into autobiographical statements and get sucked down into the whirl-pool of their own 'self-under-standing', from which they begin and with which they end, for within the darkness of that vortex they lose sight of all daylight above them.

2. *The Relevance of Historical Science*

We have been contrasting theological science for the most part with sciences dealing with impersonal objects, but what of those that treat of personal objectivities or at least have some form of subjectivity latent in their objects, such as the study of history?

Let us consider how theological science and historical science proceed in regard to the fact of Christ. Wherever theology has to do with acts of God in space and time it is no less inter-ested than historical science in the truthfulness of historical facts. Indeed its commitment to the absolute Truth of God will not allow it to depreciate historical facticity and therefore it insists on inquiring into what is historically factual and what is not, and on working out the criteria appropriate for this purpose. If therefore in theological inquiry we find ourselves acknowledging that it is God Himself who meets us in this Man Jesus Christ we are forced to take His humanity, and thus His temporal, worldly creaturehood, seriously. It is not disrespect but sheer respect for Him that makes us ask questions about Him as a historical person. Theological and historical science overlap at this point, since we are not concerned in our understanding of Christ with timeless and spaceless acts of God but with acts of God that fall within the space-time structures of human existence and activity in this world and are themselves part of a whole complex of historical happenings.[1]

How then does historical science approach the fact of Jesus Christ? It can investigate it only as a segment of historical

---

[1] This is what is implied in the theological statement that in Jesus Christ God has come to us not simply 'in man' but 'as man', for His acts are not merely transcendent to the historical Jesus, nor are they merely causally related to Him, but in Him have entered our world of space and time as human acts, creaturely events, predicated though they are of God Himself. Thus the acts of God in Jesus Christ cannot be spoken of merely as 'supra-historical' but also as genuinely historical. A similar point is made by Alan Richardson, *History Sacred and Profane*, pp. 131, 138, 184 f.

process, through controlled and tested observation, by submitting all that is claimed as evidence for it to the criterion of
perceptibility and the recognised canons of credibility with
which it operates in the investigation of all other historical
processes. In historical science, of course, we operate with data
supplied to us by others who may themselves be immediate
eye-witnesses of the events in question or only links in a chain
of tradition through which reports about the events have
reached us. For the most part we are concerned with docu-
mentary sources although they usually enshrine oral tradition
in various degrees. We subject all this to our critical interrogation to sift it for its evidential value, testing the chain of testimony and report and tracing back as far as we can the actual
steps by which it has reached us. And so we try to determine
what was directly observed and what actually happened.
This is not a simple but a complicated procedure in which we
seek both to bring to light the grounds upon which our historical
knowledge is based and to establish it evidentially upon those
grounds in such a way that we exhibit a thoroughgoing
consistency between our reconstruction of the events as they
really happened and the facts themselves, but in a measured
degree it is the rationality and coherence of our reconstruction
that enables us to discriminate the real facts from accretions and
fictions. Thus 'historical facts', as H. W. Walsh has reminded
us, 'have in every case to be established: they are never
simply given.'[1]

We get at the original events only through the subjectivity
of others, and therefore have to allow for colouring and
misrepresentation of the facts through them. Of course there
are subjectivities that rightly belong to the subject-matter
itself, for the events we seek to investigate in historical science
are human subjects and communities, with their experiences,
deeds, views, words, and their truth and falsity, in inter-action
with each other and with nature, and so we attempt to bring
to light what they actually thought, felt and said as well as

---

[1] H. W. Walsh, *Philosophy of History*, revised edit. p. 18 Cf. what Collingwood
has to say about 'evidence', *The Idea of History*, p. 247 f., and Alan Richardson's
view that historical 'facts' are judgements of evidence, *History Sacred and Profane*,
p. 192 f. This was, of course, the point made by Kant in his doctrine of judgement
in which factual and interpretative elements belong together. Cf. Kemp Smith,
A Commentary to Kant's Critique of Pure Reason. xxxvii f.

did, as distinct from what has been reported of them. And yet we do that only through reports and by analysing the testimonies of others. Because we have to distinguish what is objectively factual from the distorting forms of subjectivity with which the original events have almost inevitably been overlaid, we have recourse to checking devices such as the use of archaeological 'evidence' and we employ as working rules certain canons of acceptibility, such as consistency with our own understanding of human nature and behaviour, or congruence with our own verifiable experience and with what is conceivable in terms of it. In this way, however, there arises a tendency as John Baillie expressed it, 'to depress history into the realm of nature',[1] to assimilate historical investigation and observation to the modes of thought that obtain in the natural sciences which are also concerned to investigate observable processes, and the concept of 'observation' undergoes a subtle change. This is not deterred by the fact that in historical inquiry we are concerned with events that are past and are no longer perceptible or immediately observable, for similar situations also arise in the natural sciences, for example in microphysics or in astrophysics.

Only when something has come into being, only when an event has taken place, can it be observed. In the nature of the case we are unable to observe those processes through which what is observable emerges into observability, but once it has emerged into the realm of observable nature, it is observed for what is it, since when it has taken place it is necessarily what it is and not another thing. What we actually observe has thus the fixity or the 'necessity' of the past, and so we are tempted to think that it had to be what it now is. This temptation is particularly strong in the field of historical science, for it is only when something has ceased happening and is in the past that it becomes the object of historical inquiry. But to think of the past that it had to be what it now is, is an illusion brought on by the apparent similarity in the unchangeability of events between ontic necessity and causal necessity. It involves the serious error of confounding temporal nexus with logical nexus and of resolving away all contingency into necessity.[2] Yet it is

---

[1] John Baillie, *The Belief in Progress*, p. 67.
[2] Cf. here the 'Interlude' in Kierkegaard's *Philosophical Fragments*, pp. 59 ff.

under this illusion, apparently, that many historians, operating with the concept of a closed continuum of cause and effect as a primary canon of credibility,[1] develop a positivist and often a determinist view of history, so that at their hands historical science is always being threatened with being reduced to a form of natural science conceived after a Newtonian or pre-quantum model.

In its own proper intention, however, historical inquiry is concerned not with what is or has taken place as an unalterable state of nature, but with the *change* or *transition* in events as they result from the actions of rational agents.[2] It is into that 'dynamism' that the historian must penetrate in any attempt to reconstruct the events as they actually happened. Since the event might have happened in another way we want to understand something of the logic of its happening in the way it did, for only then do we reckon that we can understand and reconstruct the event as it really took place. Historical investigation thus seeks to probe into the happening itself in order to understand it in its own proper passage and in its own intrinsic connections with other events in the experiences and interactions of personal and social agencies. Thus we refuse simply to observe the static result of what has actually taken place but try to appreciate its inner intention or movement that yielded this specific state of affairs and even its teleological thrust into the future—only then do we reckon that we determine and assess the historical event itself.

In attempts to distinguish history from (natural) science it is sometimes argued, for example by Collingwood,[3] that the historian is concerned with the *inside* rather than the *outside* of events, that is with what can only be described in terms of thought, whereas the scientist is concerned with the external aspect of events in their extrinsic connections. On this view it is the thought expressed in the events that is regarded as the

[1] e.g. Rudolf Bultmann, *Existence and Faith*, p. 291 f. Contrast John Baillie: 'Historians have recovered their sense of the discontinuous element in history, the element which cannot be explained in terms of the unfolding of human nature, but must be assigned to extraneous or transcendent agencies.' *The Belief in Progress*, p. 171.

[2] A distinction must be drawn, however, between the story of natural processes, especially life processes, and the story of humanity; cf. Tillich's distinction between 'the historical dimension' and 'history proper'. *Systematic Theology*, III, p. 297 f.

[3] R. G. Collingwood, *The Idea of History*, pp. 213 ff.

proper subject-matter of history and the real object of the historian's inquiry. To discover what this thought is the historian must think it again for himself, but in doing this he 're-enacts' in his own mind the experience of the past, and that on this view, is what historical science is about.[1] It is certainly true that it is the historian's task to discover the intrinsic logic of historical events by interpreting them as embodying intention or as expressive of purpose, and that in this way he really is concerned with an 'inner' and intelligible aspect of historical phenomena and not simply with a bare chronicle of *res gestae*. Nevertheless in this contrast Collingwood took too idealistic a view of history and too materialistic a view of natural science. Historical events cannot be investigated or interpreted aright if they are treated as little more than the expressions of mental experience, even if we grant, as we must, that at the centre of all historical study we are concerned with personal agents and their actions. Historical events take place in the continuities of space and time, within the structures and determinisms of nature and society, where there are discrepancies in various degrees between purposes and their realization, and where intentions translated into action often yield unexpected and unintended results. Human agents are physical as well as intellectual beings, and their actions cannot be studied in detachment from the involvement in sheer nature, even though as rational subjects they are capable of a measure of self-transcendence in time as well as space, of acting creatively upon nature and of affecting the future.[2] Historical science must be particularly aware of the damaging effects of Cartesian dualism, for any attempt to find the meaning of history in what is detachable from the structured necessities of space and time and therefore in what can be mentally and freely 'reenacted', cannot escape the grave error of reading back into the past what we think and want to think in the present, so of reducing history in the end only to a mode of encountering and understanding ourselves.[3] One thing that can save us from this is

---

[1] Op. cit. p. 284 ff. Behind this lies Dilthey's notion of bringing life to dead factuality by applying to it our own inner experience of life and reliving it and so reproducing its inner form. See H. A. Hodges, *The Philosophy of Wilhelm Dilthey*, ch. v., e.g. p. 144.

[2] Cf. Tillich, *Systematic Theology*, vol. III, p. 319 f.

[3] See Gadamer's shrewd critique of this tendency, *Wahrheit u. Methode*, pp. 172 ff., and 345 f.

the inseparable relation between the mental and the physical, the actions of agents and the events of nature, but once that is given up, there is little to stop 'history' from taking off into a world of free imagination and losing contact with concrete reality. Historical facticity must be given an essential place in any genuine attempt to determine the meaning of the past.

On the other hand, we do not do justice to natural science by restricting it to the investigation of phenomena only in their extrinsic connections as if all we can be concerned with in natural events is to reach a purely statistical account of what is externally observable. Is this not to work with the old narrow notion of science that we mainly treat of particulars and generalizations and are interested in the particular only as an instance of the general, instead of the modern view of science as the rigorous extension of rationality in forms of knowledge determined by the nature of its subject-matter in various fields of inquiry and therefore exhibiting from field to field methodological differences in the way in which knowledge is gained, grounded and verified? Collingwood's exaggerated contrast presupposes that while history has to do with events that are inherently intelligible because they are expressions of rational agents, natural events are not inherently intelligible so that we cannot penetrate inside them and understand them from their inner aspects as we can historical events. This has the unfortunate effect of driving a deep wedge between science and history and damaging his understanding of history as a scientific pursuit,[1] although of course Collingwood is quite right in refusing to allow historical science to be assimilated to natural science for that would assume that historical events are merely and entirely continuous with natural events and so restrict them to interpretation on the same level in terms of the so-called 'laws of nature'. But Collingwood's understanding of natural science at this point must be challenged, when he reduces it to an external description of natural phenomena operating through observation and experiment, for natural science

[1] A similar mistake is to be seen in the fatal disjunction between *Historie* and *Geschichte* perpetrated by Herrmann, Troeltsch and Bultmann, which goes back to the same Cartesian and Romantic roots. Contrast A. E. Taylor, *The Faith of a Moralist*, vol. 2, pp. 169: "There are not really two water-tight compartments of the historical process, a 'physical' sphere and a 'mental' sphere; there is the one concrete given process with its mental and physical elements interrelated and interacting."

actually presupposes the inherent rationality of nature and is devoted to laying it bare, although this involves immense intellectual effort. That is to say, natural science as it is now pursued refuses to stop short at the level of description and does not reckon that it has really done its work until it has succeeded in developing an explicatory account of the nature of things, but to do that it must penetrate into their inner logic: hence the immense importance today of the meta-sciences.

What the scientist does in any field is to seek to achieve an orderly understanding of events in which he can grasp them as a connected and intelligible whole and so be able to penetrate into their inner rationality. He does not invent that rationality but discovers it, even though he must act with imagination and insight in detecting and developing the right clues and act creatively in constructing forms of thought and knowledge through which he can discern the basic rationality and let his thinking fall under its direction as he offers even a descriptive account of the events. Undoubtedly a two-way movement of thought is involved in working out the way in which his account of the events is related to the grounds upon which it is based, for it is the coherence in the patterns of his thought that enables him to discern the systematic connection in the nature of things and yet it is only as he reaches that discernment that he is able to separate out the actual evidence upon which his account of the events must be allowed to rest. In so far as he can reduce to consistent and rational expression the ways in which his knowledge is related to the grounds upon which it is based he is convinced that he has come to grips with the inherent rationality of things and convinced of the truth of his reconstructions—hence the crucial importance in natural science of achieving wherever possible mathematical representation of our understanding of things for it is in that way that we bring the objective rationality to view. Yet, as we have seen, we may treat this representation only as a disclosure-model through which we apprehend the reality we are investigating and not as a descriptive formula or as the equivalent of some ontic structure in the reality itself.

The task of the historian is not basically different from this, for he must pass beyond description and narration to explanation in his reconstruction of past events in an intelligible and

coherent whole. 'His way of doing that', as Walsh has summarized it, 'is to look for certain dominant concepts or leading
ideas by which to illuminate his facts, to trace connections
between those ideas themselves, and then to show how the
detailed facts become intelligible in the light of them by
constructing a "significant" narrative of the events of the
period in question.'[1] It is of course scientifically imperative
to take into account all that is implied for historical science
in the unique nature of historical happening which may be
said to lie in the interaction between rational agency and natural
causation or between intention and necessity. Hence it will
not do to offer an historical explanation of past events simply
by rethinking the thoughts or reliving the experience expressed
in them in the hope of penetrating into the intentions of the
agents, or simply by reconstructing the connection between
the events solely in accordance with their natural aspects
and so penetrating into their necessary relations. The inside
and the outside of historical events cannot be separated without
distortion in our understanding of them, for the thoughts do
not occur in a physical vacuum, and the physical facts cannot
be considered in detachment from the purposeful actions of
agents if we are to remain within the field of historical inquiry.
What is required in historical explanation is a penetration into
the movement or happening in a series of events in such a
way that we lay bare the inner logic of the interaction between
mind and nature that runs throughout them and then in the
light of it gain for ourselves such a grasp of those events in
their intelligible patterns that they become, as it were, dra-
matized before us. Considerable use of art and dramatic
imagination, of empathy and intuition, will undoubtedly
be necessary but all in order to provide us with an adequate
lens, as it were, through which our understanding can break
through to the original happenings themselves. In undertaking
this we have to be aware of the changes in modes of thought
and behaviour that have come over the human race, and therefore have to be constantly on guard against any selection and
organization of the facts governed only by what modern people
think, feel and accept in case we work up those facts wrongly
into a coherent whole by interpolating into them alien thoughts

[1] Op. cit. p. 62.

and intentions.[1] Rather must we develop modes of interrogation that subject the source-material to such critical examination that they are made to interpret themselves to us through
their own latent hermeneutic. This is not to say that we must
not employ as working rules the knowledge of human and
physical nature which we have acquired in modern times, but
we must be careful not to let these obstruct us from asking
open questions or force us falsely to extrapolate answers from
one field of inquiry to another. Perhaps nowhere more than in
historical investigation are we tempted to determine from the
outset the results of our research through questions that are
closed from behind by ready-made answers. This is always
disastrous in attempts to penetrate into the inner happening
of historical events, but it is not difficult to see that wherever in
history we may be concerned with any interaction, or alleged
interaction, between God and the world, this would eliminate
at once even the possibility of genuinely open questioning.
Yet it is just this kind of free and untrammelled interrogation
that is of the essence of scientific activity as we have developed
it in the modern world, interrogation that reacts critically
upon the presuppositions that are used in forming the questions
so that they may become open to presuppositions from the side
of the realities being investigated. Only if they are really open
from behind can they be really open in front. Whatever else
historical investigation is, as we have learned from the time of
Laurentius Valla, it is the ruthless application to written
sources of the same sort of critical interrogation to which we
subject witnesses and documents in a court of law in order to
bring out the actual truth of things from the parties themselves,
so that they, the witnesses or the documents, may be forced
to be their own interpreters and to reveal themselves in
accordance with what they actually are.[2]

[1] G. Noller, *Sein und Existenz*, persistently and successfully maintains this charge
against Bultmann's interpretation of the New Testament; see, for example, p. 99.
See also R. W. Hepburn, *New Essays in Philosophical Theology* (edit. by A. Flew and
A. MacIntyre) p. 233.

[2] Collingwood (op. cit. p. 269) is mistaken in asserting that Francis Bacon was
unaware that his theory of experimental science, as putting nature to the question,
was also the true theory of historical method, for Bacon, as lawyer and theologian,
took his method and indeed his language from Calvin, R. Agricola, and L. Valla,
who had applied forensic questioning to historical research, and formulated the
kind of interrogative logic that this involved. What Bacon did was to apply the
kind of questioning the Renaissance lawyers and historians had been developing
to the investigation of nature. See particularly here, L. Valla, *In dialecticen
adnotationes* (*Dialectical disp. con. Aristotelicos*), and R. Agricola, *De inventione dialectica*.
See above p. 70.

Before we go further, however, we must be careful to distinguish clearly the kind of rationality inherent in historical events from that inherent in natural events. When we presume that nature is inherently intelligible we presume that our understanding of its processes and states can be given some form of mathematical representation, for it is in that way, as we have noted, that we believe its rationality can come most clearly to view. We cannot treat historical events in the same way—although undoubtedly mathematical forms of thought have their due part to play even here, e.g. in the application of statistical thinking to the socio-economic aspects of history—for historical events overlap with natural events. In historical events we operate with a different kind of rationality which we have described as intention or purpose, rationality in its personal rather than in its impersonal form. There have always been scientists (and doubtless always will be) who have found it hard not to regard nature as the expression of an infinite Mind—one thinks of Pascal or Jeans—but even so rationality is expressed in natural phenomena in a different way from that in the actions of personal agents. If we may speak of the rationality embedded in nature as *number*, we may speak of the *rationality* embedded in history as *logos*, for in history we are concerned with giving a different kind of account (λόγον διδόναι) of things from that we give of natural processes, and it is therefore a different kind of *story* that we have to tell. Hence while in natural science we have to direct our interrogative methods to the realities being investigated (*commensurable events*) with a view to bringing their inner logic to view in mathematical forms, in virtue of which it is made to disclose and explain itself to us, in historical science we direct our interrogative methods to the subject-matter of our research (*word-events*)[1] with a view to bringing out its latent intentionality, in virtue of which it is made to disclose and explain itself to us so that we in the present may grasp it in an intelligible and coherent way even though it is past. It is the business, then, of historical science to develop the kind of questions that are appropriate to bringing out the distinctive logic inherent in its subject-matter, in order to let the past events being investigated bear witness to themselves, interpret and explain

---

[1] I have taken the expression 'word-event' from a recent broadcast by Alan Richardson, 'When is a word an event?', printed in *The Listener* for June 3, 1965,

themselves to us, as far as possible in accordance with what they actually were in their own time and happening. In achieving this we, with our involvement in the present, must let ourselves be put to the question with our questions, to prevent us from reading back into the past later conceptions, attitudes, and feelings that are alien to it, so that we may really learn from the past and not merely use it as a means of our self-understanding.[1] Everything depends, therefore, in historical inquiry, upon the readiness of our minds, and the openness of our questions, in face of the actual subject-matter, if we are to appreciate it in accordance with the nature and forms of the rationality intrinsic to it. In this case our interpretation of historical events will not be one that we merely put upon the facts out of our situation in the present, but one that we rather draw out of the facts themselves in the light of the word with which they are impregnated, and under the guidance of the hermeneutical processes latent in them. Here no less than in natural science we have to understand events out of themselves and find ways of letting them speak to us across the centuries out of their own intelligibility what we cannot tell ourselves through any form of self-knowledge.

In turning back to the consideration of Jesus Christ, it must be said right away that we cannot but treat this historical event as we treat other historical events. We do not treat it simply as a necessary fact of nature to be brought under general laws, but as an event that happened in the free determination of rational agency within the context of our created world of space and time and in interaction with the natural processes of this world. But if in our inquiry into this happening in its inner sequence and appropriateness we find ourselves up against a movement in which we are forced to acknowledge the personal presence, speech and action of God Himself, we must distinguish it from other historical events as one

[1] Cf. the distorted understanding of ancient documents, e.g. the Gospels or The Acts of the Apostles, that comes from reading back into their authors the memory-habits of modern people (except in the cases of those trained in the educational methods of ancient Rabbinic centres such as Safed or in pre-Communist Chinese schools) who are normally unable to repeat word for word any disquisition longer than a few sentences, whereas this was common and natural, e.g. in the Palestinian schools at the time of Jesus or in the religious schools of North Africa at the time of St. Augustine.

resulting primarily from a divine movement and learn to appreciate it accordingly. Here is a historical fact which is like other historical facts, for it belongs to a series of events in space and time brought about through the actions of personal human agents such as Mary, John the Baptist, Herod, Caiaphas, Pilate and many others. But we are convinced that there is quite another side to all this, which we indicate by saying that in this fact we encounter *the Son of God become Man*, or by saying that in Jesus Christ *the eternal Word of God has become flesh*. That is to say, here is a historical event in which God is immediately and directly engaged as active Agent, a coming into space and time in which the *becoming* is a divine act, a historical event laden with the divine Word.[1] As such it is unlike any other historical event known to us, and must be investigated and assessed by letting it bear witness to itself within the sequences of the other historical events in which it is found. This is not to posit some supra-historical event that is not actually historical, but to claim that this historical event is more than at first appears, for in its inner happening there is a personal divine movement which gives it distinctive character without detracting from its nature as fully historical event on the same plane as other historical events. Moreover, it is to claim that only as we take this into account are we able to do justice to *all* the historical evidence, without resorting to the shoddy practice of cutting away the data that offend our preconceived notions and so of tampering with the evidence by imposing upon it from without an interpretation of our own, where the 'evidence' turns out to be only what we can square with our preconceptions.

Here then is the problem with which the historical approach to the fact of Jesus Christ is faced. In observing and checking historical data and in seeking to rest our knowledge squarely upon tested evidence, we are tempted first to treat the events once they have occurred as necessary facts of nature, as

---

[1] H. J. Paton is surely right when he argues that we cannot know God's actions as they are in themselves, from God's own point of view, but it does not follow that we can consider only man's way to God and not God's way to man, as he avers, for that is just what God's Grace is. Paton apparently fails to consider the fact that God's Act and His Word are inseparably joined, and that through His Word He does reveal to us what His acts are toward us. This is part of the very essence of the Incarnation. See *The Modern Predicament*, pp. 363 ff.

belonging to the causally determined world of impersonal things and to reject everything that appears to conflict with the 'laws of nature'. This is the temptation to convert historical becoming into necessity and to reduce historical science into a form of natural science whose specific methods are unscientifically extended beyond their proper spheres.[1] If we overcome this temptation, we are tempted in the second place to treat the historical Jesus merely as an ordinary historical episode like all others. Moreover, if we work with a view of historical science that presupposes that the particular must be interpreted in terms of the general, we lapse once again back into the mistake that converts historical science into some form of natural science. In both cases we start from a notion of scientific observation that precludes from the beginning the kind of becoming appropriate to the event into which we are inquiring. Either we simply convert becoming into necessity or we convert all becoming into one single kind of becoming.

On the other hand, if we are convinced that in the historical Jesus we meet with God become Man, and so affirm of the eternal God an act of historical becoming, are we not lapsing into a contradiction? Yet since it belongs to the essence of God's revelation that He makes Himself known to man in terms of what He is not, and therefore to the essence of man's knowledge of Him that it involves a two-fold objectivity, we are surely to understand this not as a contradiction, but as what inevitably appears paradoxical when observed from the standpoint that admits of only one kind of becoming, that which obtains in simple or common historical facts. Here we have a unique historical process characterised by an inherent duality that arises from the interaction of God with historical agency.[2]

Let us state the matter in another way. If God has become Man in the historical Jesus Christ, as Christians believe, that is an event in space and time that cannot be fully appreciated by ordinary historical science concerned only with the actions of human agents that rise and fall on the stage of history.

[1] It should be pointed out that behind this lies a philosophy of 'naturalism' which, as Alan Richardson rightly notes, means the extinction of the human sciences as independent scientific disciplines, *Science, Religion and Philosophy*, p. 28.

[2] Cf. A. E. Taylor's discussion of 'the complete interpenetration of Creator and creature in an individual life', and the importance of discernment of this for historical interpretation of the Evangelical accounts of Jesus. *The Faith of a Moralist*, Vol. 2, p. 123 f.

Ordinary historical science has to do with events that do indeed have continuing effects for longer and shorter periods but which themselves die away into the past. In this event, however, in the life of Jesus Christ, we have to do with something more than a passing historical episode: with a word-act of the eternal and living God that did not pass away and that has reached out beyond the immediate context of the passing historical events, in which it first happened, into the ages that followed and into the present. In so far as that act has entered into our creaturely existence and has in that way become a fact of this world it may be 'observed' like the other facts of nature, and in so far as it has assumed form and process within our space and time in a whole complex of historical events it can be investigated as a historical happening within the context of general history, but the word-act of God itself cannot be observed or investigated merely in these ways for it cannot be treated as if it were only a dead fact of history—treated in that way it could only prove illusory, for historical inquiry could not get to grips with it in its real actuality. It requires an act of discernment beyond common historical observation and a mode of rationality on our part appropriate not only to its character as enduring historical event but also to the personal and articulate nature of the divine activity intrinsic to it. This is what we call *faith*, i.e. the adaptation of the reason given to it in the process of acknowledging God's revelation in history and of obedient response to the Word of God communicated in human form. The object to which the reason is directed in faith is not the bare act of God as such, nor the mere historical event as such, but the word-act of God in and with the historical event through which He encounters people in every age in the present, and calls for their rational acknowledgment or faith—and faith here means simply the *fidelity* of the human reason to what is actually there in the encounter, the personal presence and act of God in our human and historical existence. Divine actuality and historical facticity are thus inseparably united in the ground of our knowledge and are not to be torn apart in our continuing inquiry into the fact of Jesus Christ.

We recall that in historical investigation we are concerned with the actions of human agents in which rational intentions and physical facts interact, and that to understand a historical event we must probe into its inner intelligibility and grasp the logic of its happening. That is what we have to do in our inquiry into Jesus Christ. But as we probe into this event we find that we are penetrating into the *Logos* of God and begin to understand it from within the divine purpose of redemption, and yet we apprehend all this only as the divine acts in the incarnate Word interact with the processes of this natural world and with the historical human agencies found at that particular period. To inquire into this historical event, into the logic of its happening, is to inquire into the logic of the divine Grace at work in the life of Jesus Christ. We are thus led to interpret the historical events in the light of their own intelligibility in the incarnate *Logos* and in accordance with intrinsic processes of hermeneutic in the work of the incarnate Son. In this historical event Word and Act are one and inseparable; the divine and the human are interlocked in one particular historical life that must be understood out of itself, through its own witness to itself, and in accordance with its own self-revelation through word and act in the actual context of space and time in which it was found. Here theological inquiry into the person of Jesus Christ must be historico-theological, and historical inquiry into the fact of Jesus Christ must be theologico-historical, for we are confronted with a *complex fact that includes its own interpretation as part of its facticity*, and we are confronted with a *logos* that has embodied itself in our concrete existence in space and time and cannot be known apart from that embodiment in history. If we are to remain faithful to the fact of Jesus Christ in its integrity and wholeness we cannot allow either side of this duality to be resolved away.

Our problem with this basic duality is complicated by the fact that we have to operate at three different levels. (1) At the top level we are engaged in investigating and interpreting the historical documents of the Christian Faith. Here we work within a duality or subject-object relation between ourselves and the biblical texts enshrining the protocol reports of the original witnesses to Jesus Christ. (2) Then in these texts we have to do with an intermediate level at which witness is borne by human subjects to realities beyond themselves, as they both offer us evidence as to the fact of Christ and report to us the intrinsic meaning or truth of that fact drawn out of the fact itself. Here we are concerned with a duality or subject-object relation between the witnesses and the reality to which they bear witness and to which they direct us as the object of our consideration and faith. (3) Finally there is the ground level where we meet with God Himself in the person of Jesus Christ, where Jesus directs us away from Himself to the Father who sent Him and where the Father reveals Himself to us in the face of Jesus. Here we are thrown upon the basic duality in the unity of the incarnate Son of God, for all things have been entrusted to Him by the Father. No one knows the Son but the Father, and no one knows the Father but the Son and those to whom the Son wills to reveal Him.[1]

It is upon this basic level and the nature of the duality inherent in it that the character and significance of the other levels depend. Is this a duality, then, in which two spheres intersect, or one in which they remain permanently disparate, *Jenseits und Diesseits*, bearing upon one another only tangentially at some vanishing mathematical point? Is it a duality in which quite different realities, God and the World, interact, or is it merely the kind of duality in which we give two diverse and disconnected interpretations to the same experience? When we say that God reveals Himself in the historical Jesus, do we mean that this revelation is a factual occurrence within our space-time existence, and therefore a disclosure of God that takes place within the subject-object structures that we have in this world? Or do we mean that it is some kind of occurrence that merely touches our existence from beyond it, where our existence ceases, so that Jesus Christ (for example in His sacrificial death) is not to be regarded as an act of God *within our world* affecting and changing things in it, but only as the occasion where we become aware of a 'paradoxical' or 'eschatological' 'act' of God at the boundary of our existence where the world 'comes to an end' or our being borders on non-being, and where we are flung back upon ourselves in some form of self-understanding?[2]

[1] Matt. 11. 27; Luke 10. 22

[2] Cf. R. Bultmann, *Existence and Faith*, especially the essays, 'The Hidden and the Revealed God', and 'Revelation in the New Testament'. Contrast H. J. Paton, 'All religious faith must depend on a belief that God acts in the world and that such a belief is of necessity historical. A God who does nothing cannot be an object of worship' (*The Modern Predicament*, p. 238). Bultmann's position can be reached by abstracting the 'word' from the 'act' and turning it into a timeless *Ereignis*, but if we abstract the 'act' from the 'word' we make essentially the same mistake.

The first of these alternatives is that which historic Christianity has always taken, in which it has affirmed not only a causal and ontological connection between the acts of God and our worldly existence, but a personal participation of God in our human being and life through direct and immediate agency in human history, so that it has insisted upon the objective reality of divine acts in the space and time of this world. But if we take the second alternative the different levels of thought at which we operate are affected so radically that every statement we make about God or Jesus Christ is altered—and even when the statements are linguistically identical they mean radically different things. It makes the interpretation of historical reports and events entirely ambiguous, giving them two diverse and disconnected senses through looking at them in quite different ways.[1] This is what we find, for example, in Bultmann's two-fold approach to Jesus Christ, *historisch* and *geschichtlich*.[2] One is the approach of a positivist conception of history (*Historie*) in which, working with a closed continuum of cause and effect, almost everything in the traditional life of Jesus is rejected as editorial accretion and explained as creative projection out of the early Church, with there remaining only the scantiest evidence as to the death of this Man. In this way the historical foundations of Christianity are cut away drastically, so that a new basis for faith must be sought in essential detachment from historical facticity. But the other is the approach of an existentialist conception of history (*Geschichte*) in which historical documents are valued not for the references they promote but for the attitudes they evoke. In this way the fictitious material is not cut away for some underlying residue of fact or truth, but the manifold forms in which the New Testament material is presented are

[1] This is the kind of approach we are familiar with in connection with the 'puzzle pictures' discussed by Wittgenstein (*Philosophical Investigations*, II, p. 193) and Waismann (*The Principles of Linguistic Philosophy*, p. 360 f.) such as a drawing which when looked at in one particular way appears to be the leg of a table but when looked at in another way appears to be two human profiles facing each other, or a drawing of a die which appears now to project away from us and now to project toward us depending on the way we regard it.

[2] For the following see especially the essays of Bultmann in the various volumes of *Kerygma and Myth* (edited by W. Bartsch), *Essays: Philosophical and Theological, History and Eschatology, Primitive Christianity, Existence and Faith, Jesus Christ and Mythology.* Cf. the analysis of Bultmann's notions by G. Noller, *Sein und Existenz*, pp. 86 ff.

regarded as enshrining the thoughts and attitudes of early Christians to the other world objectified in primitive cosmological notions and as capable of yielding a meaning under existentialist interpretation that helps us to understand ourselves and find authentic existence in the present. These two approaches to the historical Jesus Christ do not have any essential link between them, for each is the limit and paradoxical antithesis of the other. Behind this of course lies Bultmann's axiomatic assumption of an infinite yawning gap between God and man or a radical dichotomy between God and the world which rejects entirely any possibility of interaction between God and nature, or between divine agency and human agency in historical events. It is this that has led him into a way of speaking about Jesus in which he has been accused (e.g. by Jaspers) of 'double thinking'. At any rate the upshot of Bultmann's approach has led to what Hermann Diem has called the reduction of one set of problems to another.[1]

If there is no fundamental interaction between God and the world then not only must the whole objective framework in which Christian Faith is expressed in the historic creeds be deemed mythological, but the objective reference in the Evangelical narratives must be discounted. Hence their 'meaning' must be sought in detachment from all reference to acts of God in the proper sense and solely within the souls of their authors and the community to which they belonged, as objectified forms of their self-expression. The theological significance of this was made clear in 1925 by an essay of Bultmann entitled 'In what sense can we speak of God?'[2] in which he first argued, rightly, that we may speak of Him not in the abstract nor as a mere 'object' but only as we are aware that we are addressed by His Word and our existence is determined by Him. However then he went on to argue, quite wrongly, that this determination of our existence by God is the only content we can give to statements about Him, for we can only speak about God by speaking about ourselves. In this event 'God' merely becomes a cipher for our *relations*

---

[1] H. Diem, *Dogmatik: Ihr Weg zwischen Historicismus und Existentialismus*, Eng. tr. by H. Knight, p. 242 f.

[2] *Glauben und Verstehen, Gesammelte Aufsätze*, vol. 1, pp. 26 ff. Cf. also H. Gollwitzer, *The Existence of God*, p. 15 ff.

with God, and nothing can then stop it from becoming a mere cipher for our relations with our fellowmen, the step that has now been taken by the 'secularising' theologians.[1] Our concern at the moment, however, is with the fact that the rejection of the subject-object form of thought that lies at the back of Bultmann's approach carries with it also a rejection of all external reference to actual historical events, so that the problem of historical reality, to cite Diem again, 'can now only be posed from within private existence as an inquiry into what has meaning for such existence'.[2] So far as historical investigation of the New Testament documents is concerned, this means that the different levels at which our thought must move are all flattened out with the objective poles telescoped into the subjective poles making the inquiry finally into a mere encounter of the historian with himself.[3] But since this implies that meaning is and must be detachable from objective physical events, the latter being without significance in themselves are gladly handed over to a naturalistic conception of history that has no compunction about demolishing them by the axe of natural law. Thus Bultmann's rejection of any interaction between God and the world ends up in travesty of historical method. The lesson to be learned from it is that it is only through interaction with God that we can be delivered from a purely naturalistic existence, and so may be delivered from our temptation to use that as the criterion for historical interpretation. In terms of historical inquiry into the documents of the New Testament this means that when we come up against the interaction between divine and human agency in historical events we are forced to take them seriously and to seek their meaning out of their own actuality.

While it may be readily granted that historical happening has a distinctive character of its own and is not to be confused with any other kind of event, and while it must also be granted that there must be a distinctive philosophy of history, it cannot be granted that in disciplined historical inquiry we operate

[1] Cf. H. Lamparter, 'Modern Theology, its Achievements and Failures', tr. by H. Hartwell, *The Bridge*, Nov. 1966, pp. 5 ff.

[2] H. Diem, op. cit. p. 243.

[3] Cf. Buber's remark that whenever man has to interpret encounters with God as self-encounters, man's very structure is destroyed. 'This is the portent of the present hour'. *The Eclipse of God*, p. 22.

with methods that are essentially different from those employed in all scientific investigation. Historical science is certainly different from every other science, but its difference falls within the scientific requirement of fidelity to the nature of the subject-matter. It is only on that ground, therefore, that the historian develops his own distinctive forms of thought and his own appropriate variations in method that demand our recognition and acceptance. It is on this basis that we must object to idealist and existentialist interpretations of history, for they conflict with the fundamental principle of science that we seek knowledge of realities out of themselves in their own intelligibility and wholeness. This means that our understanding and interpreting of historical events must be derived from their own actuality and verified on their own ground, in processes of thought in which we develop forms of knowledge appropriate to their distinctive nature. In all genuinely scientific operations we interrogate realities in such a way as to let them disclose themselves to us, so that they may yield to us their own meaning and be justified out of themselves, without the arbitrary application to them of criteria that we have developed elsewhere and subjected to our disposal.

When we speak of the 'self-disclosure' of realities we are aware that this must often be a figure of speech—i.e. when we are concerned with impersonal, dumb and dead things, for we have to force them to react to our probes in a 'yes' and 'no' way and so yield the answers to our questions. But in so far as we interrogate personal realities actual self-disclosure comes more into play, and we have to acquire more and more a disciplined readiness to listen so that we may really understand them out of themselves. When we come to deal with historical events we have to remember that they are constituted through the inter-relation of personal agencies and impersonal physical facts, so that we have to bring our forms of interrogation and learning into line with these distinctive characteristics. Here more than in the science of psychology we have to force the events to answer our questions, but here too we have to listen and learn from the realities through their own self-disclosure more than in natural science where we are concerned only with wordless phenomena. Indeed the closest analogy we have to historical inquiry is to be found in forensic interrogation with its mixture of compulsion and listening applied to spoken and written testimony in which we seek to determine what actually took place through a clarification both of intention and physical fact. Neither by itself is sufficient, for whether the testimony is spoken or written it is verified solely by reference to that to which witness is borne; only when that connection is established do we reckon that we have evidence, for then our knowledge of things is matched with grounds in the things themselves. Of outstanding importance in all this is the *logic of reference*.[1]

In all handling of historical documents—which constitutes the major part of historical investigation—the persistent question we must ask is, *What does the text actually say?* What does it want to say and what does it really succeed in saying? And in answer we must probe as deeply as we can into the lines of reference in order to clarify and establish the connection between what is said and that about which the documents speak. This is what we do in theological studies when we investigate the historical sources of Christianity and inquire into the original events to which the biblical documents bear witness. Thus when we make the Evangelical narratives the object of our study they must be allowed to refer us beyond themselves to the specific series of historical events that is their object, and we must listen to their witness to the interaction of God with our world in those events for that is manifestly what they *intend*. We must probe into that reference and test the relation between the witness and that to which witness is borne. But in order to do that we cannot detach ourselves from it and make it the mere object of our reflection, nor can we transcend the subject-object relation it involves and seek to interpret it obliquely in terms of an existential attitude to existence. In following through its intended reference we must let ourselves get drawn into its process, and operate within the subject-object relation inherent in the situation between the witnesses and that to which they bear witness.[2] We must get ourselves into the position where we can really listen to what is going

---

[1] Yet this is what was largely set aside by Dilthey in favour of a *logic of expression*, and this in turn has exercised a damaging influence upon the historical understanding and biblical interpretation of Bultmann. For a change from an objective to a subjective meaning of *Ausdruck* in Dilthey's thought, see the extended note by H. G. Gadamer, *Wahrheit und Methode*, p. 474 f.

[2] See the trenchant analysis of this by H. Diem, op. cit. pp. 282 ff.

on, for it is only in that way and at that place that we are able properly to appreciate the documents themselves and to judge what they say in the light of the object of their witness. If we fail to get that far we have already obstructed a genuinely scientific approach. But if in our probing into the historical events to which they refer we manage to penetrate into their inner happening, and then find ourselves up against the divine interaction with historical agency, we must let ourselves become implicated in that interaction, for we will not be able to reach apprehension otherwise. But if at that point we withdraw from engagement with the realities to which we are referred and seek to understand and interpret them on other ground of our own choosing where they do not actually encounter us, we will only deviate from the course of true inquiry and our questions will shoot past the realities into emptiness.

In the course of historico-theological investigation into Jesus Christ there become revealed distinctive characteristics that bear particularly upon the process of inquiry. The significance of this event is disclosed to us in the light of its own actuality as an event, for in this fact *word* and *event* coincide. This 'event' is not a 'fact' without a meaning nor a 'meaning' without a fact. Significance and factuality both belong inseparably to the essence of the event. It is a self-disclosing, self-interpreting event, yielding forth its meaning intrinsically as word out of itself. That is why the New Testament writers insisted that their message about Jesus went back to Jesus Himself as the Word of God, for He proclaimed Himself to them through a life of self-disclosure in which His words and His acts kept pace with each other, and so He supplied them in His own teaching and work with the controlling source of their witness. This means that the whole historical event of Jesus Christ must be interpreted out of its own inner intelligibility and that it will not yield its meaning when subjected to *a priori* assumptions, extraneous criteria, or frames of reference that we may arbitrarily bring to it; rather must we allow these to be questioned before the fact of Christ, and be made to give way before His self-interpretation if we are to apprehend it.

Moreover this inner conjunction of significance and fact in Christ meant to the New Testament writers that Jesus' own Word continued to be heard and to be effective through their witness to Him, so that in this way the original word-event went on happening. They bore witness to the majestic and dynamic character of that event, for it addressed them and acted upon them, and they felt their very existence challenged and affected by it. They found themselves drawn out of themselves and committed in direct engagement with God, for in this event their own lives and destinies were at stake. In Jesus Christ God's own action had assumed historical process in their midst and they were caught up in a series of decisive events in which divine agency was immediately interacting with men in deeds of judgement and salvation. That is the momentous nature of the historical event of Jesus Christ, for in its conjunction of word and act, of significance and fact, it remains active in historical human existence, so that even now, as in the first generation of disciples, people find themselves directly confronted in this event with the Word and Act of God challenging and determining their existence. This is an event that they are unable to appreciate or interpret from out of their own prior or natural existence, but only as they renounce themselves, take up the cross and follow Christ as His disciples. And then they become aware that since in this original event God had already laid hold of their human existence, as they allow themselves to become involved in it, the historical processes originally at work in Jesus press toward fulfilment in their own existence in the present.

What then does it mean to inquire into the historical events presented to us in the Gospel records? It means that we must probe into the inner movement of a historical process which embodies in actual specific events the interaction between divine and human agency in the realization of God's purpose of revelation and redemption, but which assimilates to itself an interaction between human witnesses and those particular events as the medium of its continued and effective happening. It is the task of the inquirer to penetrate within the subject-object relation between the witness and the reality attested, to follow through the reference given, and then to engage with that reality by letting himself become the object of its address and activity. If at that point he is convinced that he has come into contact with the personal presence and action of God Himself in Jesus Christ then he must assess the whole series of historical events in that light. But if he fails to be convinced he must nevertheless seek in scientific integrity to appreciate the historical process as far as possible out of itself, and not merely in the light of preconceived ideas of the historical or in the light of some alleged *intentio obliqua* that can only turn the flank of honest-to-goodness historical investigation.[1] It is the contention of Christian faith that only as we allow ourselves to enter the sphere of the divine interaction with our world in the life and teaching of Jesus can we do justice to all the historical evidence about Him, but that if we fail or decline to do so we will never be able to reach a satisfactory account of the historical Jesus Christ at any level of inquiry.[2] Each succeeding reconstruction of the events will inevitably break down as before a bewildering enigma which nevertheless keeps on insisting that we develop a method of approach and a form of knowledge with intrinsic appropriateness to it. Such is the Jesus of History who has haunted and baffled so many modern historians, for He insists on being understood as true historical event that will not submit to historical criteria we already have at our disposal but will yield His secret to those who are open and ready to consider Him in His own majestic self-presentation and self-interpretation.

A full positive account of the historical Jesus Christ (which we cannot offer here) must include an assessment of His *resurrection* as a real historical event occurring in the same sphere of reality to which we human beings belong. It is indeed from the perspective of the resurrection that the New Testament witness to Jesus is given, as well as from the perspective of the Incarnation. In the resurrection the saving intervention of God in our human being and His interaction with 'this passing world' overcome the corruption of our existence, redeeming time from its decay and futility, and result in a fully authentic historical happening, *so real* that it breaks through the day-to-day happening that crumbles away into the dust of the past and into non-being, and as such constantly provokes man's reflection on its 'meaninglessness', 'purposelessness' and

---

[1] Thus Bultmann, 'The Problem of Hermeneutics', *Essays*, p. 249.
[2] Cf. the discussion of this point by Alan Richardson in *Science, History and Faith*, espec. pp. 61 ff.

'hopelessness'. On the contrary, this is a happening that flows against the stream of decaying time and dying history, and against all threat of final illusion, to remain on throughout history as enduring reality and to confront us in the present as permanently live happening. Far from being finished and done with this is a creative event in our midst that injects final purpose into human existence and opens up an entirely new vista for it in the future. In the Incarnation, Crucifixion and Resurrection we have a momentous series of events that shatters the frame-work of what, from a natural point of view, we regard as but the on-going history of this world and forces us to develop a Christian metaphysic of history. Here we are up against one of those decisive moments in thought where radical reconstruction of prior knowledge is demanded of us and a profound shift in the meaning of certain important concepts must be carried through.

The Christian approach to history as a whole cannot but contain powerful eschatological elements, for it must offer an account of the interaction of divine acts with human agencies throughout history, and therefore of the persisting conflict between the Kingdom of God and the sin-distorted patterns of human life or the power structures of temporal and political existence; but it must also contain powerful teleological elements, for it must offer an account of the redeeming and creative work of God in Jesus Christ, and therefore of the evangelical mission of the Church in world history as through its witness to Jesus Christ the original events remain dynamically operative in our midst and press toward their consummation. Thus on the one hand the Christian approach to history must show, in the words of Karl Löwith, that 'the "meaning" of the history of this world is fulfilled against itself because the story of salvation, embodied in Jesus Christ, redeems and dismantles, as it were, the hopeless history of the world,'[1] but on the other hand it must also show not only that there is a purpose at work in human history but that this is given its true end and significance through interrelation with the eternal purpose of the divine love already incarnate in our human being in Jesus Christ but continuously at work penetrating into the

[1] Karl Löwith, *Meaning in History*, p. 187

life of mankind and gathering up our historical existence toward final fulfilment.[1]

In the nature of the case such a metaphysic of history cannot but affect the Christian's scientific approach to historical events, since he will want to relate their innermost intention to the divine purpose if he is to grasp the historical processes he studies in their own intrinsic propriety and wholeness, for to cite Löwith again, 'nothing in the New Testament warrants a conception of the new events that constituted early Christianity, as the beginning of a new epoch of secular developments within a continuous process'.[2] At the same time this must not be allowed to have the effect of imposing from above, as it were, a Christian pattern upon historical events as though a distinctively Christian history could be given, say, of the Second World War. Rather does it mean that the Christian historian must operate at different levels of thought which, far from being complete and consistent in themselves, interact with each other and are open to each other at significant points in ways that modify their operations at different levels. These are the points where the key-concepts we use have to undergo their due shift in meaning and thereby introduce subtle but all-important determinations into our outlook in reading and correlating historical evidence, if only because as points of interaction between the levels, they prevent the key-concepts and criteria operative on each level from becoming closed and rigid. In other words, the Christian's interaction with divine acts which delivers him from a purely naturalistic existence, should help to prevent him from short-circuiting historical connections, and make him more sensitive in his handling of the subject-matter as he penetrates to a profounder level of intelligibility in the events.

3. *Theology as Dogmatic Science*

It is to be hoped that the indirect comparison between theology and the other sciences which we have attempted by

[1] Cf. the enlightening way in which Nels Ferré discusses "the pull of purpose" in the meaning of history, *Reason in Religion*, pp. 216 ff.

[2] Op. cit. p. 196.

examining their mutual involvement and their likeness and difference, in the relations between the knowing subject and the object known in different fields, has served at least to clarify the scientific intention of theology as rational, human inquiry into the knowledge of God. In claiming to be a science, objective knowledge exhibiting its own grounds and employing its own independent categories, theology thereby excludes the transfer to its own field of the distinctive axioms, postulates and canons that have been forced upon us in other fields of knowledge by the nature of their subject-matter, and thereby rejects all alien dogmatisms. As a science theology is obliged to submit only to the demands of its own subject-matter and to accept only the forms, possibilities and conditions of knowledge dictated by the nature of what it seeks to know. It is thus that theology develops its own *inner dogmatics*, and this in the interest of scientific fidelity and purity. Christian dogmatics is the pure science of theology in which, as in every pure science, we seek to discover the fundamental structure and order in the nature of things and to develop basic forms of thought about them as our understanding is allowed to be controlled by them from beyond our individualism. It is through dogmatic activity of this kind that theology is directed to formulate precise and positive statements under the pressure of the truth that will allow it to come to light in its own integrity and so to advance our apprehension of it. Hence our discussion of theological science among the other sciences requires to be completed by a more definite account of this positive aspect of its activity.

It is not immediately evident why 'dogmatics' should be used to denote scientific activity of this kind, or what connection this has with 'dogmas'. In the ancient pre-Christian world 'dogma' could refer to several different things. It could mean a public decree or statutory ordinance, a judicial decision or judgement, a statement of principle in philosophy or science as laid down in some school or even by an individual teacher, or merely an opinion or belief. In the early Christian Church 'dogmas' (usually found in the plural) referred to ecclesiastical ordinances such as the sacraments of baptism and eucharist or to Christian truths especially as they were brought to decisive enunciation through the councils of the Church. Dogmas thus came to mean doctrinal propositions formulated and given out by the Church on the ground of decisions or judgements reached by the Church through corporate or conciliar acts. In the Roman Church dogmas came to signify revealed truths as they came to expression in the mind of the Church and were given authoritative interpretation through its teaching office and as such came to be identified with canonical definitions and legal ordinances. Throughout the whole Church, in East and West, the emphasis upon *dogma* came to be upon well-grounded and agreed affirmation rather than arbitrary and individual opinion, and upon positive and constructive as opposed to sceptical or merely critical thought.[1]

The concept of *dogmatic science* or of *dogmatics*, however, did not arise until after the Reformation and the change from an *a priori* to an *a posteriori* approach to knowledge emancipated from the shackles of traditional preconceptions and authoritarian interpretations. Thus *dogmatics* seems to have been applied first to the new notion of science that emerged out of the sixteenth into the seventeenth century, in which the subject-matter was explored and understood in accordance with its own interior connections, and not in accordance with external authorities. As such it came to be applied to physics, as a science proceeding through constructive inquiry rather than by way of critical philosophical questioning. A *dogmatic science* was the kind of science in which men thought of the given facts as they were forced to think of them by the facts themselves and developed 'cataleptic conceptions' under their pressure. It was the positive form of science in which a field of 'dogmatic inquiry' was fenced off from all distracting and sceptical problems in order to allow the attention to be concentrated upon the subject-matter in its own nature. While this involved critical testing of all the ideas that were thrown up in the inquiry there had always to be a return to the facts themselves when the scientists could let their minds fall under the compulsion of their natural patterns and formulate in positive 'dogmas' what they apprehended.[2] It was in this direction and in this sense that *dogmatic science* came to be applied to theology bracketed off as a field of study on its own, unobstructed by abstract questions as to essence and sceptical questions as to possibility

---

[1] This was in line with the philosophical and scientific understanding of *dogma*. See Sextus Empiricus, *Adversus dogmaticos*.

[2] Cf. here the statement of A. N. Whitehead: 'The dogmas of physical science are attempts to formulate in precise terms the truths disclosed in the sense-perception of mankind'. *Religion in the Making*, p. 47

raised before proper scrutiny had been given to the actual nature of the given realities and the actual situation in which knowledge arises between the knower and the object. Critical and epistemological questions were raised but only on the ground of actual knowledge, in the light of the inner logic of the material content of that knowledge, and with a rigid exclusion of *a priori* assumptions or external presuppositions and authorities.

Such was the origin and intention of the dogmatic science pursued in the Evangelical Churches in the seventeenth century, but before very long a significant change set in as primary place began to be given to 'logical analysis' and formal 'method' (the catch-expressions of Pierre de la Ramée and his followers). This entailed systematizing theological material in forms of thought not taken from the realities themselves but from contemporary philosophies, first in the new formalistic Aristotelianism and then in the light of the Cartesian mode of questioning the self-understanding. This had the effect of reformalizing Protestant theology severely in the scholastic manner and of overloading it with rationalistic presuppositions that were bound to be questioned before the advance of critico-empirical investigation. In this way, 'dogmatics' began to refer to a system of philosophy based upon principles dictated by reason alone, or to a system of theology grounded on first principles and analytically and logically ordered into a coherent body of truth. From its stress upon positive content and constructive procedure 'dogmatics' came to be understood as philosophical or theological dogmatizing without critical reference to the evidence of primordial realities. Thus Protestant dogmatics lapsed from its strictly scientific character in the new mode into the style and mode of late medieval scholastic science. In this changed sense of the term Roman theologians could also employ, and did begin to employ, 'dogmatics' to refer to the systematic presentation of conciliar decisions and Church dogmas, and so dogmatics became assimilated to the external authoritarianism from which as a science it had earlier been emancipated.[1]

[1] It would appear to be in this connection that the vulgar sense of 'dogmatic', 'dogmatizing' arose. A dogmatical person is one who lays down opinions in an arrogant manner without submission to critical testing or empirical reference to the realities in question.

In our day, however, there has taken place a powerful rehabilitation of *dogmatics* in the proper and original sense in which it can be applied to pure physics as well as to pure theology—i.e. the kind of knowledge that is forced upon us when we are true to the facts we are up against, and in which we let our thinking follow the witness of those facts to their own nature and reality, together with the kind of statements we are compelled to make in sheer recognition and acknowledgement of the nature of those facts. A dogmatic science of this kind, whether it be in physics or theology, will not allow another department of knowledge working in quite a different field to dictate to it on its own ground, either in prescribing its methods or in predetermining its results—that would be the bad sort of dogmatizing which unfortunately theology encounters today not infrequently from the side of 'scientism' and from some philosophical empiricists. Rather does each science allow its own subject-matter to determine how knowledge of it is to be developed and tested, since method and subject-matter cannot be separated. As we have reminded ourselves already on several occasions, the physicist is not free to think what he likes. He is bound to his proper object and compelled to think of it in accordance with its nature as it becomes revealed under his active interrogation. He is not being dogmatical when he does that—he is humbly submitting his mind to the facts and their own inner logic. So with the science of pure theology, in which we let the nature and pattern of that into which we inquire impose themselves upon our minds. It is positive, dogmatic science, but not authoritarian or 'dogmatical'.

On the other hand, we must not overlook the fact that there is a considerable difference in dogmatic science as applied to physics and applied to theology, in accordance with the nature of their respective subject-matters. Each is a dogmatic science operating on its own ground and in terms of the inner law of its own being, and the statements in each have a positive and obligatory character for they are grounded definitely on their object and are made out of a binding relation to it. In physics dogmatic statements have a necessary and (on Fermat's principle) an exclusive relation to the things about which they are made, while in theology dogmatic statements have an obedient and right relation to the Word of God as their source which precludes the acknowledgement of the rightness of any other choice (and thus excludes 'heresy').[1] The difference lies in the fact that in the objective ground of theological knowledge there is not only a demand arising from the nature of the object, that we think and speak about it in an appropriate way, but an active Word which takes us under its command, teaches us and commissions us to make it heard and known. Dogmatic statements are thus made in acknowledgement and obedience to the decisive and instructive acts of God's self-revelation in His Word and through their correlation to that revelation cannot but take the form of doctrinal decisions and propositions, i.e. not only as forms in which the divine Truth is heard but as forms in which it is proclaimed and taught.[2] If therefore the dogmatic formulations of the Church have tended to have a magisterial and judicial character, it is not properly because they have any doctrinal authority in themselves but because as dogmatic recognitions they are made to serve the authority of the Word of God. Hence they must be sharply distinguished from the objective content or irreducible datum of the divine revelation as but human formulations whose mission it is to direct us to the Word of God that it alone may preside in all our cognition and instruction of the divine Truth. They are kerygmatic and didactic at the same time,[3] so that even in their form as doctrinal pronouncements they point to an authority beyond themselves

---

[1] Dogmatic science, of course, has its own kind of authority, but it is the authority of the irreducibly given, or as A. E. Taylor expressed it, "that which is simply received, not invented by ourselves, and is therefore, in its nature, simply authoritative, a genuine control on the wilfulness of our individualism", *The Faith of a Moralist*, vol. 2, p. 221. "There is an element of the wholly given and trans-subjective which is *absolutely* authoritative, has unquestionable right to control our thinking or acting, just because it is so utterly given to us, not made by us". Op. cit. p. 236.

[2] It must be granted that the 'dogmatic' form of statement is not uninfluenced by the traditional logic of predication, in which propositions are either assertions or denials of some predicate. Positive assertions of this kind have less place in symbolic logic which is more concerned with the clarification of relations between terms and their necessary entailments.

[3] It is significant that in the earlier ages of the Church it was κηρύγματα rather than δόγματα that was used to express these doctrinal propositions, δόγματα being used for ecclesiastical ordinances, but when dogmatic propositions came to have a more judicial and legal character δόγματα came to replace κηρύγματα.

which they can only proclaim. As soon as dogmatic pronouncements attract authority to themselves they tend to be perverted and to fail in their proper intention, and so to obscure their own inner meaning. They deny the truth of being upon which they rest and have to rest in order to be dogmatic statements at all.

In dogma, in its original and proper sense, we are concerned with the objective and ultimate ground of the Church's existence, that is, with the fundamental datum of revelation that demands our hearing and acknowledgement, on the one hand, and with the right relation between the mind of the Church and that fundamental datum, on the other hand. Dogmatic thinking arises from the fact that God has acted in human history in a final and saving way, and that what He has given us in His revelation is Himself, His own divine Being: His Being in His Act, His Act in His Being. Dogmas are the corporate recognition-statements of the Church corresponding to this authoritative self-revelation and are reached only after catholic consideration and synodical formulation. They are the results of the on-going dogmatic reflection of the Church as it lets itself be taught by the Word of God and are deposited in the creeds as guides and directives to help the faithful in their conjoint apprehension of the truth and to maintain them in the steady progression of the Church's understanding of the divine revelation, especially over against arbitrary free-thinking and self-willed aberration. Thus, for example, the classical Church dogmas took their rise in the Nicene and post-Nicene theology with the struggle to articulate aright in the Church's understanding that in His self-communication in Jesus Christ God has given and reveals to us His own divine Being, and not just something of Himself. All the early Church dogmas were rooted and grounded in that fundamental datum and were directed toward its disclosure. When we turn to the Reformation we find once again that the Church dogmas took their rise in the struggle to articulate aright in the Church's understanding that in His self-revelation in Grace God has given and reveals His own divine Being, not just something of Himself. In this way the Reformation is to be seen as the struggle to regain Nicene orientation in the understanding of the Church as to the fundamental *datum* of divine revelation, but the emphasis was upon the activity of God in His self-giving and not just upon the gift as such or upon a gift that could be detached from the Giver Himself. All the Reformation dogmas were grounded in that divine Grace, and strove to let it come to view in its own wholeness and integrity. In the Early Church the stress was more on the Being in the Act, i.e. on Christology; in the Reformation Church the stress was more on the Act in the Being, i.e. on Soteriology—but they were complementary attempts to inquire into and to determine the objective and right ground of the Church's existence and understanding. That is what Christian Dogmatics is about.

The given reality with which we are concerned in dogmatics is not just a *datum* handed over to the control and manipulation of our thought, for it remains a *dandum* that must ever be given anew, for the Gift and the Giver are identical. It is God who has given and revealed Himself in Israel and in the Incarnation for men to know and understand, but He remains the Lord God transcendent in His eternal and infinite Being who cannot be comprehended even when we apprehend Him. He has given Himself to us to receive and love and know, and yet remains Lord of His self-giving. God has imparted Himself to us within our human existence in space and time, within historical being on earth, and yet as such He remains the Lord God, Father, Son and Holy Spirit, who cannot be resolved into the forms and modes of His self-impartation. Thus in the given reality of our knowledge there are specifiable and unspecifiable elements, a fact which gives dogma a rather baffling character.

We are thus forced to draw a distinction between *dogma* and *dogmas*.[1] In *dogma* we are concerned with the one ultimate ground and creative source of the understanding and existence of the Church in the communication and self-giving of God's own Being, and therefore with the ontological unity of the Church in the one God. Hence to excise dogma is to strike at the very foundation of the Church and indeed to dissolve it entirely. In *dogmas*, however, we are concerned with the Church's historical inquiry and formulations of its knowledge

---

[1] See Karl Barth, *Church Dogmatics*, I. 1, pp. 11 ff., pp. 304 ff., and I. 2, pp. 758 ff., and 812–884.

of the fundamental *datum* of divine revelation as it is communicated in the Incarnation and as it calls forth form and structure in the Church's existence and history. Hence in dogmas the Church strives to understand its own foundation and to clarify the pattern of its life and mission on that foundation. We are concerned with dogma as the objective meaning and norm of all true dogmas, the truth that they intend as they fulfil their function in directing the Church to apprehend and appropriate God's self-revelation. We are concerned with dogmas as the rational forms in the mind of the historical Church that arise out of and correspond to its one foundation once and for all laid by God in Israel and in the Incarnation, and by Jesus Christ in His Apostles—i.e. the foundation of the Church upon the Apostles and Prophets. Dogmas, however, in relation to dogma, are forms of inquiry, stages in the Church's apprehension, or cognitive instruments for proper and deeper knowledge of the divine Truth.

Dogmatics is the *science of dogma*, rather than the science of dogmas. By penetrating through historical dogmas to their fontal source it inquires into the objective logic determining dogmas and thus into the fundamental dogma to which they point. It is not the special business of dogmatics to offer a systematic interpretation of dogmas as such (that belongs to the theological discipline known as 'symbolics'), but to examine them in their historical development and formation, testing their rightness and propriety, in order to further its inquiry through them into the doctrinal content of God's Self-revelation. In the course of this inquiry it will doubtless judge their adequacy or inadequacy in the light of their inner meaning and ground in that revelation, and may indicate where and how they need to be reconstructed in order to fulfil their proper intention in the present, but as a science dogmatics aims at developing its own dogmatic forms of thought and at building its own dogmatic propositions, which may well be built securely upon the foundations laid by the dogmatic activity of the Church in the past, but which are designed as new questions in the forward thrust of inquiry in the hope that they will open up the way for a genuine advance in the understanding of the Truth. Since the classical dogmas are the deposit of the Church's common knowledge and corporate dogmatic activity in the past they are respected like the so-called laws of nature reached through scientific thinking in the past but which have to be reconstructed in the light of more advanced knowledge; they are not cast aside for within their limited range they are set more securely upon their proper foundations. But in the deepening of theological knowledge fresh dogmatic formulations are elaborated, which are related to dogma as compound analogues or disclosure-models through which the fundamental datum of revelation is understood more profoundly and precisely in its own inner unity and simplicity. In so far as this succeeds scientific dogmatics leaves its mark upon the dogmatic progress of the Church and its continuing reformation according to the Word of God.

We must remind ourselves here again that in its very character as pure science Christian Dogmatics is committed to a divine mission. This arises out of the nature of its object, as *objectum docens*, object that proclaims, interprets and defines itself, and therefore instructs us in our knowledge of it, assimilating us in our knowing to its own activity and mission. As we have seen, it is the presence and activity of the divine Word in the object of our knowledge that makes dogmatic science in theology different from any other dogmatic science, for here the positive and right forms of knowledge and statement we have to make about the object emerge not only from the pressure of its being upon us but out of its intrinsic doctrinal nature and intention, i.e. out of *objective dogma*. Hence the scientific structures of dogmatics, its compound analogues and disclosure-models, or doctrinal formulations, are not simply the theoretic instruments through which the objective reality is discerned with some exactness and precision, but the hermeneutic media through which it is heard in its own self-interpretation and articulated in our disciplined response to it. It must be granted that the essential teaching that issues out of the nature of the object and breaks through to us gets broken up in the prismatic activity of our knowing and articulating so that dogmatic constructs result, corresponding to ecclesiastical dogmas. We cannot take these as transcripts of the Word of God but as orderly, scientific reactions of our relations with the Word through which we must allow the objective reality to reveal itself to us in its own essential harmony and meaning, yet always in such a way that it is sharply distinguished from our dogmatic constructs or dogmas. That is the objective dogma toward which they tend and to which they intend to direct us. Here, then, in Christian Dogmatics *dogma* takes the place of the basic logical concept, or the ultimate unity and simplicity, which we strive to reach in our scientific inquiry in other fields, while *dogmas* take the place of the agreed and accepted scientific principles with which we operate as we advance our knowledge in the construction of theoretic models in order that we may penetrate through them more and more into the rationality and order embedded in the nature of things.

We are now in a position to re-express the nature and function of Christian Dogmatics in a more explicit way in accordance with its material content.

On the one side, dogmatics is concerned with the objectively given fact of God's self-communication: His divine Being in active and rational revelation in Jesus Christ. Dogmatics inquires into that but can never bring it under its mastery— rather is dogmatics the inquiry that opens up the space or makes room in the life and understanding of the Church for the momentous self-disclosure of His transcendent Reality and Being. It is the inquiry which allows the fundamental datum of revelation breaking through to us in the form of dogma to manifest itself and impart itself to us in divine power and grace. This dogma into which we inquire is both profoundly simple and inexhaustibly rich. It has irrefragable unity and is yet infinitely creative and expansive. It is out of that fulness that the Church receives.

On the other side, dogmatics is concerned with the Church's hearing, acknowledgement and deepening grasp of that which has addressed it and engages it, grasped it and continues to hold it. It seeks to pierce through all doctrinal formulae to reach a condensed understanding by the whole historical Church in its faithful obedience to the incarnate Word, and to articulate it in positive, dogmatic statement. The original datum, God's Act and Grace in Christ and His Gospel, continues to communicate itself to us throughout history, and as it is mediated to each generation through human agents; it continues to act creatively upon the Church in history, calling it to profounder understanding and fuller obedience. Hence in each generation dogmatics throws the Church back upon its proper object, seeks to open up a way through all historical articulations and formulations of the Truth for a better and more appropriate hearing of God's Word, in order to lay bare the basic unity, the germinal and staple Truth in its foundation in Jesus Christ, in the Holy Trinity. As in this way we refine and deepen the focus of faith and knowledge in the Church and formulate its recognition and acknowledgement of the Truth in dogmatic statements, they have behind them the concentrated understanding of the whole people of God in its witness to the one Reality of God. Thus dogmas in the proper sense are never private formulations but are the corporate recognition-acts of the Church, with historical depth and ecumenical range, and yet they point to, go back to, and are determined by, the one indivisible dogma, the Truth and Act of God in Jesus Christ the incarnate Word, who as such cannot be resolved into statements. That is the objective depth or the ontological density of dogma.

It is ultimately impossible for us to state just how dogmas are related to dogma. As we cannot state in language how language is related to things, or offer any formulation of how true scientific theory is related to the rationality of the universe, so we are faced with a corresponding impasse here. But in theological knowledge we can say at least two things. (1) As it belongs to the nature of language rightly used to be the medium through which we discern things that cannot themselves be communicated in speech, so it belongs to the nature of dogmas rightly used to be the media through which we let the one dogma, the *Prima Veritas*, reveal itself to us—hence we *listen in* through dogmas to the Reality they intend. (2) If it does not belong to the nature of language in natural science to repeat what is heard but only to give significant expression to mute being, it does belong to the nature of dogmas to echo what is heard from the divine Being as He expresses and utters Himself in His Word. Thus we may say on the ground of the Incarnation that what we strive to do in dogmas is to articulate 'what we have seen and heard of the Word of Life'. They can serve that purpose only in such a way that they are allowed to point beyond themselves to the incarnate Word who alone is the Truth of God—but that incarnate Word is also the *Way* for man to go to the Father. Here, therefore, we can get further than we can elsewhere in stating how our statements are related to what is stated, for the object about which we make our statements is the Self-statement of God to us, so that it includes in itself as part of the object of our knowledge the *way* in which He is related to our human speech of Him, through His own revealing and reconciling action in Jesus Christ. Nevertheless, it is made clear at the same time that we are far from being able to reduce this to our statements for it transcends the capacity of our human speech to specify it; nor can we argue our own way from statements about the Truth to the Truth itself, with the result that we must continually let the original and basic event of the divine self-revelation happen anew to us. It is for this purpose that God sends us His Spirit, to do what we cannot do, to be the effective relation between our understanding and speech and the Word, as well as to be the relation and action of the Word upon us. "The ring embracing God and man is closed by God Himself".[1]

Here again we are up against a primary difference between the *principia* of natural science and the *principia* of theological science, and so between the hypothetical constructions of natural science and the doctrinal constructions of theological science. While both the theories of natural science and the doctrines of sacred theology are tentative in their formulation, the latter repose upon the final and decisive Word of God, in a way that the former do not. On the other hand, because the one dogma (or the Truth and Act of God) keeps pressing through all our historical relativity in order to utter and declare itself to us in its finality over against our dogmatic formulations, we have less excuse for being dogmatical about our dogmatic formulations than the natural scientists have for being dogmatical about their empirico-theoretic constructions.

It may help at this point to recall the two-fold reference of scientific statements, which we discussed in the distinction between existence-statements and coherence-statements, and to recall that it is in the interlocking of their reference to

[1] H. Diem, *Dogmatics*, p. 290.

external existents and to one another that they have significance. Another way of expressing this, which has particular relevance to dogmatic statements, is through distinguishing them in their correlation with the object from their correlation with the subject.

Dogmatic statements have their primary intention through correlation with the object, God in His Self-revelation, or the Being of God communicating Himself and acting upon us. In this sense dogmatic statements are made primarily from a centre in God and not in ourselves, i.e. by way of recognition and acknowledgement. Certainly it is we who make them formally, but we make them within a polar relation between ourselves and God in which priority and precedence are to be given to the divine pole, for by their nature dogmatic statements derive from God's active communication of Himself in the form of personal Being and Word, and point back to Him as the goal of all our dogmatic thinking and speaking. It is when theological thinking and speaking are grounded upon the bed-rock of God's own Self-disclosure in His Being and His Act that they are essentially dogmatic, i.e. positively determined by that objective ground from beyond themselves, and not free-thinking and indefinite, i.e. uncontrolled by their proper object.

Dogmatic statements have their secondary intention, however, through correlation with the subject, or through correlation with one another within the structured inter-personal relations of human subjects to one another under the creative impact of the divine Word. They do not arise as the result of private judgements reached by individuals within their own minds, but are thrown up from within the relations of objectivity that are found in the Community of Believers; that is, where the objectivity of personal subjects encounters the objectivity of other personal subjects in their covenanted relations with God and their conjoint response to His Word, and where the ultimate judgements are reached within the corporate life and thought of the Church as it fulfils its mission under the commanding reality and presence of God's Spirit as He continuously directs it back to its centre and foundation in Jesus Christ. Dogmatic statements involve propositional relations with God as the absolute Subject and propositional relations between human subjects within the covenanted Community, for they inhere in the on-going dialogical relations between God and His people which were brought to their fulfilment in the Incarnation of the Son of God and which extend indefinitely into history on the ground of that fulfilment in Him.

Thus dogmatic statements are not only correlated with God as Subject and correlated with one another in the collective subjectivity of the Church but are directed to Jesus Christ as the centre of their correlation with God and man. However, since the primary Object of dogmatic statements is God in Jesus Christ, it must be remembered that He is Subject not only as God is Subject but as human subject hearing, believing, knowing, loving, worshipping and praising God. Thus here in the Object of dogmatic statements there is already included human subjectivity (i.e. subject-hood), so that it is the human nature of Jesus Christ that becomes the norm that we must use in determining the form of dogmatic statements as they are correlated to the human subject as well as correlated to the divine Subject. Within the perspective thus opened out we may say that dogmatic statements are correlated primarily with this Object-Subject and secondarily with the community of subjects who believe in Him and follow Him. They are statements that go down into and are enunciated out of the ontological structure of the Church as the Body of Christ—yet even here the primary reference of dogmatic statements is to their proper Object, God in His Self-giving in Christ, and only subsidiarily to the Church, and not to the Church as object but only as collective subject.

It must not be forgotten that the sole Object of dogmatic statements is the Datum of divine Revelation which does not cease to be God's own Being and Act in His Self-giving, and therefore is not something that passes over into the inner spiritual states of the Church's experience or into its historical consciousness and subjectivity. Dogmatic statements are not constructs out of the Church's acts of consciousness nor can they be reached by reading them off the subjective structures of the mind of the Church, for that would imply that the Truth of God is identical with the collective subjectivity of the Church or that the Holy Spirit is the immanent soul and mind of the historical Church impregnating it with the Truth of God. That would imply the identity of dogmas with Dogma, and a view of the Truth in which its essence is determined by its existence in the historical Church, as if the truth of a thing is not that it is what it is in God but only what it becomes in temporal tradition; but behind all this would lie a self-deification of the Church and an identification of its own evolving life with the Life of God. All this forces dogmatics to be a highly critical science in which all theological statements are to be severely tested to determine whether, in their correlation with the subject and in their claim to speak of God, Father, Son and Holy Spirit, they really do intend God, whether it really is Christ that they mean, and whether they really do distinguish the Holy Spirit from the human spirit. Dogmatics, like the Church itself, stands or falls with sheer respect for the Majesty and Freedom of God in His Word and for the transcendence of His Truth over all our statements about it even when we do our utmost to make them aright (that is dogmatically) in accordance with the rectitude of the Truth itself as it comes to light in our inquiry into the divine Revelation.

Index of Names

Index of Subjects